CW01661970

AQA AS/A-level

# Design and Technology

## Fashion and Textiles

Pauline Treuherz, Amanda Dick and Denise Davies

**Approval message from AQA**

This textbook has been approved by AQA for use with our qualification. This means that we have checked that it broadly covers the specification and we are satisfied with the overall quality. Full details of our approval process can be found on our website.

We approve textbooks because we know how important it is for teachers and students to have the right resources to support their teaching and learning. However, the publisher is ultimately responsible for the editorial control and quality of this book.

Please note that when teaching the ***AQA A-level Design and Technology*** course, you must refer to AQA's specification as your definitive source of information. While this book has been written to match the specification, it cannot provide complete coverage of every aspect of the course.

A wide range of other useful resources can be found on the relevant subject pages of our website: aqa.org.uk

DYNAMIC LEARNING

HODDER EDUCATION
AN HACHETTE UK COMPANY

**Photo credits can be found on page 343.**

Every effort has been made to trace all copyright holders, but if any have been inadvertently overlooked, the Publishers will be pleased to make the necessary arrangements at the first opportunity.

Although every effort has been made to ensure that website addresses are correct at time of going to press, Hodder Education cannot be held responsible for the content of any website mentioned in this book. It is sometimes possible to find a relocated web page by typing in the address of the home page for a website in the URL window of your browser.

Hachette UK's policy is to use papers that are natural, renewable and recyclable products and made from wood grown in sustainable forests. The logging and manufacturing processes are expected to conform to the environmental regulations of the country of origin.

Orders: please contact Bookpoint Ltd, 130 Park Drive, Milton Park, Abingdon, Oxon OX14 4SE. Telephone: (44) 01235 827720. Fax: (44) 01235 400454. Email education@bookpoint.co.uk Lines are open from 9 a.m. to 5 p.m., Monday to Saturday, with a 24-hour message answering service. You can also order through our website: www.hoddereducation.co.uk

ISBN: 9781510413498

© Pauline Treuherz, Amanda Dick, Denise Davies 2018

First published in 2018 by
Hodder Education,
An Hachette UK Company
Carmelite House
50 Victoria Embankment
London EC4Y 0DZ

www.hoddereducation.co.uk

Impression number 10 9 8 7 6 5 4 3 2 1

Year 2022 2021 2020 2019 2018

All rights reserved. Apart from any use permitted under UK copyright law, no part of this publication may be reproduced or transmitted in any form or by any means, electronic or mechanical, including photocopying and recording, or held within any information storage and retrieval system, without permission in writing from the publisher or under licence from the Copyright Licensing Agency Limited. Further details of such licences (for reprographic reproduction) may be obtained from the Copyright Licensing Agency Limited, www.cla.co.uk.

Cover photo © Shutterstock / Dahabian

Illustrations by Integra Software Services Ltd.

Typeset in India by Integra Software Services Pvt. Ltd., Pondicherry, India

Printed in Slovenia by DZS Grafik

A catalogue record for this title is available from the British Library.

# Contents

# Section 1

In this section you will learn about the following:

1.1 Materials and their applications
1.2 Performance characteristics of materials
1.3 Methods of joining and using components
1.4 The use of finishes
1.5 Enhancement of materials
1.6 Modern industrial and commercial practice
1.7 Digital design and manufacture
1.8 The requirements for textile, and fashion design and development
1.9 Health and safety
1.10 Protecting designs and intellectual property (A-level)
1.11 Design for manufacturing, maintenance, repair and disposal
1.12 Feasibility studies
1.13 Enterprise and marketing in the development of products
1.14 Design communication

# 1.1 Materials and their applications

**LEARNING OUTCOMES**

By the end of this section you should have developed a knowledge and understanding of:

- factors that may affect the choice of fabrics for textile products
- where fibres come from
- how fibres are classified according to their source
- how fabrics are tested for specific properties in industry
- how to set up simple workshop tests for specific fabric properties.

Imagine a world without fabrics. Textile materials are all around us and used for many different products including clothing, furnishings, medical applications, car interiors and engines, roads and buildings, industrial applications and safety and security products. The range of new textile materials and applications is developing all the time. Choosing the right textile material for the product is a complex process because there are many inter-related factors that must be taken into account, and choices will vary according to the type of product being made and the intended user.

For example, a fabric to be used for a school shirt will need to be strong and hardwearing, easy to care for, yet comfortable enough for a young person to wear during the school day. In contrast, the aesthetic appearance of a fabric used for a special occasion dress will probably be more important than how well it washes and if it is likely to last for a long time.

## Properties, characteristics, function and aesthetics

The properties of textile materials vary depending on the **fibres** used, and the way that the fabrics are made and finished. Functional properties such as strength and resistance to abrasion, absorbency, ability to insulate, elasticity, drape, stiffness, flammability, ease of care, colour fastness, and the ability to be heat-set are important to different degrees in different types of product. For some products, the aesthetics of a fabric are as important as how well it functions. Aesthetics is about personal taste, and what one person finds attractive may be unappealing to another.

The fibre chart below gives a general guide to fibre properties.

**Table 1.1.1** General guide to fibre properties.

| Characteristics | Absorbency | Crease resistance | Tensile strength | Abrasion resistance | Flame resistance | Thermal insulation qualities | Lustre | Resistance to build up of static electricity | Thermoplasticity | Resistance to damage by chlorine bleach | Resistance to damage by sunlight |
|---|---|---|---|---|---|---|---|---|---|---|---|
| Linen | ✓✓✓ | ✓ | ✓✓✓ | ✓✓✓ | ✓ | ✓ | ✓✓ | ✓✓✓✓ | N/A | ✓✓✓ | ✓✓✓ |
| Cotton | ✓✓✓ | ✓ | ✓✓✓ | ✓✓ | ✓ | ✓✓ | ✓ | ✓✓✓✓ | N/A | ✓✓✓ | ✓✓✓ |
| Ramie | ✓✓✓ | ✓ | ✓✓✓ | ✓✓ | ✓ | ✓ | ✓✓ | ✓✓✓✓ | N/A | ✓✓✓ | ✓✓✓ |
| Wool | ✓✓✓✓ | ✓✓✓✓ | ✓ | ✓✓ | ✓✓✓✓ | ✓✓✓✓ | ✓ | ✓✓✓✓ | N/A | ✓ | ✓ |
| Hair fibres | ✓✓✓✓ | ✓✓✓✓ | ✓ | ✓ | ✓✓✓✓ | ✓✓✓✓ | ✓✓ | ✓✓✓✓ | N/A | ✓ | ✓ |
| Silk | ✓✓✓✓ | ✓✓✓ | ✓✓✓✓ | ✓✓ | ✓✓✓ | ✓✓✓ | ✓✓✓ | ✓✓✓✓ | N/A | ✓ | ✓ |
| Viscose | ✓✓✓✓ | ✓ | ✓✓ | ✓ | ✓ | ✓✓ | ✓✓ | ✓✓✓✓ | N/A | ✓ | ✓ |
| Acetate | ✓✓ | ✓ | ✓ | ✓ | ✓ | ✓ | ✓✓✓ | ✓ | ✓✓✓ | ✓ | ✓✓✓ |
| Lyocells | ✓✓✓ | ✓✓ | ✓✓ | ✓✓ | ✓ | ✓✓ | ✓✓ | ✓✓✓✓ | N/A | ✓✓✓ | ✓ |
| Polyamide | ✓ | ✓✓✓✓ | ✓✓✓✓ | ✓✓✓✓ | ✓✓ | ✓✓ | ✓✓ | ✓ | ✓✓✓ | ✓✓ | ✓✓ |
| Polyester | ✓ | ✓✓✓✓ | ✓✓✓✓ | ✓✓✓✓ | ✓✓ | ✓✓ | ✓✓ | ✓ | ✓✓✓✓ | ✓✓ | ✓✓✓✓ |
| Acrylic | ✓ | ✓✓✓ | ✓✓ | ✓ | ✓ | ✓✓✓✓ | ✓ | ✓ | ✓✓ | ✓✓ | ✓✓✓✓ |
| Elastomeric | ✓ | ✓✓✓✓ | ✓✓✓ | ✓✓ | ✓✓ | ✓ | ✓✓ | ✓ | ✓ | ✓✓ | ✓✓✓ |

Key: ✓✓✓✓ = very good; ✓✓✓ = good; ✓✓ = average; ✓ = poor

## Cost

The cost may dictate whether a fabric is appropriate for a specific application, especially in industrial manufacture where the manufacturer has to meet the cost of materials and manufacturing processes, while also making a profit. Some fibres and fabrics are scarcer or more difficult to make so will cost more, for example silk and wool are more expensive than cotton and **synthetic fibres**, complex weaving and knitting processes will be costlier and special finishes put on to fabrics will add to the price of materials.

**KEY TERMS**

**Fibre:** a fine hair-like thread that can be spun with others to make a yarn.

**Synthetic fibre:** a fibre made entirely from synthetic polymers based on oil.

## Manufacture and disposal

How a product is to be manufactured may have an impact on the choice of fabrics; the use of a luxury fabric to make a bespoke outfit for a celebrity may be justifiable, but would not be appropriate for bulk manufactured fashion garments. The need for special manufacturing techniques or equipment may mean that certain fabrics are inappropriate.

Today, many people are concerned about the environmental impact of textiles, and therefore want products to be made from materials that are **sustainable** and can be recycled or are **biodegradable**. Many new developments in the source and processing of textile materials are helping to make textile products less environmentally damaging when disposed of at the end of their useful life.

The designer needs to take all of these factors into account when putting together a fabric specification and selecting fabrics for a particular product.

**KEY TERMS**

**Sustainable:** ensuring that all aspects of design and manufacturing activity do not have a negative impact on the environment or the lives of humans.

**Biodegradable:** a substance that can be decomposed naturally by bacteria or other living organisms.

### ACTIVITY

Write a five-point fabric specification for each of the following textile products:

- a winter jacket
- sofa cushions
- a small rucksack.

### MATHS LINK

**Calculating of quantities of materials, sizes and costs**

A shirt requires 2.35 metres of fabric that is 115cm wide, or 1.55 metres of fabric that is 150cm wide.

- The 115cm-wide fabric costs £4.78 per metre
- The 150cm-wide fabric costs £5.89 per metre.

A manufacturer is making 4,500 shirts. Calculate the percentage difference between the costs of the two fabrics.

**Answer**

First, you need to work out how much fabric is needed to produce 4,500 shirts using each fabric.

Using the 115cm-wide fabric:

4,500 × 2.35 = 10,575 metres

Using the 150cm-wide fabric:

4,500 × 1.55 = 6,975 metres

Then you need to work out the cost of producing 4,500 shirts using each fabric.

Using the 115cm-wide fabric:

10,575 × 4.78 = £50,548.50

Using the 150cm-wide fabric:

6,975 × 5.89 = £41,082.75

It is cheaper to produce 4,500 shirts using the 150cm-wide fabric.

To work out the percentage difference between the two costs, first work out the actual difference between the two costs:

50,548.50 − 41,082.75 = £9,465.75

Then divide the difference by the cost of the (more expensive) 115 cm-wide fabric and multiply by 100:

$$\frac{9465.75}{50548.50} \times 100 = \mathbf{18.73}\%$$

Using the 150-cm fabric is 18.73% cheaper than using the 115cm-wide fabric.

## Classification of materials

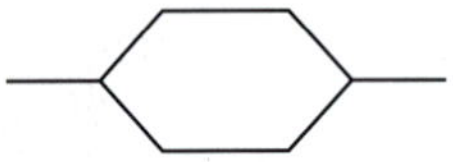

**Figure 1.1.1** Single fibre molecule.

Fibres are very fine, hair-like threads and are the basic building blocks of fabrics. All fibres – regardless of their source – are made up of atoms that are joined together to make molecules. Molecules can link together to form long chains called **polymers**.

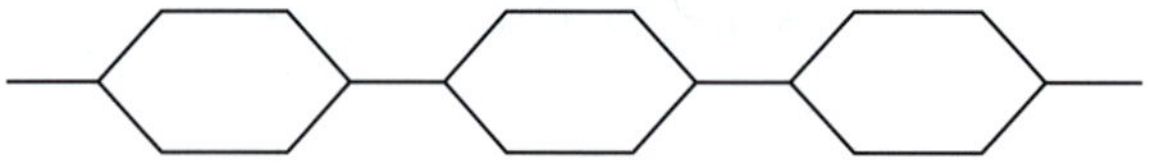

**Figure 1.1.2** Molecules joined together in a chain.

All textile fibres are made from long-chain molecules, but the combination of atoms in the molecules will vary for the different fibre types. They will usually include carbon, hydrogen and oxygen. Fibres are made from natural or man-made polymers, and have different properties according to where they come from.

**KEY TERMS**

**Natural fibre:** a fibre that comes from natural cellulose or protein.

**Regenerated fibre:** a fibre from natural cellulose that has been chemically modified.

**Polymer:** a long chain of molecules made up of fibre-forming atoms that are linked together.

Fibres must be twisted (spun) together to make a **yarn** before they can be made into a woven or knitted fabric.

Fibres ⟶ Yarns ⟶ Woven and knitted fabrics

**Figure 1.1.3** Fibres must be spun together to make a yarn before they can be made into a woven or knitted fabric.

The tables in the following sections show the classification of fibres in common use, including some brand names of fibres belonging to the fibre group.

## Natural fibres

**Natural fibres** come from plant and animal sources. Plant fibres are made from cellulose and animal fibres are made from protein.

**Table 1.1.2** Natural fibres.

| Natural fibres | | |
|---|---|---|
| Natural plant/cellulosic fibres | Natural animal/protein fibres | Natural hair/protein fibres (A-level only) |
| cotton | wool | cashmere |
| linen | silk | mohair |
| ramie | | angora |

As technologists strive to find more sustainable alternatives to the established fibres such as cotton, other sources of natural fibres are beginning to be used to make textile products, for example bamboo, pineapple and banana leaf fibres. Alginate fibres from seaweed are used in medical applications.

## Manufactured fibres

Manufactured fibres (including **regenerated fibres** and lyocell fibres) are mostly made from natural cellulose from wood pulp, or waste cotton fibres that are too short to be spun into a yarn. They have been chemically treated to modify the cellulose so that it can be made into fibres.

Regenerated fibres are first generation manufactured fibres, and were known by names such as viscose and rayon. Modal® and lyocell fibres are second generation fibres, and the most recent in the development in this type of fibre. Each time the fibre is developed the strength, softness and crease resistance has been improved. Lyocells are more environmentally friendly fibres because they are manufactured using a closed-loop system that reuses the chemicals used in the processing.

**Table 1.1.3** Manufactured regenerated fibres.

| Manufactured fibres | |
|---|---|
| regenerated fibres | lyocell fibres |
| viscose (made from wood pulp) | lyocell |
| acetate (made from cotton waste) | Modal |

**KEY TERMS**

**Polymerisation:** the joining together of small molecules to form long chains of molecules.

**Yarn:** long, continuous strands made by twisting many individual fibres together.

**Smart materials:** materials that are able to react to external stimuli or changes in their environment without human intervention.

## Synthetic fibres

Man-made fibres are made from synthetic polymers that come mainly from oil. The synthetic polymers are made by joining smaller molecules together to form a long chain. This process is called **polymerisation**.

**Table 1.1.4** Synthetic fibres.

| Synthetic fibres | Chlorofibres (A-level only) | Aramid fibres (A-level only) |
|---|---|---|
| polyamide (nylon) | polyvinyl | Kevlar® |
| polyester | fluorofibres (PTFE) | Nomex® |
| acrylic | | |
| elastomeric (Lycra®) | | |

Aramid fibres have been developed from polyamide fibres. They are technical fibres that have additional strength and durability, and are stab- and tear-resistant. Kevlar® is used to make stab-proof and bulletproof vests worn as protective wear.

Inorganic fibres come from glass, metal, ceramics and carbon, and are used for specialist applications such as micro-encapsulated and nano-fibres.

## Smart materials

**Smart materials** or intelligent materials are able to react to external stimuli or changes in their environment without human intervention. They are able to sense and react to conditions around them, for example light, heat and power. This area of textiles technology is developing all the time, especially wearable electronics that allow people to interact with their environment. Some examples of this are outlined below:

- Reactive materials include those that react to changes, such as loss of heat or presence of pollutants. Many of these fabrics are used in health and safety or sportswear applications.
- Photochromic fabrics are dyed using specific types of dye that respond to changes in UV light. This type of fabric may be used in garments that warn the wearer of the need for sun protection.
- Phase changing materials are able to help regulate body temperature, cooling down in hot conditions and warming up when it gets cooler. These materials are used for garments worn in extreme climates such as those worn by mountaineers.

## Modern textile materials

Modern textile materials are constantly being updated and new ones developed. New fibres can be engineered to have properties needed for specific purposes.

Below are some examples of new developments – there are many more.

### Microfibres

**KEY TERMS**

**Microfibres:** extremely fine fibres.

**Microfibres** are extremely fine synthetic fibres, mainly polyester and polyamide.

Microfibres are very lightweight, soft, drape well and are used for a variety of clothing products. They are often blended with natural fibres to give high performance fabrics for outdoor and sports use. **Tactel®** is a polyamide microfibre, for example Tactel Aquator® and Tactel Diablo®.

### Nano-fibres

A-level only

Nano-fibres are very tiny, varying in size from one micron to a single polymer molecule. (A micron is one-millionth of a metre; 100 microns is the width of a single human hair.) Nano-fibres are very lightweight but strong, fine and delicate to touch. When applied to a fabric as a finish, they protect it from grease and water-borne stains. They can also make a fibre more absorbent, and can be sprayed on to the human body to make a very fine, seamless skin covering.

Nano-fibres are still being developed; they open up all sorts of exciting possibilities for textiles in the future.

### Micro-encapsulated fibres and fabrics

These contain various health and cosmetic chemicals that can help to make daily life more comfortable and healthier. When the fibres are rubbed, the chemicals are released slowly and absorbed through the skin of the wearer. The chemicals break down slowly, so the effects last for a long time. For example, caffeine-encapsulated tights can help to stimulate leg veins, which reduces the risk of deep vein thrombosis (DVT).

## Methods for investigating and testing materials

When selecting possible fabrics for a product, manufacturers may carry out tests to check that potential fabrics have the performance properties required. Many of the requirements will be recommended by the British Standards Institute (BSI). There are over 10,000 British standards for almost every industry – from food to building construction and textiles to children's toys. These state the essential technical requirements – or **performance codes** – for a product, material or process to be fit for its intended purpose. For example:

- waterproof clothing really will keep the wearer dry
- fabric to be used for hotel sheets and duvet covers will stand up to repeated laundering.

Designers give fabric specifications for the product, but the method of testing must be reliable and consistent if the results are to be accurate and have the same meaning to everyone involved. BSI set standards for the test methods to be used for different performance qualities, and these are used all over the world.

To be reliable, it must be possible to repeat the test in the same laboratory conditions, using the same fabrics and obtain virtually the same results every time the test is performed. The size of the piece of fabric to be tested may affect the data obtained – a small piece may not give the same results as a larger piece. The test may need to be repeated on the same fabric or product to obtain reliable results, for example sheets need to be washed many times before any signs of wear are seen.

Industrial testing of fabrics requires specialist equipment and conditions which are unlikely to be available in the school or college workshop. However, it is possible to set up fairly reliable tests that mimic BSI tests using basic equipment. When setting up a test, there must be a logical and consistent approach. It must be clear:

- what is being tested
- how the test will be set up
- how it will be carried out
- how the data will be recorded
- how the results will be interpreted
- how results will be compared with a control.

## Flammability

It is very difficult to predict how a fabric will burn in a real situation because there are so many variables such as the style of the product, the source of ignition and whether or not there is air flow to fan the flames. In industry, a number of different tests are used to assess how a fabric will behave when burning. The following three are the most important ones used to assess how flammable a fabric is, however they do not test whether it is safe to use for a specific application.

### Industrial test 1

A sample of the fabric is held in a metal frame and a small flame from a Bunsen burner is applied to the fabric.

Test 1 shows how easy it is for a fabric to catch fire. The flame is applied to the fabric 6 cm from the bottom edge, to see how long it takes for the fabric to set alight. The flame touches the fabric for two seconds and is then removed. The test is complete if the fabric burns for more than one second. If the fabric does not set on fire, the contact with the flame is increased to three, four, six, eight and ten seconds, until it does catch fire.

### Industrial test 2

Test 2 assesses how far a flame spreads when the source of ignition is removed. The test is for fabrics that have low flammability, and measures the size of the hole burned into the fabric.

A flame is applied to a sample for ten seconds. The duration of the flaming and whether the flame reaches one of the edges are recorded. The size of the hole is measured and the duration of the afterglow is noted, as well as whether any flaming debris has fallen from the sample.

### Industrial test 3

Test 3 measures how quickly a flame spreads. A large sample of fabric is placed in the frame and three cotton trip threads attached to timers are placed at regular intervals above the flame. The flame is applied to the bottom of the sample for ten seconds, and as each thread burns through, its timer will stop. This shows how quickly the flames burned through the fabric.

## Workshop testing

For safety reasons, any workshop test for flammability must be carried out by a teacher, and done in a science fume cupboard with a fire extinguisher nearby.

Use 3 × 25 cm samples of fabrics. Attach them to a retort stand with a bulldog clip or by making a loop in the fabric with a stapler. Use a second retort stand to hold a wire marker 20 cm from the bottom of the fabric sample. Figure 1.1.4 below shows how to set up the equipment.

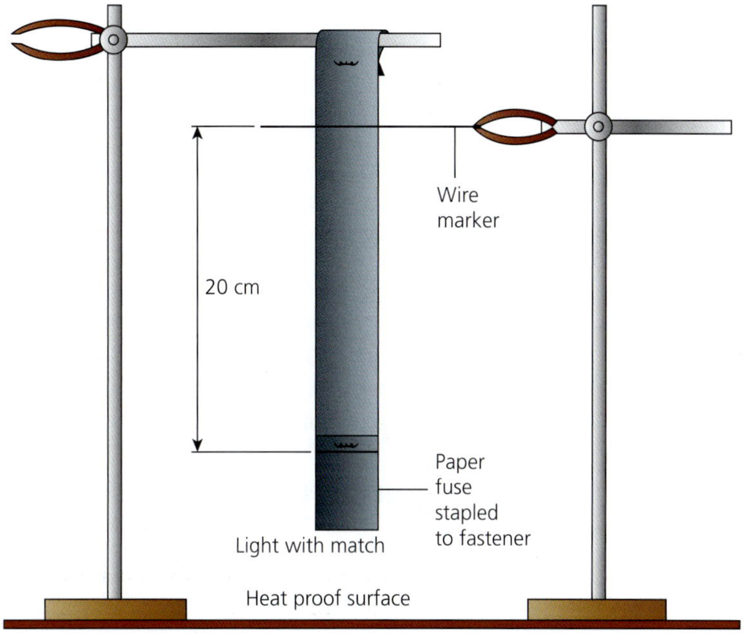


**Figure 1.1.4** Setting up the equipment to test for flammability.

Ignite the fabric with a small flame on a Bunsen burner or use a paper fuse. Record what happens when the flame comes into contact with the fabric. Record the results in a table like the one below.

**Table 1.1.5** Table to show results obtained from flammability testing.

| | Sample 1 | Sample 2 | Sample 3 |
|---|---|---|---|
| Fibre content | | | |
| Fabric construction | | | |
| Weight of fabric | | | |
| Time for burning to reach wire marker (in seconds) | | | |
| Duration of any afterglow | | | |
| Area of hole burned ($mm^2$) | | | |
| Type of residue, e.g. ash, hard bead | | | |

# Crease resistance

## Industrial testing

An industrial test for crease resistance involves creasing the fabric and measuring how quickly it recovers from the creasing. Twenty or more 1.5 × 4 cm samples of the fabric are left in standard room conditions of humidity and temperature. Once they have been conditioned, the samples are folded in half, with a slip of paper or foil inside to prevent the two sides of fabric sticking together. The samples are put under a 1,019 kg weight for 5 minutes – this gives a force of 10 newtons. The sample is transferred to a device that measures the angle of recovery after 5 minutes. The larger the angle of recovery, the better the crease resistance.

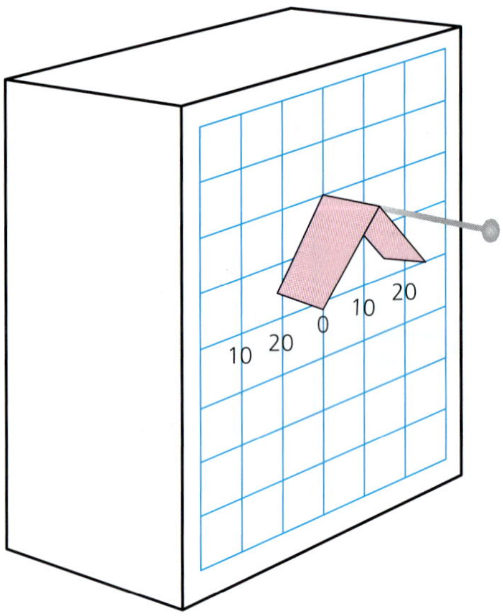


**Figure 1.1.5** Setting up a workshop test for crease resistance.

### Workshop testing

A simplified version of this test can be used in the workshop. Glue a piece of millimetre graph paper to a smooth block of wood, making sure that it is square to the edges. Push a large pin into the wood on one of the main vertical grid lines, making sure that the pin projects at a 90-degree angle. Mark a horizontal scale in millimetres about 2 cm below the pin.

Cut 1.5 × 4 cm samples of fabric and fold them in half, with a slip of paper or foil inside. Place the sample on a smooth surface and cover with a small piece of card, leaving the cut ends sticking out slightly. Place a 1 kg weight on top for 5 minutes – use a stop watch for all timings.

Use tweezers to pick up the fabric sample at the cut ends, and carefully place it over the pin so that the crease lies along the pin. The sample should be close to – but not touching – the graph paper. Leave the sample to recover for five minutes, then read off the distance between the two ends on the horizontal scale.

## Shrink resistance

Shrinkage can be a significant problem with certain fabrics and products, for example many curtain fabrics shrink by as much as 10–15 per cent when washed.

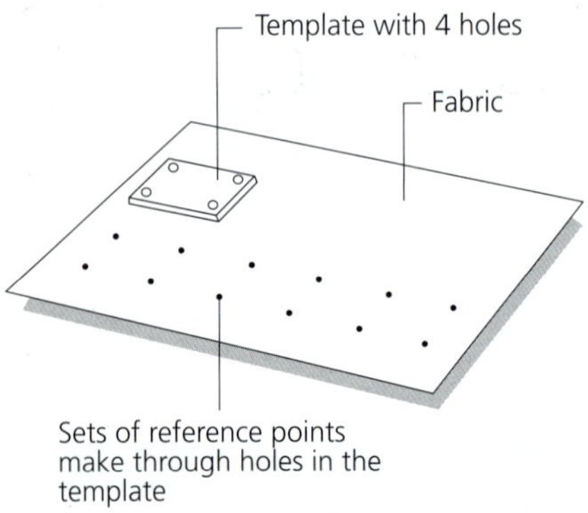


**Figure 1.1.6** Using a template to mark reference points to assess shrinkage in fabrics.

As the fabric may fray when carrying out an industrial test for shrinkage, a template is used to mark precise reference points on the fabric in permanent ink. These points are later measured and compared with the original, to assess if a fabric has shrunk. A larger piece of fabric is used and the raw edges overlocked.

The fabric samples are put into a washing machine, with pieces of polyester fabric to complete the load so that the test replicates a normal wash. The wash temperature, type of agitation, rinse and spin cycles are recorded. The samples are dried on a line, in a tumble dryer, laid flat on a rack or ironed dry. The samples are then measured between the reference points to see if there are any changes.

The percentage change in size is calculated using the following formula:

$$\text{Percentage change in length or width} = \frac{\text{original length or width} - \text{final length or width}}{\text{original length or width}}$$

If the fabric has shrunk, for example the length or width has reduced in size, the result is given with a minus sign, for example -10 per cent. If the end result has a positive sign, it means that the fabric has stretched.

A workshop test can replicate the industrial test, washing samples at different temperatures and with different types of agitation.

## Colour fastness

Colour fastness is the ability of a fabric to retain dye when washed or exposed to sunlight for any length of time. There are other types of fastness, but these are the two most important ones.

### Industrial testing

An industrial test to assess fastness compares an untreated sample with one that has been washed or exposed to UV light. They are compared using a set of grey cards called a grey scale – the grey cards show differences in the intensity of colour. The fastness is rated from one (when the colour has disappeared altogether) up to five (where there is no change of colour).

To test for fastness to light, two-thirds of the sample is covered with an opaque cover. The sample is then exposed to daylight and artificial light for a prolonged length of time before the two areas of the sample are compared using the grey scale.

When testing for wash fastness, the sample is placed between two pieces of white cotton or nylon fabric, and the layers are sewn together around all four sides. The sample is washed for 30 minutes before being compared with the grey scale, to see if there has been a change in colour or if the white fabric is stained.

**Figure 1.1.7** Testing the strength of woven fabrics.

### Workshop testing

Workshop tests can replicate the industrial test, but testing for light fastness may take weeks or even months before any differences are seen. Therefore it will not be possible to make sure that the light intensity remains the same for the duration of the test.

## Strength

The strength of fabrics depends on the fibres used, and the way the yarn and fabric are made.

**Figure 1.1.8** Testing the bursting strength of knitted fabrics.

### Industrial testing

Industrial tests for testing the breaking strength of woven fabrics involve stretching a 5 cm wide strip of the fabric until it breaks. The machine is able to exert a strong pressure on the fabric using very heavy weights. A pen recorder on the machine automatically marks the increasing force on graph paper until the fabric breaks. The sample is cut on the straight grain and at 7 cm wide, so that it can be fringed back to 5 cm along its length. This makes sure that all the threads in the sample run along its entire length. The test is repeated with samples cut in the warp and weft directions.

This method cannot be used for knitted fabrics because they have too much stretch. The test for these fabrics measures their bursting strength. A circle of the fabric is placed over a rubber diaphragm and clamped in place. Air or water is pumped in under pressure until the fabric bursts. The pressure needed to burst the fabric is called its bursting strength.

### Workshop testing

A workshop test for strength will need to be relatively simple because it is not possible to achieve the large forces needed to break the fabrics. A basic test might involve cutting similar sized samples of the fabric and making a small nick at the warp, weft and bias edges. The samples can then be torn to see which tears the most easily.

Although it is not possible to get specific results from this test, it will show the differences between different types of fabric.

## Pilling

One of the biggest causes of fabric wearing out is abrasion caused by friction when fabrics rub against each other or hard surfaces. Friction causes fibres to rub off the fabric surface until it wears into a hole. Very strong fibres such as polyamide do not break into holes; instead, small balls of the fibre tend to remain trapped on the surface of the fabric. This is called pilling.

Pilling tends to occur most in fabrics made from blended yarns, where a strong fibre is able to hold the weaker one on the surface of the fabric.

### Industrial testing

In industry, the Martindale abrasion machine is used to test the abrasion resistance of fabrics. Circular samples of the fabric are clamped on to the machine's four discs and a weight is put into each disc. Each of the test samples sits on a larger sample of plain woven worsted wool fabric, which acts as an abradant (an abrasive fabric). The test samples are rubbed in an even pattern against the abradant, and the machine counts the number of rubbing cycles made. The samples are examined under a magnifying glass at regular intervals, to see if the fabric is beginning to break down or if there are signs of wear leading to pilling.

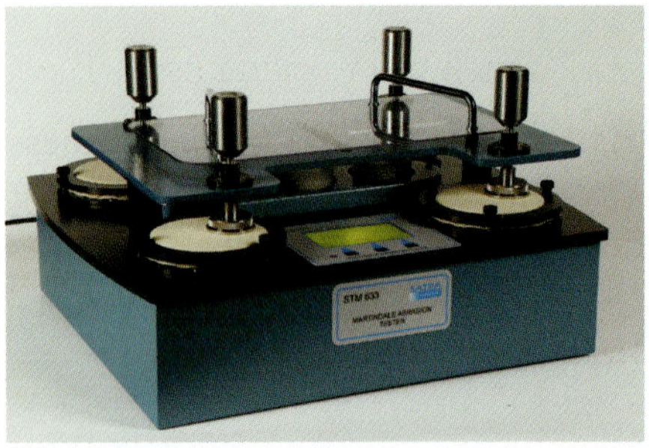

**Figure 1.1.9** The Martindale abrasion machine.

### Workshop testing

In the workshop, a simple wear machine can be made using a course round file inserted into a hand drill. A load can be made by putting about 1.5 kg of dry sand into a strong plastic bag with a string loop tied around the top so it can be hung from the end of the fabric sample. The drill is clipped to a board so that the handle can be turned to rotate the file. The diagram below shows how to assemble the wear machine.

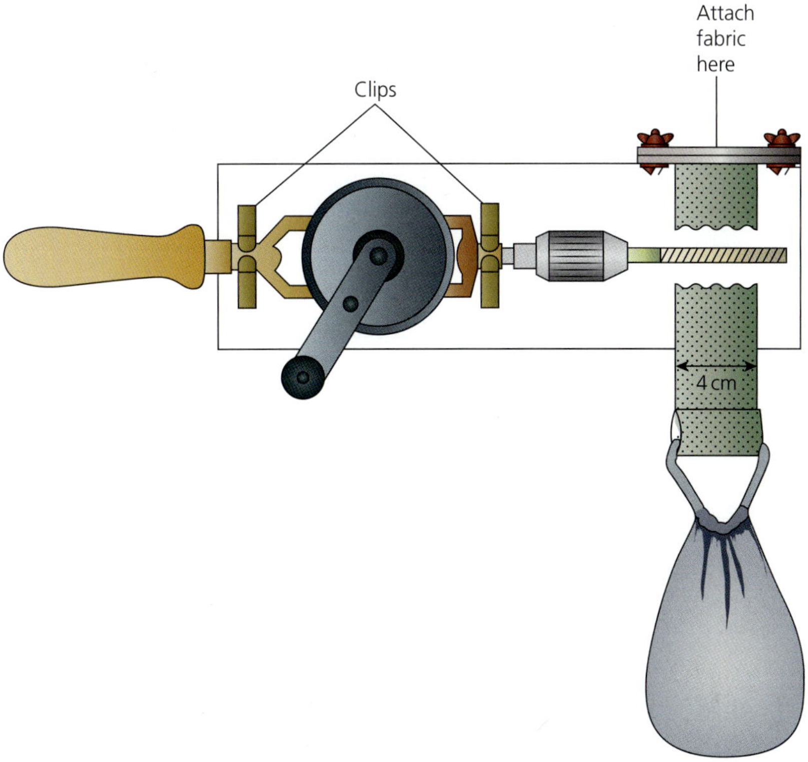


**Figure 1.1.10** A wear machine that can be used in the workshop.

The tester should be clamped onto the work bench before being used. The number of turns of the drill should be recorded for each fabric sample.

## ACTIVITY

Collect three 20 × 10 cm samples of the following fabrics:

- cotton denim
- polyester/cotton fabric – medium weight, woven with a printed design
- polyester fleece fabric
- viscose fabric – medium weight, woven
- wool fabric – medium weight, woven.

Describe the aesthetic qualities of each fabric.

Work in pairs and test each fabric sample for abrasion resistance, fastness to washing and crease resistance. Make a chart to record your results and compare them with those obtained by other students in your group.

Write a fabric specification for each of the following products:

- a school skirt for a child
- a fashion top
- casual trousers for a teenager.

Use your results to explain which fabric you would choose for each product, and compare it with one fabric that would not be suitable.

## MATHS LINK

**Analysing data obtained from testing: working out percentage shrinkage of fabrics from test results**

A curtain measuring 140 cm long by 100 cm wide is washed in a washing machine. It is line dried and then measured again. The curtain is measured and its new size is 101 cm long by 88 cm wide. Calculate:

**a)** the percentage change in length of the curtain

**b)** the percentage change in width of the curtain

**Answer**

The percentage change in size is calculated using the following formula:

$$\% \text{ change in length or width} = \frac{\text{original length or width} - \text{final length or width}}{\text{original length or width}}$$

If the fabric has shrunk (i.e. the length or width has reduced in size), the result is given with a minus sign (e.g. –10%). If the end result has a positive sign it means that the fabric has stretched.)

**a)** $\% \text{ change in length} = \frac{101-140}{140} = -0.28\%$

The curtain has shrunk in length by 0.28%

**b)** $\% \text{ change in width} = \frac{88-100}{100} = -0.12\%$

The curtain has shrunk in width by 0.12%

## KEY POINTS

- Many factors affect the functionality of textile products.
- Fibres are classified according to their source.
- Fibres are the starting point for textile materials.
- Yarns are made by twisting many fibres together.
- The properties of fibres will vary according to where they come from.
- The main sources of fibres are natural cellulose, natural protein and synthetic polymers.
- Manufacturers test potential fabrics to check that they have the required performance characteristics.
- Many fabric requirements for products will be recommended by the BSI.
- Fabric tests must be done under controlled conditions, to make sure that the results are reliable.

## Check your knowledge and understanding

**1** Place each of the fibres listed below in the correct box of the table. Use each fibre only once.

Acrylic
Cotton
Linen
Lycra
Lyocell
Polyamide
Polyester
Silk
Tactel
Viscose
Wool

**Table 1.1.6** Types of fibres.

| Natural cellulose | Natural protein | Manufactured | Synthetic |
|---|---|---|---|
| | | | |
| | | | |
| | | | |
| | | | |
| | | | |

**2** What is meant by the term 'manufactured fibres'?

**3** What are reactive materials?

**4** How do micro-encapsulated fabrics help people to live more comfortable daily lives?

**5** What is meant by the term 'colour fastness'?

## Further reading

The performance characteristics of fibres, yarns and fabrics will be covered in more detail in Chapter 1.2 of this book.

Taylor, M A. *Technology of Textile Properties*

Baugh, G. *The Fashion Designer's Textile Directory*

Hallett, C and Johnston, A. *Fabric for Fashion: The Complete Guide*

Udale, J. *Textiles and Fashion*

General information about standards: www.bsigroup.com

Information about a wide range of commercial textile tests: www.satra.com/materials

Information about testing outwear: www.gore-tex.co.uk/experience.quality/testing-outwear

The following YouTube videos show a range of fabric tests (there are many others):

- Fabric testing – tensile strength test: https://youtu.be/TN6KUrdCywU
- Textile fibres burning test: https://youtu.be/kb4tCcnA6jo
- Pros and cons of common fabrics: https://youtu.be/9QmTnHNb8ro
- Learning about fabrics: the who, what and how: https://youtu.be/-B4tfduOQ7w
- Determination of fabric propensity to surface fuzzing and pilling (Martindale method): https://youtu.be/9jg_jTohPjw
- Fabric shrinkage test: https://youtu.be/aItMu9cbTpM

# 1.2 Performance characteristics of materials

**LEARNING OUTCOMES**

By the end of this section you should have developed a knowledge and understanding of:

- the characteristics given to fibres by their physical and internal structures
- different yarns and how they are made
- different types of fabric and how they are made
- the relationship between fibre, yarn and fabric
- the meaning of technical terms relating to textiles.

If you are studying at A-level you should also have developed a knowledge and understanding of:

- different hand and machine knitting methods
- technical and modern materials
- the names of a wide range of fabrics.

This chapter is structured so that it follows the process from fibres through to yarns and fabrics, which is the order in which manufacture takes place. It is important to remember that when selecting a fabric for a particular application, the interplay between fibre, yarn, and fabric structure will affect the final characteristics of the fabric. A fibre is the starting point, but it is not a fabric. It can be manipulated in many different ways to produce a wide range of fabrics. For example, cotton can be used to make a wide range of fabrics including very fine, open weave muslin; a knitted jersey and a very heavy weight denim. To name a fabric as cotton is not very helpful because it could be any type of weight or structure.

## Performance characteristics of fibres

A fibre used for textiles must be flexible and fine, and have enough length and strength so that it is suitable for manufacturing into a fabric. The varying characteristics of textile materials are due to the differences in the basic form of fibres.

A fibre can be short – called a **staple fibre** – or a very long continuous length – called a **filament fibre**.

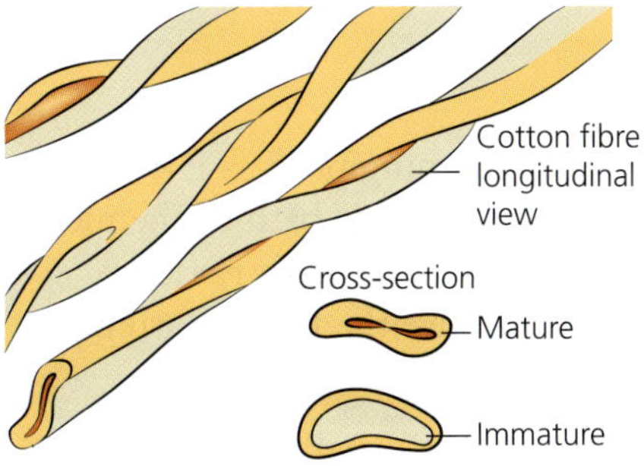


**Figure 1.2.1** The structure of cotton fibres.

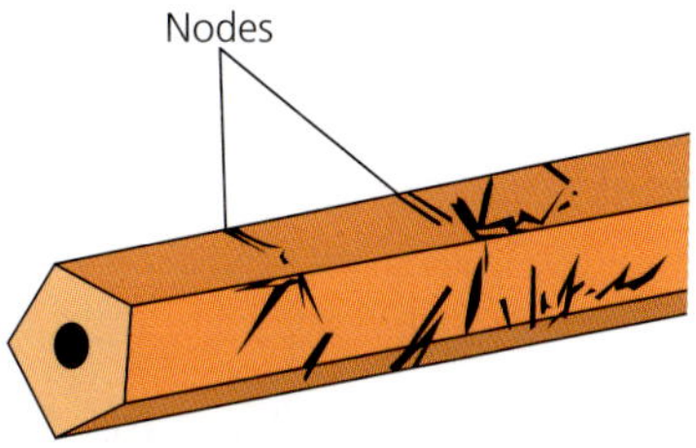


**Figure 1.2.2** The structure of linen fibres.

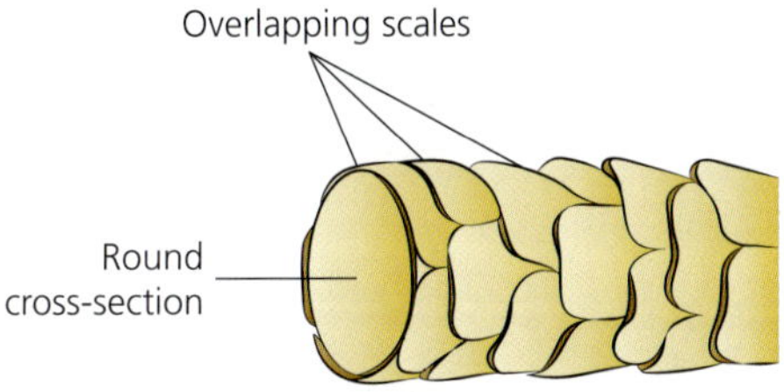


**Figure 1.2.3** The wool fibre.

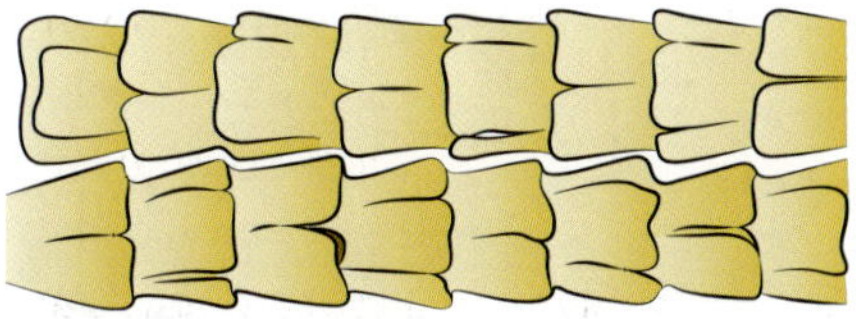

**Figure 1.2.4** The interlocking effect of wool fibre scales when rubbed together.

**Figure 1.2.5** The crimp in wool fibres.

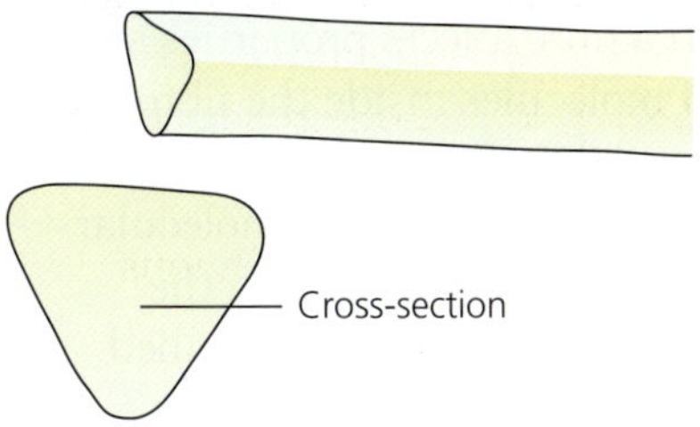


**Figure 1.2.6** The silk fibre.

All natural fibres except silk are staple fibres. All manufactured fibres are filament fibres.

The source as well as the physical shape of a fibre will have an impact on its properties. All fibres have an individual internal structure and their own naturally formed cross-section. It is possible to change (or engineer) the cross-sectional shape of man-made fibres in order to build-in specific properties. The shape and formation of the fibre length can also affect the properties of the fibre.

## Natural plant/cellulose fibres

### Cotton

An immature cotton fibre has a round cross-section, which is where the plant nutrients pass along the fibre as it is growing. When it is picked, the fibre dries out and collapses into a flattened bean-like cross-section. It also twists along its length so that it looks like a twisted and flattened ribbon.

The smooth surface prevents air from being trapped between the fibres, making cotton a poor insulator and therefore cool to wear. The flat twisted form does not reflect light well, therefore cotton does not have a **lustre**.

### Linen

Linen has a many-sided cross-section and a long, regular length to the fibres. This regular surface is able to reflect light quite well, which gives linen its slight lustre. The cross markings across the fibre length are called nodes, and these give linen its slubbed appearance. A slub is a soft lump of fibre that appears at irregular intervals along the length of a slub fibre or yarn.

## Natural animal/protein fibres

### Wool

Wool fibre is similar to human hair. The surface of the fibre is covered by overlapping scales.

The outer surface of the wool is covered with natural grease called lanolin, which makes the wool fibre water repellent.

The scales on the wool fibre can lock together when the fibre is in the presence of heat, moisture and friction. This will make the wool shrink – this property is used when making felt from wool fibres. It also explains why wool can be difficult to care for, and why it needs gentle hand washing or dry cleaning.

Other hair fibres such as cashmere and mohair have a similar shape to wool.

Wool fibres also have a natural crimp, like curly hair, and when many fibres are spun together, the crimp and the scales will cause them to stand away from each other and trap air. This is what gives wool its ability to insulate.

### Silk

Silk comes from a silk worm which spins two triangular-shaped filaments, one from each side of its mouth. These two filaments are held together with **sericin**, which is a natural gum produced by the silk worm.

## Regenerated fibres

### Viscose

Viscose filaments are manufactured fibres. The spinning process for viscose fibre involves coagulating (or setting) the liquid fibres in a bath of chemicals. The fibres set at an irregular rate, which makes tiny grooves (striations) along the length of the filaments. These striations give the fibre an irregular cross-section.

Viscose has a relatively smooth surface which is able to reflect light. As this can be an unwanted property, a de-lustering chemical is often added to the spinning solution to reduce this ability to reflect light.

The shape of the cross-section of a fibre affects its lustre and handle. The shape of the cross-section of manufactured fibres such as viscose can be changed using **spinnerets** with different cross-sections. The fibre spinning process is explained later in this chapter.

**Figure 1.2.7** Longitudinal view of viscose fibre.

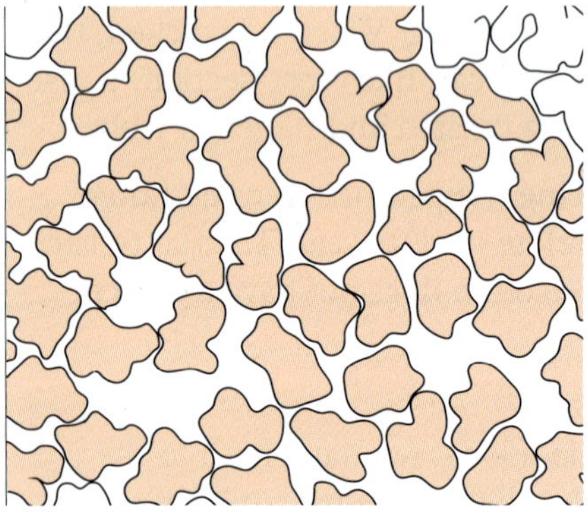

**Figure 1.2.8** Cross-section of viscose fibre.

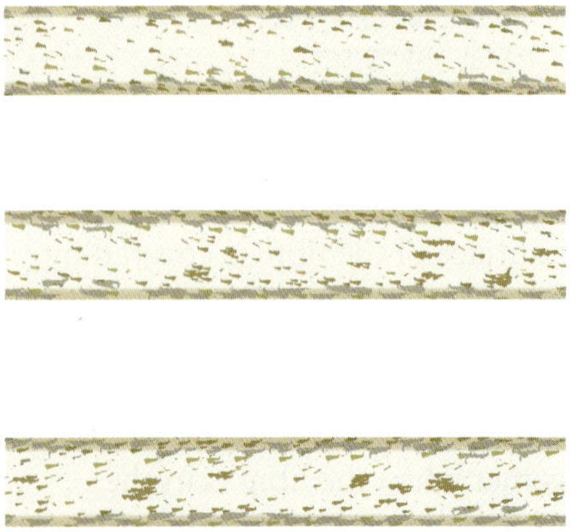

**Figure 1.2.9** Longitudinal view of nylon and polyester fibres.

## Synthetic fibres

Synthetic fibres such as nylon and polyester are manufactured. They are produced as continuous filament, and look like glass rods; this very smooth surface enables them to reflect a lot of light. Because they are so smooth, they do not trap air and are therefore poor insulators.

The cross-section of nylon can be modified to a tri-lobal shape. This means that the fibre surface will have less contact with skin when worn, therefore making it more comfortable.

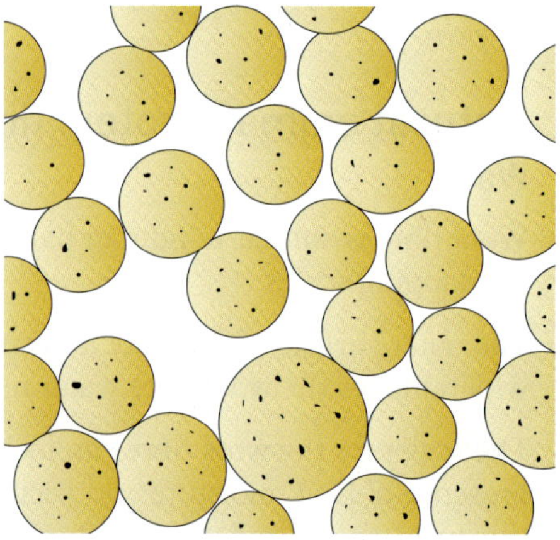

**Figure 1.2.10** The cross-section of nylon and polyester is circular.

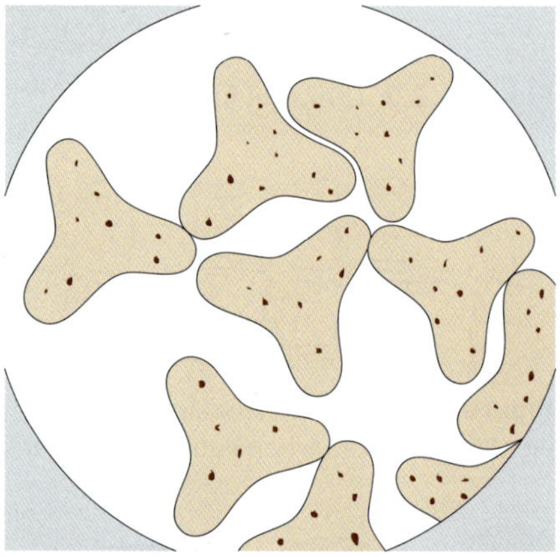

**Figure 1.2.11** Tri-lobal cross-section of modified nylon fibres.

## Fibre properties

Fibre properties are related to the internal fibre structure. The way that the chains of molecules are arranged within a fibre affects properties such as strength and absorbency. If the chains of molecules inside the fibre are tightly packed, and lie parallel to each other and to the length of the fibre, they are said to be highly oriented. In a less oriented fibre, the molecular chains are less tightly packed together and lie at various angles to the longitudinal fibre axis. All fibres have areas of high orientation – called crystalline regions – and areas of low orientation – called amorphous regions. These occur randomly throughout the fibre and not in any particular order. Each chain of molecules will be one part of a number of different areas, and this helps hold the fibre together.

Figure 1.2.12 below represents a simplified and exaggerated view of the internal structure of a fibre.

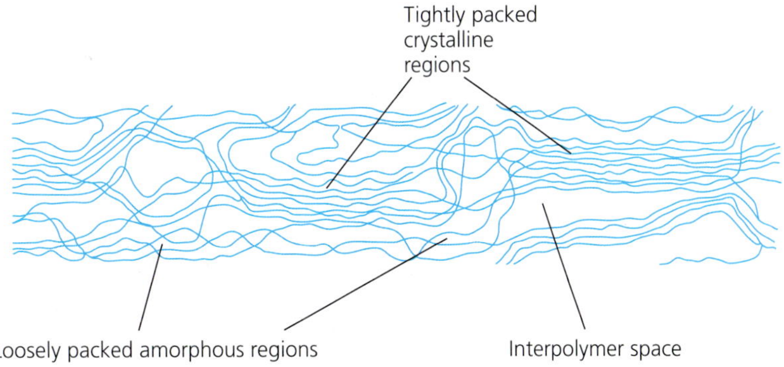


**Figure 1.2.12** Internal structure of a fibre.

A synthetic fibre starts off as a liquid spinning solution, which is forced through a spinneret. When the filaments leave the spinneret, they are still in a liquid state and have no crystalline regions at all, therefore the chains of molecules are completely disoriented. The fibre 'sets' or dries from the outside to the centre. As it is setting, the fibre is stretched, which causes the chains of molecules to become oriented and lie parallel to the fibre axis. This process is called **drawing**.

Figure 1.2.13 below is a simplified representation of the stages that a drawn synthetic fibre passes through.

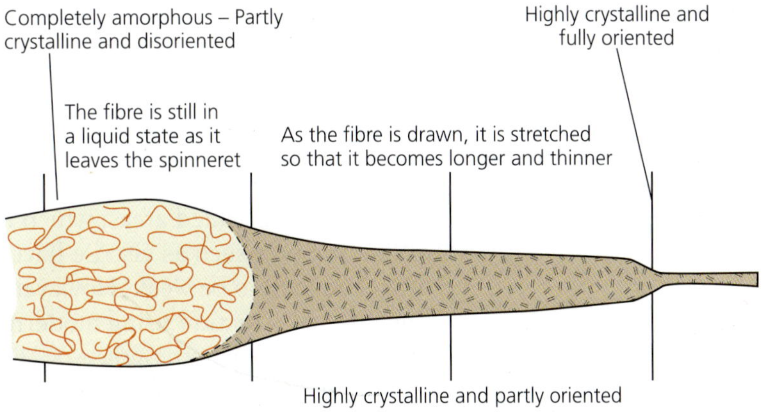


**Figure 1.2.13** The stages of a drawn synthetic fibre.

## Absorbency

A fibre's ability to absorb moisture varies considerably, and affects a number of performance characteristics:

- One of the most important is comfort when wearing a garment. If a garment is to be comfortable in wear, it must either absorb the wearer's perspiration or allow it to pass through the fabric. However, very absorbent fabrics can be uncomfortable in wet conditions – cotton denim jeans that have become soaked in the rain are a good example of this. And while an absorbent fabric is not good for making products that are intended to protect against wet weather (for example a tent or a raincoat), some products must be made from an absorbent fabric if they are to do their job properly, bathroom towels for example.

- The care of textile products is affected by the absorbency of the fibres because very absorbent fibres take a long time to dry. They also absorb water-borne stains easily, so may need to be washed more often. Absorbency is also linked to shrinkage in some fibres.
- Most dyes are applied to fabrics by using water to carry the dye molecules into the fibres. If the water is not easily absorbed by the fibres, it is difficult to dye the fabric.
- Fabrics that do not contain moisture can be affected by static electricity. A build-up of static electricity can cause fabrics to stick to each other or cling to a wearer's body, as well as giving small electric shocks which can be very uncomfortable.

It is difficult for water molecules to penetrate between the tightly packed fibre molecules in highly oriented areas of a fibre. Areas of low orientation are more easily penetrated by water because of the larger spaces between the molecules. When a water molecule goes into a fibre, it causes the fibre to swell by becoming wider. This means that the fibre length has to shorten to accommodate the increased width, therefore the fibre shrinks.

Natural and regenerated fibres are very absorbent because they have more amorphous regions. In synthetic fibres, the chains of molecules are very tightly packed therefore the water has few places to go. This is why they do not absorb moisture well.

## Strength

The strength of a fibre is related to its ability to resist breaking under tension. If the chains of molecules in a fibre are highly oriented and the fibre is put under tension, all the molecules share the load, which means the fibre is strong. If the molecules are less oriented, some of them will 'straighten out' in the direction of the fibre length when tension is applied – this means the fibre will be less strong and is able to extend more before it breaks.

Cellulosic fibres such as cotton and linen have a mixture of highly oriented and less well oriented areas, which makes them strong. Regenerated cellulose fibres such as viscose have many less well oriented areas and therefore tend to be weak. However, it is possible to manipulate (engineer) the internal structure using modern production methods, to produce viscose with better strength.

The process of drawing during the manufacture of synthetic fibres causes the chains of molecules to become tightly packed and lie parallel to the fibre axis, which gives them their superior strength.

## Elasticity

Elasticity, also known as extensibility, is the measure of how much a fibre will stretch or extend before it breaks.

The chains of molecules inside a fibre are joined sideways to each other at intervals along their length. These cross-links stop the chains of molecules from sliding past each other. The strength of the cross-links varies in different fibre types, and this strength is partly responsible for a fibre's ability to return to its original length after being stretched. In fibres with lots of highly oriented areas – for example linen – the chains of molecules do not have spaces to move in to where molecules are less tightly packed. If these fibres are subjected to excessive stretching and bending, the cross-links between the chains of molecules will break, causing irreparable damage and weakness where the breaks have occurred. This causes wrinkling and creasing of fabrics due to the weakened structure of the fibres.

In fibres with a mixture of high and low orientation areas, the chains of molecules can move when the fibre is stretched or bent. This ability to flex gives the fibres a softer handle. A fibre with good elasticity is one whose chains of molecules can recover from strain and return to their original length after stretching.

Elasticity is important especially for clothing fabrics, because fibres that are able to recover easily from stretching are able to keep their shape and shed creases easily. This type of elasticity is not the same as the high levels of stretch found in elastomeric fibres.

### Flammability

Textile materials do not catch fire unless they are exposed to a source of ignition, therefore spontaneous combustion is impossible in normal situations. Some fibres catch fire very easily while others do not set alight at all, or with great difficulty. Fibres react in different ways to flames – some burn very quickly and fiercely, and give off toxic smoke; others melt and drip. Clearly there is a serious risk of injury from burning fabrics, but those that melt and drip can be even more dangerous – the hot, molten fibre can stick to the skin, causing very serious burns.

Cellulosic fibres such as cotton catch fire easily, whereas synthetic fibres are difficult to set alight but melt and drip. Wool fabrics do not catch fire easily and tend to put themselves out very quickly. How easily a fabric catches fire and burns is a particularly important consideration when choosing fabrics for children's nightwear and soft furnishings.

### Thermal qualities

The thermal qualities of fibres can help to determine if a fabric will be warm or cool to wear. The shape and formation plays some part in the thermal qualities of a fibre. The ability to trap air – which acts as an insulator – is an important factor in deciding if a fibre will have good thermal qualities. Smooth surfaces such as those found in cotton, linen and synthetic fibres are not able to trap air, but the crimp in wool and other hair fibres gives them excellent thermal properties.

### Lustre

Lustre is the ability of a fibre to reflect light so that it appears shiny. In order to reflect light, a fibre needs to have a very smooth surface, for example silk and synthetic fibres. Lustre can add to the aesthetics of a product, but is sometimes an unwanted quality.

### Handle

The handle of a fabric is how it feels when touched or stroked. Is it rough or smooth, soft or hard, stiff or pliable, thick or thin?

These sensations also add to the aesthetics of a product, and different types of product will have different requirements.

## Different fibres and their specific performance characteristics

When choosing a fibre for a particular application, you need to be aware of the requirements of the product and try to match them to the specific qualities of one or more fibres.

### Plant/cellulose fibres

Cellulose fibres, for example cotton, linen and ramie are strong and good at absorbing moisture. This means that they can take a long time to dry but take dye well and are not subject to static electricity. They can be washed and ironed at high temperatures without damage. As the fibres do not trap air, they are not thermal insulators so are cool to wear in hot conditions. The flat, ribbon-like structure of cotton means that it does not reflect light so appears dull, but linen's more regular shape allows it to appear slightly lustrous.

Unfortunately, cellulosic fibres crease badly and shrink, but they can be given special finishes to overcome this. They are also easy to set alight, so can be dangerous.

### Animal/protein fibres

Wool and silk are both protein fibres from animals, but are quite different in many ways. Wool is soft and warm because it has a natural crimp like curly human hair, which is able to trap air. Wool does not crease easily because the crimp allows it to be stretched and then return to its original length. Wool fibres have a coating of lanolin – a greasy substance secreted by the sebaceous glands of the sheep – which makes the fibres naturally water-repellent. When subjected to heavy wetting however, it will eventually absorb water. It is very good at absorbing moisture and can absorb up to 30 per cent of its weight in water without feeling wet. As wool absorbs moisture, it is able to give off heat – a little magic trick that makes it very useful in fabrics used in cold and damp conditions, for example under layers of clothing for wet weather sports.

**Figure 1.2.14** Wool fabrics can be attacked by moths leaving holes in the fabric.

Wool does not set alight easily and when it does, it puts itself out quickly. It is hardwearing and quite strong so woollen products will last a long time if cared for properly. It does not have a lustre because the fibres are not smooth.

Wool has some disadvantages, as follows:

- It shrinks badly – known as felting. This makes it a problem to wash, but it can be given a special finish to prevent shrinking.
- Because it is very absorbent, it takes a long time to dry, especially as most wools will shrink if put in the tumble dryer.
- Wool fibres can be quite scratchy and therefore may irritate some people's skin.
- It can be attacked by moths who lay their eggs in wool fabrics; when they hatch, the larvae eat the fibres, leaving holes in the fabric.

**Silk** is lightweight, very smooth, and the shape of the fibres gives them a lustre. It is a very strong fibre but becomes weak when wet, so it needs careful washing. It is warm and absorbent, which makes it feel nice next to the skin. Although it has natural elasticity, silk can crease very badly. The triangular cross-section gives silk its lustre and softness.

## Regenerated fibres

Regenerated fibres have different properties according to their source. Standard viscose is derived from wood cellulose, and has some similar properties to cotton. It is very absorbent, but it is not a very strong fibre, especially when wet. It can also shrink and crease very badly. Most viscose fabrics are given special finishes to reduce shrinking and creasing. Viscose has a silky feel to it and a slight lustre, making it popular for fashion garments. In common with other cellulosic fibres, viscose sets alight easily.

Acetate comes from cotton cellulose and is a smooth, soft fibre that drapes well. As with other regenerated fibres, it has poor strength and resistance to abrasion, but it has a lustre and is inexpensive, so it is often used for dress fabrics and linings.

## New generation lyocells

Environmental concerns about the use of oil, the shortage of land for growing cotton crops as well as excessive use of pesticides and fertilisers has led to the development of a new group of cellulosic fibres called lyocells. The cellulose comes from sustainable wood sources – mainly eucalyptus and beech trees – and is processed in a closed-loop system where the chemicals are reused. Many new biodegradable and recyclable viscose-type fibres are being manufactured, for example lyocell and Modal. The cellulose in these new fibres has been modified or engineered to make fibres that are stronger, less absorbent and do not crease and shrink as much as standard viscose.

## Synthetic fibres

Synthetic fibres such as polyester and polyamide (nylon) are very strong even when wet, good at resisting abrasion, and are lightweight. They are very smooth to touch and can have a lustre. Most synthetic fibres are not good at absorbing moisture so they dry quickly – this is not the same as being waterproof!

Synthetic fibres do not shrink and do not crease much during normal use. They are **thermoplastic**, which means that they become soft when hot. This property means that they can be heat-set into new shapes such as pleats and creases. They should not be washed at high temperatures, otherwise they will soften and become badly creased during the washing and spinning process. The creases created during washing and spinning are not easy to remove because the fabrics melt under a very hot iron, with disastrous consequences!

The melting temperature of polyester and polyamide is about 250 °C, so while a hot iron will cause damage, the fabrics will not melt in the washing machine or tumble dryer. Synthetic fibres do not set alight easily, but will melt and drip – this molten fibre is very hot and can cause serious burns.

Polyamide turns yellow and rots after long exposure to sunlight, and is weakened and yellowed by chlorine bleaches. Polyester is not weakened by sunlight, and is not damaged by normal laundry detergents unless they are used in very high concentrations. It has slightly less elasticity than polyamide.

The shape and structure of many synthetic fibres is engineered to give them improved thermal qualities, and to enable them to wick moisture away from the body.

Although acrylic fibres are synthetic, they are produced as staple fibres; this makes them soft with a full, warm handle similar to wool. They are produced as bulky fibres, which allow them to trap air. Acrylic fibres are not very absorbent and are crease-resistant; however, they are sensitive to heat, and highly flammable unless given a special treatment.

The molecules in elastane fibres are like coiled springs, which gives them their very high ability to stretch and recover. Because they are so stretchy, they are not used on their own. The fibres are very fine, crease resistant and not absorbent.

The table of fibre properties in Chapter 1.1 (see page 3) summarises the properties of the main fibres.

## Fibre production

### Cotton

**Figure 1.2.15** A cotton plant with cotton balls.

Cotton fibres come from a plant that grows in tropical parts of the world. The seed pods of the plant are called bolls, and when they ripen, the seeds inside the boll become covered with very fine cotton fibres. When the seed pod eventually bursts, it becomes a fluffy ball which looks like cotton wool.

The cotton fibres are like hollow tubes. As the sun dries the fibres, they collapse and become flatter like a ribbon, and twisted. The fibres in the boll are short, about 2–5 cm in length.

### Linen

Linen fibres come from the stem of the flax plant. The stalk is made up of bundles of fibres surrounding a centre pith. The fibres are smooth, round tubes with a hollow centre, and have cross markings like bamboo canes at regular intervals down their length. The fibres are separated from the parts of the plant that are not wanted. The fibres are very smooth and about 3–4 cm long.

### Wool

Wool comes mostly from sheep. The sheep are sheared and the fleeces sent to the mills for processing.

Some luxury wools come from other animals, for example cashmere from goats, mohair from angora goats and angora wool from the angora rabbit. The wool fibres may be between 4 and 39 cm long, and are staple fibres.

### Silk

Silk is a protein fibre that comes from the cocoon of the silk caterpillar. The caterpillar spins the cocoon with two triangular shaped filaments, one from each side of its mouth. The filaments are held together with sericin, a

Figure 1.2.16 A silk worm and a cocoon.

Figure 1.2.17 A spinneret.

natural gum produced by the caterpillar. When the caterpillar is ready to turn into a moth, it will break through one end of the cocoon. This spoils the silk by turning it into small lengths, and means that it cannot be used as long continuous filament fibres, which are needed to make the best quality fabrics. When the cocoon is needed for silk fibres, the caterpillar is killed by submerging the cocoons into boiling water. The silk filaments can then be unwound as continuous lengths.

## Wet spinning of regenerated fibres

The wood pulp used for regenerated fibres is cleaned and the cellulose pressed into sheets. The sheets are dissolved in a solvent to make a thick, sticky liquid called the spinning solution.

The spinning solution is filtered to remove any undissolved particles, then pumped through a spinneret which has small holes in it like a showerhead. The spinneret is immersed in a bath of chemicals, which solidify the viscose filaments as they emerge from the holes. This is called **wet spinning**. The fibres solidify from the outside inwards at an irregular rate, and this gives them their distinctive striations along the length of the fibre.

The filaments are drawn (stretched) before being wound on to a spool as filament yarns, or cut into short staple lengths.

The shape of the holes in the spinneret can be changed to make fibres with slightly different characteristics.

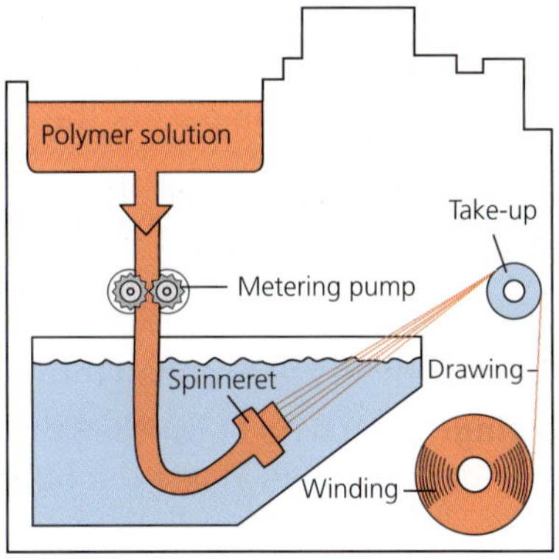


Figure 1.2.18 Wet spinning of viscose fibres.

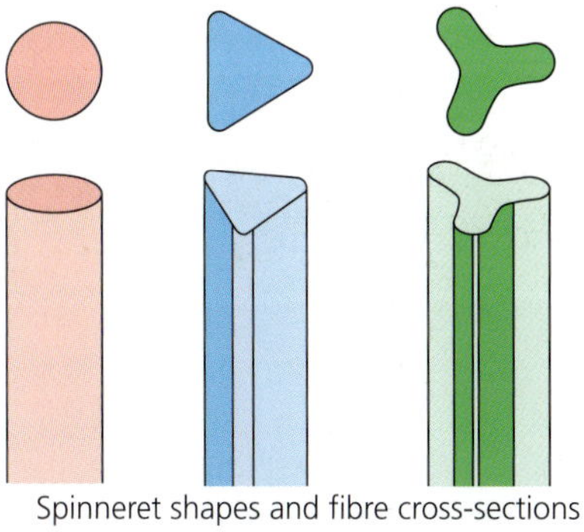


Figure 1.2.19 Changing the shape of the holes in the spinneret gives different fibre cross-sections.

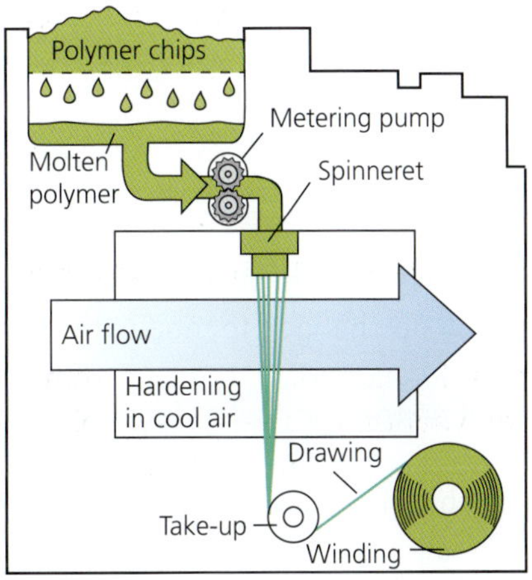


Figure 1.2.20 Melt spinning of synthetic fibres.

## Melt spinning of synthetic fibres

Synthetic fibres are made from chemicals which come from oil. The chemicals are made into a polymer, which is cut into small pieces. These are melted to make a spinning solution that is then pumped through spinnerets – the process is therefore called **melt spinning**. As the long filaments leave the spinneret, they are passed through a stream of cold air that solidifies them, before they are drawn out to three or four times their original length.

The long filaments are often cut into shorter staple fibres so that they can be mixed with other staple fibres such as cotton.

## ACTIVITY

Find samples of cotton, wool, viscose and polyester fabric. Use a probe or a needle to separate some of the yarns from the cut edge of the fabric. Untwist the yarns until you have just the fibre.

Using a hand lens or microscope, take a close look at the fibres. Sketch what you see. (You may need the help of a teacher or a science technician to use the microscope.)

Make a chart like the one below.

**Table 1.2.1** Observations of fibres.

| Fibre | Length of fibre | Appearance under lens/microscope |
|---|---|---|
| Cotton | | |
| Wool | | |
| Viscose | | |
| Polyester | | |

## KEY TERMS

**Staple fibre:** a short fibre.

**Continuous filament fibre:** a fibre that is a very long, continuous length.

**Thermoplastic fibre:** a fibre that becomes soft when hot, therefore it can be heat-set into new shapes such as pleats and creases.

**Lustre:** a natural sheen that gives a slight shine to a fibre.

**Spinneret:** the nozzle part of the spinning machine where the molten fibres are extruded.

**Wet spinning:** the fibre polymer is extruded into a bath of chemicals that set the filaments.

**Melt spinning:** the fibre polymer is melted to make a spinning solution, and the filaments are passed through a stream of cold air to solidify them.

**Drawing:** stretching of synthetic fibres as they are spun to align the chains of molecules inside the fibre.

## KEY POINTS

- The physical shape of a fibre affects its properties.
- All manufactured fibres are filament fibres, but silk is the only natural filament fibre.
- The scales on the outside of wool fibres cause it to shrink.
- The shape of the holes in the spinneret can be changed to modify the fibre's cross-section.
- The absorbency of fibres has a big impact on the comfort of fabrics made from them.
- Natural and regenerated fibres are very absorbent; synthetic fibres are virtually non-absorbent.
- Regenerated fibres are made from cellulose, therefore they have similar properties to other cellulosic fibres.
- Many synthetic fibres are engineered to give them improved thermal qualities, and to enable them to wick moisture away from the body.

# Performance characteristics of yarns

The performance characteristics of yarns are important in determining the qualities of the fabrics they are used to make.

## Yarn production

Fibres must be made into yarns before they can be woven or knitted into a fabric. Staple fibres are short and therefore need to be twisted together with other fibres to make a yarn. Many filament fibres are very fine, and need to be lightly twisted with other fibres so that they can be made into useable yarns.

It is the twist that holds the fibres together and gives the yarn its strength. A low level of twist allows the fibres to slip apart so the yarn will be weak. The yarns will be thicker and rougher to the touch. A higher level of twist increases the strength and gives a smoother, denser yarn that is more expensive than one with low twist.

### Staple yarns

**Staple yarns** are made from short staple fibres; these have to be carded, or combed, so that they all lie in the same direction, before being twisted together to form a yarn.

Filament fibres can be chopped up into short staple fibres; this means that they will need to be twisted together to make a yarn. If a filament fibre is to be blended with a staple fibre, the long filaments need to be cut into staple before being spun into yarn.

Staple yarns are hairy, which makes them good at trapping air between the fibres. This means that they are good insulators and will make fabrics that are warm. The hairy yarns can also trap moisture between the fibres. Hairy yarns have more texture than smooth yarns, and are duller in appearance.

### Filament yarns

Multi-filament yarns are made by lightly twisting continuous filament fibres together. A mono-filament yarn is made from a single, continuous filament.

**Filament yarns** are smooth and therefore do not trap air between the fibres. This means they make fabrics that are not good at insulating. Filament yarns are more lustrous than staple yarns.

**KEY TERMS**

**Staple yarn:** a yarn made from short staple fibres that are twisted together to form a yarn.

**Filament yarn:** a yarn made by lightly twisting one or more filament fibres together.

**Plied yarn:** a yarn made by twisting single yarns together to make a thicker yarn.

**Corespun yarn:** a multi-component yarn with a central core yarn that is covered by other fibres.

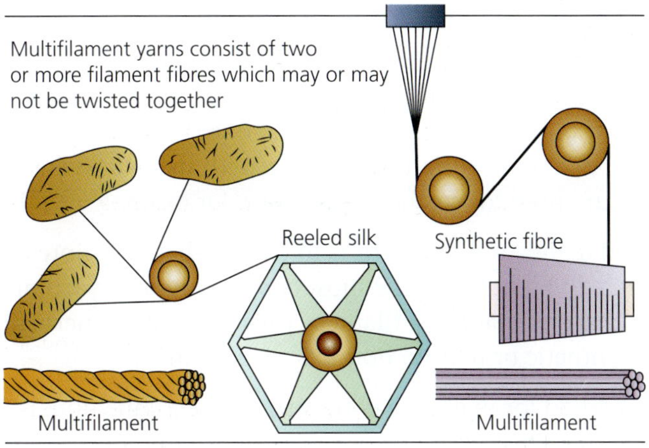


**Figure 1.2.21** Multi-filament yarn.

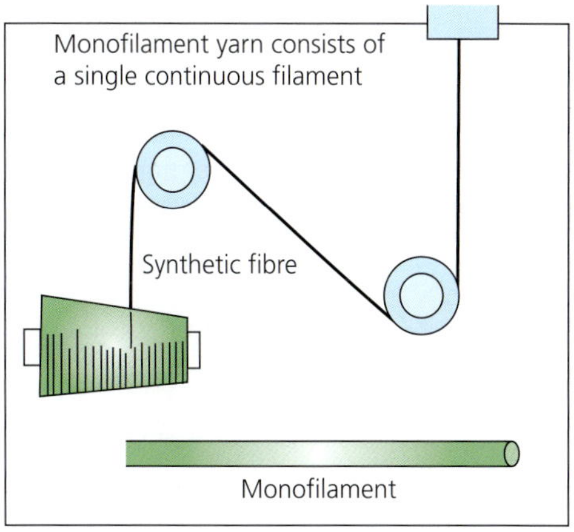


**Figure 1.2.22** Mono-filament yarn.

## Single yarns

A single yarn is one that has staple fibres or filament fibres twisted together to make one single yarn.

## Plied yarns

**Plied yarns** are made by twisting single yarns together. The ply of a yarn refers to the number of strands that make up the yarn, therefore a 2-ply yarn will have two strands, a 4-ply yarn will have four strands, and so on. Yarns with a higher ply number are more durable than those with a low number because the plies hold the fibres tightly together.

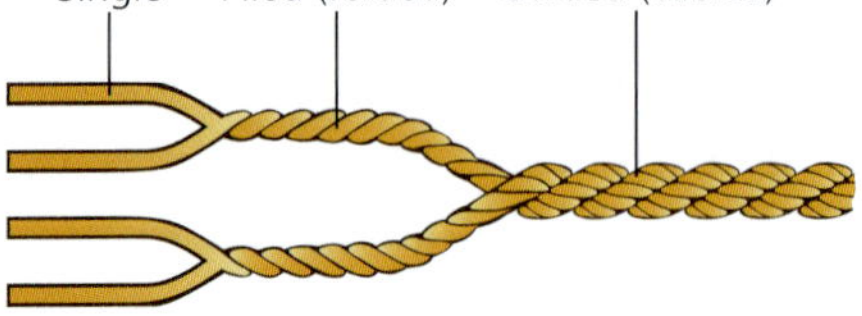


**Figure 1.2.23** Multi-ply and corded yarns.

A high number of plies does not always make a yarn thicker or heavier – that will depend on the thickness and weight of the individual strands used to make the yarn.

The single yarns are twisted together in the opposite direction to the direction that they were spun – this makes a yarn that has an even thickness with no weak places. Yarns with more than one ply can also be twisted together to make corded yarns, for example to make sewing and embroidery threads or industrial yarns that need to be very strong.

Plied yarns can also achieve special effects by using yarns made from different fibres or colours.

# Mixture and blends

Most modern fabrics contain more than one type of fibre. This is because there is no such thing as a perfect fibre, therefore manufacturers include different fibres in a blend. Blending is achieved by spinning two or more fibres together to make a yarn. This enables a fabric to be made that will be better suited to the product.

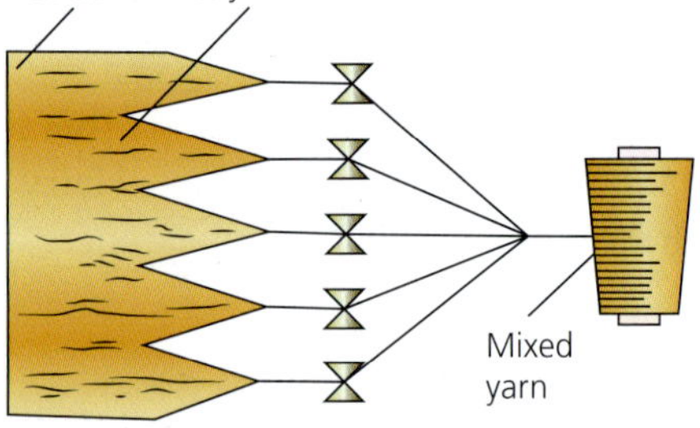


**Figure 1.2.24** Spinning a polyester/cotton blended yarn.

In order to make a successful blend, the fibres must be of the same length so that they can be mixed together before they are spun into a yarn. Therefore, if a filament fibre is to be blended with a staple fibre, the long filaments need to be cut into staple. The cut fibres are mixed together in the proportions needed for the yarn, for example 70 per cent polyester fibres and 30 per cent cotton fibres. They are then carded and spun into a yarn.

Continuous filament yarns can be twisted together to make a multi-filament yarn, for example polyester and nylon.

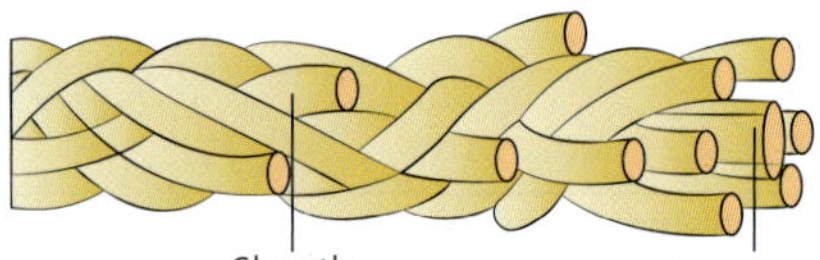


**Figure 1.2.25** The stretched elastane fibre is covered by a sheath of non-elastic fibres.

**Corespun yarns** are multi-component yarns where one component – the core – is at the centre of the yarn and is covered by the other fibres. They are important in the manufacture of stretch yarns and those used for sewing threads. The core can provide strength in a yarn where weaker outer fibres are used for aesthetic purposes, for example metallic yarns.

One method to create a core yarn is to twist a sheath of fibres around a core made from a different fibre. The most common type of yarn made using this method is one that has a filament yarn or an elastomeric fibre as the core, and synthetic or natural fibres as the sheath.

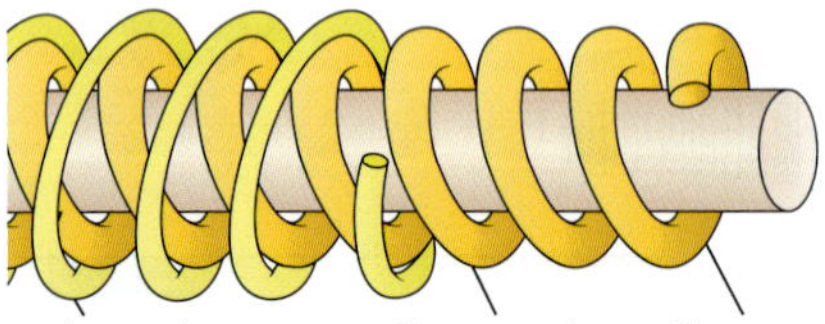


**Figure 1.2.26** Filament yarns are wrapped around the core yarn.

A second method for making a core yarn with elastane fibre is to stretch the core yarn and cover it with one or two strands of non-elastic filament yarn. The strands are wrapped in opposite directions to balance the yarn.

Core yarns are used for sewing threads because a synthetic filament core (such as polyester) gives strength, while the covering fibres (such as cotton) prevent the machine needle from overheating, and prevent the core fibre from softening during high-speed machining.

A mixture generally refers to a fabric that has been woven with different warp and weft yarns, for example a fabric made with a cotton warp and wool weft.

The main reasons for blending fibres are to:

- help reduce the cost of a fabric
- give different effects in the texture and handle of a fabric
- allow for novelty effects when a fabric is dyed
- make a fabric with specific qualities for a particular end use
- make a fabric stronger
- make a fabric easier to care for
- enable fabrics to be more crease resistant
- allow fabrics to be heat-set.

Popular blends are outlined below:

- Polyester and cotton blends are commonly used to make a wide variety of fabrics. Different percentages of cotton and polyester are included according to what the fabric is to be used for. The polyester helps to cancel out the shrinking, creasing and slow drying of cotton. The cotton makes the fabric better at absorbing moisture, and makes the fabric feel nicer next to the skin. However, polyester/cotton blends are very dangerous when set alight. This is because the cotton burns easily and holds the molten polyester in place. The fabric burns very fiercely at high temperatures, and gives off a lot of black smoke.
- Elastomeric fibres like Lycra are blended with many other fibres. Lycra gives the fabric stretch – the higher the percentage of Lycra, the more the fabric will stretch. Only very small amounts of elastane fibre are needed to give a lot of stretch, therefore elastanes are never used on their own to make a fabric. Elastane also makes the fabric more crease-resistant, but fabrics containing elastane should not be washed and ironed at high temperatures because this can damage the elastane.
- Viscose fibres are used in many blends. They help to make the fabric more absorbent and soft to handle. As viscose is cheap to manufacture, it can help reduce the price of the fabric.
- Wool is often blended with nylon for products such as socks, trousers, jackets and coats. The wool makes the fabric soft and warm, as well as making it a bit more luxurious. The nylon gives improved strength and resistance to abrasion, makes the fabric lighter in weight and helps to prevent the wool from shrinking when it is washed. The inclusion of nylon will also reduce the overall cost of the fabric.

Some other fibre blends include:

- viscose and nylon
- polyester, wool and Lycra
- cotton and Lycra

- linen and polyester
- silk and polyester
- silk and cotton
- acrylic and polyester.

## Twist, strength and bulk

The strength of a yarn depends on the level of twist as well as the fibres used. The level of twist affects the hardness of the yarn, and this will have an impact on the appearance and handle of the fabric. The smoothness or hairiness of a fabric will depend on the fibres, and whether the yarn is a staple or filament yarn.

Yarns used for sewing threads need to be very even and strong, so they are plied to ensure that they are fit for purpose.

The twist in spun yarns holds the fibres together and gives strength to the yarn. The more the yarn is twisted, the tighter and stronger it becomes. If there is too much twist put into a yarn, it will cause the yarn to twist back on itself, which will make it untwist and snarl. This is how the crinkly yarns used for crepe fabrics are made.

**Figure 1.2.27** S and Z twist yarns.

If the fabric is to be brushed, then a yarn with a low twist is needed. This allows the fibres to be teased apart easily to form the raised nap.

Twist can be put into yarns in one of two directions – S or Z. When an S twist yarn is folded with a Z twist yarn, the yarn is said to be balanced, and is less likely to untwist or snarl.

### Technical terms relating to yarns

Yarns can be very fine or very coarse, and this affects the appearance and characteristics of the fabrics made from them. Yarns have a wide range of thicknesses (diameters), and it is important to select a yarn of the correct thickness for a specific purpose.

The thickness of a yarn is not a good way to measure its size because it can vary along its length. Instead, the size of a yarn is given as tex or denier. Tex and denier are worked out by weighing a specific length of the filament fibre or yarn.

Tex is the metric system used to state the thickness of a yarn. It is the length in metres of one gram of yarn. The higher the number, the finer the yarn.

$$\text{Tex} = \frac{\text{length in metres}}{\text{weight in grams}}$$

Denier was originally used for silk yarns, but is now used for all filament yarns. It is the weight of one kilometre of yarn. The higher the number, the thicker the yarn, for example 60 denier tights are thicker than 15 denier tights.

$$\text{Denier} = \frac{\text{weight in grams}}{\text{length in km}}$$

**MATHS LINK**

**Calculating tex and denier**

**a)** Calculate the weight of a yarn with a denier of 15 and a length of 9500 metres.

**b)** Calculate the tex of a yarn with a length of 7095 metres and a weight of 325 grams.

**Answer**

**a)** $\text{Denier} = \dfrac{\text{weight in grams}}{\text{length in kilometers}}$

Re-arrange the equation to calculate weight:

*Weight in grams = denier x length in kilometres*

Convert the length in metres to kilometres:

There are 1000 metres in 1 kilometre, so 9500 metres = 9.5km

Weight = 15 × 9.5 = **142.5 grams**

**b)** $\text{Tex} = \dfrac{\text{length in meters}}{\text{weight in grams}} = \dfrac{7095}{325} = \mathbf{21.83}$

## Types of yarn

### Textured yarns

Yarns made from synthetic filament fibres are very smooth, lack texture and are poor insulators.

The characteristics of continuous filament fibres can be changed by introducing crimps, crinkles and snarls into the filaments – because the filaments can no longer lie close to each other, they are able to trap air. This means that they will be better insulators.

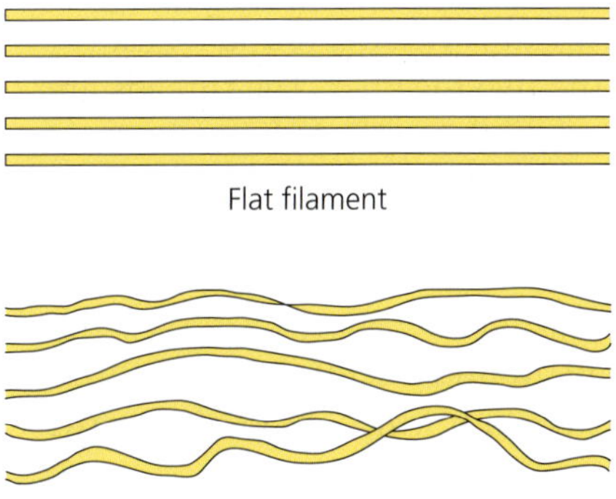


**Figure 1.2.28** Flat and textured filament yarns.

Fabrics made from **textured yarns** are more interesting. The fine tubes created in and between textured yarns help them to carry water, or allow them to wick more moisture. Textured yarns are softer, and therefore make more comfortable fabrics with more volume and less lustre. The crinkles and snarls allow the yarn to stretch out more than an untextured yarn, so they have more elasticity.

Many of the methods used to give texture to yarns depend on the thermoplastic nature of the fibres, which allows the filaments to be heat-set into the new shape.

The most important methods of texturing yarns are:

- False twist: a false twist yarn is made by twisting the yarn tightly, heat-setting it and then untwisting it. The yarn will have lots of crinkles and snarls.

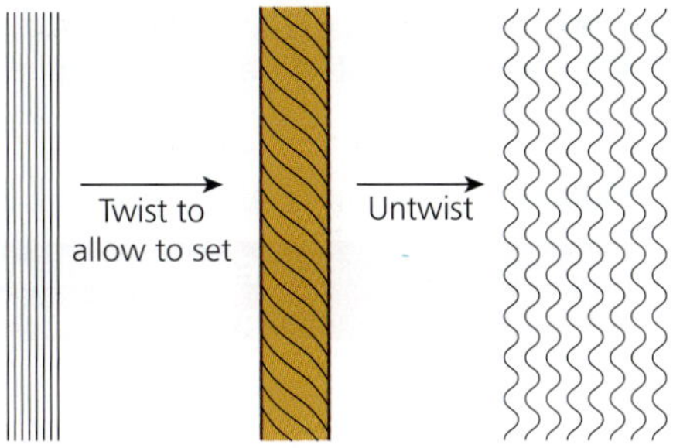


**Figure 1.2.29** False twisting of thermoplastic yarns.

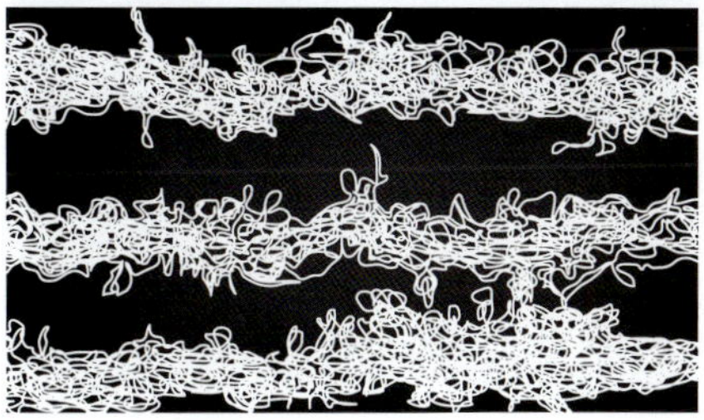

**Figure 1.2.30** Crinkles and snarls in false twisted yarns.

**KEY TERM**

**Textured yarn:** a continuous filament yarn that has crimps, crinkles and snarls set into the filaments.

## KEY TERM

**Fancy yarn:** a yarn that has irregularities and other effects added to the length of the yarn to add interest.

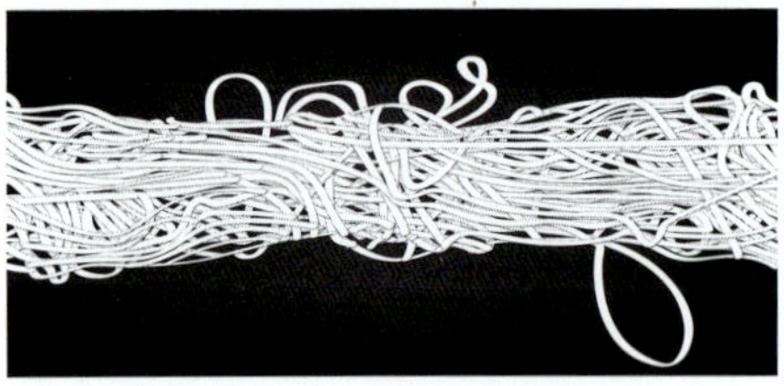

**Figure 1.2.32** Air jet textured yarn.

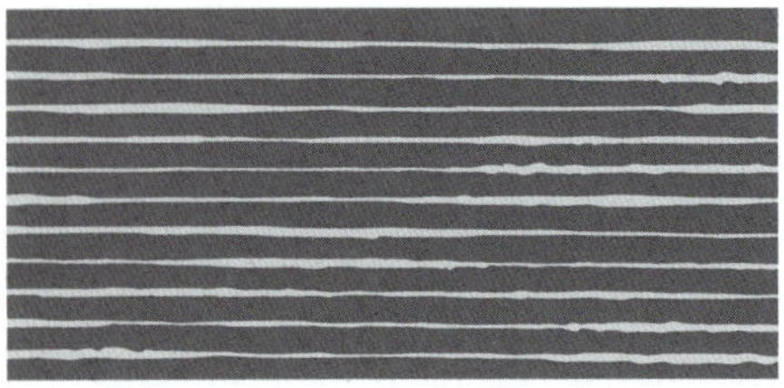

**Figure 1.2.33** Slub yarn.

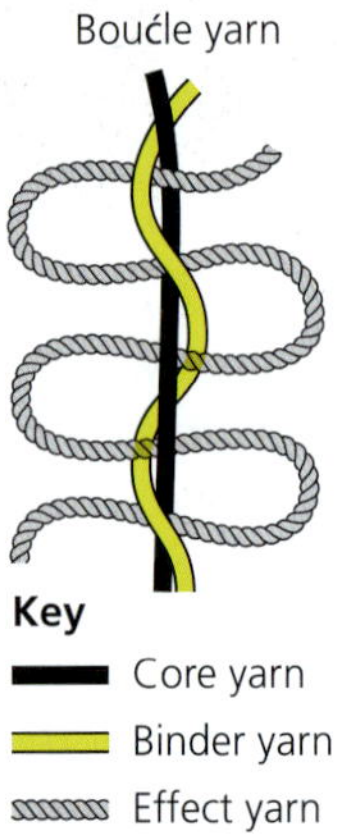


**Figure 1.2.34** The structure of a boucle yarn.

**Figure 1.2.35** Chenille yarn.

- Bulked continuous filament (BCF): a jet of hot fluid pushes thermoplastic yarns against a cold surface. This causes the filaments to cool into a saw-tooth edge-shape.

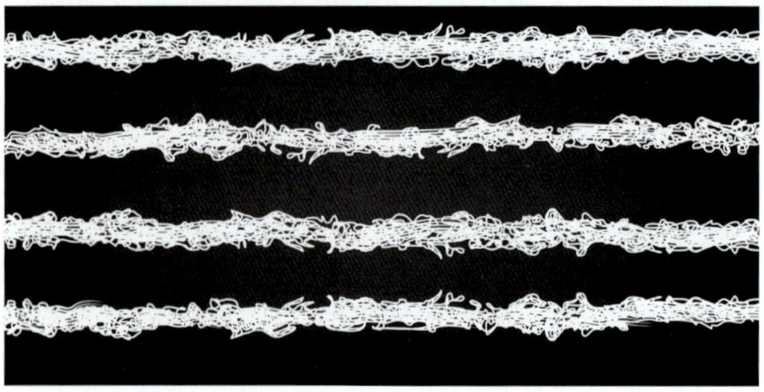

**Figure 1.2.31** BCF yarns.

- Air-jet texturing: a jet of compressed air is directed at the continuous filament yarn. This causes the individual filaments to become tangled, and creates small loops along their length. This method can be used with any continuous filament yarn because it does not depend on the thermoplasticity of the fibres.

Textured yarns are used to make fabrics for a range of applications including sportswear, underwear, swimwear, stockings and tights.

## Fancy yarns

**Fancy yarns** give texture and interesting effects to fabrics. They have irregularities and other effects added to the length of the yarn, and can be made from any fibre in either continuous filament or staple form.

The most common form is to have three different parts to the yarn: a fancy, a base and a tie thread. The fancy effect thread is twisted round a base thread. A tie thread is then used to hold the two together. The threads are often of different thicknesses in order to create the special effect.

Slub yarn is usually made by spinning thicker and thinner sections of yarn at irregular intervals. This yarn gives a fabric a similar texture and appearance to linen or wild silk.

Chenille yarn has fibres projecting from all around a central core of threads. It is produced by weaving an open net-type fabric which is cut afterwards. Chenille fabrics are soft and bulky.

Metal effect yarns are used to create fabrics such as lamé and brocades, which have sparkle and iridescent effects.

## ACTIVITY

Look at the labels in as many garments and textile products as possible. Complete the table below based on the garments and textile products you find:

**Table 1.2.2** Fibres used and reasons why.

| Product | Fibres used and percentages of each | Reasons why the fibres are used for this product |
|---|---|---|
| | | |
| | | |
| | | |

## KEY POINTS

- When filament fibres are blended with staple fibres, they must be cut into short lengths so that they can be spun together.
- Twist is important to give strength and hardness to a yarn.
- Many methods used to add texture to a yarn depend on the thermoplastic nature of the fibres used.
- Most modern fabrics are made from a blend of fibres, in order to make a fabric that is suited to the needs of the end user.
- Tex and denier relate to the thickness of a yarn, and are measured by weighing a specified length of the yarn.

# Performance characteristics of woven fabrics

Woven fabrics are produced by interlacing two sets of threads at right-angles to each other. The warp threads are fixed in the loom and run the length of the fabric. The weft threads run across the fabric from selvedge to selvedge.

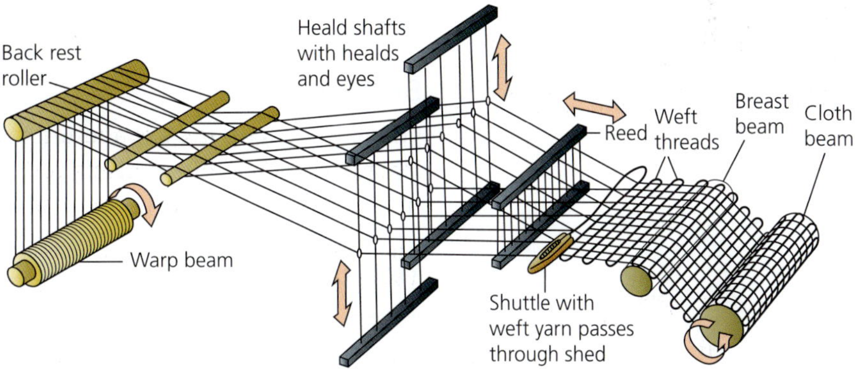


**Figure 1.2.36** A weaving loom.

## KEY TERMS

**Weaving:** the interlacing of two sets of threads at right-angles to each other to make a fabric.

**Twill weave:** a weave that has diagonal lines on the fabric, which are made when the weft yarn floats over two or more warp yarns.

**Satin weave:** the warp yarns 'float' over a number of weft yarns to give a smooth surface that is unbroken by the interruption of the weft yarns.

There are three main types of weave: plain, twill and satin. Other weaves are variations on one of these types.

## Plain weave fabrics

Plain (tabby) weave is the simplest weave.

The main features of plain weave are:

- It is the simplest and therefore the cheapest weave to produce.
- It has a plain surface that makes a good background for printing.
- It has the maximum number of interlacing points and therefore produces firm, strong fabrics which look the same on both sides.
- A variety of decorative effects can be produced by using dyed yarns. Fancy yarns can also introduce interest to the fabric.

The following fabrics are made using the plain weave.

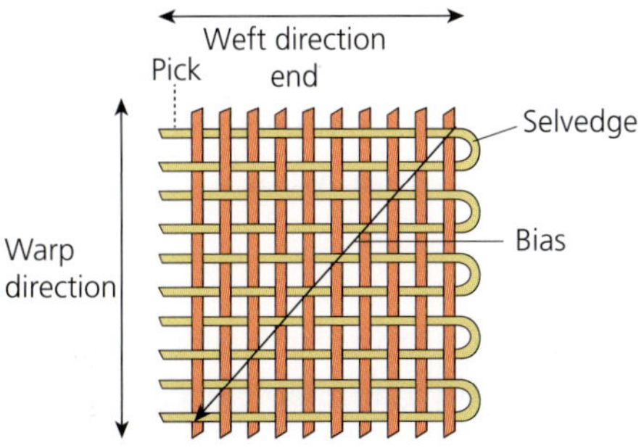


**Figure 1.2.37** A plain weave fabric showing warp, weft, selvedge and bias.

### Broderie anglaise

Broderie anglaise is a lightweight fabric with an all-over embroidered pattern that includes holes in the design. It is usually made from cotton or polyester cotton fibres.

### Calico

Calico is a medium weight cotton fabric that may be unbleached, bleached, dyed or printed. It has a slightly stiff handle because of the starchy dressing that washes out. Unbleached calico is used for making toiles because it is easy to work with. One limitation of calico is that it shrinks very easily.

### Canvas

Canvas is a firm, stiff fabric with a slightly ribbed texture, and is available in a range of weights. It can be used as an alternative to denim in clothing. It is used also for footwear, upholstery, tents and awnings. It is usually made from cotton or polyester fibres.

### Chiffon

Chiffon is a very lightweight, sheer fabric which is made from highly twisted and continuous filament yarns, using an open weave. Chiffon is a very soft and delicate fabric made from polyester, viscose or silk.

### Muslin

Muslin is a very light, loosely woven fabric made from cotton. When used for clothing, the fabric may be embroidered.

### Shirting

Shirting is a light to medium weight crisp fabric that is produced in stripes, checks and plain fabrics and usually made from cotton or cotton/polyester blends. It is used for shirts and other garments.

### Taffeta

Taffeta is a smooth, slightly stiff, crisp fabric with indistinct weft-way ribs. It is made from filament yarns such as polyester and silk, and makes a rustling sound when rubbed. When different coloured yarns are used in the warp and weft, the fabric has an iridescent two-tone effect, and the colour changes as the fabric moves and reflects light from different angles. It is used for linings and evening dresses.

### Voile

Voile is a very lightweight, open textured fabric made with 2-ply, highly twisted yarns. It is usually made from cotton, silk or manufactured continuous filament fibres, but it can also be made from wool.

### Winceyette

Winceyette is a medium weight, soft, warm cotton fabric with a brushed surface. It is often used for nightwear, but is highly flammable because of the raised surface.

### Chambray

A-level only

Chambray is a light to medium weight cotton fabric, made with a coloured warp and white weft, which gives the fabric a slightly speckled appearance.

### Flannel

A-level only

Flannel is a fabric with a slightly raised surface that gives the fabric a soft handle. It is available in different weights, and can be made using wool and wool blends or polyester/viscose blends.

### Organdie

A-level only

Organdie is a lightweight, crisp fabric that has been chemically treated to give it a durable, stiff, transparent finish. It is usually made from cotton, a polyester/cotton blend or 100 per cent polyester.

### Poplin

A-level only

Poplin is a medium weight fabric with a soft sheen and a fine rib that is made using a weft that is thicker than the warp. Traditionally made from mercerised cotton yarn, it is now often made using a cotton weft and nylon warp, a polyester weft and nylon warp, or 100 per cent polyester.

### Sheeting

A-level only

Sheeting is a wide fabric with a close weave and smooth surface. It is used for making sheets, duvet covers and pillow cases. It is usually made from cotton or cotton/polyester blends.

## Twill weave fabrics

Twill weaves produce diagonal lines on the cloth, which are created when the weft yarn floats over two or more warp yarns at regular intervals. On each successive row, the weft moves along one warp yarn to create the distinctive diagonal pattern. Different twill weave patterns are made by varying the number of warps that the weft yarns pass under and over on each row.

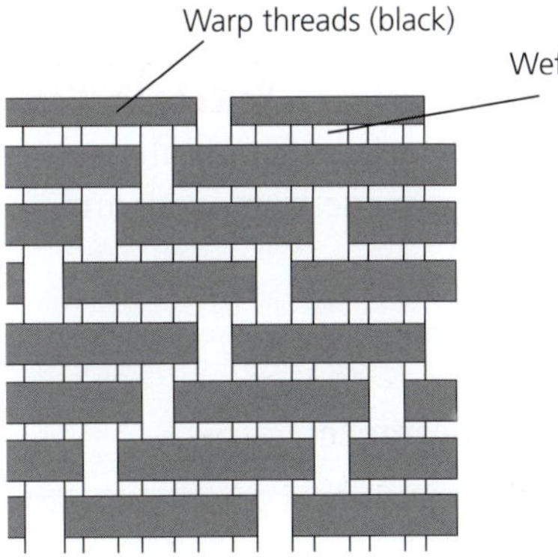


**Figure 1.2.38** A 3/1 twill weave.

The main features of twill weaves are:

- It is the hardest wearing weave.
- It is more complicated to produce and therefore more expensive.
- Fabrics have a definite right and wrong side.
- Because of their uneven surface, twill weaves show dirt less than other fabrics.
- It makes a firmer fabric, which is more likely to fray because there are fewer interlacing points.
- There are more variations possible with twill weaves.

### Cavalry twill

Cavalry twill is a firmly woven warp-faced fabric with a raised and very pronounced diagonal line on the front. The fabric is available in a variety of weights, and usually made from 100 per cent wool or 100 per cent cotton.

### Denim

Denim is a warp-faced twill made with a white weft and a coloured (usually blue) warp yarn. Denim is usually made from cotton, but small amounts of elastane are often included.

Figure 1.2.39 Tartan fabric.

Figure 1.2.40 Dog's tooth check fabric.

Figure 1.2.41 Herringbone tweed.

### Drill

Drill is similar to denim but is usually bleached. It is a heavy weight strong cotton fabric, which is often used for work or casual clothing.

### Gabardine

Gabardine is a tightly woven warp-faced fabric with a distinct steep twill line and a smooth appearance on the front. It is usually made from wool or cotton fibres, but can also be made from 100 per cent polyester.

The weave is so tightly packed that the fabric can sometimes resist water, especially when made using wool fibres.

### Tartan

Tartan was originally a twill woven woollen fabric made in Scotland, with each Scottish clan having its own distinctive pattern and colour. Today it is woven with a plain or twill weave, using a number of colours to give the traditional large check pattern overlaid with warp and weft stripes. Wool is still used to make the fabric, but other fibres such as acrylic or a polyester/wool blend are also used.

### Dog's tooth check

A-level only

Dog's tooth check is sometimes called houndstooth. The twill weave uses two colours to make a 'star' effect. It is usually made from wool fibres.

### Herringbone tweeds

A-level only

The herringbone weave is made by reversing the direction of the twill at regular intervals to give a zig zag striped effect. This is most effective when different colours are used for the warp and weft. It is an iconic fabric usually made from wool fibres to give a course and textured fabric.

### Serge

A-level only

Serge is a closely woven fabric with a slightly raised surface. Originally an Italian fabric made from silk, it is now almost always made from wool and used for tailored outfits.

## Satin weave fabrics

Satin weave fabrics have a smooth and lustrous appearance.

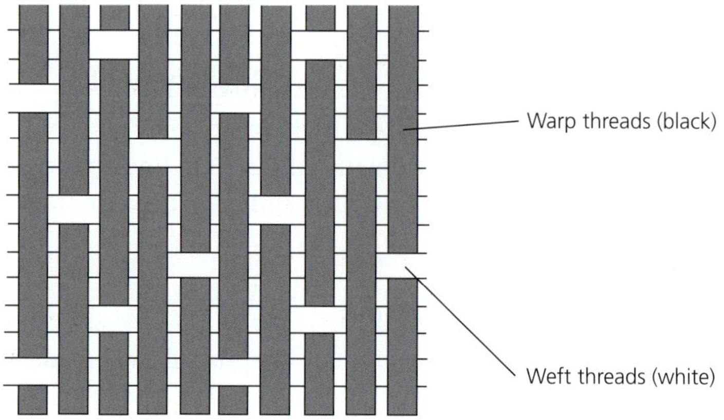


Figure 1.2.42 Satin weave.

The main features of satin and sateen weaves are:

- The weft yarns are almost completely hidden by the warp yarns, which 'float' over them in satin weaves, e.g. satin.
- Satin weaves fray easily because the threads do not interlace very often.
- Satin weave fabrics have a right and a wrong side.
- Satins with the highest lustre are made from filament yarns.
- The floats snag easily, therefore satins are not very hardwearing.
- There are not many variations possible.

Fabrics made from satin and sateen weaves include the following:

### Satin

Satin is a warp-faced fabric made in many different weights and qualities. The front of the fabric is very smooth and lustrous, and the back is dull. The lustre is enhanced by the use of continuous filament yarns that are usually made from silk, polyester or regenerated fibres. Satin fabrics are soft and drape well.

### Sateen

Sateen is a weft-faced fabric with a lustrous surface, although with less lustre than satin. As the fabric is made from spun yarns, short fibres are noticeable on the surface of the fabric. It is often made with mercerised cotton yarns or polyester/cotton blends.

### Lightweight satins

Lightweight satins are often used for linings and lingerie. Very lightweight satins are usually made from polyester, acetate, viscose or silk fibres, making them ideal for applications where a bulky fabric would be unsuitable.

### Duchesse satin

A-level only

Duchesse satin is a medium weight satin fabric with a slightly stiff drape. It is used for formal garments.

### Heavy bridal satins

A-level only

Texturised, multi-filament yarns are used to make heavy weight satins. These have shorter floating yarns on the surface and a slightly less lustrous surface than standard satins. The heavy weight ensures that the fabric holds its shape, and is therefore good for sculptured formal designs.

## Brocades and Jacquard

Jacquard is a type of weave (or knitting) which produces complicated patterns, often designed and controlled by computer programmes. The designs often contain intricate, curved patterns based on floral images with textured surfaces. Because the fabrics take a long time to make, they are often very expensive.

**Figure 1.2.43** Brocade fabric.

Brocade is a heavy-weight, woven Jacquard fabric where areas of the design often look like embroidery. It is often made with wool, cotton or silk blends including rayons and polyester. Sometimes metallic yarns are used in the fabric. The fabrics are used for garments and furnishings.

**KEY TERMS**

**Three yarn system weave:** a weave with a third yarn woven in with the warp and weft, to make a fabric with a raised surface.

**Jacquard:** a type of weave (or knitting) that produces complicated patterns, often with intricate shapes.

## Three yarn system weaves

Three yarn system weaves have a third yarn woven in with the warp and weft. This third yarn makes tufts or loops of yarn, which stand up from the body of the fabric.

### Velvet

Velvet is made using a warp pile weave, which has loops that are cut as part of the weaving process.

One method of producing velvet is to weave two cloths face-to-face, with the third (pile) warp alternating between the two fabrics. The pile warp is specially woven in to form the pile.

A knife moves back and forth at the front of the loom, and cuts the pile warp as the fabric moves forward and is woven. This produces two separate pieces of velvet at the same time.

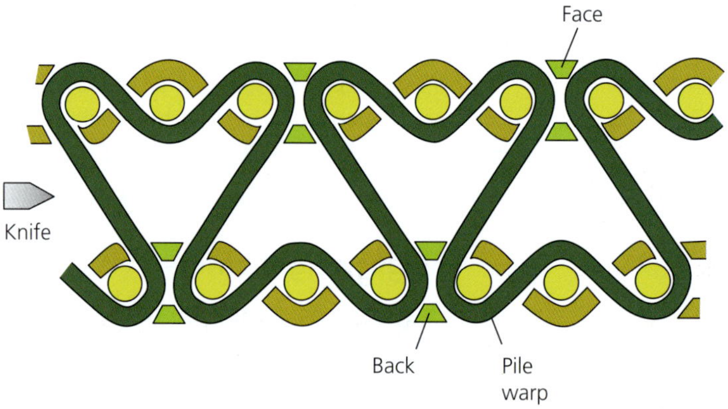


**Figure 1.2.44** Diagram to show velvet manufacturing using a warp pile weave.

### Corduroy and needlecord

Corduroy and needlecord are made using ribbed weft pile weaves which have cut loops produced after weaving. The pile runs parallel to the selvedge. The cords can vary in width to give jumbo cord (very wide) or needlecord (very fine).

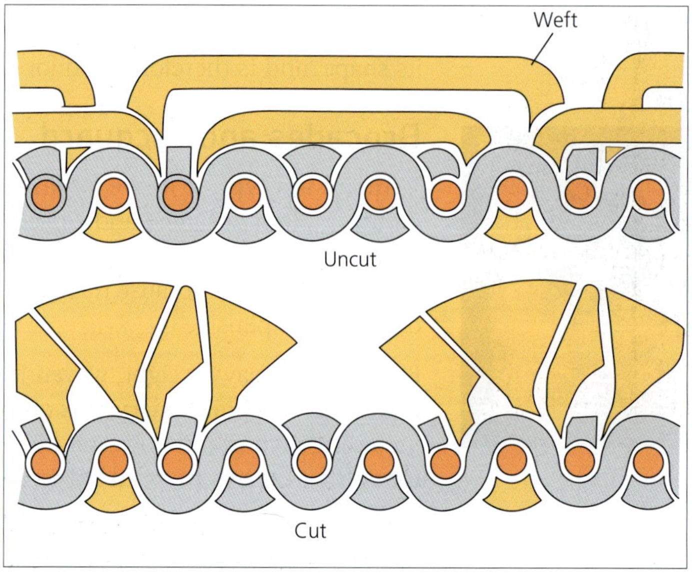


**Figure 1.2.45** Stages in making a ribbed cut pile fabric.

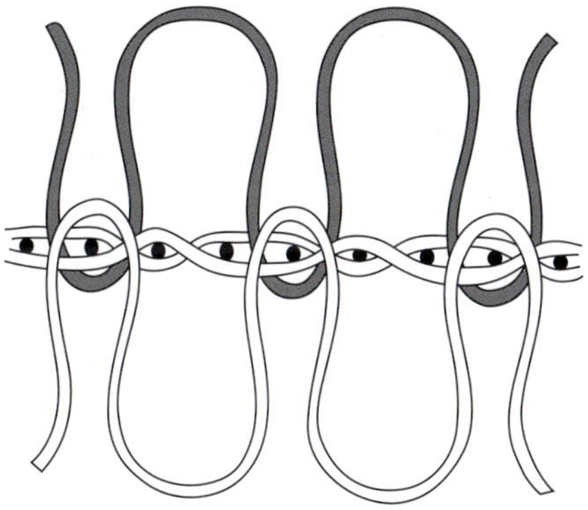

**Figure 1.2.46** A terry weave showing the loops above and below the main weave.

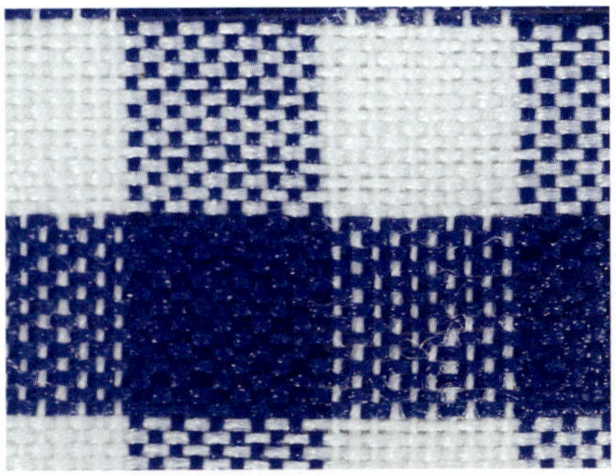

**Figure 1.2.47** Checked gingham fabric.

**Figure 1.2.48** Madras fabric.

**Figure 1.2.49** Bouclé yarn.

### Uncut loop pile weaves

In uncut loop pile weaves, the pile warp remains slack, and loops above and below the fabric to form the pile. Towelling fabrics are produced using this weave.

## Special woven effects

A-level only

By using different coloured yarns in the warp and weft, it is possible to introduce a checked or striped pattern in the fabric.

### Checks and stripes

Stripes that run down the length of the fabric are made by having blocks of two or more different coloured warp yarns and one colour in the weft. Checks are made by having blocks of different coloured yarns in both the warp and the weft.

### Gingham

Gingham is a lightweight fabric woven in a plain weave, with two different coloured yarns in both the warp and the weft to give an even sized check. Gingham can also be a striped fabric, which is produced by having two different colours in the warp and one colour in the weft. It is usually made from cotton, and is often used for school dresses.

### Tartan

Tartan is described in the twill weaves section of this chapter.

### Madras

Madras is a lightweight plain weave cotton fabric with a large colour woven check pattern and often in bright colour combinations. Authentic Indian Madras is completely handwoven, using yarns dyed with vegetable dyes that will bleed and blend together when the fabric is washed.

## Fabric effects created using fibres and yarns

A-level only

### Bouclé and crêpe fabrics

Bouclé is a plain weave fabric with a textured bumpy feel. It is a hairy, bulky fabric and often has different colours, which adds weight to a design. Bouclé fabric is often made from 100 per cent wool or a wool blend, or 100 per cent acrylic or acrylic blend.

Crêpe fabric has an irregular, finely textured crinkled or puckered surface, which is achieved using a crêpe yarn. The yarns are made by twisting them very tightly so that they twist back on themselves. The fabrics vary from very lightweight to heavy crêpes, and are usually made from wool or polyester fibres. The weave is either a plain weave or a special crêpe weave that is very irregular so that there is no obvious pattern to it. Crêpe fabrics are soft and drape well. Variations on the basic crêpe fabric include crêpe de Chine and satin-backed crêpe.

### Crinkle and permanent creasing

Crinkle and permanently creased fabrics can be achieved using thermoplastic fibres such as polyester in the fabric. The fabric is set into

Figure 1.2.50 Bouclé fabric.

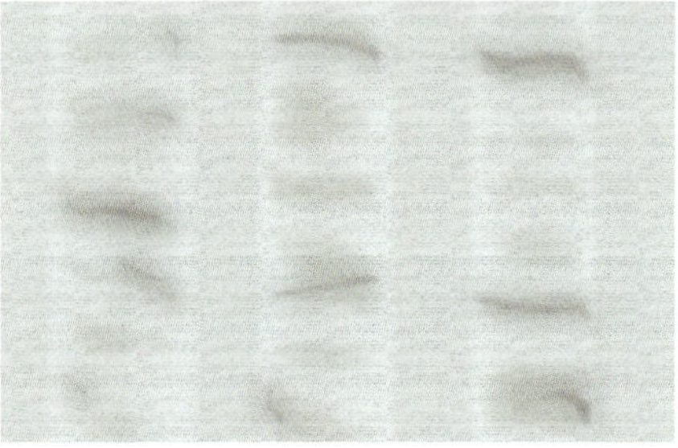
Figure 1.2.51 Seersucker fabric.

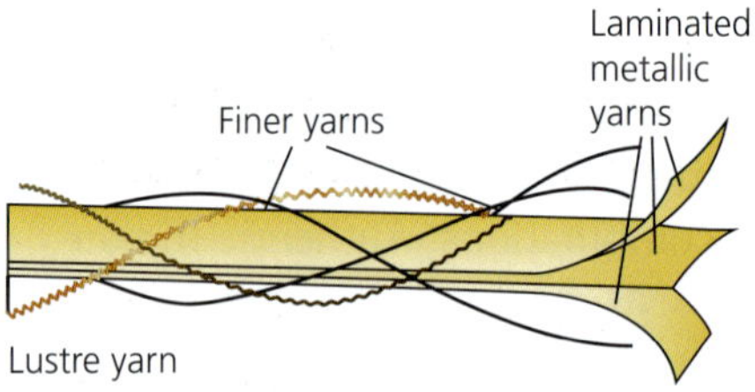

Figure 1.2.52 Structure of a metal effect yarn.

random pleats or creases using heat, which softens the thermoplastic fibres. When the fabric cools, the creases remain in the fabric.

Seersucker is a cotton fabric that has crinkled, lengthwise stripes. The effect is achieved on cotton fabrics in one of two ways:

- by printing a striped pattern on the fabric using a caustic soda solution – this causes the printed lines to shrink, which makes the fabric crinkle
- by having alternate groups of warp yarns arranged tight and loose in the loom, so that the stripes made are alternately crinkled and flat.

## Metallic fibres

Most metal effect yarns are made by sandwiching sheets of aluminium foil between sheets of clear plastic film. The laminate is then cut up into a flat, ribbon-like yarn.

It is possible to use other metals such as gold and silver to make yarns, but these are very expensive and rarely used.

## Use of dyes to give multi-coloured fabric

Fibres take dye in different ways. Using different fibres in a fabric means that it is possible to achieve interesting colour effects – dyeing the fabric using different types of dyestuff allows one fibre to take one dye and the other(s) to take a different dye.

## Use of thermoplastic fibres

The most important use of thermoplastic fibres is in making fabrics crease- and shrink-resistant. During processes such as dyeing, fabrics are pulled and distorted so that they are no longer the width or shape that they were when they left the loom. Many fabrics are made from a blend of fibres, including some that are thermoplastic. At the end of processing, the fabric is fed through a stenter machine. Small pins along the sides of the machine gradually pull the fabric into its intended size and shape. The holes from the stenter are often seen along the edges of fabric.

Once the fabric dimensions are correct, the fabric is heat-set using the thermoplastic qualities of the fibre blend, to permanently hold the size and shape. The fabric will not shrink, and will only crease if the fabric is washed at too high a temperature by the end user.

### ACTIVITY

Make a catalogue of special effect fabrics. Name and describe each fabric, and sketch a product that could be made from each.

### KEY POINTS

- The plain weave is the simplest weave, and produces firm strong fabrics that look the same on both sides.
- There are many variations of the twill weave, depending on how many warp yarns the weft passes over.
- Satin weaves are not very strong because of the lack of regular interlacing of the warp and weft, and are prone to snagging.
- Fabrics with a textured surface can be produced using fancy or textured yarns.
- The most important use of thermoplastic fibres in a blend is to heat-set the fabric so that it does not shrink or crease.

## Performance characteristics of knitted fabrics

Knitted fabrics consist of yarns looped together in a variety of ways. The two main types of looping are weft knit and warp knit. Other knitted fabrics are variations on one of these types.

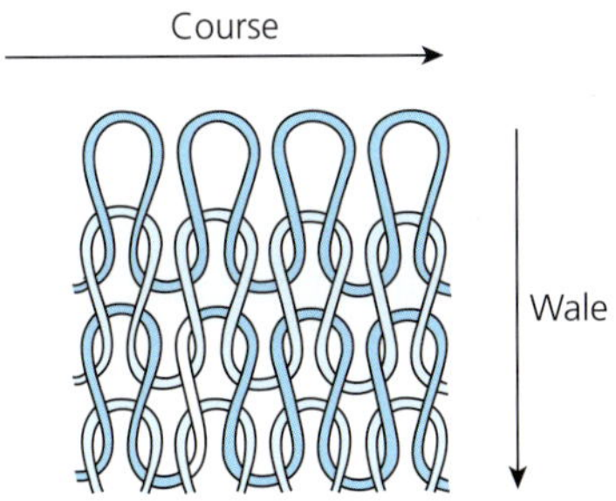


**Figure 1.2.53** Front of fabric.

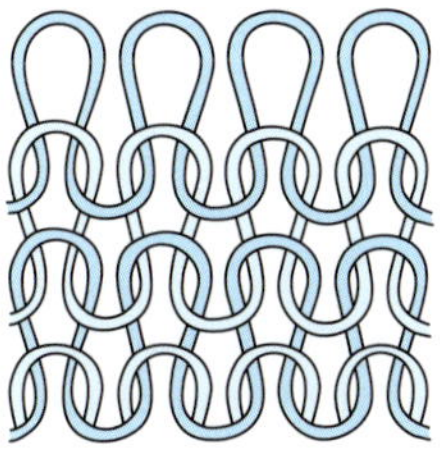

**Figure 1.2.54** Back of fabric.

### KEY TERMS

**Knitting:** knitted fabrics consist of yarns looped together in a variety of ways.

**Weft knit:** is made when one yarn travels the width of the fabric.

**Warp knit:** is made when many separate yarns are interlaced sideways.

**Hand knitting:** weft knitting to make individual garments, sometimes using traditional patterns.

**Fully fashioned knitting:** garment parts are weft knitted to the exact shape and size required, and stitched together to make the garment.

### Weft knits

Weft knit is the simplest type; it can be produced by hand, on a domestic knitting machine or industrially. To create weft knit, one yarn travels the width of the fabric, in the same way that a weft thread goes across from selvedge to selvedge in a woven fabric. Each successive row of loops is drawn through the previous row of loops in the fabric.

The horizontal row of loops is called a course; each vertical row of loops is called a wale.

The main features of weft knit are:

- It has a lot of stretch and is easily distorted, especially when washed.
- It drapes softly, and easily takes the shape of the figure.
- Fabrics do not crease easily.
- Fabrics trap air and are good insulators in still air. However, moving air is able to get through the gaps in the fabric therefore making it cool to wear in these conditions.
- It ladders easily if snagged.
- There is a distinct back and front (face) of the fabric.

Variations of weft knit include single jerseys (stockinette), double jerseys (interlock), rib knits, sliver knits (pile-type fabrics) and Jacquard knits (complex patterns with different coloured yarns). Weft knitting can also produce tubular fabrics.

Polyester fleece is a weft-knitted fabric that has an extra yarn knitted into it. The fabric is brushed on both sides to give a soft dense nap, which is able to trap air. This makes it a good insulator.

### Warp knits

Warp knit is a more complicated structure – it contains many separate yarns that are interlaced sideways. The loops are formed along the length of the fabric in the same way that the warp thread runs parallel to the selvedge of a woven fabric.

The horizontal row of loops is called a course; each vertical row of loops is called a wale. In more complicated warp knits, the needles travel sideways for two or more wales before making a new loop.

The main features of warp knit are:

- It is less stretchy than weft knit, and therefore produces a firmer fabric.
- Fabrics do not ladder and cannot be unravelled ‘row by row’.
- There is greater scope for the production of a variety of fabrics.
- It is faster than weft knitting, and the cheapest method of fabric production using yarns.

Variations of warp knit include tricots, locknit fabrics, knitted velour, Raschel knits and knitted lace fabrics.

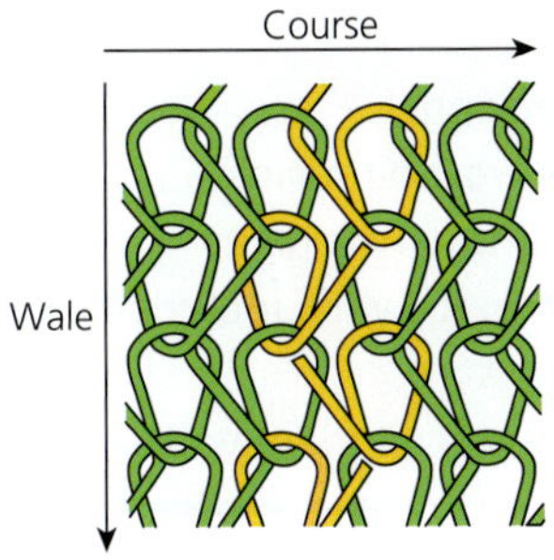


**Figure 1.2.55** Basic warp knit fabric.

## Hand and machine knitted methods

A-level only

Hand knitting can produce a variety of weights of fabric, and makes an individual product. There are many traditional styles of hand knitting, for example:

- Aran based on cable, diamond and lattice patterns
- Fair Isle, which produces multi-coloured patterns
- Guernseys, or ganseys – fishermen's jumpers with patterns based on cables.

Machine knitting can be done on a flat-bed domestic knitting machine, or flat or circular industrial knitting machines. Single-bed machines have a row of needles that produce a fabric with a knit front and purl back. Circular machines make a tube of knitting that is very fast to produce. Knitting is a faster process than weaving, so there are economic benefits to using knitted fabrics.

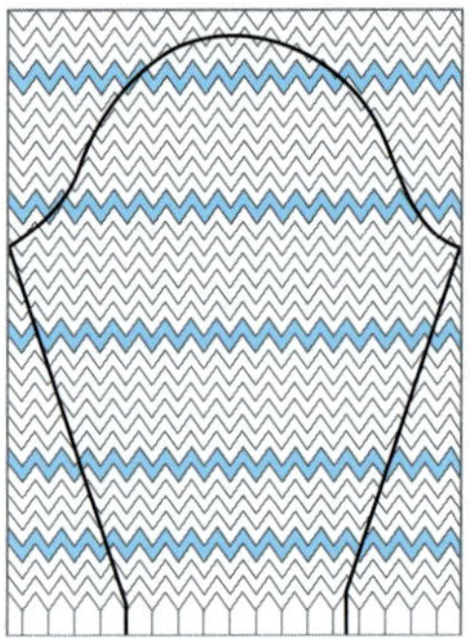

**Figure 1.2.56** A panel knitted sleeve.

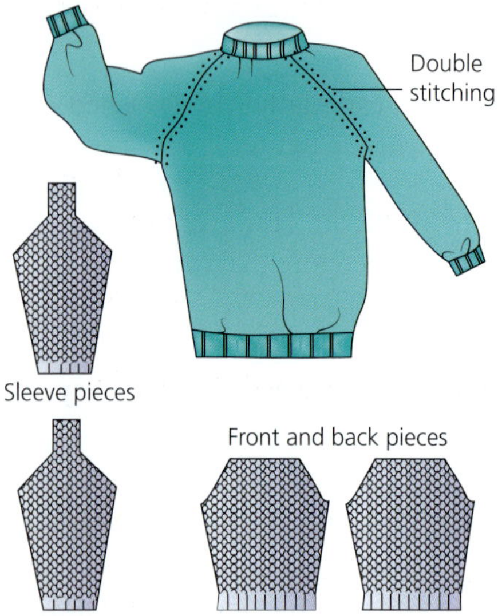


**Figure 1.2.57** Fully fashioned panels used to make a jumper.

### Panel knitting

In panel knitting, fabric is knitted in individual panels of a specific width and length, and with a finished-off edge at the start. It is used for sleeve or skirt panels.

### Fully fashioned panels

With fully fashioned panels, the garment parts are weft knitted to the exact shape and size required, and can be stitched together directly to make the garment. This method means that the fabric does not need to be cut to shape, and reduces waste. Fully fashioning is used in the manufacture of high-quality garments. All hand knitted garments are fully fashioned.

### Whole garment knitting

A knitted garment is usually made by knitting the separate parts and then sewing them together afterwards. This takes time and involves additional costs in the manufacture.

Whole garment knitting knits a garment three-dimensionally in one piece, on a computer controlled knitting machine. Because there are no seams, the garment is more comfortable to wear and it can have greater fluidity than when seams break up the garment's flow. Manufacture is more sustainable because only the yarns and threads required for each garment are used.

The seam-free garments lend themselves to sports, medical and wearable smart technology.

**ACTIVITY**

Collect samples of plain and twill weave, and weft and warp knitted fabrics. Work in pairs to unravel the fabric and watch what happens using a hand lens. In what ways is the structure of the two types of knit different?

How does the structure of the knitted fabrics differ from that of the two woven fabrics?

**KEY POINTS**

- Knitting creates a very different structure to weaving.
- Knitted fabrics do not have a warp and weft like woven fabrics.
- Tubular fabrics are weft knitted on a circular knitting machine.
- Polyester fleece fabrics are weft knitted with an extra yarn included.
- Warp knit fabrics have less stretch than weft knits.
- Warp knitting can produce a greater variety of patterns than weft knit.

## Performance characteristics of non-woven fabrics

**KEY TERMS**

**Non-woven fabric:** fabrics made directly from fibres that have not been spun into a yarn.

**Wool felt:** a thick, compact fabric made from wool fibres, using their natural felting ability to matt together in the presence of heat, mechanical action and moisture.

**Needle felt:** a felt made from synthetic fibres that are matted together by mechanical action using barbed needles.

**Bonded fabric:** a fabric made from webs of fibres held together by an adhesive, a solvent, or thermoplastic fibres.

**Non-woven fabrics** are made directly from fibres that have not been spun into a yarn. They include felts and bonded fabrics.

The main features of non-woven fabrics are:

- They are cheap to manufacture because fabrics are made straight from fibres.
- Because there is no 'grain', they are cheaper to use.
- They do not fray when cut.
- They are not as strong as woven or knitted fabrics.
- They do not drape as well as woven or knitted fabrics.

Typical uses for bonded fabrics include disposable products, interfacings, filters, insulation and liners. New developments have allowed non-woven fabrics to be given special characteristics and finishes appropriate to the intended end-use. For example:

- flame retardant, non-woven fabrics for disposable headrest covers on public transport
- the use of carbon fibres to make fabrics for military and filtration uses
- non-woven fabrics for insulation and decoration of car interiors
- Tyvek used in buildings
- fabrics impregnated with beneficial chemicals, such as those used in bandages and wound dressings.

These new fabrics are usually stronger and can be washed. Because they do not fray, they are easily cut using lasers.

### Felts, adhesive and heat bonded

A-level only

Felt made from wool fibres uses the natural felting ability of wool to cause the fibres to matt together using heat, mechanical action and moisture. A downside of felt made from wool fibres is that it is expensive.

Bonded fabrics are made from webs of fibres that are held together in various ways:

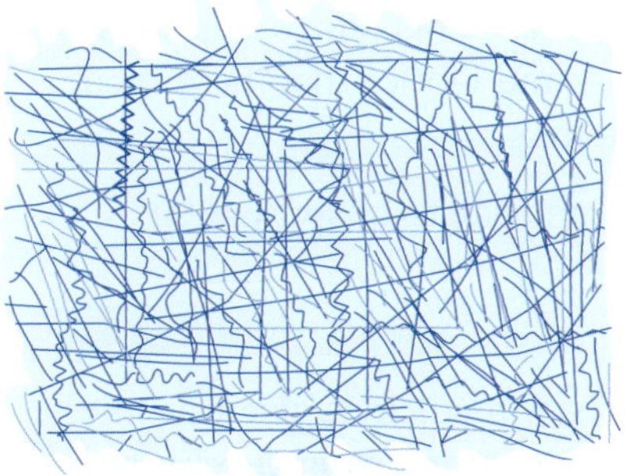

**Figure 1.2.58** Bonded fibre fabric.

- Adhesive bonding uses a special adhesive that is applied by spraying, dipping or spreading. The web is then pressed.
- Solvent bonding uses a solvent to soften and fuse the fibres together at the points where they touch.
- Thermal bonding utilises the thermoplastic properties of some or all of the fibres, to fuse the fibres together using heat and pressure.

#### Needle-felt

**Needle felts** are made from synthetic fibres such as acrylic, nylon and acetate. These are matted together by mechanical action – barbed needles entangle the fibres to produce a dense, felted fabric.

## ACTIVITY

As a class, make a collection of fabric samples. Mount them onto a large sheet of card and write the following information next to each fabric:

- name of fabric
- fibre content
- fabric structure, e.g. plain weave, weft knit, felted
- typical uses.

You may wish to arrange your samples according to the fibre content, for example all cotton fabrics on the same sheet. You could put the sheets of card on the classroom wall and add to them during your course. You could also photograph the completed fabric collection so that it can be used for revision at a later date.

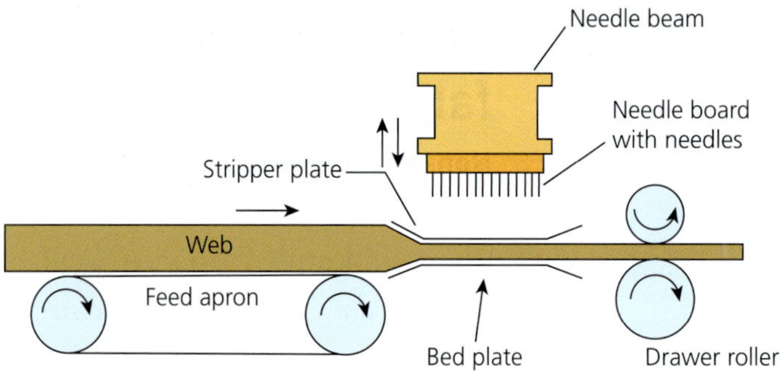


**Figure 1.2.59** The principle of needle felting.

## KEY POINTS

- The term 'non-woven' refers specifically to fabrics that are made directly from fibres, therefore knitted fabric cannot be classed as non-woven.
- Non-woven fabrics are cheap to make and use because there is one less manufacturing process. Also, they do not have a grain so can be cut in any direction.
- Non-woven fabrics are used for many disposable products because they are inexpensive.
- Non-woven fabrics are being developed and modified to give them a wider range of uses.

## KEY TERMS

**Smart material:** a material that is able to react to its environment. It changes its properties as they are needed, and reverts back to its original form.

**Modern material:** a new material that has been developed from its original form. It has special qualities suited to specific uses, but is not a smart material.

**Micro-encapsulated:** the inclusion of health and cosmetic chemicals into the hollow centres of microfibres.

**Nano-fibre:** extremely lightweight and strong fibres that are less than one micron in diameter.

# Smart materials

Smart or intelligent materials are able to react to their environment and change their properties as needed. They are able to sense and react to conditions around them, for example light, heat and power.

Smart materials include those that can warn users of changes – such as a loss of heat or the presence of pollutants – and fabrics that incorporate electronic components, such as music systems.

Many of these materials are used in health and safety or sportswear applications.

Smart materials:

- can monitor body functions and administer medicines/give warnings
- can maintain a personal microclimate, for example Stomatex®, Outlast®
- can provide buoyancy and support, for example bodysuits for medical/physiotherapy support
- can have chromatic properties, and change colour in response to specific situations
- can have shape memory, for example Corpo Nove shirts, which adjust to differing temperatures
- are self-cleaning, for example nano-technology fabrics that are triggered by sunlight
- can use biomimetics that imitate nature, for example Fastskin®, Stomatex
- can generate solar power when exposed to sunlight
- can sense and track movement, for example SensFloor® Smart carpets.

## Technical textiles

**Technical and modern materials** include the following examples:

- Gore-Tex®
- Kevlar® and Nomex®
- phosphorescent textiles
- reflective textiles using glass beads
- fabrics that wick moisture away from the body, for example Coolmax®
- micro-encapsulated fibres, for example those that release scents
- fabrics that protect against bacteria, for example Purista®, Chitopoly®
- fabrics with electronics, for example GPS systems
- geotextiles
- materials using nano-technology
- microfibres.

### Phosphorescent materials

Phosphorescent materials glow in the dark by transforming invisible energy forms into light. Phosphorescent dyes can be incorporated into synthetic fibres and yarns, used for textile printing pastes or applied as a surface coating.

Phosphorescent textiles are used in high visibility safety clothing for workers in dark areas where there is no light source. They are used in novelty clothing and fabrics to give glow-in-the-dark effects.

Polyester glow-in-the-dark thread can be used for novelty effects, and continues to work for more than 50 washes.

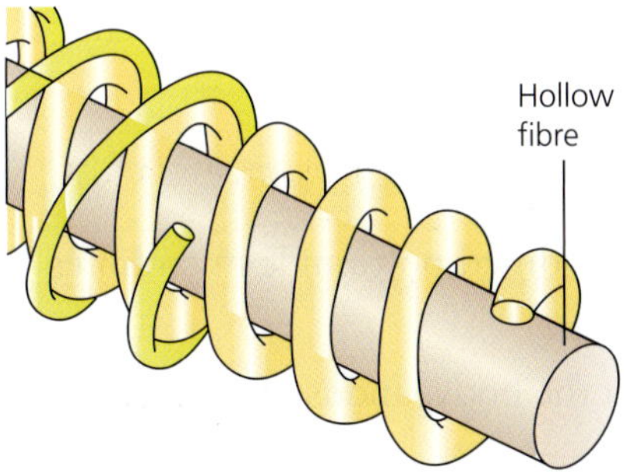


**Figure 1.2.60** Micro-encapsulated yarn.

### Micro-encapsulated fibres and fabrics

Various health and cosmetic chemicals can be incorporated into the hollow centres of microfibres. The chemicals are released slowly, and absorbed through the skin of the wearer. The chemicals break down slowly, so the effects last for a long time. This technique is also used to include ceramic molecules in a fibre.

The micro-encapsulated microfibres are covered with other fibres in a similar way to producing a core-spun yarn.

### Ceramic and carbon fibres used in the production of nano-fibres

A-level only

Ceramic and carbon fibres are important in the production of nano-fibres because they are extremely lightweight and very strong. The tiny fibres are made using an electro-spinning process, and are collected in the form of sheets that resemble non-woven felt. The fibres are very lightweight and have excellent covering power, so that a sheet of fabric the size of a football pitch can be folded down to the size of a sugar cube.

These sheets of fabric can be used as breathable membranes. They allow perspiration to pass out of sportswear garments, and at the same time, prevent large water droplets and other potentially harmful particles passing through.

Carbon fibres are used in the production of electro-conductive fibres, which are in turn used to make intelligent fabrics or wearable computers.

**ACTIVITY**

Investigate the latest developments in smart, modern and technical textiles – internet websites and labels on garments are a good place to start.

Prepare a 5 minute PowerPoint to present to your class, which brings them up to date with the newest materials and what they are used for. Include a sheet of notes that can be given to each member of the class.

## Ceramic fibres to give a fabric UV protection properties

A-level only

Ceramic molecules can be incorporated into synthetic fibres, either by coating them with ceramic particles or by encapsulating them within the fibre. The inclusion of ceramic molecules in a synthetic fibre can give the fabric UV protection properties, for example Esmo® and Sunfit® fabrics. Ceramic molecules can also make fabrics that are able to regulate body temperature, for example Thermolite® – a lightweight fibre with a hollow core.

**KEY POINTS**

- Many smart materials are used in health and safety or sportswear applications.
- Reflective textiles include glass beads to reflect light, therefore they are technical and not smart.
- Carbon fibres are important in the making of electrically conductive fibres and fabrics, as well as nano-fibres.

# Commercial names of fibres and fabrics

Manufacturers often develop a basic fibre or yarn to make a new fabric with enhanced properties. Some fabrics are innovative and are made by a particular manufacturer. The names of these materials then become registered trade names which cannot be used by another company. Some of the best-known names are given below.

## Tactel®

Tactel® is the brand name of a number of modified polyamide microfibres which are produced by the Invista company.

Tactel® Aquator wicks moisture away from the body, and is often used for underwear and sportswear fabrics.

Tactel® Diablo is a lustrous fabric that drapes well and is used for hosiery and lingerie fabrics.

## Lyocell®

Lyocell® is a new generation of viscose-type fibre made by the Lenzing company. It is produced from managed forests so it is more sustainable than standard viscose. It is the same basic fibre as viscose and Modal®, but the manufacture uses a different solvent which is easier to filter and reuse in the closed-loop system.

## Modal®

Modal® is a new generation of viscose-type fibre made by the Lenzing company. It is produced from managed forests so it more sustainable than standard viscose. The Modal® fibres are stretched more than viscose after spinning, which makes them stronger.

**Figure 1.2.61** The Lycra® logo is often shown on swing tickets of products containing authentic Lycra® fibres.

### Lycra®

Lycra® is the brand name of the elastane fibre produced by the Invista company. Products containing Lycra® fibres often carry a swing ticket with the Lycra® logo.

### Polar fleece®

Polar fleece® is made from recycled plastic bottles. It is a weft-knitted fabric which has an extra yarn knitted into it. The fabric is brushed on both sides to give a soft dense nap, which is able to trap air. This therefore makes it a good insulator.

**ACTIVITY**

As a class, make a collection of labels or advertisements for some brand names of fibres and fabrics. Write notes to explain what makes each material special.

## Summary of performance characteristics of fabrics in relation to end use

### Strength

Fabrics such as those made with a plain weave tend to be strong. This is because the structure has the maximum number of interlacing points, and therefore produces firm, strong fabrics that do not tear or fray easily. Satin fabrics are weak, even when made with strong fibres, because they fray and snag easily.

Non-woven fabrics are weak because they have little structure.

### Durability

Many things affect the durability of a fabric. Often a fabric becomes worn out not because it has developed a hole or fallen apart, but because its appearance is spoiled. Some structures are more easily spoiled than others. Pile weaves can break down fairly quickly when subjected to friction – the third yarn can easily fall away from the background weave, leaving bald patches.

Knitted fabrics, especially those made using a weft knit, can snag easily, leading to yarns pulling away from the fabric and the development of ladders.

Pilling is a major cause of fabric spoilage because it can quickly make fabrics look shabby and discoloured.

Some finishes, for example brushing, can weaken the basic structure of the fabric so they will wear away more quickly.

## Elasticity

Knitted fabrics have much more elasticity than woven fabrics because the loop structure allows the fabric to move in different directions. Obviously, fabrics with an elastane content will have greater elasticity than those without.

## Flammability

Fabrics that trap air can support combustion. If a fabric with trapped air is made with fibres that set alight easily, the fabric will be highly flammable, for example brushed cotton. A brushed fabric made with fibres that do not set alight easily will not be flammable, for example Polar fleece. Fabrics with an open structure will also support burning.

## Thermal qualities

Thermal qualities relate to a fabric's ability to keep a person warm or cool. Air is an insulator, therefore fibre, yarn or fabric structures that are able to trap air will be good insulators. Sometimes a fabric that will keep a person cool is required, so a smooth one that does not hold air will be needed.

## Absorption

Fibres such as cotton and wool, which are naturally absorbent, will obviously make fabrics that are able to absorb moisture. Although synthetic fibres are completely non-absorbent, they can be made into fabrics that are able to absorb moisture if the yarns made from them are textured. They can also be made absorbent if the fabrics are loosely structured, because moisture is able to pass through them by the process of wicking.

## Water-resistance

Water-resistance is about how easily water can pass through a fabric. Most fabrics will allow water through because it is able to penetrate through the gaps in the weave or knit structure, or will be absorbed by the fibres wetting the layer underneath them. A water-resistant fabric will have a special finish applied, or will be a laminated fabric with water-repellent qualities. However, most of these fabrics will eventually allow water to pass through, for example in a very heavy and prolonged downpour of rain.

## Stretch

Stretch can be incorporated into a fabric through the use of elastomeric fibres or by using a weft-knitted structure.

## Formability

**Formability** relates to a fabric's ability to be manipulated and deformed without being damaged. Fabrics that contain thermoplastic fibres can be heat-set so that they adopt new shapes such as pleats, and – providing that too much heat is not applied – the fabric will not be damaged.

## Handle

The handle of a fabric will depend on the fibre content, yarn structure and fabric structure. Some fibres feel very smooth, for example silk, while others are rougher, for example wool. Staple yarns can feel hairier than filament yarns if they are made with a hairy fibre. Some fabric structures such as satin feel softer and smoother than others, for example tweed. Handle can depend on personal preferences.

**Figure 1.2.62** A full drop pattern repeat.

## Drape

**Drape** is related to the way a fabric hangs or falls. A loosely structured fabric such as an open weave or knit will fall more softly than a stiffer fabric made with a tight weave, or a bonded fabric that has limited flexibility.

## Weight

The weight of a fabric can have an impact on how it hangs and drapes, as well as how it will wear in use. The fibre, thickness of the yarn and fabric structure contribute to the fabric's weight. For example, a loosely woven chiffon made with fine polyamide fibres will be much lighter than a fabric made from a tightly knitted woollen fabric that uses a thick yarn.

## Rip-proof

A-level only

Rip-proof – also called Ripstop fabric – is designed to resist ripping or tearing, and is often used for outdoor products and those used for extreme wear clothing. It has a distinctive woven-in raised square pattern, which gives it strength. It is usually made from 100 per cent nylon or polyester microfibre.

**Figure 1.2.63** A half drop vertical stripe repeat.

## Terms related to fabrics

The language of textiles includes special names for some features of fabrics. The main ones are explained below.

### Pattern repeat

The pattern repeat is the way in which the design fits together when repeated over and over to make a printed fabric. The design must fit evenly into the width of the cloth, however, lengthways is less of a problem because it is only limited by the size of the equipment used for the printing process.

The repeats are a crucial part of the overall design because the appearance of a fabric may be spoiled by the design having unintentional lines, spaces or gaps.

The design may be full drop, half drop (a vertical stripe) or brick repeat (a horizontal stripe).

The pattern repeat must always be taken into consideration when calculating quantities of fabric needed for a product, especially if the pattern is required to match up across seams in garments or furnishing products. The larger the pattern repeat, the more fabric that is likely to be needed. It is sometimes necessary to consider where the pattern will be placed on a product, so that it is centred with the product shape; this may well lead to wastage of fabrics.

**Figure 1.2.64** A brick repeat pattern.

### Directional pile

Pile fabrics have an additional yarn in their structure that stands up from the base fabric, for example velvet. When brushed, the fabric feels rougher to the touch in one direction, and when viewed from different directions, the fabric can appear to be different colours.

These fabrics must be cut with a one-way layout so that all the pattern pieces are placed in the same direction, otherwise the colour will differ across the product. This usually requires extra fabric to allow for the uneconomical layouts needed.

### Nap

A nap is a raised surface made by brushing the fabric surface after weaving. As with a directional pile, the fabric will feel different when brushed in opposite directions, therefore will require a one-way pattern layout.

### Texture

Textured fabrics such as satin, crêpe and some knitted fabrics must be cut using a one-way layout to avoid the shading effect caused by the way light is reflected off the fabric surface.

**KEY TERMS**

**Formability:** a fabric's ability to be manipulated and deformed without being damaged.

**Drape:** the way a fabric hangs or falls.

**Directional pile:** a fabric with a raised surface that appears to change colour when viewed from different angles.

**KEY POINTS**

- Fabrics must be selected so that their qualities match those required in the product.
- Pattern repeat must be taken into consideration when planning the layout of pattern templates to make a product.
- The way in which a repeating pattern is arranged can have a big impact on the aesthetics of a product.
- Taking pattern repeat into consideration often requires extra fabric for a product.
- Directional fabrics must be cut with a one-way layout, which may require extra fabric to be purchased.

## Check your knowledge and understanding

1 What is the difference between a staple yarn and a filament yarn?
2 Give three reasons why fibres are blended to make fabrics.
3 How can an elastane fibre be blended with a cotton fibre?
4 Name three different fabrics made using a three-yarn weaving system.
5 Give three reasons why a jersey fabric is often used for sportswear.
6 What type of fibre is Modal?
7 What three conditions are needed for the making of wool felt?
8 Explain how Polar fleece is made.
9 Give three important reasons why thermoplastic fibres are used in fabrics.
10 Explain what affects the thermal qualities of a fabric.

## Further reading

Hallett, C. and Johnston, A. *Fabric for Fashion*

Baugh, G. *The Fashion Designer's Textile Directory*

Willard, D. *The Fabric Selector*

Udale, J. *Textiles and Fashion*

www.textiles4u.co.uk

www.innovationintextiles.com

# 1.3 Methods of joining and using components

**LEARNING OUTCOMES**

By the end of this section you should have developed a knowledge and understanding of:

- a range of different seams and their appropriateness for different applications
- how to sew challenging fabrics
- different types of thread and their uses
- the use of fusible fleece
- the selection and use of different fastenings
- a range of different trimmings
- the selection of components and e-components
- the use of interfacings, underlinings, linings and interlinings.

## Seams

A seam is used to permanently join pieces of fabric together. There are different types of seam, and the seam which is appropriate for both the fabric and the product should be selected.

A good seam will be even, strong and protected from fraying. The choice of seam for a product depends on a number of factors:

- The type of fabric being used – is it thick or thin, opaque or see through, does it fray easily?
- The type of product being made – will it be subject to hard wear or need regular laundering?
- Should the seam not be seen easily or is it a decorative feature?

Seams should be sewn accurately – a crooked seam will make its presence seen. If the seam is wider than the allowance given on the pattern template, the product will be too small; if the seam is narrower, the product will be too big. Inaccurate seam allowances may mean that some parts of the product do not fit together correctly, for example when joining patchwork pieces.

Seams can be divided into two groups: those that need to have an edge finish, for example open seams, and those that are self-finishing, for example French seams and fell or double machined seams.

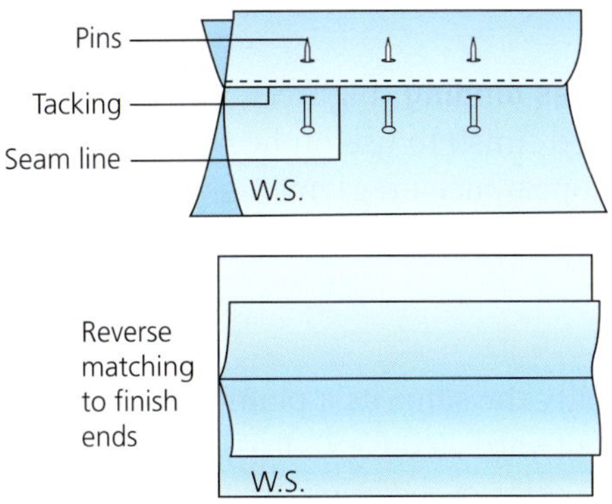


**Figure 1.3.1** Making a plain seam.

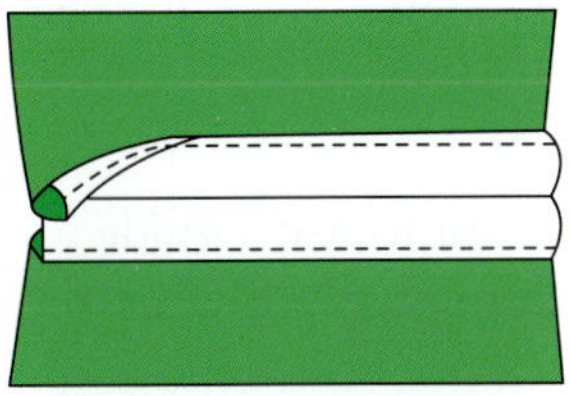

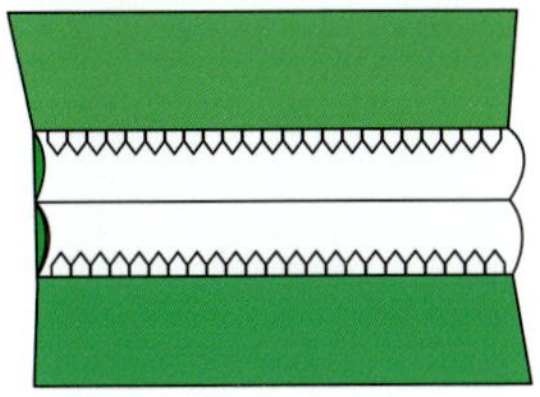

**Figure 1.3.2** Neatening raw edges with edge stitching and zig zag stitching.

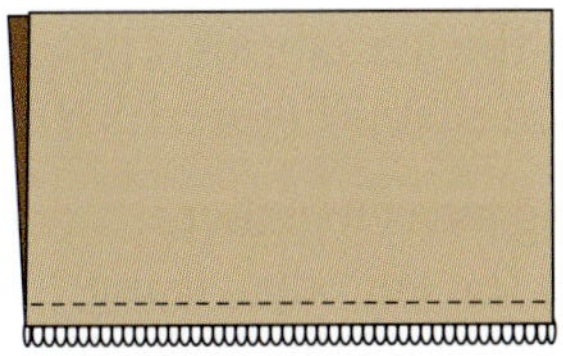

**Figure 1.3.3** Neatening raw edges with overlocking.

**Figure 1.3.4** An overlocked seam.

**Figure 1.3.5** Seam turnings neatened with pinking.

## Edge finished seams

### The plain or open seam

Plain (open) seam is the simplest, least visible seam used in many applications. It is not seen on the right side (RS) of the product unless a transparent fabric is used, and it gives a flat finish.

To make the plain seam:

1. Place the two pieces of fabric to be joined so that the right sides are facing each other, and with the edges to be joined level with each other.
2. Stitch along the seamline – this is usually 15 mm from the edge. Be sure to secure the stitching at both ends by reversing the stitching for about 5 mm.
3. Press the seam turnings flat.

The raw edges of the seam turnings need to be protected against wear, especially fraying of woven fabric. Fraying looks untidy and may eventually cause the seam to fall apart. If a knitted fabric is used, the unfinished edges can unravel or curl up. The finishing or seam neatening method chosen will depend on the fabric used and the position of the seam on the product.

## Edge stitching

The edges of the turnings can be turned under by 5 mm and stitched. This method is suitable for medium weight fabrics. On thick fabrics, the raw edges can be neatened by using a zig zag stitch on the raw edges without turning them under.

## Overlocking

Overlocking is a quick way to neaten seams, and gives a strong and neat finish. On light and medium weight fabrics, both turnings can be neatened together. The majority of seams on industrially made garments are finished with overlocking.

When the overlocker is used with two needles, it can stitch the seam at the same time as trimming and neatening the edges. This saves time, and is an ideal seam to use on knitted and stretch fabrics because it has more give than other types of seam.

## Pinking

If the fabric is firmly woven and does not unravel easily, the raw edges can be pinked with pinking shears. For a stronger finish, the seam turnings can be stitched 6 mm from the edge before you pink. Pinking is not suitable for products that will be washed frequently or are subject to hard wear.

### KEY TERMS

**Seam neatening:** finishing the raw edges of a seam so that they do not fray.

**Trims:** additional components that add a finishing touch and interest to a product.

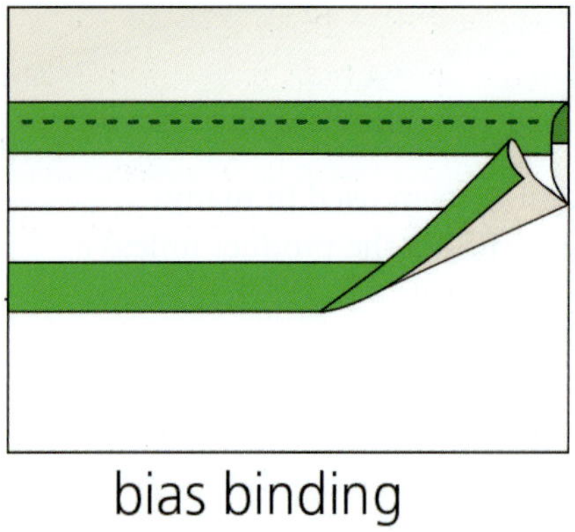


**Figure 1.3.6** Seam turnings neatened with binding.

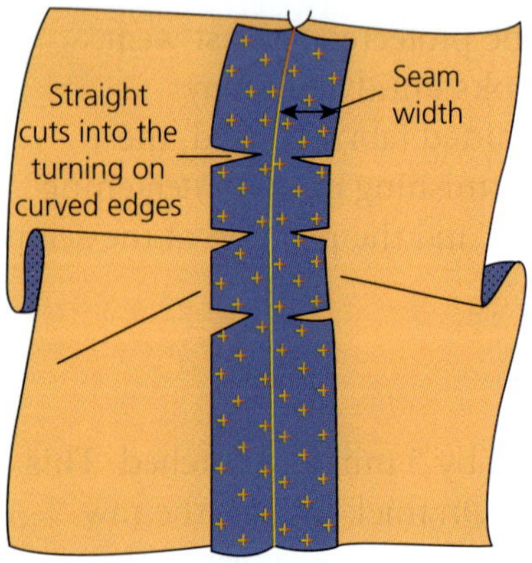


**Figure 1.3.7** A curved seam with the turning snipped.

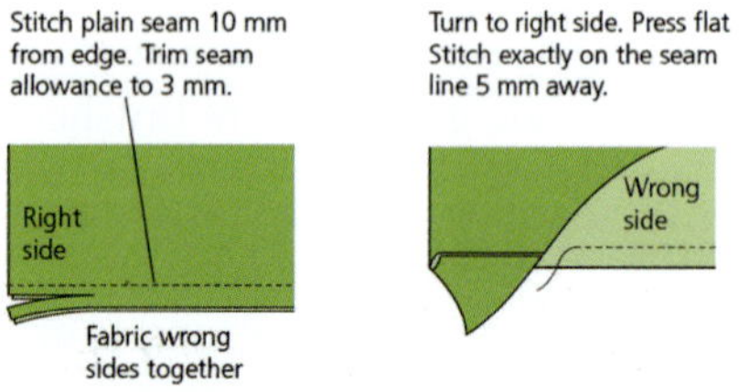


**Figure 1.3.8** Making a French seam.

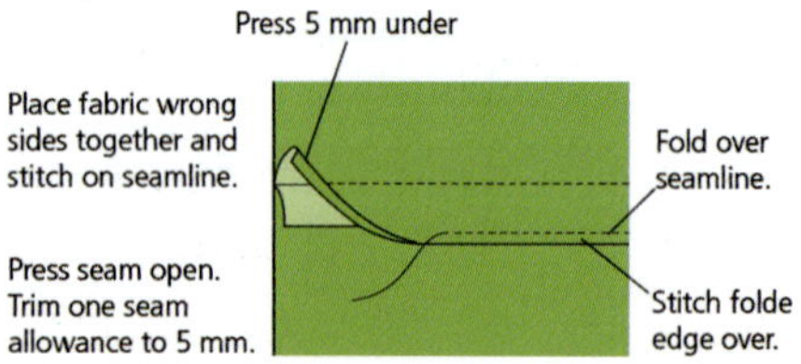


**Figure 1.3.9** Making a fell seam.

## Binding

The seam edges can be neatened with **bias binding** (Figure 1.3.6) but it is a time-consuming method. This is a good finish to use on heavy fabrics or ones that fray badly. It gives a neat appearance on garments where the seams might be visible, for example unlined jackets.

### Curved seams

A curved seam (Figure 1.3.7) is essentially the same as a plain seam. The seam may curve inwards (concave) or outwards (convex). It is important to remember that the seamlines of the two sides of the seam are to be matched – on a concave edge, the cut edge will be shorter than the seamline, and on a convex edge, the seamline will be shorter than the cut edge. This means that when pinning the fabric edges together, the convex side will need to be eased to the concave edge with the seamlines matched.

To achieve a smooth finish when stitching, it is important to use a guide on the sewing machine and stitch at an even speed. Using a slightly shorter stitch length can be helpful.

The turnings will need to be snipped at regular intervals so that they will lie flat when the seam is pressed open. The raw edges, including the clips, will need to be protected from fraying.

## Self-finished seams

### French seam

A French seam gives a neat and strong finish on fine and sheer fabrics because all of the raw edges are enclosed. The seam is not seen on the outside of the product, but it can be bulky if used on thicker fabrics. The following steps outline the process of making a French seam (Figure 1.3.8):

1 The fabrics to be joined are pinned with the wrong sides together, matching any notches. Sew the seam 10 mm from the cut edge, using the guide on the sewing machine to keep the sewing straight. Make sure you reverse the stitching at the start and end of the seam to prevent it coming undone. Remove any tacking and press the seam turnings open.
2 Trim the seam turnings to 3 mm then turn the fabric so that the right sides are facing, making sure that the first seam line is exactly on the line of the fold. Pin the seam, then sew it again 5 mm from the folded edge.
3 The seam is usually pressed so that it lies towards the back of the product.

### The double machined or fell seam

The double machined or fell seam is a strong, flat seam with two rows of stitching and all the raw edges enclosed. One or both rows of stitching are visible on the outside of the product, and the seam is often used as a decorative feature. It is usually pressed to the back of a garment. The steps for making a fell seam (Figure 1.3.9) are as follows:

1 If both rows of stitching are to be seen on the outside of the product, the fabrics to be joined are pinned with the wrong sides together, matching any notches. Sew the seam 15 mm from the cut edge, using the guide on the sewing machine to keep the sewing straight. Make sure you reverse the stitching at the start and end of the seam. Remove any tacking and press the seam turnings open.

2 Trim the turning on one side of the seam to 5 mm. Press the second turning over the first, turning the raw edge under by 5 mm. Pin in place then stitch the folded edge to the product, making sure that the stitching is close to the folded edge. If only one row of stitching is to be seen on the product, the right sides of the fabric to be joined are placed together at the start.

### The lapped or overlaid seam

This seam gives a flat, decorative finish and is used when the line of the seam is part of the garment style, as well as making a join. It is made by following the steps outlined below:

1. Fold the seam turning to the inside of the product, on the part that is to be the top part of the seam, and tack in place (Figure 1.3.10). This part of the seam is called the overlay.
2. Lap the overlay over the lower part of the product so that the seamlines are on top of each other. Pin and tack in place.
3. Stitch close to the folded edge of the overlay on the outside of the seam (Figure 1.3.11).
4. Neaten the seam turnings on the back of the seam.

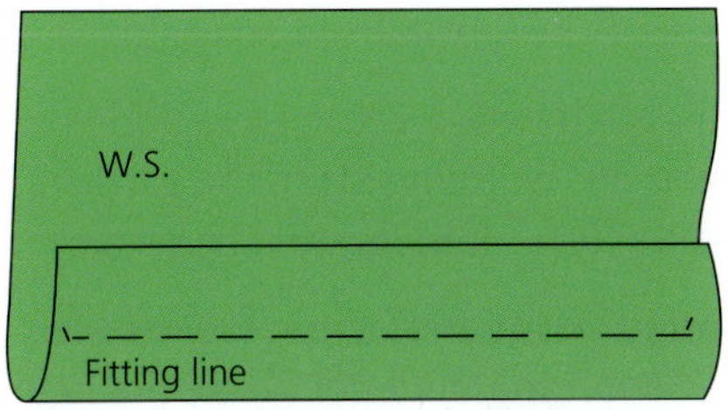


**Figure 1.3.10** Turn the seam allowance of the overlay to the inside.

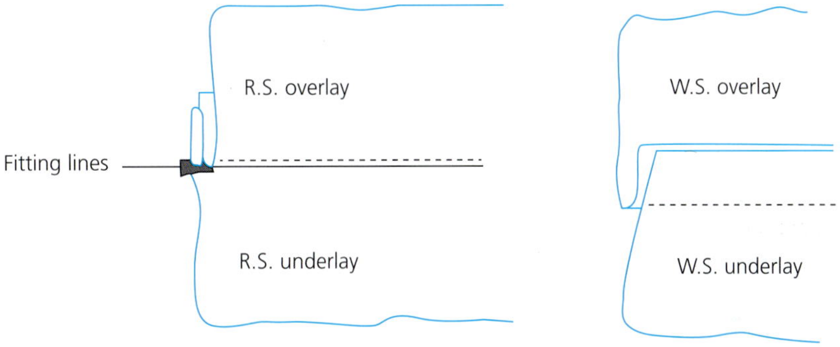


**Figure 1.3.11** Sewing a lapped seam.

## Working with more challenging fabrics

Some fabrics need to be handled with greater care – because of the way they are constructed or their pattern – in order to achieve good results in the finished product.

### Knitted fabrics

These fabrics stretch, especially weft knits, and this needs to be taken into account when working with them. The seam needs to have a little give in it otherwise it will snap when under tension. Use a stretch stitch on the sewing machine if possible, or use smaller stitches because they do not break as easily as long ones. A ballpoint needle is used on the machine because it is able to penetrate the fabric more easily than a standard needle.

A plain seam should be used because it lies flat, and the turnings should be neatened with overlocking if possible, to retain the stretch qualities. When pressing seams open, press over a roller or with strips of brown paper between the turning and main fabric, to prevent an impression of the turning showing on the right side of the garment.

Seams that go across the body, for example shoulder and waist seams, should be prevented from stretching by stitching bias or straight tape in with the seam. Pockets and buttonholes should be backed with an appropriate interfacing to prevent them from stretching and sagging. Take care not to stretch the fabric when putting in zips. Interfacings are covered in detail later on in this chapter.

### Stretch fabrics

These include fabrics that contain elastane fibres and have stretch in both directions of the fabric. They must be sewn with a stretch stitch and polyester sewing thread, so that the seams will not prevent the fabric from stretching in use.

Seams should not be taped unless there is a need to stop them stretching. A fine or ballpoint needle is needed to prevent the fabric from snagging.

Stretch fabrics should be pressed under a dry cloth with a warm iron, and pressing over a roller to prevent an impression on the right side of the garment. Using steam on a stretched seam can permanently set it in its stretched state.

Buttonholes and pockets should be supported with interfacing. If possible, machine stitch narrow hems because hand stitching may not allow the hem to stretch with the fabric.

### Checked fabrics

Checked fabrics may need to be cut out using a with nap layout. This means that all the pattern pieces must lie in the same direction so that any shading or pattern runs in the same direction on the finished product. The placement of the checks must be considered before the fabric is cut, especially large check patterns. Centre seams – such as those at the front and back of a garment – must be placed so that they are in the centre of a check or on a dominant line of the check. To make sure that the checks match across seams when they are stitched, the seam lines and not the cutting lines should be matched (Figure 1.3.12).

**Figure 1.3.12** The checks have been centred and matched across the opening of this shirt to give a pleasing appearance.

When cutting checked fabric on the bias, cut pieces on single fabric to make sure that the checks form a chevron across centre seams.

Seams need to be pinned and tacked carefully so that the checks match accurately. Using a walking foot on the sewing machine will help to stop them moving as the seam is stitched.

### Directional fabrics

A fabric with a nap (e.g. velvet), shading (e.g. satin and brocade), or a one-way printed design is known as a **directional fabric**, and must be cut with all of the pattern pieces facing the same direction, to avoid shade and pattern variations in the finished product.

**KEY TERMS**

**Directional fabric:** a fabric that has a definite one-way pattern or nap, which appears to be a different colour when viewed from different directions.

When stitching nap fabrics such as velvet, the presser foot on the sewing machine will push the top layer of fabric over the lower layer, resulting in an uneven seam. To prevent this, the fabric must be pinned with the pins at right-angles to the seam and carefully tacked in place, keeping pins and tacking stitches in the seam turnings as the velvet is easily marked. Using a walking foot on the sewing machine will help prevent the top layer of fabric from moving. A plain seam is the most appropriate for velvet because it is flat and requires only one line of stitching.

Satin and velvet should be stitched with a fine, sharp needle so that the fabric is not snagged. Both of these fabrics fray easily, therefore seams should be neatened as soon as possible using an appropriate technique.

Velvet should never be pressed on the right side as this will flatten the pile. It should be pressed over a needle board, or another strip of velvet, to prevent the pile from flattening and an impression showing on the right side of the fabric. Care is also needed when pressing satin to avoid an impression on the RS, especially if the fabric is made with synthetic fibres; a roller should be used under the seam.

### Sheer fabrics

Sheer fabrics such as chiffon and organza are very delicate as well as being see through, and their soft, loose weave causes them to fray and distort easily. Seams and interfacings will be visible on the outside of the garment, while trimmings and fastenings can snag the fabric and may be too heavy for the fabric.

When cutting these fabrics, they should be weighted down before the pattern is pinned in place, to prevent the fabric from distorting and sliding away from you. Use sharp pins and scissors or a rotary cutter so that the fabric is not snagged. The sewing machine can mangle the delicate fabric, therefore seams should be stitched between layers of tissue paper, and the fabric held taut as it goes through the machine to prevent puckering.

Fine French seams are the most appropriate for sheer fabrics; overlocking can look unattractive from the outside of the garment. If interfacing is necessary, use the same fabric so that a solid shadow is not seen on the outside of the garment. Facings are best replaced with bindings at neck and armhole edges, to maintain a translucent appearance.

Press the seams over a thick towel to prevent a ridge showing on the RS. The iron temperature should be suitable for the fibre content.

**ACTIVITY**

Make a sample of each of the four main seam types: plain, French, double machined and lapped. Sketch or photograph a garment where each seam type might be used.

If possible, make a seam in each of the following fabric types: checked, jersey, sheer, velvet and satin. Make notes on the problems associated with each of these fabric types.

## Threads

Threads are needed to sew products together, or to add decoration. There is a very wide range of threads for different purposes (Figure 1.3.13), and selecting the most appropriate ones is as important as choosing the right fabric. Some threads are used for specific purposes such as tacking, overlocking, buttonhole and quilting threads.

It is important to buy the best quality threads that you can afford, because cheap threads rarely give satisfactory results. They can also cause

**Figure 1.3.13** A variety of sewing threads.

problems with the sewing machine as they form lint – a dusty residue – around the moving parts. Lint can clog up the machine, making it noisy and slow.

## Sewing threads

- General purpose sewing threads used to construct products are usually made from polyester, but are sometimes made from cotton or silk. They are available in 100 m, 250 m and 500 m reels, or 1,000 m and 7,500 m for commercial use, and are dyed in many different colours so that they will blend in with the colour of the fabric used.
- Polyester sewing thread has some give in it, so is suitable for use with fabrics containing synthetic fibres and those that have some stretch. But it can melt when a hot iron is used to press fabrics.
- A polyester/cotton thread is core-spun with a cotton sheath around a polyester core, making it better able to stand up to a hot iron.
- Cotton threads are suitable for use with cotton or linen fabrics.
- Silk threads work well with silk and woollen fabrics.
- Buttonhole thread (usually called twist) is a thicker thread made from polyester or silk, and is used when making hand-stitched buttonholes, sewing on buttons and top-stitching.
- Overlocking threads are usually made from polyester or nylon, and are sold on large cones.
- Elastic thread is made from a polyurethane core covered with a polyester sheath. It is used for shirring and threading through knitted edges such as cuffs and necklines, to maintain shape.
- Invisible thread is made from nylon, and is colourless. It can be used for machine and hand stitching where an invisible stitch is required. It is heat-sensitive and will melt under a hot iron.
- Fusible thread is used in the bobbin of the sewing machine to temporarily stitch applique and trimmings in place. Ironing then fuses them to the main fabric, so that they do not need to be tacked before permanently stitching them.

## Embroidery threads

There is a vast range of embroidery threads (Figure 1.3.14) made from many different fibres, for example cotton, silk, wool, viscose, multi-coloured and metal.

- Stranded cotton thread has six strands which are usually separated according to the thickness needed. The thread is used for a variety of decorative techniques.
- Quilting thread is used for quilting and is made from cotton. It has a special waxed finish that stops it from tangling and gives added strength.
- Machine embroidery thread such as Gutermann Sulky and Madeira thread are fine, glossy threads that are suited to machine embroidery.
- Tapestry wool is a soft, thick thread made from wool and used for embroidery on open weave fabrics.
- Pearl cotton has two non-divisible strands, and is a smooth and lustrous thread suitable for many hand embroidery techniques.
- Soft cotton thread is a thick thread used for embroidery on open weave fabrics.

**Figure 1.3.14** Some embroidery threads.

## Special effect threads

Metallic effect threads are made from a polyester and polyamide blend or rayon, and give a lustrous 3D effect. When used on a sewing machine, it is advisable to use a special metallic thread needle.

Metallic threads have a polyester, viscose or nylon core with a coloured metallic foil wrapped round. They can be difficult to use on a sewing machine because the foil tends to split, showing the core. They also tent to twist as they are sewn. Using a special metallic thread needle and a mesh sock, or thread net over the reel of thread on the machine, is the recommended practice.

Variegated threads are multi-coloured threads that change colour at regular intervals, and are used for embroidery and quilting.

Glow-in-the-dark threads are made from coated polyester that is charged by exposure to bright light, and will glow for several hours in the dark.

### ACTIVITY

Visit a local or online shop that sells sewing and knitting resources and research the types of thread available for hand and machine sewing. Make a chart like the one below to show your findings.

**Table 1.3.1** Types of thread available.

| Type of thread | Fibre content | Number of metres on spool | Cost | Possible uses |
|---|---|---|---|---|
| | | | | |
| | | | | |
| | | | | |
| | | | | |

### KEY TERMS

**Fusible fleece:** a heat-sensitive web that has adhesive on both sides and is used to join two pieces of fabric together, using heat and steam to melt the adhesive.

# Fusible fleece

**Fusible fleece**, for example Bondaweb®, is a special type of heat-sensitive web that has adhesive on both sides. It is used to join two pieces of fabric together, for example when putting an appliqué shape onto a fabric.

Fusible fleece should only be used on small areas of a product. It can be used to hold hems in place temporarily, but is not suitable for a permanent hem on products, particularly products that will be washed often, because washing removes the adhesive, which means the hem will fall down.

# The use of fastenings

Fastenings are used to close an opening on a product, and many fastenings are used as decorative features on a product as well as being functional. The following points need to be considered when selecting a fastening for a product:

- Will the fastening need to be able to stand up to regular laundering?
- Is it a child's garment, which therefore needs a fastening that is easy to open and close? (Some fastenings, by law, are not allowed to be used on children's clothing.)
- Is the fastening intended to be hidden, or a decorative feature?

- Will the fastening be strong enough for the intended use?
- How is the fastening applied? Is the equipment needed easily available?
- What type of fabric is the product made from? (A heavy fastening on a lightweight fabric will distort the shape of the product, and some fastenings may snag delicate fabrics.)
- Will the fastening keep the opening adequately closed without gaping or slipping out of place?
- What is the cost of the fastening in relation to the type of product and the method of manufacture?

Fastenings should be stitched on to double fabric for strength. The two parts of the fastening must be sewn exactly opposite each other so that they match evenly when fastened, with the opening flat along its length.

**Figure 1.3.15** A selection of buttons.

## Buttons, buttonholes and loops

Buttons can be flat with two or four holes, or a dome shape with a shank. A shank is a stem that holds the button away from the fabric so that there is room for it to fasten. They come in many different sizes, colours and shapes, and can be made from plastic, glass, metal and wood. Buttons need buttonholes or loops to fasten through (Figure 1.3.16). Buttons can be decorative or purely functional, but need to be selected carefully – they can spoil the appearance of a product, be too heavy or lightweight for the fabric or be too large or small for the style of the product. They should also have the same care instructions as the product they are to be used on.

Most sewing machines have a buttonhole feature so that, with a little practice, neat buttonholes can be made easily and quickly. Every machine makes buttonholes in a slightly different way, so it is best to follow the instructions in the sewing machine manual.

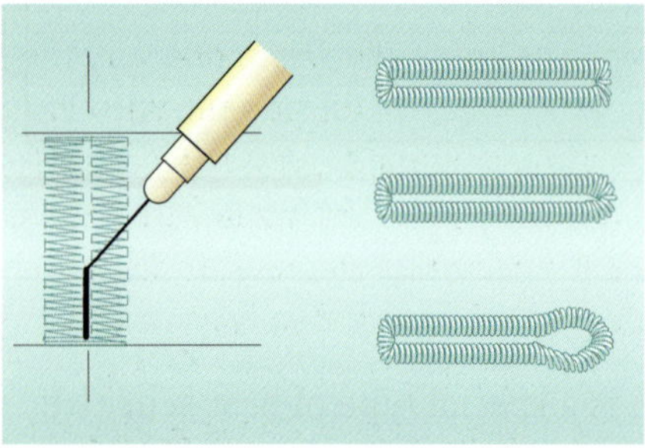

**Figure 1.3.16** A variety of machined buttonhole styles.

Buttonholes must be sewn on a double layer of fabric that has been strengthened with interfacing. When testing the buttonhole, it is important that it is done on the same fabric that has been used for the product, and with the same interfacing.

Decorative loops called Rouleau loops can be used with a button, instead of a buttonhole. The loops are made from very narrow cross-cut strips of fabric, and are used with small domed buttons for best effect.

## Zips

Zips have a slider that opens and closes the zip teeth. Zips come in many different types; some of the most used are closed end, open end, invisible and jeans. Most zips have a polyester coil which makes them lightweight. Some zips have metal teeth that are attached to both sides of a zip tape – these are most often used on jeans or for decorative purposes. Plastic moulded zips are very similar to metal zips but the teeth are made of plastic.

Open-ended or separating zips are designed to come apart so that a garment can be opened completely, for example jackets and coats. Two-way zips have two sliders, and can be opened from both ends.

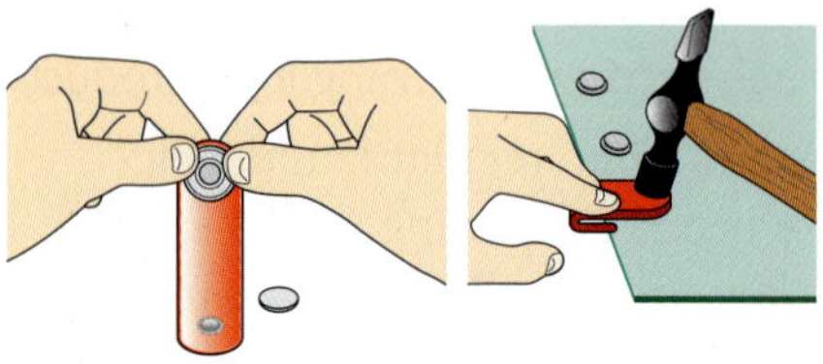

**Figure 1.3.17** Attaching poppers.

Invisible zips are designed to be unseen when put into a product. Trouser zips are curved at the lower end so that they fit the shape of the front trouser seam.

Zips come in a wide range of lengths or can be bought by the metre. They are made in many different colours, or can be dyed to match a specific fabric when bought commercially.

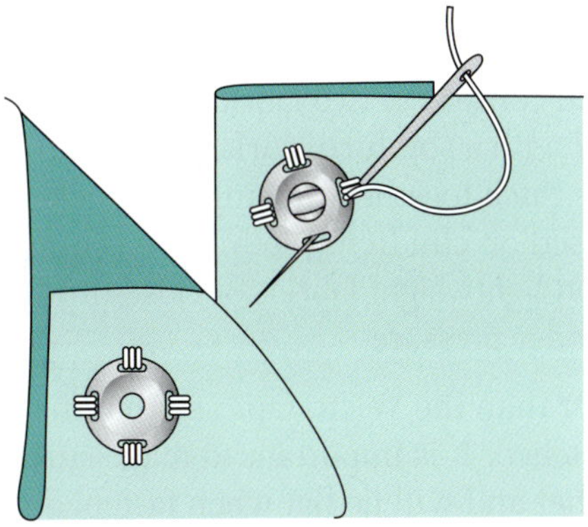

Figure 1.3.18 Attaching press studs.

## Poppers

Poppers (also known as snap fasteners) are a decorative fastening made up of two circular metal or plastic sections that lock into each other. They are a flat fastening, and are useful for openings where there is not much strain because they can pop open easily.

Poppers are bought as a kit that includes a special tool, and are applied using a hammer. The instructions that come with the kit should be followed carefully. It is important to make sure that the two parts of the poppers are lined up with each other, otherwise the fastening will not lie flat. Once they are hammered in place, it is very difficult to remove the poppers because there will be a hole in the fabric where they have been placed.

Press studs are similar to poppers but are not decorative. They are stitched on by hand using a buttonhole or straight stitch. The two parts must be aligned with each other – this is best done by putting a pin through the centres of the two halves. The ball part should be sewn to the overlap, and the socket part sewn to the underlap.

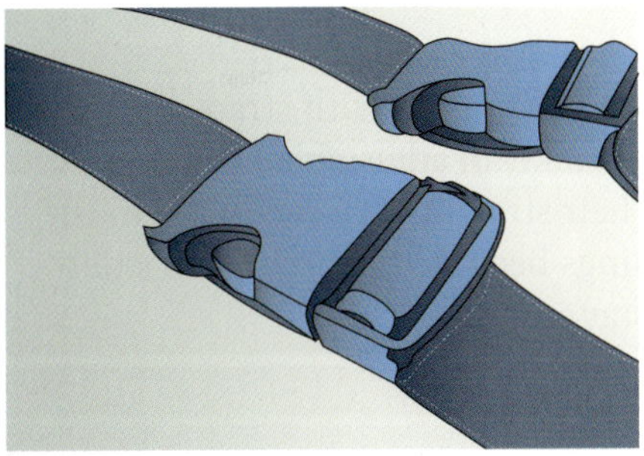

Figure 1.3.19 Parachute clips.

## Clips

Parachute clips are two-piece functional fastenings made from plastic but they can also be decorative. A pronged part of the clip fastens into a box section. The two parts of the clip have a slot at their outer ends so that a braid or strap can be threaded through and held in place with machine stitching. The straps are machine stitched to the product.

Figure 1.3.20 A belt with a buckle fastening.

## Buckles

Buckles and straps are used as decorative fastenings. They are not very secure fastenings because the two sides can slip out of alignment with each other. The fastening has two parts – a strap with a buckle at the end, and a second strap to fasten into the buckle. The strap can be made from fabric or a strong tape. One strap needs an eyelet hole at the end so that it can fasten with the buckle. The second strap is usually folded in half so that the prong of the buckle can fit through a hole in the fabric fold. The straps are sewn to the product so that they are level with each other. Buckles are also used to fasten belts.

## Clasps

Clasps are decorative two-part fasteners, usually made from metal but can also be plastic. One side of the clasp fastens into the other. Clasp fastenings are used on a range of products such as jackets, cloaks, swim and beachwear, as well as bags.

Figure 1.3.21 A range of clasp fastenings.

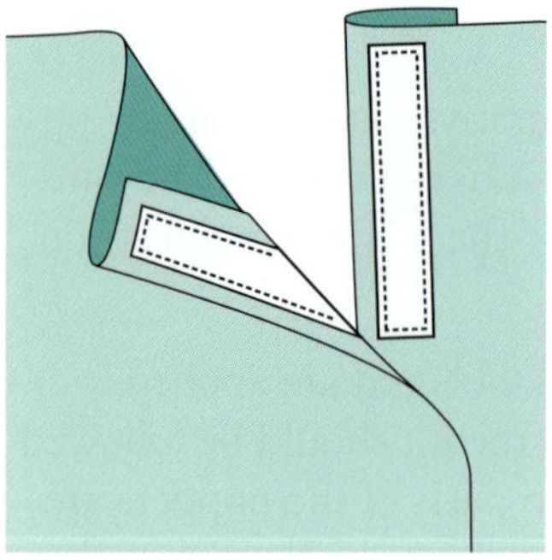

Figure 1.3.22 Attaching Velcro.

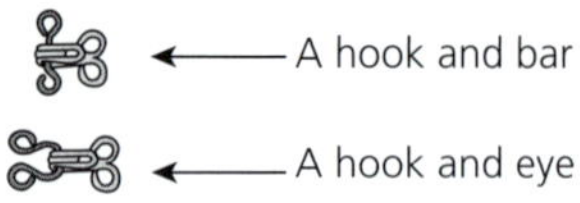


Figure 1.3.23 Hooks and eyes or bars.

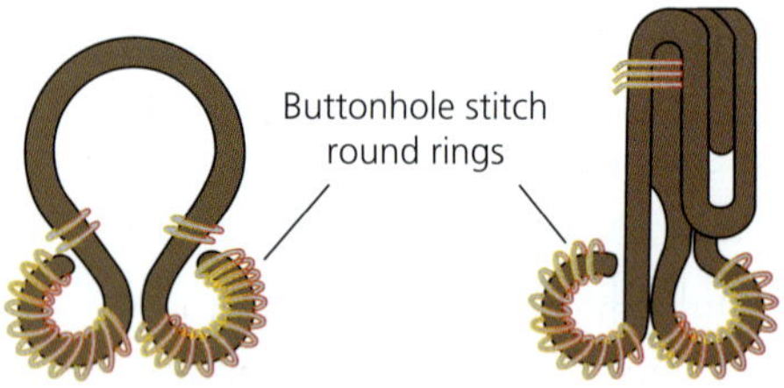


Figure 1.3.24 Sewing on a hook and eye.

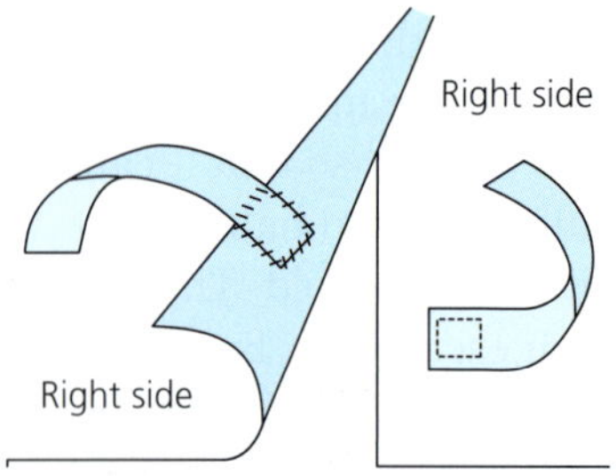


Figure 1.3.25 Ties used on the opening of a product.

Figure 1.3.26 A decorative frog fastening.

## Velcro®

Velcro is a touch and close fastener, which consists of two fabric tapes – one tape with tiny nylon hooks and the other with a soft furry surface. When the tapes are pressed together, the two layers catch together, making it a quick and easy fastening, therefore it is often used on children's clothing. It is quite a thick fastening so should not be used on lightweight fabrics or close-fitting garments. It is easily unfastened when under pressure.

The edges of the product should be wider than the Velcro tapes so that the edges of the tapes do not show when fastened. It is important to make sure that both tapes are aligned with each other and will lie flat when fastened. To attach, sew the soft side to the underneath of the overlapping part of the opening by machining it close to the edges of the tape. The harder hook side is sewn to the underlapping part of the opening.

## D-rings

D-rings are two metal or plastic D-shaped loops, used with straps or braid that is threaded through the two rings to make an adjustable fastening. A strap is attached to the two rings along their straight edge and sewn to the product. They are not very secure fastenings because they rely on friction between the strap and the two rings to stay in place.

## Hooks and eyes

Hooks and eyes are a two-part fastening made of metal, and applied with hand stitching. The hook fits into the eye, and the eye may be a curved loop (used when the edges to be fastened meet each other) or a straight bar (used when the edges to be fastened overlap each other). These fastenings are meant to be discrete, and are often used at the top of a zipped opening or on a waistband.

The hook and eye are sewn on by hand using buttonhole stitch (Figure 1.3.24). The stitching should not go through to the right side of the product to ensure the fastening is unseen. The top of the hook should be held in place with three straight stitches, so that it remains flat on the product.

## Fabric and ribbon ties

Ties are a decorative fastening that can be made from ribbon, fabric, bias binding, cord or tape. They are stitched to the product by hand or by machine. The short edges may need to be neatened to prevent fraying. If the tie is made from fabric or bias binding, the long edges will need to be turned in and sewn together to make a neat edge.

## Frog fastenings

Frog fastenings are decorative fastenings made from a narrow braid, and consist of a ball button that is fastened with a loop.

### ACTIVITY

As a class, make a collage of images showing different fastenings used on a range of products.

Make notes on their appropriateness for the product. Have any of the fastenings been used in an unusual or innovative way?

# Trims

**Trims** add the finishing touch to a product, and can be used creatively to add interest. Many are applied after the product has been completed, but some are sewn in during construction. Trims should be selected so that they are appropriate for the product without interfering with the balance of the product, and should have the same care requirements as the product's fabric. Some are not colourfast, and many are very delicate because they are not resistant to abrasion, and easily snag. Many are used to emphasise a style line, or add colour and pattern to a product.

There is a huge variety of trims on the market, and their use will often be dependent on fashion trends.

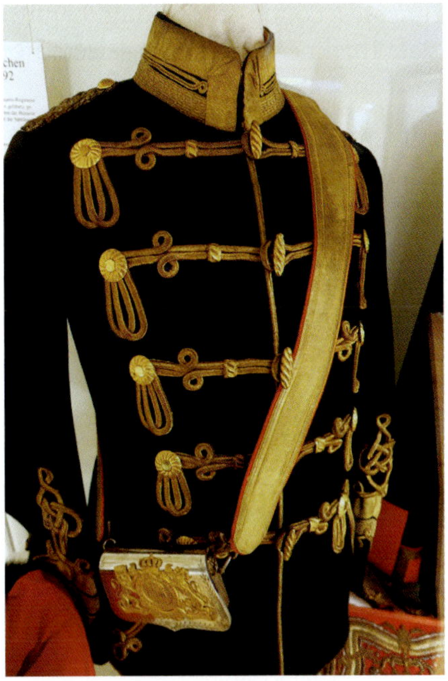

**Figure 1.3.27** Soutache braid.

## Braids

Braids come in many different styles and widths, and are made of many different materials. Some of the most popular are outlined below.

**Flat braid** is often used as a decorative border, for example to outline a pocket or hem edge. It is stitched to the product along both edges, and is often used in combination with other braids. It can be woven or embroidered.

**Soutache** is a narrow-woven braid with a shine. Because it is narrow and flexible, it can be used in rounded designs and can be combined with buttons and frog fastenings. It is usually hand sewn in place because it is narrow.

**Ric rac braid** has a wavy edge and usually comes in two widths. It is popular for children's clothes and craft projects. It can be sewn on by machine or hand.

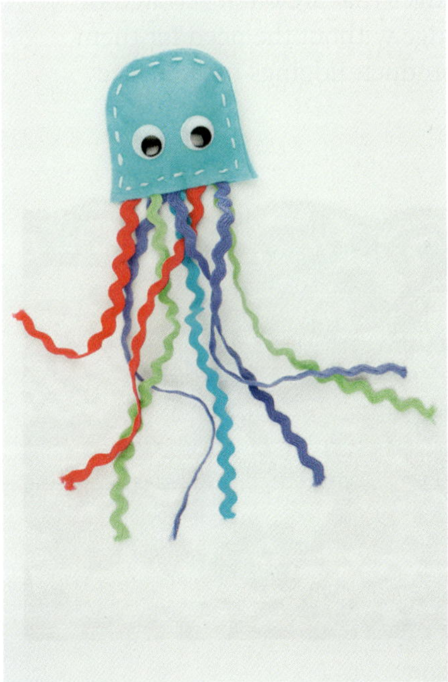

**Figure 1.3.28** Ric rac braid.

**Passementerie braids** are often made from rayon to give them their lustrous look. They are bulky and heavily textured, often with metal threads incorporated into them. They are usually used on formal garments such as suits, jackets and eveningwear, and form part of the design. They are usually sewn on by hand because of their bulk.

## Ribbons

Ribbon is used for decoration and sometimes to make a fastening. Ribbons are woven, and both long edges are self-finished. They are usually made from polyester or polyamide but can also be made from silk, and are produced in a wide range of patterns and solid colours. Satin and velvet ribbons are very widely used but taffeta, organza and grosgrain are also popular.

**Figure 1.3.29** Passementerie braid.

**Figure 1.3.30** A very wide variety of ribbon is available.

## Piping

Piping is used to define a shape, add decoration or add strength to an edge. It is made by covering a cord with fabric – usually cut on the bias – and is sewn between the two sides of a seam. Piping cord is made from cotton or polyester, and comes in a number of thicknesses; cotton cord should be pre-shrunk before use. A cord of the appropriate thickness should be selected for the product.

To make piping, fold the fabric strip in half lengthways with the wrong sides facing. Place the piping cord inside the fabric strip and pin along the long edges. Stitch the cord in place using a zip foot on the machine.

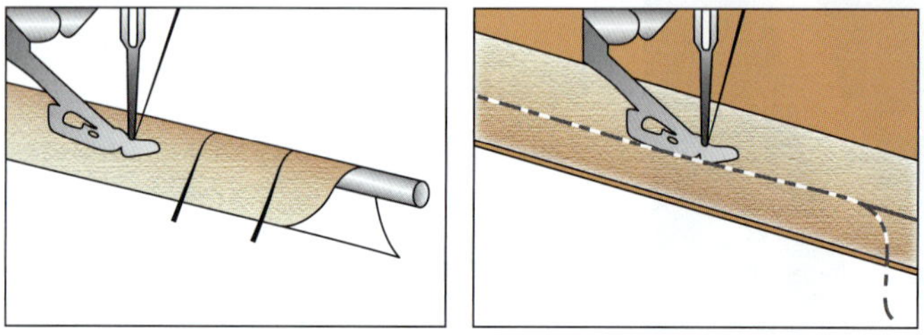

**Figure 1.3.31** Making piping.

Ready-made polyester piping trim can be bought in a wide range of colours.

## Edging

Edges can be embellished in many different ways using a variety of trimmings. Edgings have two finished edges that are often serrated or scalloped, and so can be applied to an edge without the need for them to form part of the construction of the product. Edgings include lace trimming, braids, fringing and ribbons.

**Figure 1.3.32** Lace edging with a finished edge.

## Bindings

Binding is used to neaten raw edges, and may be decorative or functional. Binding is made from strips of fabric cut on the cross/bias grain of the fabric, and shows on both sides of the edge. Because it is cut on the cross, it is able to bend and stretch around curved edges.

**KEY TERMS**

**Bias binding:** a narrow length of fabric cut on the cross of the fabric, and used to finish raw edges.

**Shirring:** a decorative gathering often done with elastic thread used on the back of the product.

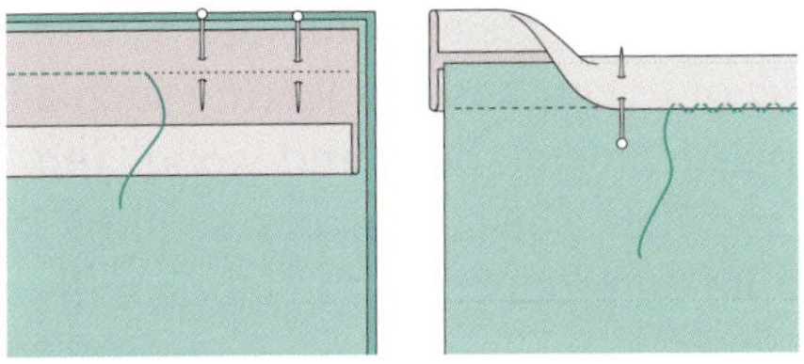

Figure 1.3.33 Applying a binding.

Figure 1.3.34 Fringing gives a sense of movement to a garment.

Figure 1.3.37 Beads and sequins used on the Emmanuel ball gown made for Princess Diana in 1986.

Bias binding can be bought as a pre-manufactured component and is available in many colours and patterns. It is normally 15 mm or 25 mm wide, and has the outer edges folded inwards so that they meet in the centre of the wrong side of the binding. You can make your own binding using bias cut strips of the fabric used to make the product; a bias binding maker tool is useful to help achieve an even width.

The seam turning/seam allowance must be removed before the binding is applied or the product will be too big.

## Fringing

Fringing is applied to the edge of a product to give a decorative and softening effect and, when used on garments, to add a sense of movement. It was very popular in the 1920s as a decoration on the straight dresses that were worn at the time. Fringing is made from many narrow strips of material closely joined together on a top band, and may be made from many different materials including rayon, silk, cotton, suede, leather and beads. Fringing is not a very durable trim and is rarely washable.

## Lace

Lace is a delicate trim with light, open designs that snag easily. Lace edging is a narrow trim that can be scalloped on one or both edges. It is usually made from cotton, polyester, nylon, rayon or silk, and comes in a range of widths and patterns. It can be applied as a flat band or gathered onto an edge. When stitching lace on by machine, a fine, sharp needle must be used so as not to snag the fabric.

Figure 1.3.35 A selection of lace edgings.

Figure 1.3.36 A lace appliqué.

Lace appliqués are single motifs that are used alone or with others, and can be used to emphasise a feature such as a neckline. They are usually sewn on by hand.

## Beads

Beaded trims are usually quite narrow, and are often added to garments and other products to add lustre and sparkle and to emphasise style lines. There are many different shapes and colours of beads available, including chains of pearl or rhinestone beads that are hand stitched to the product. Sequin trims allow a lot of sequins to be applied quickly without the need to sew them on one by one.

**Figure 1.3.38** A selection of diamanté trims.

Beads can also be sewn onto a product singly to create an elaborate pattern, outline a shape in the pattern of the fabric or to emphasise a feature such as a collar. Beads can be made from glass, plastic, metal, bone and wood, and include pearls, seed beads, bugle beads, rocailles, shisha mirrors, sequins and crystals. Beads add texture and weight to a product, so the fabric will need to be heavy and firm enough to support them.

### Diamantés

Diamantés are artificial diamonds, for example Swarovski® diamantés and rhinestones, and are used to add sparkle to a product. They need to be glued onto the product; some are pre-glued ready to attach – the glue is activated with a little heat.

## Components, e-components and their appropriateness for a range of products

All of the components including thread, fastenings and trims contribute to the success or otherwise of a product, and should be selected with as much care and thought as the main fabric. Components need to be:

- appropriate for the style of garment and overall effect wanted
- appropriate for the fibre content, structure and weight of the fabric used
- able to be cared for in the same way as the fabric used
- safe for the end user
- appropriate for the user's needs
- readily available within the constraints of a budget
- added to the product using the manufacturing facilities available.

**E-components** are used to add decorative and functional effects to textile products using electronics. In order to make these effects, an electronic circuit must be incorporated into the product. E-components are used in textiles to include:

- lights
- sound effects
- tracking devices such as GPS
- temperature and moisture sensors
- monitoring devices for medical applications
- communication systems such as integrated phones.

The basic circuit for an e-component needs a battery holder – usually a coin cell battery, a device such as an LED light and conductive thread which joins them together and completes the circuit. The conductive thread can be used like standard sewing thread, and is made from polyester or nylon coated with a metal such as copper or silver, which makes the thread electrically conductive. Because the batteries are very low voltage, the electronics can be safely used in textile products with no risk of electrocution. The devices can be standard electronic components or ones that are made specially for use in textile products. These specially made components are much smaller, making them easier to use with textiles.

**ACTIVITY**

Collect a range of different trimmings and mount them in a sketchbook or notebook. Sketch a product to show how each trim could be used in an interesting way.

**KEY TERMS**

**E-components:** components that use electronic circuits to add decorative and functional effects to textile products.

**ACTIVITY**

Use a simple electronic circuit to include an LED light in a small decorative product of your choice.

You can find information about how to make an electronic circuit at: www.tes.com/teaching-resource/electronics-in-textiles-6206400.

# Interfacings, underlinings, linings and interlinings

Most products have more than one layer of fabric. Many of these extra layers are hidden inside the product, but have very useful and important functions. The main uses of these additional layers are explained below.

## Interfacings

Interfacing is an extra layer of fabric used under the outer layer of fabric in small areas of a product. Many parts of a product need to be interfaced to give them strength, crispness and shape, or to prevent the fabric from stretching. For example:

- behind fastenings to strengthen the fabric
- in collars and cuffs to give shape
- in waistbands to stop them from stretching
- underneath embroidery to add strength and body.

The correct choice and use of interfacing is important in making a high-quality product. The weight of the interfacing needs to be chosen with care – if it is too heavy it will make the product too stiff and unable to hang correctly, but if it is too light it will not support the fabric adequately. The colour choice is also very important – a black or grey interfacing will show through light coloured fabrics and spoil the appearance. Interfacing needs to be applied before the construction or decorative process is started in order to be effective.

Interfacing fabrics can be woven, non-woven, knitted, sew-in or iron-on (fusible). Non-woven interfacings have no grain and therefore can be cut in any direction, making them very economical to use. Woven and knitted interfacings must be cut on the same grain as the part of the product that they are attached to.

Fusible or iron-on interfacings are coated on one side with a heat-sensitive adhesive. They are applied to the fabric using heat and steam, which causes the adhesive to melt and fuse the interfacing to the fabric. When applying fusible interfacings, always protect the iron and ironing board cover with an additional cloth, to prevent any misplaced adhesive from spoiling other fabrics.

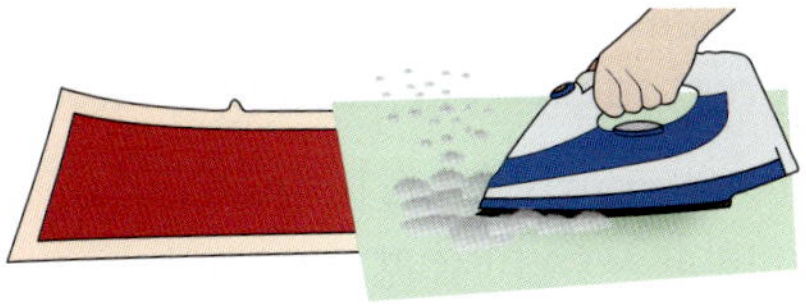

**Figure 1.3.39** Use heat and steam to apply fusible interfacing.

A fusible interfacing must be tested on the fabric before using it because it tends to make the fabric stiffer than a non-fusible interfacing, and is not suitable for very fine or see-through fabrics.

It is important to follow the manufacturer's instructions when applying fusible interfacings – if they are not fused correctly, they will bubble and come away from the fabric, which will spoil the appearance of the product. Leave the fabric to cool before moving it from the ironing board, to give it time to stick properly.

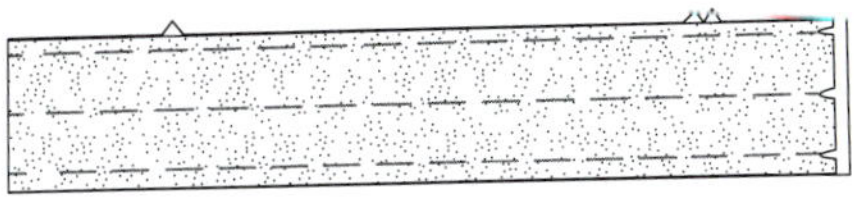

**Figure 1.3.40** Fusible waistband interfacing.

Fusible waistband interfacings are specially made for interfacing waistbands, and have perforated slots along the centre and edges. These slots make it easy to fold the waistband in half in a straight line and give a guideline for the seam turnings.

## Underlinings

An underlining acts as a backing for the outer fabric of a garment. It is cut to the exact shape and size of the outer fabric that it is used on, and the two layers are then treated as one layer when the garment is made.

Underlining is used to:

- make sheer and lace fabrics opaquer so that they are less see-through
- keep the shape of sculptured styles such as bell-shaped skirts, where the fabric used does not have enough body
- help stabilise soft or loosely woven fabrics so they do not pull away at the seams.

Underlining does not make a fabric stiff like interfacing, and it does not neaten raw edges on the inside of the garment. The whole garment can be underlined or some parts can be the top fabric only, for example sleeves. A garment that has been underlined may also be lined (see 'Linings' below).

The underlining fabric should have the same care instructions as the top fabric, and be slightly lighter in weight so that it does not dominate the top fabric. Suitable fabrics include cotton lawn, cotton muslin, lightweight satins and organza.

## Linings

Lining is used on the inside of a garment and is a separate layer of fabric. The main reasons for using linings are to:

- make the inside of a garment more attractive
- cover the internal seams and interfacings so that they are protected from wear
- make a garment easier to put on and take off, especially jackets and coats
- make a garment warmer to wear
- make rough or itchy fabrics more comfortable to wear
- prevent garments from clinging to the body
- help garments to keep their shape
- help garments to hang well
- add interest or a quirky feature to a garment such as a jacket, through the use of a contrasting coloured or patterned lining
- protect the outside of the garment from perspiration and body oils.

A garment can be fully or partially lined – trousers are sometimes lined for part of the front legs so that they do not go baggy at the knees, and skirts are sometimes lined at the back only to prevent them from 'seating' in wear.

Lining fabrics are usually specially made for the purpose. A lining fabric should be soft, pliable, slippery and of a suitable weight that does not interfere with the hang of the garment. It should have the same care instructions as the main fabric.

Most lining fabrics are satin, plain and twill woven fabrics made from polyester, acetate and silk. Stretch linings are available for use with stretch fabrics.

An antistatic finish is useful in preventing the lining from clinging to other garments.

### ACTIVITY

Sketch the outline of a coat or jacket, and label it to show where each of the following could be used:

- interfacing
- interlining
- lining
- underlining.

Attach swatches of fabrics that would be appropriate for each of the layers.

## Interlinings

An interlining is an additional layer of fabric put into the garment after any underlining or interfacing, and before the lining is added. It is used to give extra warmth to garments such as coats. The fabric should be light and not bulky (sleeves are not usually interlined because of the added bulk). Suitable fabrics include polyester wadding, lightweight polyester fleece, lambs' wool and brushed cotton fabric. The simplest way to add the interlining is to sew it as one with the lining.

### KEY POINTS

- A well-made seam that is right for the fabric and the product is important for the success of the product.
- A thread is not just a thread or cotton – there are many different types for a wide range of uses, and few are made from cotton.
- Fastenings need to be chosen carefully, with consideration given to the end-user and function of the product.
- Trimmings can be used to enhance the aesthetics of a product.
- Many garments have hidden additional layers of different fabrics, which are needed to make them suited to their intended use.

## Check your knowledge and understanding

1 Name two self-finishing seams.

2 Name two directional fabrics.

3 Name three different types of zip.

4 Explain why a Madeira thread is used to zig zag stitch an appliqué to a product.

5 What is the difference between an interfacing and an interlining?

## Further reading

Baugh, G. *The Fashion Designer's Textile Directory*

Betzina, S. *More Fabric Savvy*

Shaeffer, C. *Claire Shaeffer's Fabric Sewing Guide*

Willard, D. *The Fabric Selector*

Working with plaid fabric: www.craftsy.com/blog/2014/05/working-with-plaid-fabric

A presentation and other information about electronic textiles: www.julieboyd.co.ukle-textiles

The following YouTube videos:

- How to sew underlining by Professor Pincushion: https://youtu.be/ECnb6-oMxeg
- How to add underlining to a skirt: https://youtu.be/OvU-ee3aLe0

# 1.4 The use of finishes

**LEARNING OUTCOMES**

By the end of this section you should have developed a knowledge and understanding of:

- how finishes can improve some fabrics and make textile materials more functional and aesthetically pleasing
- the different mechanical and chemical finishes that can be applied to textile materials
- how laminated fabric finishes work.

If you are studying at A-level you should also have developed a knowledge and understanding of:

- a wide range of chemical finishes and their applications.

## Fabric finishes

Fabrics need to be fit for their intended use, and consumers have high expectations about how a textile product will perform over its lifetime. Many fibres used to make fabrics have disadvantages, however, it is possible to cancel out some of these disadvantages; for example, shrinking and creasing can be reduced by applying a **fabric finish**. An applied finish is an additional process that is intended to improve the appearance, performance, wear or handle of a fabric in relation to its intended use. It is usually the last stage of the fabric processing.

Applied finishes always cost money, so a manufacturer will need to think about how important it is to put a special finish onto a fabric depending on what it is to be used for. Many products require more than one applied finish to make them acceptable to consumers. Sometimes new finishes are developed to enable novel products to become available.

Some finishes can weaken a fabric and therefore may reduce its useful life, while others are needed to improve the safety of a product. Not all finishes last the lifetime of the product – some are temporary and are removed after the first washing or cleaning, some last through a limited number of washings and some last for the life of the product but are not as effective after several washings.

**ACTIVITY**

As a class, make a collection of swing tags/information labels that are attached to new textile products and give information about finishes that have been used. Make notes about the type of product they are attached to and the fibre content of the fabric used. Consider why the finish has been used on that product.

Present this information as a revision aid to be shared with other students in your class.

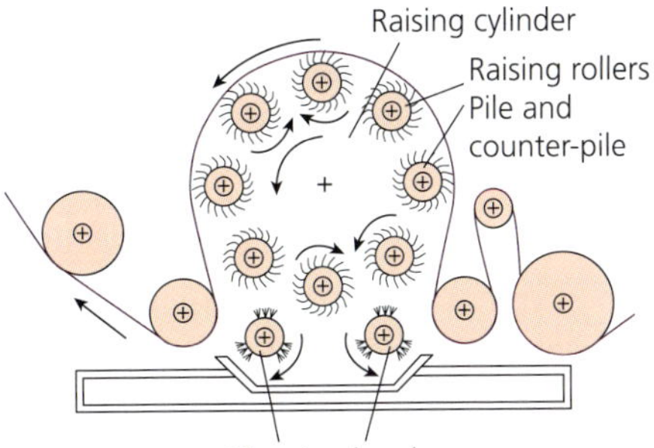


**Figure 1.4.1** The raising process.

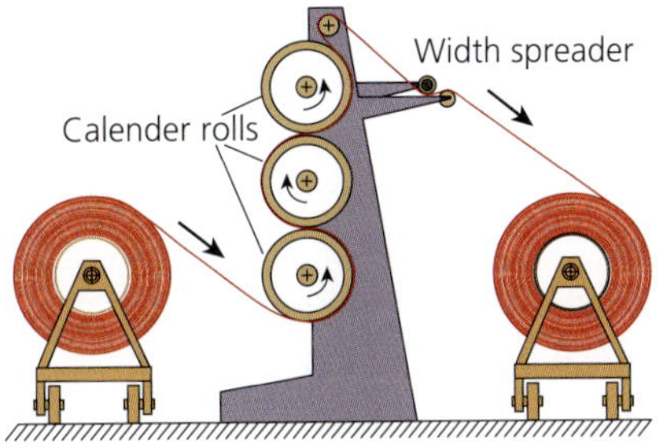


**Figure 1.4.2** The calendaring process.

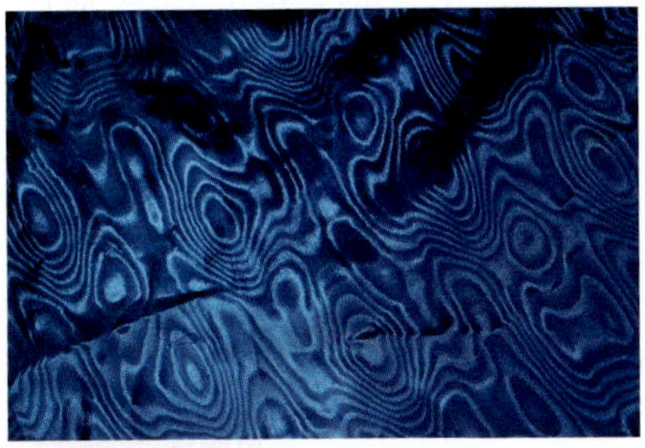

**Figure 1.4.3** Moiré fabric.

**Figure 1.4.4** Embossed fabric.

# Mechanical finishes

**Mechanical finishes** use dry processes that are applied physically without the use of water or chemicals. They are used to modify the fabric surface.

## Brushing/raising

A brushed or raised finish produces a nap and traps air – for example on cotton fabrics – and makes a fabric softer and warmer to wear, but more flammable. It is a durable finish, often used on cotton fabrics and polyester fleece fabrics.

The fabric is passed through a raising machine that has a number of rollers covered with small wire hooks. As the rollers rotate over the surface of the fabric, they tease out some of the fibre ends so that the fabric becomes fluffy. This can cause the fabric to become weaker.

## Calendaring

Calendaring is used to smooth and compact the fabric surface, produce a lustre and emboss patterns. Calendaring is similar to ironing because it uses heat and pressure to smooth the fabric surface. The effects of calendaring are usually short-lived.

The fabric is passed through heated rollers that can be set to rotate at different speeds and at varying temperatures. If the rollers rotate at different speeds, the friction caused flattens and polishes the surface of the fabric giving it a lustre, for example on cotton fabrics.

Moiré effects have a watermark pattern which is produced when two ribbed fabrics are calendared together. It can also be made using specially engraved rollers.

Calendaring can be done to compact the surface of fabrics with thermoplastic fibres. The warp and weft yarns are pushed closer together so that the fabric is less porous, for example when making polyester fabric for the sails of a boat.

## Embossing

The calendaring process can be used with engraved rollers that emboss a pattern into the fabric. This will disappear when the fabric is washed and ironed, unless a fabric with synthetic fibres is used so that the pattern can be heat-set. The embossed pattern can be made more permanent on cotton fabrics by impregnating it with a synthetic resin.

## Heat-setting

Fabrics that contain thermoplastic fibres can be heat-set to enable a range of functional and aesthetic finishes to be applied.

Many fabrics used for fashion and furnishing products contain some polyester fibres. Dimensional stability is an important requirement so that fabrics do not shrink or crease. The fabric is stretched to its correct dimensions and held flat with the width and length of the fabric at right-angles to each other before passing through a heated chamber. When cool,

Figure 1.4.5 Pleated polyester georgette fabric.

**KEY TERMS**

**Fabric finish:** an applied finish is an additional process to improve the appearance, performance, wear or handle of a fabric.

**Mechanical finish:** use dry processes that are applied physically without the use of water or chemicals.

**Heat-setting:** using the thermoplastic nature of synthetic fibres to set a fabric into a specific shape or size.

the fabric retains the set size and shape unless subjected to temperatures that will soften the thermoplastic fibres.

A textured or pleated finish can be achieved on polyester fabrics or blends containing a minimum of 60 per cent polyester. Heat and pressure are used to heat-set the fabric into the desired shape. This process can also be used on cut pattern pieces or completed garments, to create fashionable effects such as a creased look.

## Stone and sand washing

A-level only

Stone and sand washing adds a soft peach-skin surface with a worn, scuffed appearance. The pebbles or sand wear away the surface of the fabric, softening and ageing it. This enhances the appearance and feel of the fabrics, but will weaken them and also damages the machinery used.

Newer treatments use enzymes to give a stone-washed effect on fabrics, especially denim. These treatments reduce the environmental impact of the finish, cause less damage to both fabrics and machinery and are more controllable so that there is less variability in the quality of the finish.

**ACTIVITY**

You will need two pieces of smooth surfaced, plain weave cotton fabric approximately 15 $cm^2$, a hand lens and a wire brush. Using the hand lens, examine the surface of the fabric.

Use the wire brush to make a nap on one square of fabric. Examine the surface of the brushed fabric and compare it with the un-brushed sample. What are the differences?

# Chemical finishes

**Chemical finishes** are wet processes that use chemicals and heat, and may also use water. Chemical finishes change the fibre structure or fabric properties in order to improve their characteristics.

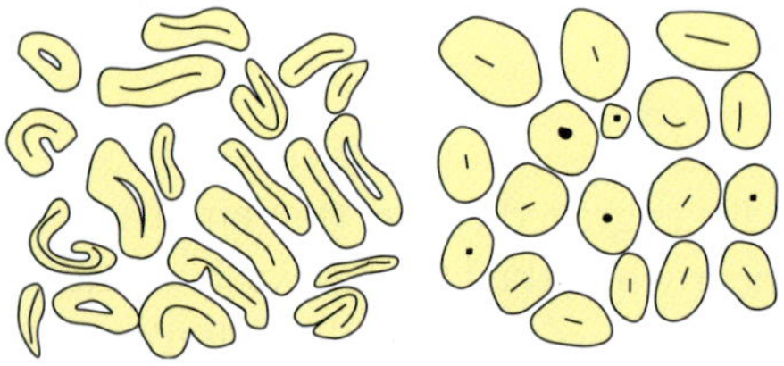

Figure 1.4.6 The effects of mercerisation on cotton fibres.

## Mercerisation

A-level only

Mercerisation is used on cotton fabrics. The process involves treating the fibres with caustic soda – a strong alkali that causes the cotton fibres to swell and shrink. This changes the ribbon-like flat fibre to a smoother one with a circular cross-section. Mercerisation adds strength, gives lustre and makes the cotton better at absorbing dyes. The process is important when processing cotton for sewing threads.

## Flame retardancy

Most textile materials will burn given the right conditions, but some are more flammable than others. Flame retardant finishes prevent the fabric from setting on fire, or prevent it from burning quickly.

Fabrics made from cellulosic fibres are very flammable, while synthetic fibres are described as inherently flame retardant because they do not set fire easily. They tend to melt rather than burst into flames.

Fabrics used for nightwear are required by law to be flame retardant. Cotton and viscose fabrics used for nightwear can be treated with Proban® or Pyrovatex® – these are finishes which contain a polymer that is trapped within the fibres, and is not removed by laundering.

Proban and Pyrovatex flame retardant finishes can make the fabric stiff and reduce its tearing strength. They are expensive to apply and can degrade with washing.

Zirpro® is a flame retardant finish that is used on wool fabrics when a high level of protection against flames is required.

Metal coated fabrics are used to make garments that can protect against flames, for example aluminised clothing worn by welders in industrial situations.

## Water resistance

Water resistant finishes have two main functions:

- They prevent staining from water-borne stains.
- They protect fabrics from being penetrated by rain and water.

Water resistant finishes protect fabrics from staining so that they are easier to care for, and are not spoiled by stains that can be difficult to remove. The use of silicone treatments such as Scotchgard® are effective in protecting fabrics from water-borne stains and prevent penetration by water.

Teflon® is a surface finish that provides an invisible barrier to prevent water and oil-based stains from penetrating the fibres. It is used on clothing (particularly school uniforms), household products and in commercial applications. It is also used as a finish to make products resistant to rain, for example raincoats and tents. Teflon does not affect the feel, appearance or breathability of the fabric, and makes it easier to iron.

Finishes that use nano-technology make fabrics hydrophobic – they are able to repel water and allow stains to be rinsed off with water. NanoSphere® is a finish that is used on products made by many fashion brands.

## Non-iron/crease resistance

Non-iron/crease resistant finishes make fabrics easy-care and reduce the time spent caring for textile products. Crease resistant finishes also mean that fabrics do not develop creases easily when worn or used.

Fabrics made from cellulosic fibres – cotton, linen and viscose – are particularly prone to creasing due to a result of changes to the molecular structure of the fibres. The finish is applied by passing the fabric through a liquid containing synthetic resins – these resins enter the fibres in the form of small molecules. The fabric is then held flat and smooth while it is heated, to cure the resin. The curing causes the resin molecules to join together and link with the fibre molecules, so that they are held permanently within the fibre. This type of finish will last the lifetime of the product.

These finishes also make the fabrics resistant to shrinking, but can reduce a fabric's tearing strength and resistance to abrasion.

KEY TERMS

**Chemical finish:** are wet processes that use chemicals and heat and may use water.

## Shrink resistance and antifelting

### Shrink resistance

Cellulosic and wool fibres are especially prone to shrinking when laundered. Cellulosic fibres shrink because they swell when wet, causing the fibre length to shorten. This can be prevented by the use of resins, which enter the fibres as small molecules and are joined together within the fibres by the curing process. (See 'Non-iron/crease resistance' above.) Resin treatments used on cellulosic fibres perform a double function of making the fabric shrink resistant as well as crease resistant.

### Antifelting

A-level only

Wool shrinks in a very different way to cellulosic fibres. In the presence of heat, moisture and friction, the overlapping scales on the wool fibres become entangled with each other and lock together – this irreversible process is called felting. One finish modifies the surface of the wool fibre by using a small amount of nylon polymer to coat the scales, so that they are smoother and not able to lock with each other so easily. Wool treated in this way is called Superwash wool. Wool can also be given a machine washable finish by applying a Teflon coating.

Inter-fibre bonding is a process that fastens the fibres together using a soft polymer, which sticks to the surface of the fibres and makes bridges – called inter-fibre bonds – between them. Fabrics treated in this way are machine washable.

## Mothproofing

The chemical structure of wool includes a sulphur molecule that makes it particularly attractive to moths and is not present in silk fibres. A clothes moth can lay as many as 50 eggs on wool fabrics that are stored in dark places, such as the back of unventilated wardrobes. When the eggs hatch, the grubs feed on the wool fibres.

The mothproofing process involves impregnating the wool fibres with chemicals that make the fibres inedible, and protect the fabric against moth attack.

Mitin® and Dielmoth® are mothproofing finishes.

## Antipilling

Pilling is the formation of small balls of fibre on the surface of the fabric. It occurs on many fabrics, especially those made from wool and synthetic fibres as well as blended fibre fabrics. Antipilling finishes use polymers or solvents, which form a film on the fabric surface to prevent the fibre balls from forming.

Biopolishing is a newer treatment that uses enzymes to remove the fibres protruding from cotton, wool and viscose fabrics, leaving a softer and slightly shinier fabric. This treatment helps the fabric to stay looking new for the lifetime of the garment.

## Hygienic (sanitised)

Bacteria and microorganisms can lead to infection as well as causing staining and deterioration of fabrics. These organisms breed in warm, damp conditions and are not effectively removed by washing, especially at the low temperatures encouraged to reduce energy use. Antimicrobial finishes that inhibit their growth can be used for underwear, socks, textiles used in hospitals and for medical purposes, active sportswear, bedding and textiles used for catering.

It is possible to incorporate antibacterial substances into the spinning solutions for regenerated and synthetic fibres to give a permanent finish. Treating the fabric surface is more complex, but is the method used in the majority of cases.

Purista is a treatment used on cotton fabrics. The finish controls the growth of microorganisms that cause unpleasant odours, helping to keep garments such as socks fresher for longer.

Chitosan is a naturally sourced antibacterial found in the shells of crustaceans such as crabs and shrimps. It is a useful finish for people with delicate skin and allergies, and is used mostly with natural fibres. It can be applied as a surface finish, or as a micro-encapsulated finish to viscose and polyester fibres.

Silver has antimicrobial qualities, and is used in textile materials that have healing and medical benefits. Bacteria can be controlled by impregnating synthetic yarns with particles of silver. Yarns made from ceramic yarns also have antibacterial properties.

**Figure 1.4.7** Sanitized® finish used on underwear.

### ACTIVITY

As a class, collect the following products: a school blazer, a pair of denim jeans, a fashion shirt, a pair of sports socks, a woollen jumper. Complete the chart below.

**Table 1.4.1** Products and finishes

| Product | Fibre content | Fabric structure | What finish could be applied? | Reasons why finish might be needed |
|---|---|---|---|---|
| School blazer | | | | |
| Denim jeans | | | | |
| Fashion shirt | | | | |
| Sports socks | | | | |
| Woollen jumper | | | | |

## Laminating as a finishing process

A **laminated** fabric is made up of two or more layers. These very thin layers are held together with an adhesive, or thermoplastic fibres that are heat-set to fix the layers together.

Typical laminated fabrics include Gore-Tex®, Sympatex® and fake leather fabrics backed by a woven fabric to give them stability.

### KEY TERMS

**Laminating:** making a fabric using two or more thin layers, which are held together with adhesive or by heat-setting thermoplastic fibres.

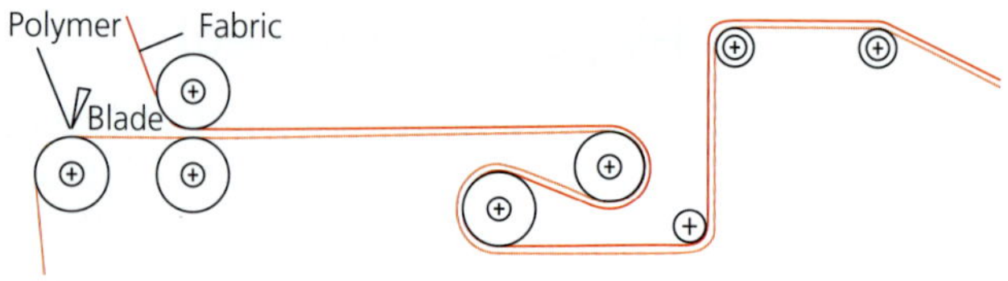


**Figure 1.4.10** Laminating using an adhesive.

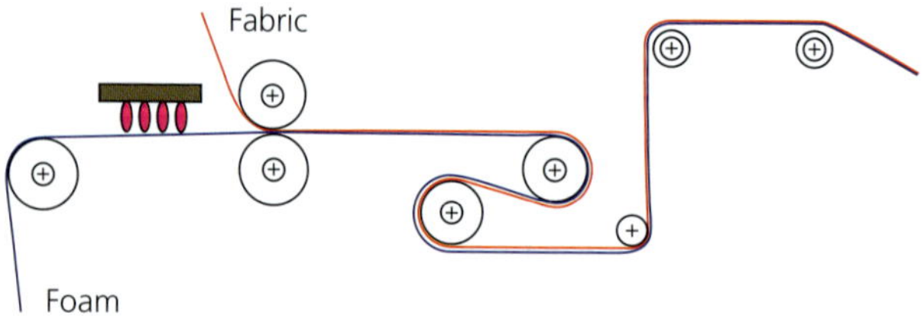


**Figure 1.4.10** Laminating using foam.

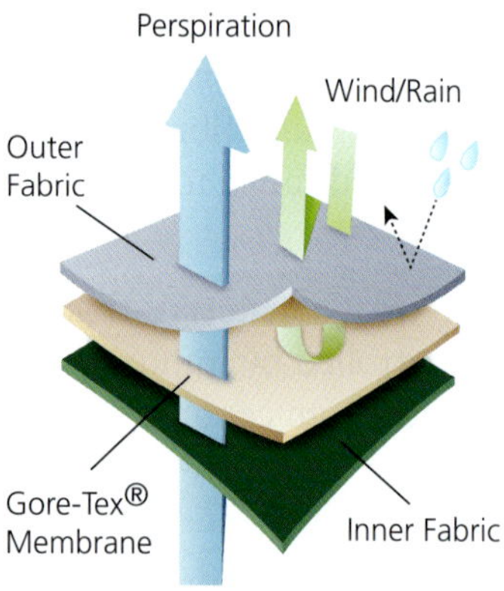


**Figure 1.4.11** How Gore-Tex fabric works.

## Gore-Tex

Gore-Tex is a laminated fabric that is totally waterproof and windproof, but also allows for perspiration to pass through – this makes it a breathable fabric and allows for skin to be kept dry. It is used for outdoor wear, sportswear, shoes and bags, tents and awnings. It is also used in many fashion applications because the membrane can be laminated to many different fabrics, including those with elastane fibres without losing any of its special qualities.

The non-woven Gore-Tex membrane is a very thin polytetrafluoroethylene (PTFE) film that has 9 billion microscopic holes per 2.5 $cm^2$. These holes are too small for rainwater to pass through, but large enough to allow perspiration to escape. The Gore-Tex membrane is usually laminated to a high performance outer fabric – usually nylon – and a softer inner lining layer.

The handle and feel of the fabric are not affected by the membrane, and newer, very lightweight fabrics that can be folded up and packed into a very small space have been developed.

## Sympatex

Sympatex fabrics have a non-porous water-loving (hydrophilic) polyester membrane that creates weatherproof, breathable fabrics. Perspiration is forced out through the hydrophilic membrane to the outside of the fabric where it can evaporate. The system can be used with a wide range of fabrics.

## Bonded fabrics

A-level only

Bonded fabrics are made by laminating a top fabric to a lightweight, woven backing fabric. This provides stability, strength and a firmer handle for the fabric without spoiling its handle or appearance. The two layers of fabric are held together with an adhesive. Fake leather is an example of a bonded fabric.

**ACTIVITY**

To revise this section, make a collage of pictures of products made using Gore-Tex fabric.

Draw a diagram that shows how Gore-Tex fabric works.

**KEY POINTS**

- Fabric finishes are applied to improve fabric performance and meet consumer expectations.
- Some finishes can have negative effects on the fabric.
- Finishes are additional processes and cost money, so are only applied when needed.
- Some fabrics are given more than one finish to make them suitable for the intended end use.
- The range of finishes is constantly developing, with new ones used to improve the aesthetics and functionality of fabrics.
- The chemicals used to make and apply some finishes can have a negative effect on the environment.
- Some finishes can help reduce the negative environmental impact of products, for example crease resistance.

## Check your knowledge and understanding

1. Name three different finishes that use the thermoplastic qualities of synthetic fibres.
2. Give two drawbacks of brushing a cotton fabric.
3. What causes cellulosic fibres to shrink?
4. What causes wool fibres to shrink?
5. Explain how the Gore-Tex membrane makes a fabric weatherproof and breathable.

## Further reading

Hibbert, R. *Textile Innovation*

Fabrics and finishes: www.textiles4u.wikispaces.com

Textile finishing: www.tikp.co.uk/knowledge/technology/finishing/textile-finishing/

Gore-Tex: www.gore-tex.co.uk

The following YouTube videos:

- Textiles – industrial finishing processes: https://youtu.be/ZkuX2gyXkrM
- Mechanical textile finishing – sanding, napping and shearing: https://youtu.be/yeB2IfDfzg4

# 1.5 Enhancement of materials

**LEARNING OUTCOMES**

By the end of this section you should have developed a knowledge and understanding of:

- how colour and pattern are put onto fabrics
- different embroidery techniques
- how quilted fabrics are made.

If you are studying at A-level you should also have developed a knowledge and understanding of:

- how fabric is prepared for dyeing and printing
- different dyeing and printing techniques.

Colour and pattern are major considerations when consumers select textile products for particular end uses. Colour is created when light is absorbed or reflected by different surfaces. It can be applied to textile products by surface decoration in the form of dyeing and printing, and also through the use of embroidery and trimmings.

## Surface decoration – dyeing

There are many different dyes available for colouring fabrics; most of them have been developed for a particular application. Textile dyeing involves the permanent application of a colourant to a fabric to give a uniform all-over colour. In order to be successful, the colourant must be able to be absorbed by – or react with – the textile fibre. It must also be soluble so that it can go into the spaces between the fibre molecules.

### Vat, discharge and resist

In commercial manufacture, dyeing is done on a very large scale in a dye-bath called a vat. The vat contains the dyestuff, water and added chemicals to help the dye attach itself to the fabric. This is called the dye liquor. Dyeing in a vat gives the fabric a solid all-over colour. Fabrics are dyed in batches of several hundred metres, and each batch is given a number. The batch number allows manufacturers of textile products to make sure that all parts of a product are cut from the same dye batch, to avoid colour shade variations.

The process of dyeing consists of three basic steps:

- Immerse the textile into the vat.
- The dye attaches itself to the textile fibre.
- Fix the dye within the fibre.

**Figure 1.5.1** A discharge dyed pattern with most of the original colour removed.

**Figure 1.5.2** The chemically printed spots resisted the blue dye.

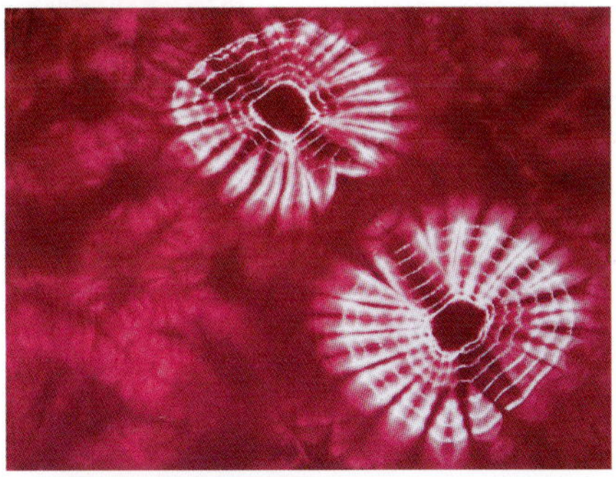

**Figure 1.5.3** Tie-dyed fabric.

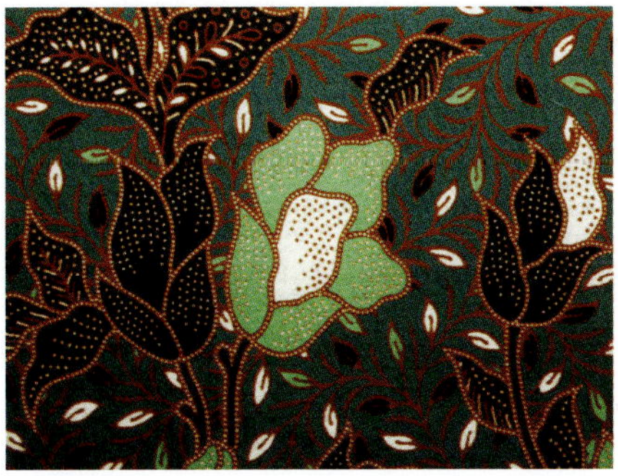

**Figure 1.5.4** A fabric decorated with batik.

The dye liquor is usually heated to help the dye penetrate the fibres, and the fabric is moved continuously so that the dye attaches itself evenly. Once the fabric is the desired colour, the excess dye is removed and the fabric is cleaned with detergents. If this is not done, the fabric may develop faults such as losing colour when washed or streaking of the colour.

The process of dyeing normally involves putting colour onto a fabric but, can also be about removing colour or preventing colour from going onto the fabric. In dyeing, this can be achieved using discharge or resist techniques.

A discharge technique uses a chemical deactivator to remove colour from the dyed fabric. The design is printed or painted onto fabric that has already been dyed, and the deactivator removes the colour completely, leaving an off-white shade or a lighter tint of the original colour.

A resist technique involves the fabric being printed with chemicals that prevent dye being taken up in the chemically treated areas. This is usually used when a small design is to be put on a single-coloured fabric, for example white spots on a red background.

Tie-dye is another method of resist dyeing. The fabric is twisted, folded or knotted and tied tightly with string to prevent dye from reaching some parts of the fabric. The fabric can be dyed with just one colour, or re-tied in different ways before being dyed with other colours. It is difficult to predict exactly how the pattern will turn out.

Batik is a resist method that uses wax or rice paste to prevent the dye from colouring the fabric. Hot wax or rice paste is applied to parts of the fabric by hand, using a tjanting tool or brush. When the wax or paste has dried, the fabric is dyed and the parts covered with the wax or paste resist the uptake of dye, therefore remain undyed when the wax or paste is removed.

Many commercially produced fabrics that have a tie-dye or batik design have had the pattern printed on to them because it is very costly to produce these effects by hand.

## Fibres, yarns, fabrics and finished products: when dye is applied

Textiles may be dyed at various stages in the processing – from the fibre to the finished article:

- Spin or dope dyeing: the dye is added to the spinning solution of man-made fibres before spinning the fibre. This method results in the textiles having good light and wash fastness.
- Stock dyeing: the fibres are dyed in a loose form before being spun into a yarn. This method has the advantage that if the dyeing is uneven, it will be removed by the blending processes that follow when converting the fibre into yarn.
- Yarn dyeing: yarns are dyed before being made into fabric. This gives them good fastness to washing and wearing, so they are almost always used to make high-quality shirt and suit fabrics. Dyed yarns are used to produce certain colour and pattern effects on fabrics, for example stripes and checks.
- Fabric dyeing: also known as piece dyeing, this is the process by which woven or knitted fabrics are dyed in long lengths (Figure 1.5.6).
- Garment dyeing: basic ready-made garments such as T-shirts are dyed as required. This allows manufacturers of fashion products to apply colour at the last minute, as and when there is consumer demand for the latest shades.

**Figure 1.5.5** Yarn is wound on to cones after it has been dyed.

**Figure 1.5.6** Fabric is piece dyed in very long lengths.

**Figure 1.5.7** The effects of crocking when dye from jeans rubs off onto light coloured fabrics.

**ACTIVITY**

As a class, design a set of experiments to test the colour fastness of a coloured fabric.

You should test the fabric for wash fastness, light fastness and rub fastness. (Make sure you read Chapter 1.1 of this book before you start.)

## Dye fastness

**Dye fastness**, also known as colour fastness, is the ability of a fibre or fabric to retain dye during manufacturing processes, and during the use and care of the product by the consumer. Degradation of colour can occur in three different ways:

- fading – colour is lost into the atmosphere
- crocking – colour is lost through abrasion
- bleeding – colour is lost in water.

When a fabric manufacturer selects a dye for a particular application, colour fastness must be considered and will usually form part of the specification for the product.

Fabrics may need to have fastness to the following:

- Washing: this will be important for clothing that is worn regularly.
- Dry cleaning: solvents used in the dry-cleaning process can cause some dyes to fade.
- Light: furnishing products that are regularly exposed to sunlight, for example curtains, must be able to resist the bleaching effects of the sun.
- Perspiration: this will be important for underwear and fashion products.
- Rubbing (crocking): this can cause localised loss of colour, for example at the knees of trousers, or the transfer of colour from one product to another, such as dye used on denim jeans which can transfer to light coloured seating (Figure 1.5.7).
- Bleaching: the use of chlorine bleach will remove colour from most fabrics, however for swimwear, the dye must resist the effects of the chlorine in swimming pools.

## Dyeing in response to consumer demand and seasonal trends

A-level only

A consumer will be heavily influenced by colour and colour trends when selecting textile products, and designers planning a new range or collection of textile products will take careful notice of colour trend predictions. Colour forecasters analyse and interpret the moods and preferences of consumers, so they can make accurate predictions about colours that will be popular at least one year (sometimes two years) ahead of the fashions. These trends are shown at trade fairs such as Premier Vision, which is held twice-yearly in Paris.

If fabrics are to be made from dyed yarns, the choice of colours for the up-coming season has to be made much earlier, to allow time for the fabric to be manufactured once the yarns are dyed. Fabrics that are piece dyed can remain in their greige state (see page 83) until they are needed to be dyed a specific colour, making it easier and more economical to respond to market demand using Just in Time (JIT) manufacture. This type of manufacture is explained in more detail in Chapter 1.6.

Basic shaped products can be held in an undyed state and dyed to order as colour trends and customer demand change.

## Surface decoration – printing

Printing creates patterns or designs on fabric, and is an important way of adding colour to fabric to give a surface decoration. The process may involve putting colour onto a fabric, or preventing colour from going onto the fabric. Printing has a number of advantages over dyeing:

- There is a greater scope for designing.
- More colours can be used in the design.
- Complicated designs can be produced.
- The methods of printing are varied.
- It is usually less costly than dyeing.

Printed fabrics can be distinguished from woven fabrics because only the printed side shows the design clearly. This is because the dye applied during printing does not penetrate right through the fabric. The dyes used for printing need to be made into a viscous paste using a thickener such as a starch, gum or **alginate**.

### KEY TERMS

**Degradation:** the gradual breakdown of a dye leading to loss of colour in a product.

**Dyeing:** the permanent application of a colourant to a fibre or fabric, to give a uniform, all-over colour.

**Dyestuff:** a coloured substance used to add colour to textile materials.

**Alginate:** a gel-like substance that comes from brown seaweed.

**Dye fastness:** the ability of a fibre or fabric to retain dye.

**Greige cloth:** a fabric in its natural state as it comes from the loom or knitting machine.

**Printing:** a process of creating a design on fabric through the application of colour.

**Surface decoration:** any form of decoration put onto a ready-made fabric to add colour and/or texture.

### Preparing a fabric for printing

A-level only

When the fabric comes from the loom or knitting machine, it is not ready to be dyed or printed on straight away. At this stage, it is referred to as Grey (greige) or loomstate cloth, and it often has a natural creamy colour.

Fibres – especially the natural fibres – have natural impurities in them, for example fats, waxes and salts. There will also be other impurities picked up during the processing, for example oil and dirt from machines, and 'size' (starch) added to strengthen yarns before weaving. These have to be removed before the fabric can be dyed or finished, otherwise the colour or finish will not attach itself evenly to the fabric.

The following are some of the important preparation processes.

#### Desizing

Size is a starch, gum or gelatine type of substance which is applied to warp yarns before they are woven into fabrics. This helps to strengthen them so they are more able to stand up to the constant movements of the loom. Most of these substances are soluble in water so they can easily be removed by washing.

#### Scouring

Scouring removes fatty and waxy impurities that would prevent the fabric from being 'wetted'. Cotton fabrics are scoured by boiling them in caustic soda solution. This method would not be appropriate for wool fabrics because they would be damaged by the heat and the alkali; instead they are moved through warm detergent solutions to remove the fatty deposits in the fibres.

More modern methods involve 'washing' the fabrics in solvents to remove the oils and greases.

### Bleaching

Fabrics are sometimes bleached to obtain a fabric that is evenly white before colour is added. Cotton fabrics are bleached using carefully controlled amounts of hypochlorite bleach or hydrogen peroxide. Wool is often left in its naturally creamy colour – It is never treated with chlorine bleaches because these would damage the scales on the wool fibres. Wool can be bleached using hydrogen peroxide (as used to bleach human hair), or by using sulphur dioxide gas.

Synthetic fibres are naturally white and therefore do not require whitening treatments.

## Techniques for printing as a surface decoration

There are a number of different printing techniques that can be used to put a pattern onto the fabric. The choice of method will depend on the quantity of fabric to be printed, the effect required and the cost of the process. Most commercially printed fabrics are produced using screen printing, as this is a cost-effective way of printing large quantities of fabric.

### Direct

A-level only

The design is printed directly onto the fabric using any one of the methods described below.

### Discharge

A-level only

The fabric is dyed and then printed with a paste that contains chemicals. These chemicals destroy the dye in areas according to the printed design. This is a similar process to discharge dyeing.

### Hand (block and stencil)

Block printing is one of the earliest forms of fabric printing, and uses wooden blocks to transfer the pattern to the fabric by hand. The design is marked on the surface of the block and the background cut away. Each colour in the design is applied using a different block. Colour is applied to the block by dipping it into the printing paste or by using a roller, and the block is pressed firmly onto the fabric. The registration of each repeat of the design must be carefully positioned. Pins at each corner of the block join up exactly so that the pattern continues without interruption. When more than one colour is used, the whole fabric is printed with the first colour, dried and then printed with the next colour. Block printing is a very slow process and is not used much commercially because of the expense. It is sometimes used for very artistic designs in a craft workshop or with small-scale print runs.

**Figure 1.5.8** Block printing by hand.

A stencil is a piece of paper or card with the design cut out of it. It is placed on the fabric and the print paste is applied with a roller or spray diffuser. Like block printing, it is only used for small-scale printing and in craft workshops.

### Rotary/flatbed screen printing

Screen printing is developed from the Japanese method of stencilling delicate patterns on fine fabrics. Most fabrics used for clothing and furnishings are screen printed because it is a fast and economical method. The two main methods used commercially are rotary and flatbed.

Rotary screen printing is the most popular method of screen printing because it is quick and efficient. It also allows a greater quantity of fabric to be printed in a short time. It is suited to designs with large repeats, and complex designs that have more than five colours.

The screen is a seamless metal mesh roller, and the design must fit on the roller so that it prints the repeating design accurately along the fabric length without any overlaps or gaps. The designs are usually prepared using computer aided design (CAD) software, and a screen is prepared for each colour in the design. All of the rollers are fitted onto the printing machine. The stationary blade (called a squeegee) is fitted through the centre of the roller, and the dye is automatically fed in through a pipe attachment. Each screen roller prints one colour across the width of the fabric.

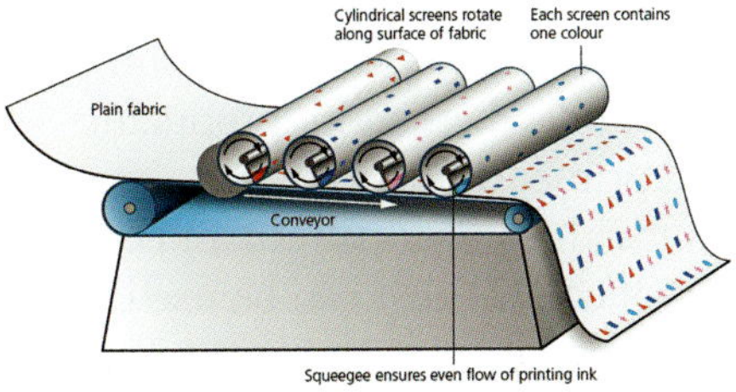

**Figure 1.5.9** Rotary screen printing.

While the rollers are revolving in one direction, the conveyor belt carrying the fabric moves in the opposite. The cloth travels under the rollers and is printed by each in turn.

Flatbed screen printing involves stretching a finely woven mesh fabric over a metal or wooden frame to form a screen. The screen is coated in a chemical that is sensitive to UV light. The parts of the design that are to be printed are blocked off and the screen is exposed to UV light, so that the chemical becomes insoluble in those areas not blocked off. When the screen is washed, the unexposed chemical is removed and the print paste will be able to pass through the mesh. A separate screen is needed for each colour in the design.

The fabric to be printed is on a roll at one end of the printing table. The fabric is fed onto the table by means of a conveyor belt, which carries the cloth under the printing screens. When the fabric stops, the screens are lowered onto the printing table. The screens are placed side by side a few centimetres above the table, and are lowered onto the cloth when printing commences. Each screen prints a different colour across the width of the fabric. Two fine squeegees move across the screens, pressing the printing paste through the mesh of the screen. After the blades have pressed the dye through to the cloth, the screens rise and the conveyor moves the fabric along into position under the next screen.

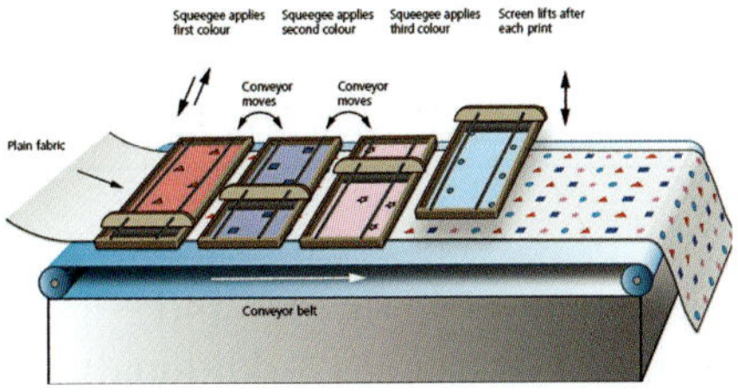

**Figure 1.5.10** Flatbed screen printing.

With both methods of printing, the fabric goes to a drying chamber at the end of the printing table. The dried printed fabric is finished by passing through a steaming chamber, acid baths and a scouring unit to fix the dye and remove the gum used in printing. The fabric may be given any further finishing processes that are required.

## Transfer/dye sublimation

Transfer (or dye sublimation) is similar to ironing transfers onto fabric, and is a low-cost technique suited to short print runs. It is most effective when used on fabrics from synthetic fibres or blends with synthetic fibres. Transfer printing allows the designer to use many different colours, and to change the design quickly as and when required.

The design is printed onto a special type of paper, which is wound onto a roller and placed in position in the machine. The design is the full width of the cloth to be printed.

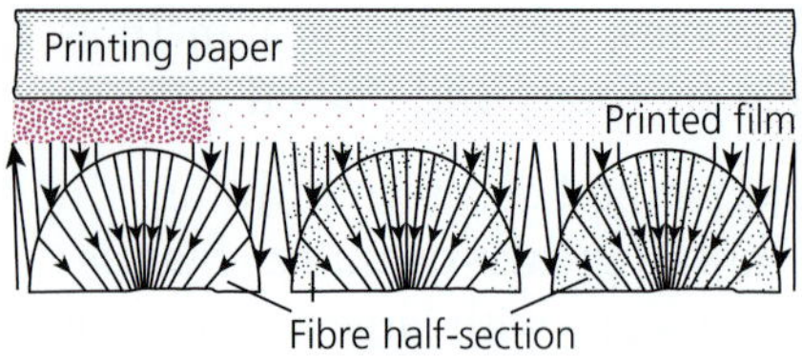


**Figure 1.5.11** Principle of sublimation printing.

The fabric (which is on another roller) is placed opposite the design paper roller, and both fabric and paper are brought together in a dry heat press. This transfers the design from the paper to the cloth. The temperature of the heat press is high enough to cause the dye to turn into a vapour, which then transfers, under pressure, to the fabric. This is also known as sublimation printing.

### Digital printing

Although digital printing (sometimes called inkjet printing) has developed rapidly in recent years, it is not yet an economic method for high volume printing of fabric and garments, but it is a feasible method for producing sample lengths. The ability to link a digital printer directly to CAD equipment allows a designer to experiment with endless pattern and colour variations. There is no limit to the number of colours that can be used in a single print, and no problems with the scale of the pattern repeat. The finished print is a very high quality, and often used on bespoke products (see Chapter 1.6).

The pattern is printed directly onto the fabric or garment, in the same way that a printer linked to a computer prints on paper. Most digital printers can print onto any fabric if an appropriate ink is used. Once the fabric is printed, the colour is set using heat or steam.

Digital printing of fabrics works well with JIT manufacture (see also Chapter 1.6) because the designs go straight from the computer software to the printer. This means that there are very short lead times and no minimum print run. New designs can be produced very quickly and used on any fabric, so manufacturers are not dependent on stock fabric.

Digital technology is also capable of printing a cutting outline directly onto a fabric, to allow for bespoke and sample garment production.

**ACTIVITY**

As a class, make a collection of fabrics or images of products showing fabrics that have been:

- digitally printed
- screen printed
- resist dyed
- discharge printed (A-level only).

## Embroidery

Embroidery adds colour and texture to a fabric by using threads and yarns to make stitches and various combinations of stitches. Additional trimmings and components such as beads and sequins can be added.

### Hand embroidery

Hand embroidery stitches can be divided into four basic categories:

- Flat stitches are usually straight stitches that lie on the surface of the fabric, for example back stitch, running stitch and satin stitch.
- Linked stitches are formed when a loop of one stitch is linked to another, for example chain stitch and feather stitch.
- Looped stitches are made when a loop of the thread passes around the needle and each stitch interlinks with the next, for example loop stitch (sometimes called blanket stitch) and fly stitch.
- Knotted stitches are made when the thread is twisted around the needle to form a knotted or raised surface, for example French knots.

Embroidery threads are usually thicker than regular sewing threads, and so need to be used with needles that are specifically for embroidery.

**Figure 1.5.12** Fabric for hand embroidery is held taut in an embroidery ring.

Crewel needles have a sharp point and a long eye so that thread can easily pass through.

An embroidery ring or frame is often used to hold the fabric while it is being stitched. The frame helps to hold the fabric taut so that the stitches do not cause the fabric to pucker.

## Machine embroidery

There are two basic types of machine embroidery:

- pre-programmed or computer controlled embroidery
- free machine embroidery.

### Pre-programmed stitches

All sewing machines can do zig zag stitch, which allows some basic decorative stitches to be made. Most machines also have a number of decorative stitches that are pre-programmed into the machine, and the sewer simply has to set the stitch length and width required.

Pre-programmed stitches can be combined and used in many ways to create interesting effects, especially when combined with fabric strips, ribbons and other trimmings.

Computerised sewing machines have a very wide range of pre-programmed stitches, and can also stitch motifs that have been designed on a computer or downloaded from a website and scanned into the machine by the user.

Dedicated embroidery machines are computerised machines that only sew embroidery designs. The designs are stored in the machine's memory or on a card that is inserted into the machine, or the user can develop their own designs on a computer and transfer them to the machine. The fabric is held in a special embroidery hoop attached to the machine, which will automatically sew the design and stop when it is completed. These machines do not have feed dogs that feed the fabric under the machine, allowing the hoop to move freely. There is no foot pedal, instead they are operated using a start button.

In industry, a central computer can control large machines with multi-heads that can stitch more than one colour and sew hundreds of the same design at one time.

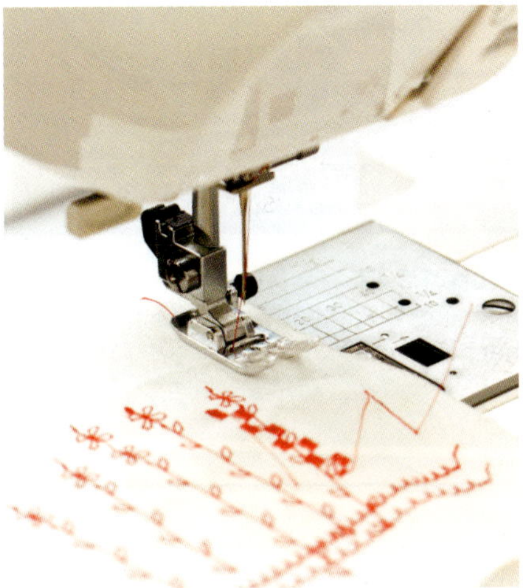

**Figure 1.5.13** Pre-programmed stitches can be built up to create designs.

**Figure 1.5.14** Dedicated embroidery machines automatically sew designs.

### Free machine embroidery

In free machine embroidery, the fabric is moved under the needle to draw the pattern on the fabric. The machine foot is removed and a free machine embroidery foot is fitted. The feed dogs are covered or lowered so that the fabric can be moved freely to achieve individual patterns. The fabric must be held taut in an embroidery hoop and kept flat on the base of the machine. Very lightweight or flimsy fabrics should have an underlining or interfacing behind them to support the stitches. The machine is threaded in the usual way using a thread specially made for machine embroidery – regular threads can keep breaking. The presser foot must be put down even though it has been removed, in order to operate the thread tension.

**Figure 1.5.15** Computer controlled industrial machines can sew hundreds of designs at the same time.

**ACTIVITY**

Look online to find a tutorial showing how to do free machine embroidery. Use free machine embroidery to make a small decorative panel. Include some additional materials as you stitch, or add them after the stitching is complete.

The hoop with the fabric is moved around as the machine sews, allowing the stitching to go in different directions to build up a unique design. The design can be developed by using straight and zig zag stitches, adding additional fabrics or by painting parts of the fabric before stitching.

Free machine embroidery takes practise, but can be used to achieve some exciting effects.

**Figure 1.5.16** Free machine embroidery is done by moving the fabric under the needle.

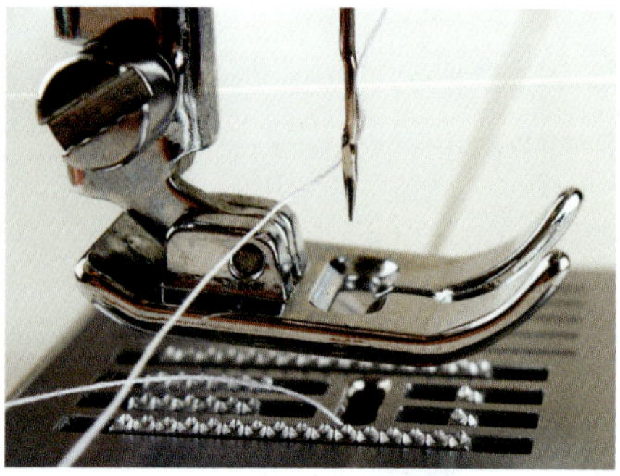

**Figure 1.5.17** The feed dogs on the machine must be lowered for free machine embroidery.

## Quilting

Quilting is a functional and decorative technique that gives texture and form to fabric.

The simplest type of quilting involves placing a layer of wadding between two layers of fabric and then stitching through all the layers. The layer of wadding traps air so the fabric acts as an insulator, and the added thickness makes a more protective fabric. This is called English quilting.

**Figure 1.5.18** English quilting is made up of a layer of wadding between two outer fabrics.

The three layers are laid on top of each other, making sure that the grain line runs in the same direction on the top and bottom layers of fabric. The layers are pinned and tacked together, starting in the middle and working outwards to keep the fabric flat.

The layers are stitched together in a pattern, usually based on straight lines, and using a long machine stitch to allow for the thickness of the fabric. The lines can be marked on the fabric using tailor's chalk, or a quilting foot can be used on the machine to guide the stitching.

Quilting can be combined with patchwork to give a more decorative effect.

**Figure 1.5.19** English quilting combined with patchwork.

Italian quilting is purely decorative, and does not add warmth to a product. Two layers of fabric are stitched together in a design that has parallel lines. Cord is inserted between the lines of stitching so that they stand out in relief.

Trapunto quilting is also a decorative technique. Two layers of fabric are stitched together to make a design that has small enclosed areas. These are padded from the back of the work by making small slits in the backing fabric. A small amount of padding is inserted and the slits stitched together.

### ACTIVITY

Make small samples of English, Italian and Trapunto quilting.

How could you incorporate them into fashion products?

### KEY POINTS

- Dyeing is usually about putting colour onto a fabric, but it can also be about removing colour or preventing colour from going onto the fabric.
- Fabric needs to be cleaned in preparation for dyeing and printing, otherwise the colour will not attach.
- Screen printing is the most used commercial method of printing a design onto fabric.
- There are many different types of embroidery, including stitches worked by hand and machine.
- English quilting adds warmth and decoration to a product, but Italian and Trapunto quilting are purely decorative techniques.

**Figure 1.5.20** Italian quilting is a decorative technique based on parallel lines.

**Figure 1.5.21** Trapunto quilting is the decorative technique of padding small enclosed areas of a design.

## Check your knowledge and understanding

1. What is the difference between dyeing and printing?
2. Name two resist methods of dyeing fabric.
3. What is the basic difference between flat bed and rotary screen printing?
4. What type of needle is required for hand embroidery?
5. Explain briefly how a quilted fabric is able to insulate a person.

## Further reading

Briggs-Goode, A. *Printed Textile Design*

Grey, M. *Raising the Surface*

Grey, M. and Campbell-Harding, V. *Stitch, Dissolve, Distort: With Machine Embroidery*

Healey, E. *Stitch, Fabric and Thread: An Inspirational Guide for Creative Stitchers*

Udale, J. *Textiles and Fashion: Exploring printed textiles, knitwear, embroidery, menswear and womenswear*

Wolff, C. *The Art of Manipulating Fabric*

Interactive CDs from www.pumpkin-interactive.co.uk/collections/design-technology-and-textiles

The following YouTube videos:

- Digital printing: https://youtu.be/L5uJ-YVSEro
- Printed fabric production: https://youtu.be/zuR2x0lorLg
- Factory tour – dyehouse: https://youtu.be/L76Hz30tvWE
- Dyeing and finishing: https://youtu.be/Dh5WCGHQ5D8

# 1.6 Modern industrial and commercial practice

**LEARNING OUTCOMES**

By the end of this section you should have developed a knowledge and understanding of:

- different manufacturing systems
- how computer systems are used in manufacturing.

If you are studying at A-level you should also have developed a knowledge and understanding of:

- a wide range of modern manufacturing systems
- global manufacture.

Fashion is one of the most important industries in the world, and is made up of a number of inter-related and complex processes. New textile and fashion products are continually appearing in the shops. People buy new products, even though ones they already own may not be worn out. They want the latest fashions or technological developments, because they are concerned with their image, and how other people see them. But the world of fashion is not just about pandering to people's illusions about themselves; it is a multi-million-pound industry, driven by the need to make profit.

This complex industry has three essential parts – designing, manufacturing and distribution. Manufacturers need to make interesting, new and different products if they are to stay in business. Once the products have been manufactured, they have to be sent to the retailers so that they can be sold to consumers. A designer will generally be expected to work with the manufacturer, in order to ensure that products are capable of being manufactured efficiently and safely, and to the final specifications.

## Scales of production

There are different types of production systems. The manufacturer will choose the most appropriate system for the type of product being made. Some products must be made quickly and efficiently to keep costs down, while other products are one of a kind and made for individual customers, so will be very expensive.

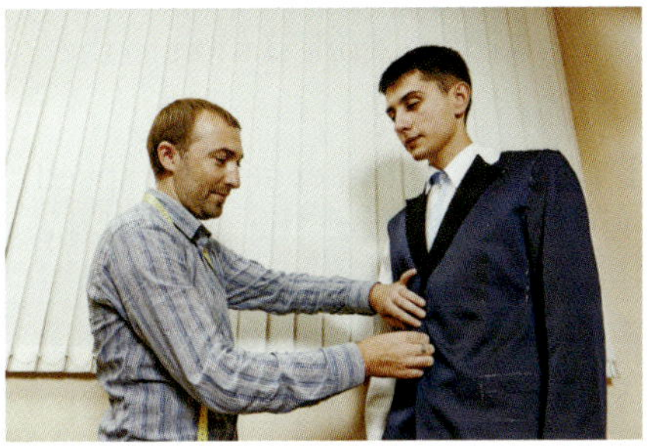

**Figure 1.6.1** A tailor making a bespoke suit for an individual client.

## One-off, bespoke production

One-off production is also called job, individual, make through and bespoke production. One highly skilled craftsperson produces a single garment or textile product over a number of days or weeks (Figure 1.6.1). Each product is made only once or only in very small quantities. This method may be used to make a theatre costume or an outfit to fit an individual customer. The garments are usually unique and finished to a very high standard. They are very expensive because of the labour costs and the use of costly materials.

## Batch production

A team of workers make a specified number of identical products, which may be made in one production run or in **batches** repeated at certain times. A batch can range from two or three products to 100,000 or more. In a large factory, many batches of different products for different customers and delivery dates will be processed at the same time. This involves complex planning, which will add to the costs of manufacture. Seasonal products such as fashion tops or trousers are made using batch production.

## Mass/line production

Very large quantities of products are made over and over in assembly line production. Machines are in continuous use for long periods of time so they are very specialised and expensive. The machinery and the operator skills are very specific for the job in hand. A number of operatives work on the production line – each does one part of the manufacture before passing the product to the next person, who does a different job. The work flows through the factory in a straight line and every operation is timed; the production plan is drawn up to make full use of every machine and every operative. The bundles of work move from one work station to another on a conveyor system, usually controlled by a computer, or in crates wheeled around by porters.

Workers become skilled at doing one part of the manufacture, but may need to be re-trained to do other types of work. The system enables them to make identical products very quickly but can be very boring for the workers, who do the same task over and over again (Figure 1.6.2).

**Figure 1.6.2** Working on a production line.

This system is also called synchronised or progressive bundle production because the products are put together as they progress through successive **sub-assembly** and main assembly operations in bundle form.

Mass production reduces time and costs, but the whole production can quickly halt if there is a problem. Also, changing the line to make a different product can take a long time. Mass/line production is not usually used for clothing because styles change so often. Some factories may specialise in products that do not change often, for example jeans or school shirts.

## Unit production systems

A-level only

Unit production systems (UPS) have been in use for many years as a mechanical system. In 1983, a major advance was made when computers began to be used to plan, control and direct the flow of work through a manufacturing system. The unit of production is the complete product, not a bundle. The bundle is taken automatically from one work station to the next to create the complete product.

The rate of production is pre-determined, and the computer sets the speed at which sections of the product are taken to the operator. The parts of the product are taken by overhead conveyor to as close to the operator's left hand as possible, reducing the amount of movement needed to position the item to be stitched. Some operations can even be carried out without removing parts from the hanger.

All of the components for one garment are loaded into a carrier at a workstation specially designed for this purpose. The carrier is divided into sections, each of which has a quick-release clamp to prevent the components from falling out during movement through the system. When a batch of garments has been loaded into carriers, they are fed past a mechanical or electronic device, which records the number of the carrier and sends it to its first destination.

When the operator has completed work on one carrier, a push button at the side of the sewing machine activates a mechanism, which transports the carrier back to the main line. As one carrier leaves the station, another is automatically fed in to take its place. When the carrier leaves the station, it is recorded on the data collection system, and then sent on to its next destination.

One of the most important advantages of a UPS is that it allows a factory to respond quickly to changes in the fashion market, because it allows as many as 40 different styles to be produced at the same time.

## Quick response manufacturing

A-level only

Modern fashion retailing depends on garments being produced according to consumer demand. During manufacture, the different parts of the garment are cut out and moved around the factory to the operatives, who sew them together. This is called **work in progress**. If the parts of the garments spend a lot of time in the factory waiting to be sewn together, this will add to the manufacturing costs as space must be found for storage, and workers must be paid to move the parts around as they are needed.

In quick-response manufacturing (QRM), workers operate in teams or production cells/modules. The workers share tasks and equipment, and become more skilled because the job they do changes day by day according to what is being made. The machinery used is more versatile than that used in mass production and workers will be skilled at using a variety of different machines. Each module is responsible for its own performance and the quality of work produced.

Working as a team means that products are made quicker than one person working alone, and allows for some flexibility so that they can respond quickly to changes in demand. This means that a product is completed from start to finish by a multi-skilled operative moving around machinery in a horseshoe arrangement. Three operatives might work together in a horseshoe of eight machines to complete individual garments. The garment will be passed quickly from one operative to another as they become free to process it, allowing garments to be assembled very quickly.

### KEY TERMS

**Work in progress:** the different parts of the garment that are cut out and ready to be sewn together.

**Sub-assembly:** parts of the product are assembled on a separate line before they go to the main production line.

**Batches:** a specified number of identical products that may be made in one production run.

## Section

A-level only

The section system is a development of one-off manufacture – it is on a larger scale to reduce costs. Workers specialise in making one major component of a garment and sew it from start to finish.

For example, if a shirt were being made, one person would make the fronts including sewing on the pockets and making the button and buttonhole bands; another person would make the back of the shirts and it would then be passed to the next worker, who would join the fronts to the back. This would continue until the shirts were completed.

The workers are versatile and able to carry out a number of different processes, and the factory is organised according to the different operations needed for particular garments.

## Vertical in-house production

A-level only

Vertical in-house production is where high street retailers do their own designing, manufacturing and distribution. This allows lead times to be shortened so that products are in the shops more quickly. It also reduces costs of outsourcing manufacture. Marks and Spencer and Zara are two popular high street retailers who operate this system.

### ACTIVITY

Explain how scales of production can affect the production times and costs of manufacturing. Present your work in a grid like the one shown below.

**Table 1.6.1** Scales of production and how they affect production times and costs of manufacturing.

| Scale of production | Type of product made | Time (long, short) | Cost (high, medium, low) |
|---|---|---|---|
| One-off/bespoke | | | |
| Batch | | | |
| Mass | | | |
| QRM | | | |

# The use of computer systems

The fashion industry is completely reliant on effective computer systems at every stage of design, manufacture, distribution, retailing and planning. There are complex production networks that span many different businesses, and frequently cross international boundaries. In addition, sales are seasonal and can be unpredictable, therefore the windows for completing and delivering orders can be very tight. Effective planning, production scheduling, process control and stock management are therefore essential for success.

## Manufacturing systems

### Modular/cell production

A-level only

Modular/cell production is when workers operate in small teams to enable products to be made as QRM. This system is covered in detail above.

**KEY TERMS**

**Just in Time (JIT):** a stock control management system that ensures fabrics and components arrive at the factory just as they are needed to go onto the production line.

### Just in Time

**JIT** is a stock control management system that ensures fabrics and components arrive at the factory just as they are needed to go onto the production line. The manufacturer will have a production plan for each product that is made. This will give information about the materials and components needed, and at what stage of the production process they are needed.

The different materials needed for the product come directly from the supplier and arrive at the factory when they are needed, where they go straight onto the part of the assembly line where they are needed. This means that stock is bought in the quantities required for each batch of products and not stored in warehouses. This saves money on warehouse space and wages for workers because the products are not being continually handled, therefore fewer operatives are needed. The materials will also be of the quality agreed between the supplier and the manufacturer.

The whole process is controlled electronically using the barcodes attached to every item. The barcodes are read by scanners at each stage of manufacture, and the information is stored on a central computer system. This allows manufacturers to place orders quickly when fashions change so that they can be more flexible in their working practice. Because the computerised system controls stock levels, manufacturers do not have large quantities of stock that may not be needed. This means that there is less waste of materials, which is cost effective and better for the environment.

### Quick response manufacturing

You learned about QRM earlier in this book. Computer control can help manufacturers respond quickly to changes in the market and save on production costs by using quick response methods. QRM systems were first developed in Japan to enable manufacturers to respond quickly to market demands, especially when orders for individual styles were in small lots.

QRM systems – where workers are multi-skilled – allow for small batches of a wide range of products to be manufactured quickly. They use a system of job rotation within the team so that workers do not become bored so easily, and have greater job satisfaction. Because of this, they have greater ownership of their work and are likely to produce better quality products. These teams are called quality circles. The products move quickly through each section of the manufacturing process, giving a rapid response time.

### Flexible manufacturing systems

A-level only

A flexible manufacturing system, such as QRM, is one that is able to respond quickly to changes in demand, for example fad designs, garments to meet unexpected weather conditions or products to celebrate an unexpected event.

**Figure 1.6.3** Mass customisation allows trainers to be personalised for individual customers.

Flexible manufacturing systems allow for the manufacture of smaller orders so that consumers can get items specially tailored for their needs in a very short period of time. This is called demand activated manufacture.

Since 2006, a new process called demand-based flow is often used by companies who sell via the internet. When a consumer orders something from an online retailer, they are often told that there will be a two week or longer delay. This allows the manufacturer to produce goods as they are ordered, and is based on demand-pull rather than schedule-push manufacturing. This demand-activated system will become more important as retailers and manufacturers work to match demand with real time purchasing power of the people, and avoid expensive waste.

**Mass customisation** allows manufacturers to meet orders for individual customers by modifying standard designs at low cost. If manufacturers can change designs quickly at minimal cost, then shorter runs become cost effective, to the point where each customer can be provided with exactly what they want.

KEY TERMS

**Mass customisation:** the modification of standard designs to individual customers' requirements.

**Electronic data interchange (EDI):** a system that allows computers to exchange information electronically in a standard format between business partners.

## The use of computer controlled systems in production, distribution and storage

Computerised systems are used throughout the design and manufacture of textile products, and these have been covered in detail in this and other chapters of this book.

Distribution and storage of finished products is also controlled by sophisticated computerised systems.

The growth of globalised manufacture makes air freighting an important way of delivering goods to and from almost any location in the world. Air freighting is expensive in terms of cost and environmental impact, so it is important that full use is made of available space on a plane, and that as many different products as possible are shipped at the same time. Computer controlled systems can help to collate collections and deliveries, and make sure that a range of products from the same or different manufacturers are grouped together, ready to be transported at the same time.

Transport and distribution services for clothing have become very sophisticated, and a number of specialist companies provide comprehensive 'logistical' support in the form of customised vehicles, fully computerised warehousing facilities and full electronic data interchange (EDI) linkage with both suppliers and customers.

An increasing number of garment manufacturers no longer have their own warehousing facilities and instead rely on these specialist companies, some of whom have large international networks and offer additional services such as garment re-finishing immediately prior to delivery to retail outlets. Many fashion products go straight from the factory to the retailer, with no necessity for warehouse storage. Movements of products use a JIT stock control system controlled by EDI barcode systems, which track the progress of the products through the manufacturing and distribution stages.

## The use of standardised and bought-in components made by specialist manufacturers

Components are added to products to make them functional or to add detail, style and individuality. The type of components used on a product

**ACTIVITY**

Create a visual aid to help with your revision – take each computer system in turn and draw some diagrams to show how computers aid manufacturing, distribution and storage.

changes in line with fashion trends, and the latest collections will be shown at trade fairs all over the world.

Some manufacturers specialise in making components such as embroidered panels, logos, collars, cuffs and other trims. It is more economical for manufacturers to buy these pre-manufactured components because they do not need to invest in the specialised machinery needed to make them. They can also buy the type and number of components needed, and as they are needed, using a JIT stock control system.

Components are made in standard sizes, for example zip lengths, bias binding widths, and interfacing fabric widths, according to the type of product being manufactured. This makes efficient use of manufacturing systems because machines can be programmed to deal with these pre-set sizes.

## Sub-assembly

When planning for manufacture, the different stages in the manufacture are grouped together into key areas of production. Sections of the product may be made as sub-assemblies. This is where some parts of the product are assembled on a separate line before they go to the main production line. This may be a separate line in the factory, a different factory or even a factory in a different country. It will have specialised machinery or workers who are especially skilled in a particular type of production such as embroidery.

**ACTIVITY**

Outline the manufacturing stages used to make a fashionable pair of trousers.

Which parts could have been made as sub-assemblies? List the components used.

Sub-assembly of certain parts of the product by specialist manufacturers helps to reduce manufacturing costs, and enables the finished product to be high quality because the sub-assembled part will be quality checked before it leaves the factory.

Sub-assembly also facilitates JIT manufacture because parts can be bought in as and when needed.

## Global production

A-level only

Many textile products are designed in one country and made in another. The designers and manufacturers can easily communicate via the internet, and computer-generated information about a final design can be sent anywhere in the world in just a few seconds. The information can be fed directly from the computer into manufacturing systems to make the product.

Electronic communication allows the factories to be anywhere in the world. Many of the factories are huge – some the size of a football pitch – with rolls of fabric delivered to the cutting room where it goes straight onto the cutting tables. Once cut, the bundles of cut pieces are distributed to the machinists, sewn together and delivered to the retail outlet within a matter of hours.

A factory will make products for many different brand names using the same machines and workers. However, different designs, materials and different levels of quality are needed, depending on the target market group.

## Offshore production

Products are made overseas because labour is often cheaper or materials may be more readily available. Some overseas manufacturers have skilled workers who are able to perform specialist tasks. Many textiles products sold in the UK have been made in other countries. The environmental costs of manufacturing products overseas – such as air pollution and the use of fuel for planes and boats – and the ensuing consequences for employment in the UK, are issues that need to be considered.

Other social and moral issues surrounding overseas manufacture may be related to working conditions and pay for those employed in the production of fashion and other textile items.

## Imports and exports

The UK fashion market trades with many different countries within the global market place, especially the Far East and eastern Europe. The scale of trade depends on many factors such as labour and material costs, international trade agreements, tariffs and currency exchange rates.

Manufacture of fashion products in the UK has declined over many years as low-cost products made overseas have been imported. Many British manufacturers now specialise in making small batches of high value and specialised products, and these are the main exports from the UK.

British retailers that have outlets overseas provide export markets for those manufacturers who supply their shops, for example Paul Smith and Marks and Spencer.

## Branded goods

Brand image is very important to some consumers who will want to buy products that enhance their personal image by purchasing from specific designers or retailers, for example Levi jeans and Nike trainers. A brand name can give the consumer assurances about the quality of the product and consistency in the standard of the manufacture, and help to differentiate one designer or retailer from another. A well-known and respected brand name will help to increase sales because consumers have confidence in the quality of the products.

Brand names may apply to a specific range of co-ordinated products that have a particular theme, for example clothing, accessories and cosmetics.

A brand name is also used to give a corporate image to a company, for example a corporate colour scheme, logo and trademark that appears throughout the company's offer on packaging, workers' uniforms and advertising materials.

Strong brand names can help to sell products in the global market place, especially to those consumers who have high levels of disposable income to spend on the latest fashion trends.

**Figure 1.6.4** The Levi brand is synonymous with denim jeans.

**Figure 1.6.5** The trademark Nike tick gives a recognised brand image.

**Figure 1.6.6** A strong image can help sell fashion goods in the global market place.

**ACTIVITY**

As a class, make a collection of brand labels associated with fashion and textile products.

What different images do they convey to the consumer?

Where are the products made?

## Contracted goods

A contract manufacturer makes branded or labelled products for another company. These products may be based on their own or the customer's designs and specifications. For example, a manufacturer may make a number of products for different retailers, even though those retailers will be in competition with each other for customers. Each product will carry the individual retailer's logo or trademark.

A manufacturer may be unable to produce all of the goods that have been ordered, so will look for other factories that are able to take on the order. These goods will be made under the original manufacturer's name, even though they have been made elsewhere.

There is a strong relationship between material cost, form, manufacturing processes and the scale of production:

- the development of designs that use materials economically and with regard to their characteristics
- the use of manufacturing processes which increase accuracy and reduce waste
- the savings to be gained when comparing bulk production with one-off production
- the advantages of JIT manufacture.

# Efficient use of materials

Please note this section refers to section 3.1.7 of the AS Level specification.

All of the materials used to make a textile product – fabric, thread and components – add to the cost of making the product, so it is important to make the best use of them and avoid waste. Further information about using materials efficiently can be found in Chapter 2.7 of this book.

## Developing designs that use materials economically

When developing new products, a designer will make prototypes to check that the design works. Part of this modelling will include looking at how the design might be modified so that fabric can be used more efficiently and economically. For example, making a section of the product slightly shorter or narrower may have little impact on the aesthetics or functioning of the product but could result in much less fabric being used. For example, the pattern pieces can be placed closer together on the width of fabric being used. Removing a seam from a product can result in big savings of thread and manufacturing time, when making a large batch of the products commercially.

Some fabrics need to be cut in a specific way because of how they are made or how they are designed, for example those with a one-way design or a nap. This can add considerably to the cost of making the product because the layout is likely to be quite wasteful of the fabric.

The designer's choice of components used on products can affect the costs – a zip may be cheaper than buttons, which require additional manufacturing processes and materials to make the buttonholes. Using beads and embroidered decoration will cost more than a printed design, which is simpler to apply.

## Manufacturing processes that increase efficiency

The quality of the finished product is important in keeping costs down and avoiding waste; faulty goods cost manufacturers money and customers will not continue to buy their goods in future.

Modern manufacturing systems can help make products accurately and reduce the amount of waste material produced, which is better for costs and environmental impact. Systems that use computer control usually produce greater reliability with accuracy of manufacture, and are often cheaper to run because they use materials in an economical way and need fewer operatives. They can also run 24 hours a day and 7 days a week without the need for breaks. Further information about automated manufacturing systems can be found in Chapter 1.7 of this book.

## Savings between bulk and one-off production

Costing is an important consideration when designing and making a textile product, and a budget will be set at the start of the process. Products are designed and manufactured for specific consumer markets; bespoke products will be more expensive than mass produced fashions because the costs of labour will be higher, and often more luxurious fabrics and components are used.

Manufacturers are able to save money by buying fabrics and components in bulk as and when they are needed. The style and colour of many textile products are determined by changes in fashion, therefore buying fabrics as and when they are needed using a JIT system can save money as unused materials are not wasted.

Some basic materials such as interfacings and white thread are used in large quantities and are not affected by changes in fashion as much as some other materials. By buying these in even larger quantities, the manufacturer may be able to negotiate a bigger discount with the supplier, helping to make even greater savings.

## The advantages of JIT manufacture

JIT manufacturing systems are covered in detail earlier in this chapter.

## KEY POINTS

- The scale of manufacture is important in ensuring efficiency.
- Computer control extends throughout all manufacturing systems, and is essential in making sure that work is organised and completed efficiently.
- JIT and quick response methods of manufacturing allow for quick changes in fashion.
- JIT manufacture can save money on materials and costs of storage.
- Fabrics and components must be used as economically as possible to reduce costs
- The more of the same product that is made, the less each unit will cost.
- Large factories situated all over the world produce fashion goods for many different brands.
- A brand name is important in conveying impressions of quality, and can help sell fashion products.

## Check your knowledge and understanding

1 What is a bespoke garment?

2 What are standardised components?

3 Give two reasons why sub-assembly systems are used when manufacturing fashion products.

4 What is meant by the term 'section' manufacturing?

5 Give three reasons why the fashion industry is highly reliant on computer systems.

## Further reading

Hannelore, E. *Clothing Technology*

Sinclair, R. and Morgan, S. *Textiles Technology*

Down, J. *Textiles to GCSE*

The following YouTube videos:

- Dress shirt factory/manufacturer: https://youtu.be/4zhjVkTVJ1E
- Garment production: https://youtu.be/x7LN-MZNvec
- Drake's London bespoke shirts: https://youtu.be/vKfAoYezu4g
- Trousers production in a UPS system: https://youtu.be/v03vPLGMNaM
- How it's made – jeans: https://www.youtube.com/watch? v = C8vA0UwLS70

# 1.7 Digital design and manufacture

**LEARNING OUTCOMES**

By the end of this section you should have developed a knowledge and understanding of:

- how software programmes are used in the development of design ideas
- the importance of pattern design systems (PDS) in the design of fashion products
- automated manufacturing systems.

If you are studying at A-level you should also have developed a knowledge and understanding of:

- the benefits of using production, planning and control (PPC) systems
- how EDI is used in retailing and marketing.

Computer aided design (CAD) and computer aided manufacturing (CAM) are used extensively throughout the textiles industry, and are important at every stage of the design, manufacture, packaging, distribution and selling of the products. Today's manufacturing systems are totally dependent on these technologies, for example JIT manufacture. Many companies have invested significant sums of money in CAD and CAM systems. This is so that they can compete effectively in the global marketplace where quick changes in fashion and efficient manufacture are the order of the day.

## Computer aided design

CAD is used in all areas of the design process – from generating ideas to presenting them to the client. CAD software packages make a seamless link with many computer controlled manufacturing processes. CAD has made the process of designing garments much quicker and cheaper because physical samples are not required as early in the process or as frequently, as was the case when designs were produced manually.

### The advantages and disadvantages of using CAD compared to manually generated alternative

CAD systems save time and money, and often allow designers to be more creative with their ideas.

The designer has access to databases of designs that have already been used, and these can be adapted into new designs. Having instant access to existing designs saves time re-drawing garments because the changes can quickly be made on screen.

Using software for experimental work involving colour, pattern, shape and style saves time and physical resources such as paper, coloured inks and paints as well as fabric. This not only saves money but also has a positive impact on the environment.

Different parts of the design and manufacture process are often in different places and countries, so being able to send electronic copies of ideas and specifications means that there is a faster interaction between the client, designer and manufacturer. This allows decisions to be communicated more quickly and client feedback on proposals to be received earlier.

The disadvantages of using CAD and CAM are few – the initial set-up costs for the systems are high, and efficient use of them requires every company involved in the various processes to have compatible systems.

## The use of CAD to develop and present ideas for products

The client will want to look at the first design ideas and choose some for development. The ideas will need to be presented clearly. A designer will probably use a **presentation board** to show ideas. The presentation board will have sketches of the products, and some samples of the fabrics and components that could be used. Images on the presentation board can be easily and accurately generated using CAD. Ideas can be presented using real life images of collections, ranges and colourways in high quality, interactive 3D. Changes to the design can be made quickly without the need to start afresh, and this shortens the time needed for development. It enables important design decisions to be made before a physical sample is produced, saving both time and money. Once the pattern is made, the **pattern design system (PDS)** can be used to create virtual samples, therefore reducing the costs of making fabric samples and enabling them to be sent electronically to the client or manufacturer. This allows any errors to be detected and corrected at an early stage of the development, and before the factory produces the first prototype sample.

### KEY TERMS

**Pattern design system (PDS):** a computer programme that makes pattern templates automatically from a 3D model.

**Presentation board:** a collection of illustrations, samples and colourways used to present final ideas to a client.

**Virtual prototype:** a prototype product modelled on a computer but not actually made.

## How CAD is used in industrial applications A-level only

In industry, designers use a computer programme called a PDS (see above). Some of the ways that designers use this CAD system are described below.

- Designing repeat patterns for fabric prints, embroidery designs, knitted or woven patterns: these patterns can be more complex and accurate, and sent directly to the manufacturing equipment. Software allows the designer to rotate motifs and plan repeat patterns accurately, so that they fit within the fabric width or the size of the product. Photographs and images can be downloaded or scanned in and manipulated to create new patterns (Figure 1.7.1).
- Creating databases of patterns and designs that can be used as a starting point for new ideas: many new fashions that appear in shops are often very similar to those of a previous season, with minor modifications such as different colours or applied patterns, therefore using existing products as a starting point saves time.

**Figure 1.7.1** CAD software is used to develop patterns for fabric.

**Figure 1.7.2** Computer programmes can be used to experiment with colour and pattern.

- Designing new products that can be shown in different colourways and with different applied patterns: CAD software usually has a Pantone colour palette that can be used to accurately represent the colour that will be on the product (Figure 1.7.2).
- Experimenting with colour, pattern and texture on 3D images of a garment: image mapping allows the designer to show what the pattern and colour will look like on a garment (Figure 1.7.3).
- Making a **virtual prototype** that can show how a garment will move when on a human body, and how it will look in different colour ranges: virtual prototypes are quick to make and change, and do not use fabric therefore they are cheaper and more environmentally friendly (Figure 1.7.4).

**Figure 1.7.3** A CAD programme allows a fabric design to be placed on a garment to see what it looks like.

**Figure 1.7.4** Virtual prototypes show how a garment will look and move when worn by a human.

When a final design has been chosen for bulk manufacture, a pattern or template is made. If it is a fashion product, the patterns will be developed from basic blocks stored in the system. If the product has been manufactured before, the existing pattern will be used again. The computer

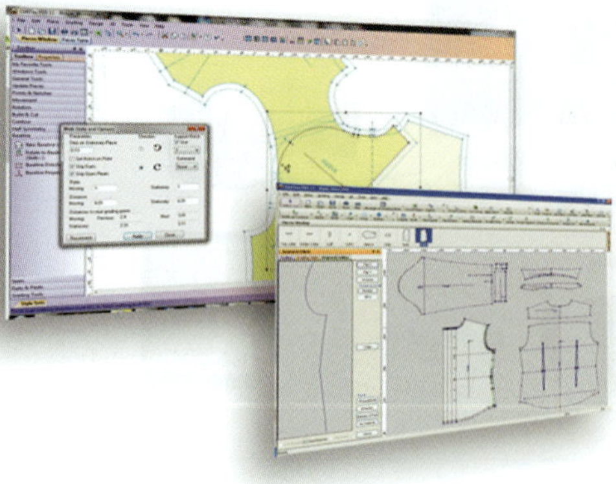

Figure 1.7.5 The computer can make pattern templates instantly from a 3D model of a garment.

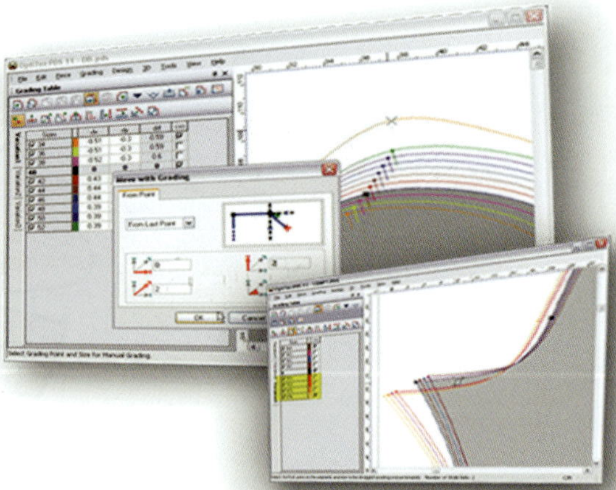

Figure 1.7.6 Grading a pattern.

programme has pattern shapes for basic products. These patterns are called standardised designs, and are adapted to make the new template.

The CAD software enables fast, efficient pattern development. This allows for complex darts and pattern shapes to be made quickly, reducing time spent on pattern development and therefore reducing costs. The computer makes the new patterns accurately with the right number of pieces, and includes seam allowances for the garment developed as a 3D model (Figure 1.7.5). Patterns are also graded so that they can be used to make different sized garments.

The PDS software reduces time spent re-drafting patterns from scratch, reduces material costs, ensures accuracy and decreases reliance on highly skilled operators.

In a fully automated factory with integrated systems, the pattern templates will be sent to the fabric laying and cutting system. The PDS can produce a **lay plan**, which shows where the pattern pieces should be placed on the fabric.

CAD systems can also show the likely costs of making the product through the use of spreadsheets.

## Computer aided manufacturing

CAM uses automated machines that are controlled by computers, and is often used in conjunction with CAD. CAM is used to replace a manual operation, which means that a machine can work continuously. The quality is more consistent, with fewer faulty goods produced. CAM systems can also work with materials and chemicals that might be harmful to humans.

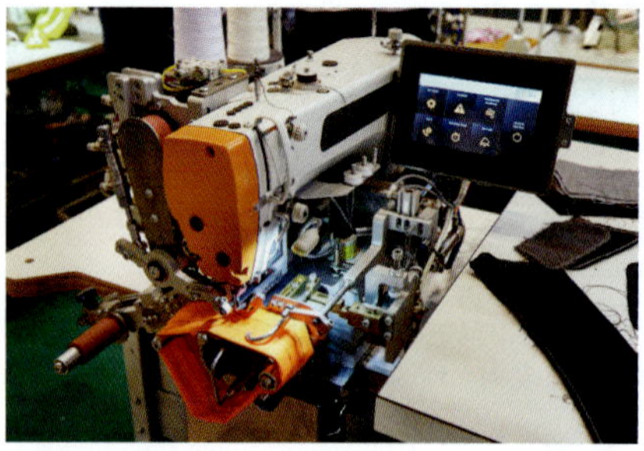

Figure 1.7.7 A CNC machine is programmed to sew collars.

When a designer uses CAD software to produce a design, it can be programmed into a manufacturing machine as numerical data so that the machine will be able to cut or sew the product part automatically. This is called computer numerical control (CNC) (Figure 1.7.7). The numbers are like the co-ordinates of a graph. They control the movements of the sewing machine so that once set, they can be repeated precisely. The instructions

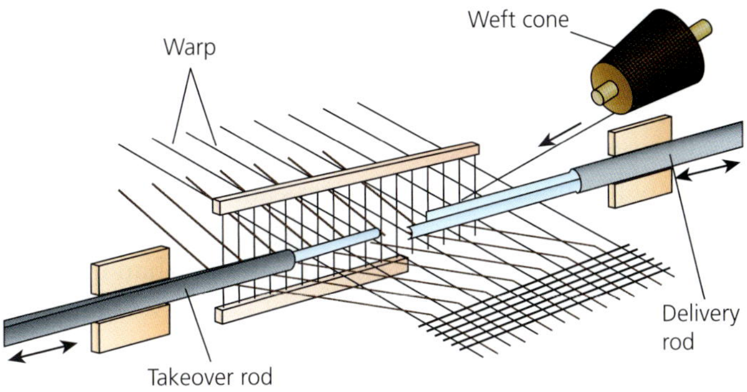

**Figure 1.7.8** A rapier system uses two gripper rods to insert the weft.

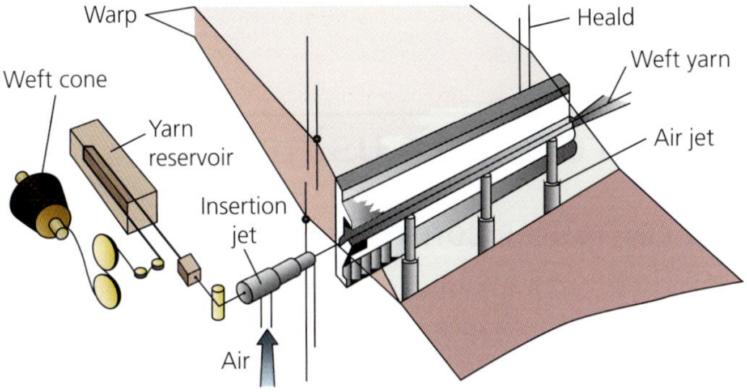

**Figure 1.7.9** An air jet weaving machine uses pressurised air to push the weft across the fabric width.

can be stored electronically, and downloaded and programmed into the machines very quickly so that changes can be made easily as required. Highly specialised machines carry out identical operations, which need to be repeated many times. These include automatic dart sewers, buttonholers, automatic patch pocket setters, pocket flap sewing machines, hemmers and seam sewers.

Some automated sewing machines require additional operations to be included, for example picking up sections of the garment or components that are to be sewn in place.

## Fabric manufacture

The move from manual to power-driven looms took place during the Industrial Revolution in the 1880s as steam- and water-powered looms were invented. After the Second World War, the demand for fabrics at an affordable cost meant that the processes of weaving and knitting had to be made faster. Modern weaving looms are automated, enabling the weft threads to be inserted more efficiently, and allowing for different colours to be put into a woven pattern at the correct time. The CAD software used to design the fabric can send instructions to the looms or knitting machines that make the fabric in any country of the world.

When making woven fabrics on automated looms, the main methods used for the weft insertion are:

- using a gripper or rapier to carry the weft across the fabric width at high speed. The gripper system carries a single yarn across the fabric in one direction only. The rapier system has a rod with a gripper that takes the weft to the centre of the fabric, where a second rod picks it up and carries it to the opposite side. With both methods, the weft has to be cut and secured at each edge.
- in water and air jet looms, using water or pressurised air to insert the weft by carrying it across the width of the fabric.

**Figure 1.7.10** An automated circular knitting machine.

Weft and warp knitting machines are also controlled by computers, enabling them to produce plain and patterned fabrics very quickly. Circular knitting machines are used extensively in commercial manufacture, and they produce tubes of fabric called tubular knits. These are usually split along one side to give a flat fabric. The latest knitting technology is able to produce seamless garments from a computerised design package.

Jacquard weaving and knitting machines produce very complex patterns that require each yarn to be individually controlled. This was originally done using a punched card but now uses computer control.

**Figure 1.7.11** An inkjet printer used for digital fabric printing.

## Fabric printing

Designs for fabric print are usually developed using CAD software, and the movement of the fabric and print screens are controlled by computer

**ACTIVITY**

Investigate different fabric manufacturing processes such as weaving, knitting and Jacquard weaving. You could find information by searching for video clips online which explain the different processes.

**KEY TERMS**

**Barcode:** an optical, machine-readable label that uses black lines to represent data.

**Lay plan:** a diagram showing how pattern templates are to be placed onto fabric ready for cutting out.

**Stepped lay:** different lengths of fabric used in a multiple layered fabric layout.

software. The designs for heat transfer printing are made on a computer and transferred to the printing paper using automated equipment.

Digital printing is done entirely through the use of CAD and CAM, and is becoming more commercially viable as the costs of the equipment have fallen and technology has improved. The process allows the design to be taken directly from the design software to the fabric, with no need for designing on paper. The printing inks use pigments rather than dyes because they are cheaper and give better wash and light fastness. Pigments can be printed onto a wide range of fabrics without the need for special preparation processes, and fix directly to the fabric, making them more economical and more environmentally friendly.

Further information about this process can be found in Chapter 1.5 of this book.

## Manufacturing processes using CAM

### Lay planning and computer controlled cutting

When a product has been selected for manufacture, the fabric will be ordered. Before it is cut into pattern shapes, it will be inspected to look for flaws such as imperfections in the dyeing or printed pattern, holes or frayed sections. This checking can be done using automated machines, and once the roll of fabric has been checked, it will be labelled to say it is fit for use. **Barcode** labels are used to identify the fabric, and all the details including any faults are kept on a computerised control system. The rolls of fabric are stored in numbered positions in automatically controlled warehouses.

Many layers of the fabric are cut out at the same time. Sometimes the spreading out of the fabric is controlled by computers, which make sure that the edges of the fabric are laid exactly on top of each other, and that any patterns on the fabric are in the same place on each layer. An automated spreading machine is designed for repeatability and productivity for volume manufacture, and will ensure tension-free spreading of fabric, providing accurate and consistent spread length. It is capable of spreading woven or knit materials from either rolls or folded packs, and can adapt to most common spreading requirements and multiple lays, although it is not suitable for very delicate fabrics that can be easily distorted. It allows for **stepped lays** where some groups of fabric layers have different lengths to allow for the placing of different sized pattern templates. It accurately aligns fabric edges so that parts can be nested closer to the beginning, end and edges of the spread. This eliminates end loss and optimises material utilisation. It also provides quality and reliability.

In a factory that uses a PDS, the computer can produce a lay plan which shows where the pattern pieces should be placed on the fabric so that:

- there is minimum wastage
- different sizes can be cut together to reduce waste
- all of the pattern pieces are cut out
- any pattern in the fabric – for example checks and stripes – is taken account of so that the pattern is symmetrical across the centre of the

Figure 1.7.12 An automated spreading machine.

Figure 1.7.13 A computer controlled cutting machine.

Figure 1.7.14 An automated machine uses a jig to sew a pocket flap.

garment and across horizontal seams such as pockets. In a high-quality garment, care will be taken to ensure that any pattern not only matches across vertical seams but also across body panels and sleeves
- pattern pieces are cut on the correct grain of the fabric, taking one-way design or nap into account.

Fully automatic computer controlled cutting machines use knives, laser beams and high-pressure water jets to cut through the fabric. The lay plan is sent straight to the cutting machine, which cuts the fabric automatically without the need for pattern templates.

The cut-out pieces are put into bundles according to the size, colour batch and the order in which the garments are to be sewn together, and labelled before being sent to be sewn. Often the labels provide information which can be read by computers. This means that a product's progress through the manufacturing process can be checked.

## Automated buttonholing

Automatic buttonhole machines use CNC machines, which remember the sequence of stitches to repeatedly make buttonholes of the same shape and size. When a number of buttonholes need to be made on the same garment, the space between them is programmed into the machine's computer. The buttonholes are cut automatically before or after they are stitched.

Computer controlled button sewing machines automatically space the buttons and remember the pre-programmed stitch patterns for buttons with two or four holes. The buttons are usually fed automatically from a storage magazine.

## Making and sewing of pockets

A pocket sewing machine uses a jig and a template to automatically place and stitch patch pockets onto garments. This is called a profile sewing system.

The flat pocket is hemmed at the top edge then fed onto a template. The pocket is placed over the garment section in the exact place where it is to be stitched, and the edges are automatically folded under. A jig holds the pocket down while the machine stitches it to the garment in a pre-determined pattern.

## Seam stitching

Long seams such as those used on the legs of trousers can be stitched on an automated profile machine. Automated machines are programmed to make fell seams in jeans and trousers.

## Pressing

Some sections of a product may need a fusible interfacing. This can be applied using a conveyor fusing press with the pressure, temperature and time controlled by computers to give an even finish.

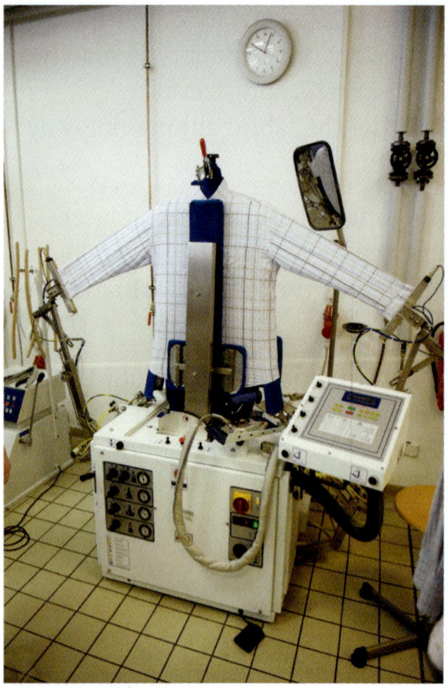

**Figure 1.7.15** A computer controlled pressing machine that can store different pressing programmes in its memory.

**Figure 1.7.16** A computerised embroidery machine.

**Figure 1.7.17** A dress made from laser cut fabric.

Finished products are pressed before leaving the factory. A steam dolly is a specialist pressing machine used for skirts, trousers and dresses. The dolly is inflated inside the clothes using steam and air, which makes the creases fall out.

Pressing of completed garments can also be controlled by computers.

## Computer controlled decorative processes

Embroidery is an important decorative process used on many textile products. When done manually, it is a very labour-intensive process, which makes it very expensive. Computer controlled machines can be used to produce logos and embroidery quickly and accurately using many different coloured threads. The designs can be sent directly from the CAD software to the embroidery machine.

## Laser cutting

Fabrics can be enhanced by the use of cut-out decoration or etched patterns. Lasers can cut very intricate patterns on most fabrics and, because the design and laser cutter are computer controlled, the patterns can be repeated as often as necessary. The heat from the laser beam seals the edges of the fabric at the same time as it cuts, stopping the edges from fraying.

By varying the depth of the cut, a pattern can be etched into the fabric. This is particularly effective on thicker fabrics such as denim and velvet.

### MATHS LINK

**Calculating speeds and times for machining**

A machinist can sew 442 stitches per minute.

In a seven-hour shift:

- 5% of the time is allowed for changing threads on the machine
- 2% of time is spent discussing issues with a supervisor
- 7% of time is used to cover rest and personal requirements.

Calculate the number of stitches that will be made during the shift.

**Answer**

7 hours = 420 minutes (7 × 60 minutes)

- 5% of the 420 minutes is allowed for changing threads: 420 × 0.05 = 21 minutes
- 2% of the 420 minutes is spent discussing issues with the supervisor: 420 × 0.02 = 8.4 minutes
- 7% of the 420 minutes is used to cover rest and personal requirements: 420 × 0.07 = 29.4 minutes

Total time spent on these other activities = 21 + 8.4 + 29.4 = 58.8 minutes

Time for machining = 420 − 58.8 = 361.2 minutes

If a machinist can sew 442 stitches per minute: 442 × 361.2 = **159,650.4**

**The number of stitches completed in the shift is 159,650.**

**ACTIVITY**

Make samples of decorative techniques using as many of the computerised machines as you have in your school or college. You might choose to:

- stitch a motif or small embroidered design using a computerised sewing or embroidery machine
- digitally print a small panel of fabric from your own computer-generated design
- design and print a panel using heat transfer
- use a laser to cut a pattern into fabric
- use a laser to etch a design into a fabric.

## Virtual modelling

A-level only

In addition to the production of virtual prototypes, digital body scanners allow for mass customisation of standard designs, where mass produced garments are modified one at a time based on the customer's needs. A 3D body scanner is used to collect the customer's measurements, and a body form is produced. The customer selects fabrics, styles and design features, and the garment is virtually modelled so that the selected garment can be seen on an accurate representation of the customer's body. A PDS then creates an individual pattern based on the body measurements and the garment is made using a QRM system.

### Pattern design systems

In addition to helping with the design of garments and developing pattern templates, the PDS can be used to present images and virtual prototypes. Catalogues of garments and product ranges can be put together by the designer and used to show the products to clients. These can be accessed at any point in the pre-production, production or merchandising process.

Modern manufacturing also allows for customised fit for individual orders. The PDS can create customised fit using data from high tech 3D body scanners, or body measurements taken with a tape measure. The system can simulate texture, draping and fit of garments by displaying them on a realistic, virtual human body form, so that the customer can see how the final product will look and drape on their own body.

### Computer controlled printing to produce sample fabric lengths

Digital printing allows a pattern to be printed directly onto fabric so that it is possible to print short lengths of fabric directly from a computer design programme. This allows designers to experiment with endless pattern and colour variations with minimum costs and time involved. This makes it ideal for producing short sample lengths to show to individual clients, to display at a trade fair or to use in the manufacture of specialised and bespoke orders.

**Figure 1.7.18** A machine-readable barcode.

## Electronic data interchange

A-level only

**EDI** is a system that allows the computer-to-computer exchange of documents in a standard format between business partners. It removes the need for paper documents such as purchase orders, invoices and shipping documents by exchanging them electronically.

EDI systems are used extensively in the fashion and textiles industries, the best known being the use of barcodes to represent data about the product to which they are attached. They are read by special optical scanners and applications software (apps) such as those found on smartphones.

Barcodes are attached to most products sold in retail outlets, and are scanned at the checkout. The cash register transmits the barcode number to the shop's central point of sale (POS) computer, which sends the price of the product back to checkout. This is referred to as an **electronic point of sale (EPOS)**. The information is transmitted to the shop's stock list, which records the number of items sold and can help decide when and how many to reorder from the manufacturer. Reordering is often done automatically as stocks of a particular product become low.

Large retailers have centralised storage depots where goods are received and dispatched straight away to the shops that need them without having to store them. The whole process is controlled electronically using the information on the barcode labels. This means that money is saved on warehouse space as well as wages for workers, because the products are not being continually handled therefore fewer operatives are needed.

Information gathered from EPOS is used for marketing purposes, and to collect data about the type of products sold. Many large retailers have loyalty cards, which customers scan each time they shop. The barcodes on these cards identify the individual consumer, allowing the retailer to customise their marketing based on each shopper's buying patterns. At the checkout, customers may be offered special discounts or offers based on information generated by the loyalty card. Data about what individual customers are buying will also be used by the retailer as part of their market research to inform the development of new products and marketing strategies.

Some barcodes include a hyperlink to a shop's web page. This link can be read by smartphones, and used by a shopper to browse the website and find the best price for the product.

Using EDI networks to analyse consumer trends allows all areas of the textile industry to meet consumer demands better, and enables consumers to get specially tailored items in a very short period of time. The use of simulation and computer integration will ensure that the fashion and textiles industry will be able to react to consumer demand, leading to **demand activated manufacture**. This helps fashion manufacturing to be more sustainable by reducing waste created by over-production – manufacturers only produce the products that have been ordered by consumers.

### ACTIVITY

As a class, write a short leaflet to show all the ways in which barcodes and other machine-readable codes are used when selling and marketing fashion and textile products.

- How do these EDI-based codes collect information about individual consumers?
- In what ways is the information used for marketing purposes?

# Production, planning and control networking

A-level only

> **KEY TERMS**
>
> **Electronic data interchange (EDI):** a system that allows the computer to exchange information electronically in a standard format between business partners.
>
> **Electronic point of sale (EPOS):** a self-contained electronic checkout that accepts all forms of payment, and also updates stock levels.
>
> **Demand activated manufacture:** using digital technology to produce fashion products on demand as they are ordered by customers.

A production, planning and control (PPC) system is concerned with planning and controlling all aspects of manufacturing, including materials, scheduling machines and people, and co-ordinating suppliers and customers. The design of a PPC system should be adaptive and allow for changes in the market, different customer requirements, changes in the supply chain and be able to deal with other problems as they arise.

Implementing an effective PPC system helps manufacturers to remain competitive in the ever-changing fashion environment. The current market requires more styles, smaller orders, increased product complexity and much shorter lead times. An effective system will allow production to plan movements from warehouse to manufacturer, and to the distribution streams involved. Production can be planned in a global environment as information can be quickly shared with all the companies involved in a product's manufacture, regardless of where in the world they are based.

Production planning is the technique of foreseeing every step in a long series of separate operations needed to manufacture the product. Each step needs to be taken at the right time and in the right place, and carried out with maximum efficiency. It helps the manufacturer to work out the materials, manpower, machinery and money required in order to produce a specified level of output in a given period of time. Because of the complexities involved, a computerised system is clearly necessary.

Advantages of a computerised PPC system include:

- Improved use of available capacity and the ability to constantly monitor flow of production. Improved 'on time' availability and supply of materials and components.
- Fewer production stoppages and lower excess costs due to 'waiting time'. Improved control of 'work in progress' means reduced use of overtime to solve problems. Improved production performance therefore lowers air freight and late delivery penalties.
- The ability to respond quickly when requirements change. Alternative planning solutions can be implemented. Reduction in lead times through improved control.
- Central storage of all information in a single place to allow improved decision making.
- More efficient planning of processes and machine requirements. This is particularly useful in businesses with multiple manufacturing sites.
- Visibility of all orders and their status. It provides the planner with a mechanism that can be used to effectively manage free capacity and the allocation of orders at the most appropriate factory/supplier.
- Efficient planning for style change-over.
- The facility to track orders throughout the supply chain and to deal quickly with transport and delivery issues.

## Availability of materials

When a design has been approved for manufacture, it will be necessary to source all of the materials needed for production. Some are standard materials and will be readily available, but others will need to be specially made for a specific product. These special materials might include printed fabrics, embroidered panels or a specific type of button, and these will have longer delivery dates. The PPC system will be used to co-ordinate the different delivery dates so that all the materials needed will be available when needed to start production.

Most manufacturing companies use a JIT system of buying fabrics and components, and it is important that materials needed for each product are delivered just as they are needed. A computerised planning and control system allows a company to keep track of what has been ordered, and know exactly when it will be delivered, so that it can go directly onto the production line without the need for storage. Late deliveries can cause serious hold-ups in the production and have financial implications for the manufacturer.

## Scheduling of machines and people

Successful manufacture depends on careful planning so that the machines required for a specific product – and the people needed to operate them – are available as and when needed. Some processes take longer than others, and this will need to be factored in when planning work schedules. Each operation in the manufacture will be timed and used to make a production plan.

Extra machines and operatives will be required for processes that take the longest, otherwise there is likely to be a bottleneck at those stages, leading to operatives at the next stage of manufacture having to wait for work.

It is important to ensure that all workers on the production line have work throughout the year. A PPC system is essential in the planning of when the different styles will be made if a company is to keep its trained workers, and avoid having money tied up in stock that will not be put on sale until some weeks in the future.

### ACTIVITY

Co-ordinating suppliers and customers

Investigate how production is planned and controlled by watching one or more of the videos listed below. Discuss with your class how the principles might be applied to the manufacture of a specific fashion product of your choosing.

- www.youtube.com/watch?v=Vjdil2nBCf0
- www.youtube.com/watch?v=hfQGHh5NIXI
- www.youtube.com/watch?v=Mdyyyu41dZ4

### KEY POINTS

- CAD and CAM are important at every stage of the design, manufacture, packaging, distribution and selling of fashion and textile products.
- Modern manufacturing systems are totally dependent on CAD and CAM technologies.
- A PDS does many of the tasks that used to be done manually, but in a much shorter time and with a greater degree of accuracy.
- Virtual prototypes and modelling are used in the development of designs, and in the customisation of standard designs to meet an individual consumer's needs.
- CAD/CAM is not a machine or a technique, but is many different and specific computer controlled processes.

## Check your knowledge and understanding

1. Give three benefits of using a PDS.
2. Describe three different ways that CAM is used to add decoration to fabrics.
3. Explain how a computer generated lay plan for pattern templates can benefit a manufacturer of fashion garments.
4. Name three different sewing processes that can be done using CNC controlled machines.
5. Explain how information on barcodes is used by retailers of fashion products.

## Further reading

Hannelore, E. *Clothing Technology*

The following YouTube videos:

- The basics of automated weaving, including the Jacquard loom: https://youtu.be/TyhDkd8Iabs
- The manufacture of seamless garments: https://youtu.be/asQzJN6pmh4
- How pockets are sewn onto garments: https://youtu.be/oaOtX1btpUM
- Automated dart stitching: https://www.youtube.com/watch? v=8FXBLID4BRg
- Issues related to automated garment construction: https://youtu.be/BA96-WX-oXc
- Automated shirt manufacture: https://youtu.be/sv536cciOiQ

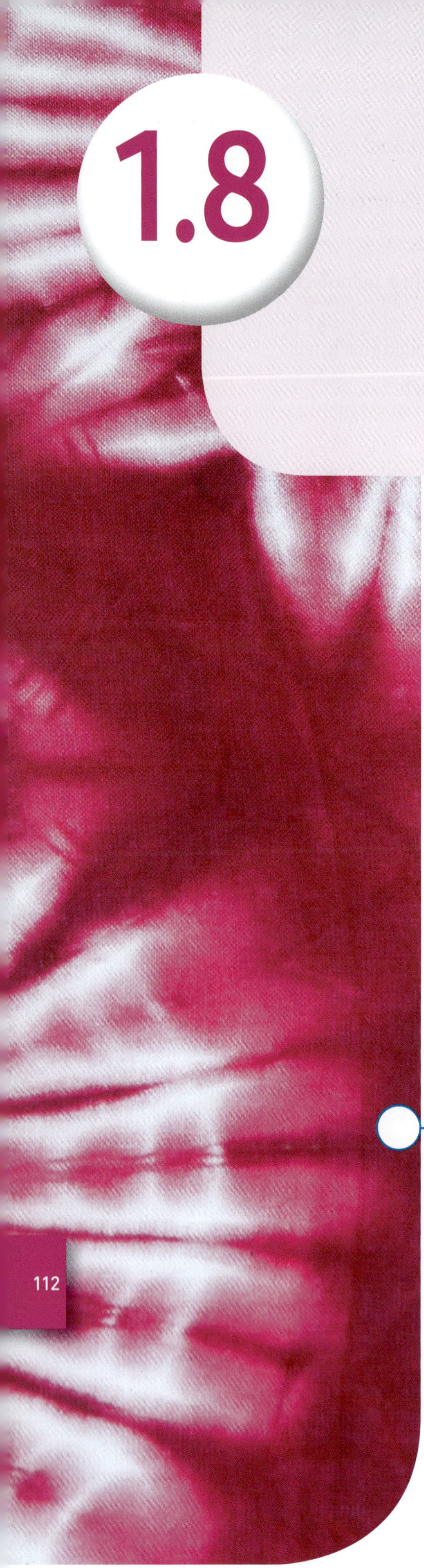

# 1.8 The requirements for textile, and fashion design and development

**LEARNING OUTCOMES**

By the end of this section you should have developed a knowledge and understanding of:

- product development and improvement, to meet specification criteria and to be fit for purpose
- how the critical analysis of existing products can lead to the development of new designs
- the application of ergonomic and anthropometric principles in the development of design ideas
- consideration of aesthetic and functional qualities when developing new design proposals
- the development of products that are inclusive in their design, so that they can be used by a wide range of people including the disabled, children, the elderly, transgender people and gender nonconformists.

Fashion and textile products are developed to suit the requirements of the target market, and to make sure that they will appeal to the consumer and perform well in use. Existing products are often used as a starting point for new design ideas, but further developments take place in order to create **ergonomic** and **inclusive** products that are relevant to the consumer and new fashion trends.

## Product development and improvement

In commercial practice, some new textile and fashion product designs are completely new designs, while others are developed directly from existing products. In a company, many new product designs are updated versions from previous collections. Sales figures indicate which are the best sellers, and these items are given fresh appeal for the coming season by:

- updating colours to the next season fashion colours
- using fabrics that are in line with the textures and prints of the next season
- including trims and components that are going to be popular
- adding the latest embellishments such as embroidery details that are predicted to be desirable
- modifying sleeve length, neckline and hemline to new fashionable shapes
- incorporating any other styling feature that will be fashionable, such as a larger collar.

Existing products are updated following the guidelines given in trend forecast mood boards, video presentations and trend reports. Trend forecasts are bought from companies who research and predict future fashion trends. (For further information, please refer to Chapter 1.13.)

Product developers will also be aware of their competitors' most successful ranges. They will analyse why these ranges appeal to shoppers and perhaps incorporate elements of the best features into some of their own designs.

## Study and critical analysis of existing products

An existing product can be studied to get information about the design of the product, how it was made and why the product appeals to the target market. Through critical analysis, an opinion can be formed about the success of the manufactured item, how it performs and whether it is fit for purpose. Examining and understanding the weaker aspects of an existing product can also be seen as an opportunity to develop a new and improved product design. By understanding more about why certain design decisions were made, you can be inspired by the successful features seen in products.

**Figure 1.8.1** Student exemplar of existing designs by Marina Hoermanseder.

In the student exemplar below (Figure 1.8.1), inspiration has been taken from the work of Marina Hoermanseder. The student focuses on the straps and buckles, corset shapes, fabrics and colour combinations seen in this designer's work. Each detail is carefully selected by the student, and analysed to explain how the fashion silhouette, the choice of materials or the particular technique is going to inspire their own design ideas.

This student has used the internet to get information, whereas in the fashion industry, designers and product developers are also able to attend designer fashion shows to get ideas. The fashion collections of **couture** designers include complex designs with specialist fabrics and exclusive techniques. The design concepts are sometimes controversial and may be too extreme for high street fashions. However, these existing products give other designers themes and features to incorporate into their own designs. Garments designed for high street fashion can be made with similar but less expensive materials and less complex techniques. Aspects of the shape and style seen on the catwalk can be interpreted by designers for wider appeal to high street shoppers.

Fashion designers also take inspiration from fashion and textile products in historical and cultural collections in museums and galleries. Analysis of these existing products can lead to fresh interpretations of past designs. Alternatively, elements of designs from different cultures can be combined with a more conventional approach to fashion, to make an exciting new product; for example traditional African print fabrics made into fashionable skater-style dresses (a short A-line dress fitted at the waist, and named after ice skating dresses).

**Figure 1.8.2** Celebrity style.

In Figure 1.8.2, a celebrity poses for cameras at a red-carpet event in a black sheer top and a black leather skirt. The fashions worn by celebrities can have an immediate impact on high street designs. Product developers are quick to pick out the main features of the celebrity dress, and modify existing designs to reflect the latest trends. Similar garments are soon seen for sale in high street shops. Celebrities and the most popular style setters on Instagram influence fashion trends.

**ACTIVITY**

Find out how the fashion designer Hussein Chalayan was inspired by Turkish ethnic costume in his autumn/winter 2002 ready-to-wear fashion collection. Present your findings on a page of existing product research, which includes reference to Turkish ethnic costume and Hussein Chalayan's A/W 2002 collection. Visit this website to find out more: www.vogue.com/fashion-shows/fall-2002-ready-to-wear/chalayan.

## The design, development and manufacture of fashion clothing and textiles products to meet specification criteria

A design specification is written to list the design criteria for a product design. It clearly communicates the instructions to the designer and the production development team. The final design is tested against the design specification to make sure the design fulfils the requirements. In the student exemplar below (Figure 1.8.3), the design specification is given for a wedding dress, and the student knows that it will be used to test ideas against.

Design Specification

**Figure 1.8.3** Student exemplar design specification.

In industry, after checking against the design specification, the fashion design drawing is interpreted by the pattern designer or cutter, who then makes pattern pieces for the prototype design. For completely new garments, the new pattern can be developed from a block pattern. They can also be made using the moulage technique – where pieces of fabric are draped onto a mannequin to work out each pattern piece shape. To develop an existing product, the original pattern may need some adjustment.

**Figure 1.8.4** Pattern cutting room at Top Shop headquarters.

The prototype for the new product design is made by the sample machinist, who uses factory production techniques to construct the garment. In Figure 1.8.4, the product development team are making the first samples in a navy-blue fabric; the employees on the left are pressing the pieces of fabric during garment construction.

The prototypes are made to trial materials and techniques, and they are tested and evaluated to find out about:

- fitness for purpose
- **aesthetic** appeal
- wearability
- fit on a live model.

It is an opportunity to sample different versions of the same design to find out, for example, if less expensive fabric could replace the original choice of fabric. The team would consider:

- drape and movement in use
- colour matching with garment trims and lining
- texture, pattern direction and scale in the made-up garment
- light reflectance from the fabric surface
- performance characteristics such as crease resistance in use.

The development team might recommend:

- adjusting features such as collar size, or shape or position of pocket(s)
- using alternative trims and components
- adjusting shape, length or styling to give a better fit or ease of movement.

**Figure 1.8.5** A garment technologist tests a dress for size and fit on a live model.

**Figure 1.8.6** Student exemplar – testing a stage costume.

**Figure 1.8.7** Student exemplar – testing accuracy of beading techniques.

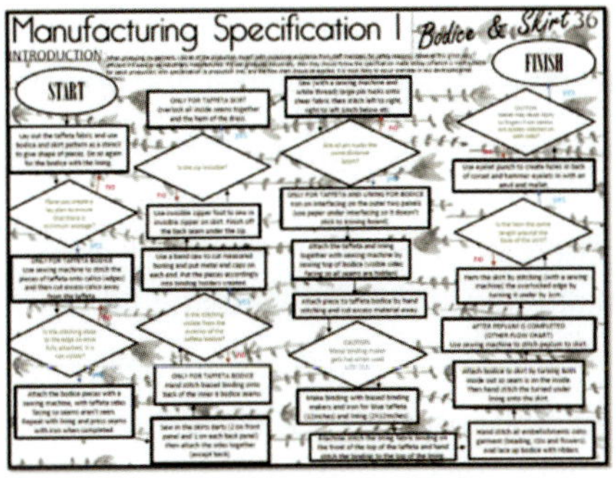


**Figure 1.8.8** Student exemplar – manufacturing specification flow chart.

Once the new product design meets the design specification and is agreed, a product specification and manufacturing specification can be written to record all the information about the product design and how to manufacture it. These are important documents because they are used as a contract between the designer and manufacturer, and they ensure that information is clearly communicated from designer to factory workers, and that the products are manufactured correctly, to the required standard. A sample garment is made using production techniques and processes, and checked against the manufacturing specification. The sample is submitted to the client for style and fit approval. When approved, a final sample is taken from the production line with all the correct labelling, tickets and packaging included. This sample is sent to the client, along with the specification. This becomes the **gold seal standard**, against which all subsequent garments can be checked for accuracy.

## Fitness for purpose

A successful product is deemed 'fit for purpose' if it is useable and works as intended. The designer will check the design specification, and make sure that suitable fabric and components are selected to meet the new product requirements. For example, the product may need to be easy-care and durable. The techniques and processes used to manufacture the product must be appropriate for the fabrics and components, and must result in a product that will look right, perform well in use and be within budget. The garment technologist in Figure 1.8.5 is testing the dress for size and fit by trying it on a standard sized model.

In the student's work (Figure 1.8.6), the stage costume is tested to see if it is fit for purpose. The dress is worn by a model on stage, and the audience give feedback on the aesthetics and effectiveness of the design. By getting a performer to wear the dress and switch on the LED lights (which embellish the garment), the student is able to see whether the dress works well for the intended purpose.

## Accuracy of production

In the student example (Figure 1.8.7), a range of possible beading techniques are investigated to find out how the final piece can be embellished accurately. By sampling techniques, the student is able to trial a variety of methods and materials, and decide which approach is most appropriate.

The student manufacturing specification in Figure 1.8.8 gives the quality control checks for a bodice and skirt. It is essential to examine the work at each stage of making, to see if the correct method has been followed within the given tolerances. If a mistake has been made or the standard of work does not meet requirements, the piece can be corrected. By following the flow diagram and checking at set intervals, the accuracy of production is increased.

In industry, quality checks are made by testing samples of the manufactured product at intervals during the production schedule. It is important to check garments during the production run, so that they are made accurately and consistently within the tolerances listed on the manufacturing specification.

**Figure 1.8.9** Student exemplar – product analysis leading to original design idea.

**ACTIVITY**

Update your wardrobe.

Find an existing product such as a dress or fashion top that you bought from a high street shop last year. Take some photographs of the garment, analyse it closely and record your findings.

Research some new fashion trends using free websites such as trendtablet.com or nellyrodilab.com. Use inspiration from one of the new trends to redesign your garment. Illustrate your new design in colour.

### How the critical assessment of products can lead to the development of new designs

In the student example (Figure 1.8.9), existing product analysis leads to a new fashion design. An existing garment is scrutinised and the style, construction, colour, fabric choice and embellishment are recorded. The information collected during analysis inspires a new design idea for a long dress, which incorporates some of the elements of the original garment.

## Critically assessing products and developing new design proposals

New textile and fashion products can be designed and developed by students in a similar way to commercial practice. Critical analysis and **disassembly** of existing products can lead to the development of new designs. Some existing products may be very simple, however, the basic design could be taken and further developed by the student. The new design could include some more complex features, more interesting use of materials and a wider range of decorative embellishment. A current best seller could be redesigned to include the next fashion trend.

Existing products are closely examined to find out about:

- construction of the product – how it was put together and which processes were used, for example whether any parts were made using a sub-assembly
- decorative techniques
- the shape and size of each separate piece of fabric
- fabric type, construction method and fibre content.

The existing product can be measured, sketched and photographed to record the information. It can be methodically taken apart step-by-step, to find out exactly how it was made. Each deconstructed piece of fabric can then be traced onto paper. The findings of analysis and disassembly of an existing product can be used as a starting point for new designs. The templates made from tracing around the fabric pieces can be developed into new pattern pieces.

## Working with a variety of materials to produce creative and original products

The materials selected for a new product design will determine the success of the piece. Materials need to be appropriate and suited to the purpose and function of the product, but they should also have aesthetic interest and appeal.

A variety of fabrics can be featured in the design. For example, sheer fabrics give transparency and lightness while silky or metallic fabrics reflect light. Knitted or lacy fabrics can add textural interest. Woven fabrics that fray easily at cut edges can be exploited to create textural features using fabric manipulation techniques such as ruffles.

A wide variety of trims such as braids and ribbons can be included to add more pattern, colour and texture to a product. Tassels can add movement to the piece, and beads and sequins can reflect the light from a textured surface. Interfacing is used to create more rigid panels and wadding to make quilted 3D features. Buttons made from a variety of materials or self-covered buttons – or additional 3D features such as 3D flowers – bring textural contrast and interest to fabric surfaces.

**Figure 1.8.10** Baby carrier with adjustable straps to make it fit a range of adult and baby sizes.

## Considering aesthetics, ergonomics and anthropometrics when designing products and prototypes

Textile products and fashion clothing must look attractive, and be suitable for the people using or wearing them. The aesthetics or beauty of the design should be considered, so that the appearance of the product is pleasing to look at and handle.

When designing and developing products and prototypes, designers find out about **anthropometrics** and **ergonomics** – the standard measurements of the average human body, and how people buying and using the product will interact with it.

The baby carrier in Figure 1.8.10 is designed to fit a range of adult and baby sizes. Anthropometric data has been used to guide the size of the carrier and the range of adjustments that can be made to the length of the straps.

Designers need to know about the size and shape of the typical person that they are designing for, so they can design a garment that fits, or a product that functions properly. Anthropometric data lists the dimensions of each part of the body. This information is used to create the sizing system. The data will vary between countries according to characteristics in different populations, and size charts may be unique to each country. However, for global markets, it is essential to use a standardised sizing system so that products are easily identified across the globe for size and fit.

| SIZE | EXTRA SMALL | | SMALL | | MEDIUM | | LARGE | |
|---|---|---|---|---|---|---|---|---|
| UK | 4–6 | | 8–10 | | 12–14 | | 16–18 | |
| USA | 2–4 | | 6–8 | | 10–12 | | 14–16 | |
| EURO | 32–34 | | 36–38 | | 40–42 | | 44–46 | |
| | INCH | CM | INCH | CM | INCH | CM | INCH | CM |
| BUST | 32 ½–33 ½ | 82–85 | 34 ½–35 ½ | 88–90 | 37–38 ½ | 94–98 | 40–42 | 102–107 |
| WAIST | 24 ½–25 ½ | 62–65 | 26 ½–27 ½ | 67–70 | 29–30 ½ | 75–77 | 32–34 | 81–86 |
| HIP | 35–36 | 89–91 | 37–38 | 94–97 | 39 ½–41 | 100–104 | 42 ½–44 ½ | 108–113 |

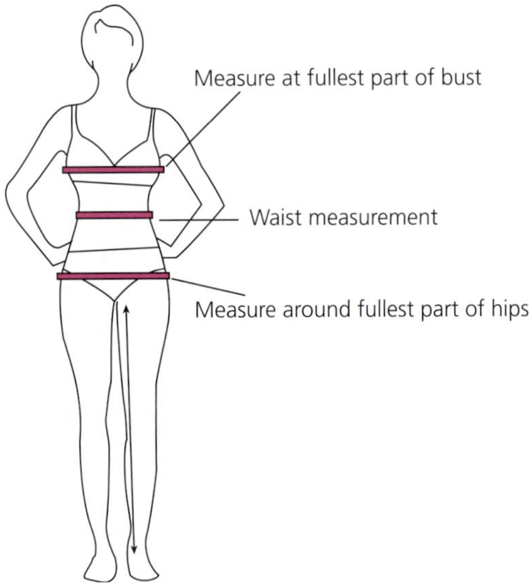


**Figure 1.8.11** Size chart for UK, US and Europe.

Accurate anthropometric data can be generated from 3D body scanning. Researchers also carry out body motion analysis to find out how the body moves. The anthropometric data and body motion analysis data can be used with 3D garment design computer programmes, to design patterns for garments that include ease allowance to improve fit.

Ergonomics is concerned with the way that people and products interact. The children's rucksacks in Figure 1.8.12 have been specifically designed to be ergonomic – bags like these are designed to put less strain on children's backs. A specially sculptured back panel allows more air to circulate, and provides extra padding. The straps are well-padded and sculpted for better fit over the shoulders.

The 'Easy Button' is an ergonomic component which is designed especially for use by the elderly or those with dexterity difficulties. The shape of the button is easier to grip and push through the button hole than a uniformly shaped button.

Figure 1.8.12 Ergonomic school bag.

These buttons have been ergonomically designed for elderly people.

Figure 1.8.13 Ergonomic buttons.

## Inclusive design

Standard fashion items are designed for a particular target market, and products are usually intended for a specific consumer gender, age range and perhaps personality profile. Fashionable clothing has largely been for those of average shape and physical ability, and designed for gender stereotypes. The design of the resulting clothing or textile product is therefore exclusive to the needs and aspirations of a narrow range of people in society. Inclusive design, on the other hand, is about designing fashion and textile products for a wide range of diverse people.

### A market for products that are inclusive in design

There is an increasing market for fashionable clothing for older or disabled people, as well as those with body shapes outside the average proportions. As the average body weight increases in the population, fashion brands such as Evans have targeted consumers who are referred to as 'plus size'. It has been recognised that fashionable clothing should be available to a wider range of consumers.

Transgender people and gender non-conformists may require fashion and textiles products that are more inclusive in terms of shape, style, fit, colour and material choice. Fashion design that avoids **gender stereotypes** – with androgynous or gender-neutral designs – is inclusive. For example, the high street retailer Zara has a unisex fashion range called 'Ungendered', which is not restrictive in its appeal. Selfridges also promote their 'Agender' range for genderless shopping.

Issues have been raised about overly thin, size zero models being used to promote fashion clothing in advertising and on the catwalk, and how this influences people to feel dissatisfied with their own healthier body weight and size. The clothing promoted is not inclusive. Recently however, there has been a move towards more inclusive fashion advertising with more realistically shaped models.

Conventional feminine pinks and masculine blues for babies and children may be restrictive for those in society who wish for more inclusive colour ranges in fashion products for this age range. Older gender non-conformists may also find the colours and styles of conventional fashions limit their choice.

Typical clothing for disabled people, those with special needs or those over the age of 60 has often lacked aesthetic appeal. Many fashion and textile items designed for these demographics appear to be obviously made for someone with particular needs, and until recently, very few clothing companies have taken fashion trends into consideration for these groups of people. However, there are some new businesses that sell fashionable **adaptive clothing**. This means that the clothing has been specially designed for easy dressing with carers in mind, or for those who can dress themselves but have restrictive body movement or lack of finger dexterity. Such clothing might fasten in places that the carer can reach more easily, and buttons and zips are replaced with Velcro or press studs. The clothing is designed with sections available, to allow for medical equipment or incontinence pads to be worn.

## Development of products that are inclusive in design

To be commercially successful, inclusive mainstream fashion and textiles products must be accessible to as many people as possible, without losing aesthetic appeal. Products should be easy to use, comfortable, fashionable and flexible in how they can be worn or used. Garments need to be fashionable and easy to put on and take off, and be adjustable for size to fit. The style and colour of clothing needs to challenge gender stereotypes.

This could be achieved by:

- selection of fastenings that are easy to use, for example magnetic clips
- use of elastane in fabrics for added stretch, and to ease fit
- additional ribbons at points for grasping, such as at waistband openings
- bound or French seams to add more comfort for those with sensitive skin
- use of colour, pattern, shape, style, fit and materials that are gender non-specific
- use of new technologies, for example micro-encapsulation with antibacterial chemicals to keep clothing fresher
- online shopping using new technology to create bespoke garments. This is where the shopper can select from a stock of fabrics and components to help design a customised garment. The bespoke manufacturing may incorporate options suited to a wider range of consumers.

### ACTIVITY

Research genderless fashion and analyse what makes fashion gender neutral. Present some examples on a page to illustrate the points you make.

### KEY TERMS

**Adaptive clothing:** garments designed to meet the needs of people with limited mobility and dexterity.

**Aesthetics:** the beauty or tastefulness of the look of a product, and how attractive it is to the consumer.

**Anthropometrics:** the measurements of the size and shape of the human body.

**Couture:** fashionable, made-to-measure or bespoke clothes.

**Gold seal standard:** a production sample product – including the packaging materials – used to check quality control production samples against.

**Disassembly:** to take apart step-by-step, or to deconstruct.

**Ergonomic:** the relationship between people and the products they use.

**Inclusive:** universal design, design for all, people-centred design and user-focused design.

**Gender stereotypes:** over-generalisations about the characteristics of people based on their gender.

## KEY POINTS

- Many new product designs are updated versions of existing products.
- Through critical analysis, a judgement can be made about the success of an existing product, how it performs and whether it is fit for purpose.
- Specifications are used to test designs, prototypes and manufactured products.
- Critical analysis and disassembly of existing products can lead to the development of new designs.
- When designing products, designers consider the standard measurements of the average human body, and how the consumer will interact with the product.
- Inclusive design is about designing products for a wide range of diverse people.

## Check your knowledge and understanding

1. How are current best sellers updated for the following season?
2. Why is it important to write a specification?
3. If a winter coat is 'fit for purpose', what features would you expect to find in the coat's design?
4. What is the difference between anthropometrics and ergonomics?
5. How can clothing be made more inclusive?

## Further reading

Winters, W. *Who's Wearing the Pants?*

Ecouterre: www.ecouterre.com

Red Dot Award – Design Concept: www.red-dot.sg/en

The rise of genderless fashion: www.bonafide-supernova.com

Samples: www.fashion-incubator/the-13-different-kinds-of-samples

# 1.9 Health and safety

**LEARNING OUTCOMES**

By the end of this section you should have developed a knowledge and understanding of:

- the requirements of the Health and Safety at Work Act
- safe working practices
- the legislation that exists to protect consumers.

If you are studying at A-level you should also have developed a knowledge and understanding of:

- safety precautions associated with specific manufacturing processes
- the concept of risk assessment.

Health and safety issues are very important. Factories in the textiles industry can be very dangerous places with machines that are designed to cut, pierce and press fabric. Chemicals that are hazardous to health and the environment are used in many processes. Many machines have moving parts, and some get very hot – these can cause serious injuries.

Health and safety also applies to products, and designers and manufacturers must ensure that the textile products they make do not cause harm to the consumer when used as intended. There are a number of laws and standards relating to the safety of textile products, for example flammability. Failure to adhere to these rules can be very costly for designers and manufacturers – they are likely to lose consumer confidence in their products, lose sales and may have to fight court cases brought against them for negligent practices.

## Safe working practices

Employers are required to ensure that their employees work in a safe environment. Employees are responsible for their own health and safety as well as that of other workers around them, and must follow all rules and regulations. This applies to students in schools and colleges as well as workers in factories. Unsafe working conditions or practices are called **hazards**, and a **risk assessment** assesses the workplace to ascertain what could be harmful to workers or the environment.

### Health and Safety at Work Act

The Health and Safety at Work Act (1974) was passed to protect employees from hazards in the workplace, and makes employers criminally liable for failure to meet the regulations. Every employer is required by law to make sure that employees work in a safe environment.

This Act has four main effects on the workplace:

1. It makes employers criminally liable for failure to meet regulations.
2. It set up the Health and Safety Executive (HSE) which is responsible for checking that the Act is being followed. HSE and local authority inspectors visit workplaces to make sure that health and safety regulations are being followed.
3. It gives employees the right to be represented on health and safety matters.
4. It places an obligation on employees to use safety equipment.

The Act requires businesses to make a risk assessment of their activities, to identify possible dangers and make sure that everyone can work safely. The company must appoint a Health and Safety officer who will check the workplace for possible risks, and puts into place the necessary procedures and/or equipment to reduce risks for employees. This will include making sure that:

- all equipment, tools and machinery are safe to work with, and are regularly tested for safety (equipment is labelled and dated as proof of testing)
- all workers wear suitable protective clothing
- the working environment is safe and healthy
- all processes are safe and do not damage the employees' health.

**Figure 1.9.1** Warning signs used in the workplace.

In addition to the Health and Safety at Work Act, the Health and Safety (First-Aid) Regulations state that all workplaces should appoint a person to be in charge of first aid, and workplaces should have a clearly marked and well stocked first aid kit.

Employees must follow all rules and instructions, and make sure that any actions they take do not affect their own health and safety or that of other workers around them. Health and safety signs, posters and warnings must be put up in all working environments.

This Act also applies to you and school or college workshops.

## Control of Substances Hazardous to Health

Many different substances such as dyestuffs, bleaches, chemicals used to apply finishes to fabrics, adhesives and cleaning materials are used in the manufacture of textiles, and these can have harmful effects on people's health and well-being if they are not stored and used correctly. These effects include:

- chronic lung diseases
- rashes and other skin problems
- complaints arising from inhalation of fumes
- asthma
- eye irritation.

**Figure 1.9.2** Hazard warning symbols warn of dangers when using certain substances.

The Control of Substances Hazardous to Health (COSHH) regulations form part of a company's risk assessment, and employers have a duty to protect employees and others who may be exposed to hazardous materials. In order to be covered by the COSHH regulations, hazardous substances must carry a warning label to show that they are irritants, flammable, corrosive or toxic.

Good working practice when dealing with hazardous substances removes the risk of legal action against the employer, and helps to make sure that employees do not become engaged in disputes and industrial action, which would disrupt production.

## Safe working practices and identifying potential hazards

A safe and healthy working environment will include:

- clean and tidy work areas to help prevent tripping and falling; textile waste can also be a fire hazard
- clearly marked fire exits that must be kept free in case of an emergency
- well-lit and ventilated work areas so that people are not working with fumes, for example when dyeing fabric, or textile dust that can irritate the lungs or eyes
- adequate breaks for workers so they do not lose concentration
- ergonomically sound seating so that workers do not develop back and shoulder problems after working for long periods of time
- no eating or drinking at the work station because food and drink may become contaminated with hazardous substances.

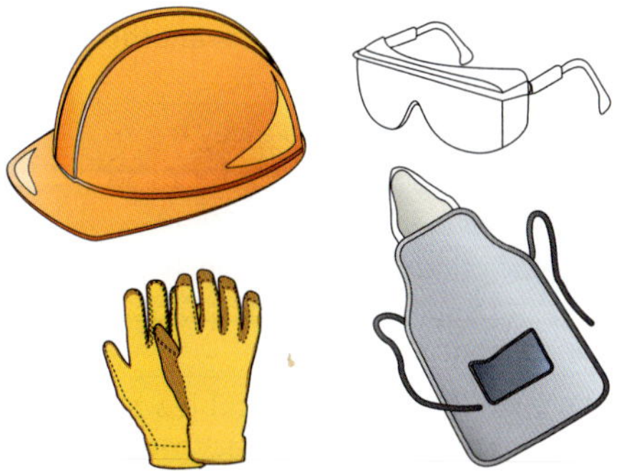

**Figure 1.9.3** PPE.

Safe working practices include proper training for the job, so that operators are aware of potential dangers and know how to work machines safely and efficiently. Some machines, for example sewing and cutting machines, need to be fitted with guards to protect the operators from injury. Machines should have emergency stop buttons so that they can be quickly switched off in the event of an emergency.

Some processes require operatives to use **personal protective equipment (PPE)**. This is special safety clothing and equipment such as overalls, masks, goggles, gloves, hard hats and special footwear. For example, chainmail gloves for those engaged in cutting fabrics, goggles and masks for people working with certain chemicals and steel-toe boots for workers who move heavy rolls of fabric.

Fork-lift trucks are commonly used to move materials from one part of a factory to another, and operatives need to consider their own safety as well as that of other employees; often there are marked out areas, outside of which the trucks are not allowed to operate.

Electricity can kill if not treated with respect. Frayed cables should be replaced immediately, and qualified electricians should do electrical repairs. Plugs, sockets and electrical appliances should not be allowed to get wet or touched with wet hands. The Electricity at Work Regulations (1989) require electrical equipment to be maintained at a safe condition, and it is good practice to have circuits and equipment tested regularly by a qualified electrician, and labelled to indicate that it is safe to use.

### KEY TERMS

**Risk assessment:** a process used to identify possible dangers in the workplace.

**Hazard:** an unsafe working practice or process.

**Personal protective equipment (PPE):** special protective clothing or equipment used when performing hazardous tasks.

### Health and safety in the school or college workshop

When working on your textiles projects, it is important that you work safely and are aware of the need to maintain a safe environment for those working around you. Following the correct instructions for using tools and machinery, and being aware of possible risks, is very important for everybody's safety.

The table below lists the risks in certain areas of the school textiles workshop.

**Table 1.9.1** Risks in the school textiles workshop.

| Personal safety | Safety when handling materials | Safety when working with tools and equipment |
|---|---|---|
| Follow all safety rules and obey instructions. | Handle chemicals such as dyes with care, so they do come into contact with your skin. | Keep hands away from cutting blades, and use safety guards as required. |
| Tie hair back so it will not get caught in machinery. | Wear protective clothing when necessary. | Put tools and equipment away in the correct place after use. |
| Wear protective clothing when necessary. | Take care with hot liquids such as water or batik wax. | Check the correct operating temperature for equipment that gets hot, e.g. an iron. |
| Sit correctly and at an appropriate height when working or operating machines. | Make sure that you are using correct chemicals by checking the label. | Make sure that hot or heavy equipment is kept on a firm level surface so it cannot topple over, and stand irons in an upright position. |
| Make sure walkways and working spaces are clear by placing bags safely under tables, or in a specially designated area of the workshop. | Clean up any spills immediately so they do not cause slipping and falls. | Leave tools and equipment clean after use so they do not contaminate the work environment. |
| Do not eat or drink in the workshop. | Use the correct tool for the job. | Switch machines off at the socket after use, so others do not start them accidently. |
| Do not fool around with other students. | | Keep hands and fingers away from moving parts of machines, for example the needle on a sewing machine. |
| Concentrate on what you are doing at all times. | | Make sure that you are properly trained to use the equipment, and only use it under supervision. |
| Know what you are expected to do in case of an emergency. | | Make sure that electrical cables are out of the way so they do not become a trip hazard. |

## Health and safety in industrial contexts

A-level only

There are laws concerning safety in the workplace, and all employers are required to abide by them. There can be serious consequences if these laws are broken.

Most companies in the UK textiles industry treat the issues of health and safety very seriously, and go to great lengths to make sure that safety regulations are enforced throughout the manufacturing and supply chains. All safety procedures are controlled by government legislation, European safety laws and codes of practice. These cover a number of areas including use of tools and equipment, materials handling, signs and symbols, use of protective clothing, working with computers and working with chemicals.

Disposal of waste materials is an important consideration, and all manufacturers must follow strict rules and guidelines on safe and environmentally friendly ways of disposing of these kinds of materials.

In the textiles industry, waste materials include:

- dyes and chemicals such as solvents or toxic substances used when applying finishes to fabric
- water used in processes such as bleaching and dyeing
- waste fabrics and components that might be flammable or contain toxic chemicals
- packaging materials.

Wherever possible, waste materials should be reused and recycled rather than being sent to landfill or incinerated. Water used in the processing of fabrics must be filtered and cleaned to remove toxins, before it is allowed to be discharged into sewers.

## Safety precautions that should be taken with specific manufacturing processes

### Risk assessment

An important part of a health and safety officer's job is to carry out risk assessment. This means identifying possible areas of danger and how they can be avoided. This procedure will be done for every process that a product goes through, and will relate to the use of equipment, the general working area and the procedures themselves. A risk assessment process includes:

- writing down the risk
- classifying the risk as high, medium, low or minimal
- identifying the safety equipment and clothing needed
- creating a safety manual or safety guidelines
- creating a code of practice for all users of all equipment
- ensuring that all employees are fully trained on the equipment they will use
- making sure that the correct safety labels are on all equipment, and relevant safety signs are next to the equipment.

Some of the most common hazards and safety guidelines associated with commercial textiles manufacture are outlined in the table below.

**KEY TERMS**

**Code of practice:** a voluntary set of rules and guidance provided by a professional body to direct a company's way of working.

**Table 1.9.2** Common hazards and safety guidelines.

| Process | Risk | Safety guidelines |
|---|---|---|
| Handling large rolls of fabric | Back injury<br>Foot injury if rolls fall<br>Head injury if rolls fall from a height | Use lifting equipment.<br>Never attempt to lift heavy rolls alone.<br>Wear steel toe-cap shoes.<br>Wear a hard helmet. |
| Spreading and cutting of fabric | Hand/finger injury from spreading or cutting machines<br>Inhalation of dust from fabric cutting<br>Dust in eyes when cutting | Ensure safety guards are in place.<br>Handle equipment correctly.<br>Wear chainmail gloves.<br>Wear a breathing mask.<br>Wear safety glasses. |
| Using fusing presses, e.g. when applying fusible interfacings | Hand/finger injury<br>Burns from press | Use the press correctly.<br>Wear protective gloves.<br>Be aware of first aid procedures. |
| Using sewing machines | Hand/finger injury from sharp parts<br>Hair/clothing becoming caught | Make sure that needle guards are in position.<br>Fit emergency stop buttons to machines.<br>Tie long hair back and secure loose items of clothing. |
| Using pressing equipment | Burns or scalding from hot equipment or steam presses<br>Finger/hand injury from presses | Be trained to use equipment.<br>Turn off steam before using a machine.<br>Have emergency stop buttons on machines. |
| Dyeing and printing of fabric | Inhalation of dyestuff or solvents<br>Staining of skin<br>Dye dust in eyes<br>Chemical spills | Wear appropriate PPE such as a dust mask, protective gloves, safety glasses and overalls.<br>Clean any spills up immediately. |

| Process | Risk | Safety guidelines |
|---|---|---|
| General working areas | Tripping and falling<br>Electric shock<br>Eye strain or repetitive strain injury when working with computers<br>Injuries caused by fork lift trucks and other moving equipment | Keep all work areas clear and tidy.<br>Ensure that all electrical equipment is safety tested regularly.<br>Take regular breaks when working with computers.<br>Ensure areas of moving equipment operation are clearly marked out.<br>Be trained to use moving equipment. |

**ACTIVITY**

Make a list of eight items of tools and equipment used in the textiles workshop. Complete the table below.

**Table 1.9.3** Risks in the school textiles workshop.

| Tool or equipment | Risk | High, medium or low risk | Precautions to avoid accidents |
|---|---|---|---|
| | | | |
| | | | |
| | | | |
| | | | |
| | | | |
| | | | |
| | | | |
| | | | |

## Safety in products and services to the customer

Textile products must be safe for the consumer to use, and must comply with a range of safety standards and specifications. In many cases, safety of products is a legal requirement, and manufacturers have a responsibility for the goods they produce. The BSI provides advice on the safety standards for a wide range of products, including those made from flame-resistant materials.

The legislation outlined below sets out how consumers can be protected from poor quality and unsafe products. Other legislation and codes of practice relate to design and manufacturing issues relating to textiles. These include safety standards in children's clothing, flammability of textiles, the use of toxic dyestuffs and metal contamination.

Metal contamination can happen when pins and needles are left in textile products during manufacture. In order to ensure that these do not pose a danger to the consumer, factories are subjected to stringent anti-metal contamination procedures. These include:

- Machinists may only have one needle at a time, and all other needles are kept in a secure container.
- If a needle breaks, all the pieces must be found.

- A supervisor must dispose of the broken needle.
- The product must pass through a metal detector if all pieces are not found.
- If all bits of the needle are not found, the product must not enter the supply chain.

## Legislation used to protect consumers

There are many laws designed to protect consumers when buying goods and services, and it is important to remember that legislation is constantly updated.

Laws that relate to the design and manufacture of textile products include:

- The General Product Safety Regulations (2005): These regulations place a responsibility on businesses to supply safe goods. Clothing must comply with any relevant safety legislation. Where there is no specific legislation, the safety of the product will be covered by these general regulations.
- The Furniture and Furnishings (Fire Safety Amendment) Regulations (1993): These regulations cover the fabric furnishings used in public places. In the UK, fire brigade officers usually decide on the flammability requirements for buildings and their contents, where the public has access. This kind of public building includes schools, hospitals and places of entertainment such as cinemas, nightclubs and concert halls.
- The Trades Descriptions Act (2011): This act promotes good practice by prohibiting false descriptions of products. Therefore a coat described as waterproof must not allow water through, and a top labelled as silk must not be made from polyester.

Day-to-day enforcement of safety legislation is the responsibility of trading standards officers who have the necessary powers to take action if they believe a product to be unsafe or falsely described. They can suspend unsafe products and can prosecute suppliers of unsafe products.

### Consumer Rights Act

The Consumer Rights Act came into force on 1 October 2015, and applies only to sales after this date. It replaced three earlier Acts: the Sale of Goods Act (1979), the Unfair Terms in Consumer Contracts Act and the Supply of Goods and Services Act.

The new act simplifies consumer protection laws, and reflects the different ways that consumers buy goods and services today. For example, many consumers now buy goods online rather than from a high street shop. The law clearly sets out the consumers' rights when buying goods and services, and how they can enforce their rights. The act applies to sales made in shops or other physical locations as well as online, sale goods and second-hand goods. Consumers buying goods 'at a distance' have additional rights.

As with the Sale of Goods Act, the Consumer Rights Act requires that all products – whether physical or digital – meet the following standards:

- As described – this means that the goods must match any samples shown or any description given at the time of purchase.
- Satisfactory quality – goods should not be faulty or damaged when the purchaser receives them. Satisfactory quality may vary according to the type of goods, for example a designer outfit would have a higher standard of quality than a top bought in a bargain fashion shop.

- Fit for purpose – this means that the goods must be fit for the purpose they were supplied for, in addition to any specific purpose that the purchaser made known to the retailer before agreeing to buy the goods.

If goods do not meet these criteria, the purchaser has a legal right to reject them and get a full refund – as long as they do this within a specified timeframe (see below). The purchaser's rights are against the retailer and not the manufacturer, and what they are entitled to depends on how much time has passed since they bought the goods.

The right to reject is limited to 30 days from the day that the product was purchased, after which it is no longer legally necessary to give a full refund if the item develops a fault. This right to a refund does not apply to purely digital products such as music, games or apps that are bought as downloads. Consumers can however ask for a digital product to be repaired or replaced if it develops a fault. And if this is not possible or is unsuccessful, they have the right to receive a price reduction.

If outside the 30-day right to reject period, a purchaser has to give the retailer one opportunity to repair or replace goods or digital content. If the repair or replacement is not possible or is unsuccessful, a refund or price reduction can be claimed. However, the customer cannot ask the retailer to make further attempts at a repair or replacement. This right extends for six months after the purchase.

After the first six months, the purchaser still has a right to ask for a repair or replacement, but the retailer has the right to deduct some money for the use of the goods within this time. If the product is a car, the retailer can deduct money after one month.

The purchaser has six years to take a claim to the small claims court for faulty goods in England, Wales and Northern Ireland, and five years in Scotland.

These rights do not apply if you simply change your mind about a product – although many retailers will allow an exchange if the goods are in good condition and you have proof of purchase, to show goodwill.

### Sale of Goods Act

The Sale of Goods Act (1979) has been replaced by the Consumer Rights Act (2015), and now only applies to goods bought before 1 October 2015.

The Sale of Goods Act requires all goods to be:

- as described
- of satisfactory quality
- fit for purpose.

If they are not, the retailer is in breach of contract, therefore the Sale of Goods Act gives you rights to a refund, repair or replacement if something you buy develops a fault.

To get a refund on a faulty item for any item purchased on or before 30 September 2015, you need to reject it and return it within a reasonable time after purchase. What is considered to be a 'reasonable time' will depend on the product and the type of fault.

**Figure 1.9.4** A warning label must be permanently attached to nightwear that does not meet the BSI standard for flammability.

## Children's clothing

Children are particularly vulnerable to dangers such as choking, strangulation and injury from flammable materials. Nightwear – like many other textile materials – can burn rapidly when set alight, leading to serious injury – especially in children and the elderly. Therefore legislation and performance codes have been set up to set standards for flammability and to make the public more aware of the dangers.

The Nightwear (Safety) Regulations 1985 refer to nightwear made for children over three months and under thirteen years of age, as well as adult's nightwear. Nightwear (pyjamas, babies' garments and cotton terry towelling bath robes) must meet flammability performance requirements set by the BSI. The regulations also specify labelling requirements; nightwear that does not meet the flammability requirements must carry a permanent label with 'KEEP AWAY FROM FIRE' in red letters (Figure 1.9.4). Nightwear that meets the BSI flammability requirements must carry a permanent label with one or both of the following forms of words:

- 'LOW FLAMMABILITY TO BS 5722' in black letters
- 'KEEP AWAY FROM FIRE' in red letters.

Apart from the Nightwear Regulations, there are no other specific regulations relating to the safety of children's clothing, and all other aspects of safety are covered by the General Product Safety Regulations (2005).

The BSI has set a number of standards relating to the safety of children's clothes. These include guidelines on the mechanical safety of children's clothing, which provide advice on design, fabric and component selection and assembly techniques. They cover all children's clothing such as dressing-up costumes and ski-wear that is intended to be worn by children up to 14 years of age, and include information on a wide range of features such as drawstrings, cords, loops, zip pullers, adjusting tabs, shoulder straps, halter necks, tied belts and sashes and belt loops.

A British and European code of practice relating to the mechanical design and manufacture of children's clothing specifies that:

- the hoods of children's outer garments must not be designed to be secured by means of a cord drawn through the material because this could be a strangulation hazard. A child's outer garment is defined as 'a raincoat, overcoat, anorak or other garment suitable for use as outer wear, having a measurement not exceeding 44 cm across the chest when the finished garment is laid out as flat as possible
- there must not be cords or ribbons accessible to a child's mouth because they could be a choking hazard
- there must not be zips in trousers for boys under five years of age.

## British Standards Institute

The BSI sets standards that are accepted UK guidelines for industry and commerce, and often works with similar standards authorities in other countries. Many of these standards relate to textiles, and include those relating to sizing, labelling, safety and testing methods.

The BSI set strict guidelines about how tests are set up and conducted. They regularly test samples of a range of products, and award certification to say that the product conforms to a stated British or European standard.

Figure 1.9.5 The BSI kitemark.

This assures the consumer that an acceptable quality can be expected. Goods that have been passed as satisfactory by the BSI usually carry the kitemark symbol on a swing label. This reduces the risk of someone buying a product which could be defective in some way.

Standard sizes are important for designers, manufacturers and consumers, for example in the sizing of duvet covers and sheets. Clothing sizes are regularly updated and are based on anthropometric data collected from thousands of people. There are often wide variations in sizes because of current fashion shapes and variations between manufacturers. Some large retailers do their own size surveys and make their clothes to fit their customer profile – this can explain the differences in the sizes in clothes bought from different shops.

Labelling textile products with the fibre content and their percentages is mandatory in the UK, and the information must be understood by consumers in the country where the product is sold.

An origin label must be included if, without one, a consumer might be misled as to the real origin of a garment. An example of this would be a garment made in China but with the British flag on the label.

Providing care instructions is not a legal requirement in the UK, but is strongly encouraged. Nightwear garments are required to carry labels regarding their flammability.

## Measures to ensure the safety of toys

Many toys are made from textile materials, for example soft toys and dressing-up clothes. Some potential dangers are:

- toys with small components that could come off and be a choking hazard, for example buttons, beads, eyes and electronic components
- toys with loose pile fabric or hair that sheds easily and therefore becomes a choking hazard
- strings or cords that are longer than 30 cm, which can wrap around a child's neck and become a strangulation hazard
- toys and dressing-up clothes that are flammable.

Members of the British Toy and Hobby Association (BTHA) must make sure that all of their products conform to the relevant safety standards. This includes EN71 - the European standard for toy safety testing.

### Lion Mark

Figure 1.9.6 The Lion Mark logo is put on toys that have been classified as safe for children to use.

The Lion Mark (Figure 1.9.6) was developed in 1988 by the BTHA. It is a symbol of toy safety and quality for the consumer, and can only be used by members of the BTHA. All members of the BTHA must adhere to the Code of Practice, and ensure that all products conform to EN71 safety standards.

## Advice to consumers

Labels and packaging on textile products carry a lot of information about the product, including its intended use and safety advice. Some of the labelling is controlled by UK and EU legislation, and some is provided by the manufacturer or retailer. Labels can take different forms; permanent labels are stitched into the product, swing tickets are attached to the product and other labelling is printed or stuck onto the packaging.

Figure 1.9.7 A QR code.

**Figure 1.9.8** A swing ticket advising the consumer that the dye may rub off onto light coloured fabrics.

**Figure 1.9.9** The cover fabric is not match resistant, but the furniture has an interliner which passes the specified test. The furniture meets the filling requirements and is cigarette resistant.

## Manufacturer's instructions

Manufacturers of textile products sometimes label products with additional information or advice about how a product should be used. For example, a top made from a delicate fabric may have an advisory label telling the consumer to avoid catching it with rings or other jewellery.

Quick response (QR) codes and augmented reality (AR) labels appear on many products. They allow consumers to use a smartphone or tablet to activate a link, website or video that gives more information about a product.

Some fabrics may shed fibres or have loose dye that can discolour other fabrics, and manufacturers attach advisory labels to such products.

## Safety warnings

In addition to the labelling of nightwear, safety warnings are required to be attached to upholstered furniture. The Furniture and Furnishings (Fire Safety) Regulations (1988, amended in 1989, 1993 and 2010) set levels of fire resistance for domestic upholstered furniture, furnishings and other products containing upholstery. Each item of new upholstered furniture (with the exception of mattresses, bed bases, pillows, scatter cushions, seat pads, loose covers sold separately from the furniture and stretch covers) must carry a label at the POS indicating its ignition resistance.

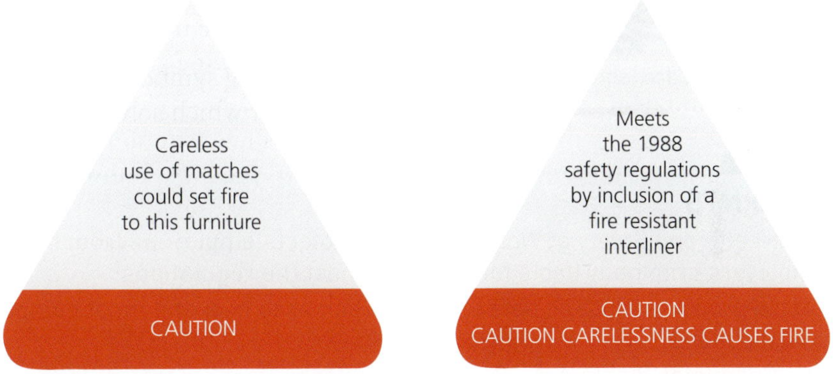


**Figure 1.9.10** These labels indicate that the furniture meets the filling requirements and is cigarette resistant. This applies to the likes of baby nets, and the word 'product' may be substituted with the word 'furniture' on the second side of this label.

**Figure 1.9.11** This label indicates that the furniture meets the filling requirements, and is both cigarette and match resistant.

**Figure 1.9.12** The basic care label symbols.

## KEY TERMS

**Care label:** a label with symbols to explain how a textile product should be washed, dried and ironed.

## ACTIVITY

As a class, make a collection of care labels (Figure 1.9.13) from different products. For each label, explain how the recommended care relates to the fabrics used. How might the fabric be affected if the care advice was not followed?

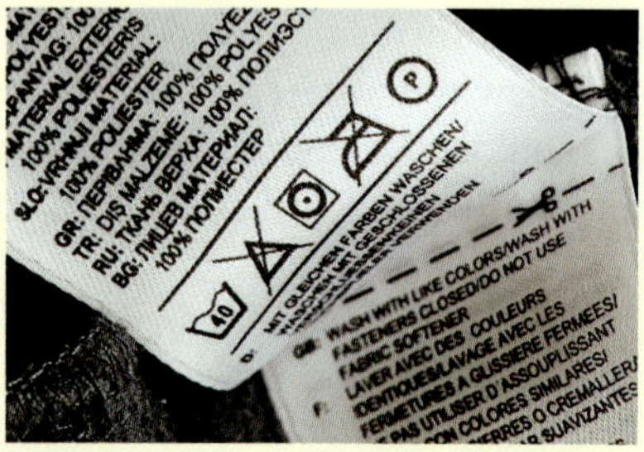

**Figure 1.9.13** A care label.

## Aftercare advice and care labelling

**Care labels** are put into textile products to tell the consumer how to care for and clean the product. The care advice recommended will depend on the fibre content of the product, as well as any special finishes or components that may have been used on the product.

The information is given in the form of five basic symbols which relate to washing, bleaching, drying, ironing and dry cleaning. The symbols are the international care labelling code (ITCLC), and are adapted to make the information relevant to the product.

Any symbol that has a cross through it means that process should not be done to the product.

The wash symbol has a number inside the wash tub – this indicates the maximum temperature in °C at which the product should be washed. Lines underneath the wash tub relate to the amount of agitation that is safe for the product: no line means full agitation, one line is reduced agitation and two lines is minimum agitation. A hand in the wash tub means that the product should be hand washed only.

The bleaching symbol relates to the use of chlorine bleach.

Drying symbols indicate if the product should be tumble dried, drip dried, line dried or dried flat.

Ironing symbols indicate the temperature of the iron using dots – the more dots, the higher the ironing temperature can be.

The dry-cleaning symbol will have the letters A, F or P in the circle, to tell the dry cleaner which solvents are safe to use on the product.

## KEY POINTS

- The Health and Safety at Work Act (1979) protects employees from hazards in the workplace and makes employers criminally liable for failure to meet the regulations.
- Textile products must be safe for the consumer to use, and must comply with a range of safety standards and specifications.
- The Consumer Rights Act (2015) simplifies consumer protection laws and reflects the different ways that consumers buy goods and services today.
- Legislation about flammability relates to nightwear as well as furniture and furnishings.
- Some codes of practice apply specifically to children's clothing and soft toys.
- The advice on care labels is related to the qualities of the fabric from which it is made.

## Check your knowledge and understanding

1 What are the four main effects of the Health and Safety at Work Act?

2 What three requirements must goods meet under the Consumer Rights Act?

3 What does this symbol tell the consumer?

(a)

(b)

4 What is the difference between an act and a code of practice?

## Further reading

Down, J. *Textiles to GCSE*

Fire Safety Advice Centre: www.firesafe.org.uk/furniture-and-furnishings-fire-safety-regulations-19881989-and-1993

HSE: www.hse.gov.uk

Legislation: www.legislation.gov.uk

Which?: www.which.co.uk/consumer-rights/regulation/consumer-rights-act

www.performancetextiles.org.uk/safety.html

# 1.10 Protecting designs and intellectual property

A-level only

**This topic is for A-level only. If you are studying at AS Level, you do not need to cover the content in this section.**

## LEARNING OUTCOMES

By the end of this section you should have developed a knowledge and understanding of:

- the importance to the designer of copyright and design rights, patents, registered designs, trademarks and logos.

It is important for fashion and textile designers to know how to stop other people from using their art and design work without permission. Art and design work is **intellectual property**, and it can be protected from being stolen or copied.

Designers' intellectual property can be protected by copyright, design right, patents, trademarks and by registering designs. Some protection is automatic and free, but better protection can be gained by paying a fee and registering work. This can help when drawing up an agreement for others to pay to use the work, and makes taking any necessary legal action more straightforward.

## Copyright and design rights

To copyright artwork, illustrations or photographs, designers mark them with © - the copyright symbol, the designer's name and the year they were created. This will protect work, and stops other people from using it without permission. The copyright protection for artistic work lasts for 70 years after the artist's death. If a designer wishes to sell or allow others to use their work, they can license the copyright and make an agreement between them and the person who wants to use it. There is no register for copyright work.

To design right a design, a designer will sign and date copies of their design drawings and get them verified by a solicitor, who keeps them in case of any future dispute. A textile design is automatically protected by design right, and this lasts for 15 years after creation or for 10 years after it was first sold. Better protection is possible by registering the design.

## KEY TERMS

**Intellectual property:** ideas or creations such as inventions and artistic work, which are owned by the creator.

**Emblem:** a symbol, sign or design used as an identifying mark.

**Trademark:** a distinctive sign used to identify and promote a brand, product or organisation.

**Hallmark:** a mark stamped on a product to show its origin, and to show it is a genuine item.

**Counterfeit:** a deceptive copy of an item to look like the original, for illegal sale.

**Figure 1.10.1** Desigual® trademark.

## Patents

A patent is used to protect something new and inventive. This type of protection is not meant for aesthetic, creative or artistic work. A patent protects an invention or how a product works, and prevents others from manufacturing, using, selling or importing the new invention without the inventor's permission.

A designer needs to apply for a patent, which can be difficult to get; it is expensive and usually takes around five years to obtain. The application for a patent provides a detailed description of the invention with diagrams to explain how it works. It lasts for 20 years but has to be renewed each year.

## Registered designs

A designer can protect the shape, decoration and appearance of a product by registering the design. Once registered, a number is allocated to the design and, if appropriate, this can be displayed on the product. To be registered, the design must be the designer's own new design with no offensive words or images and no protected flags or **emblems** included in the design. The design protection lasts for up to 25 years, although registration needs renewing every five years.

## Trademarks

A **trademark** is a distinctive sign used to identify and promote a brand, product or organisation. It can include words, logos, colours and sounds, but must not contain offensive words or images, nor use official flags, **hallmarks** or emblems. Trademarks must be renewed every ten years. When you see the symbol ™ after the trademark, it shows that has not been registered – using an unregistered trademark offers businesses certain rights under common law, but more protection is gained by registering the trademark.

The fashion clothing brand Desigual® has a distinctive trademark. It is the company name written in a simple plain font but with the 's' reversed to make the trademark stand out.

A trademark must be new and unique to be registered. The ® symbol is used to show that a trademark is registered and protected against being used by others. It makes it more straightforward for designers to take legal action against counterfeiters.

Trademark infringement is the unauthorised use of a trademark, which is identical (or confusingly similar) to an existing trademark, in a way that is likely to cause deception or mistake about the source of the product. Luxury fashion brands often have their designs copied and made into cheap versions, which are sold on the street or in other shops.

Burberry is a long-established luxury fashion company that is well known for its famous red, camel, black and white check design. The check was first used in the lining of Burberry's trench coat in 1920. During the early 2000s, when it was particularly fashionable to wear designer brands, the Burberry check was copied by counterfeiters many times. The Burberry check was very popular with 'chav' celebrities, and football hooligans adopted the check as a symbol of their group identity. The violent and antisocial behaviour of football fans dressed in the Burberry check led to

## KEY TERMS

**Logo:** a graphic symbol or design that is used alongside the name of a business.

**Figure 1.10.2** Westwood logo on a shop front.

## ACTIVITY

Design a trademark and logo for a new shop with branches at Britain's top tourist destinations. Think of a name for the business. Use the Crown jewels for design inspiration.

**Figure 1.10.3** Crown jewels at the Tower of London.

the wearing of Burberry check garments being banned at some football venues. Burberry struggled to survive this unwanted association and in order to recover its business, removed the check design from most of its products. More recently, further trademark infringements have been brought to court. New people have been accused of copying the Burberry check as well as the Burberry equestrian Knight **logo**, to advance their own image and increase profit.

## Logos

Logos are graphic symbols or designs that are used alongside the name of businesses. It is important that they are memorable and connect people with the products or services offered by the company. The logo colours, shape, font and image all need to work together in a simple design that represents the business. The logo is a visual identity and must be recognisable because it is used on company products, packaging, advertising, promotional material and stationery.

The fashion designer Vivienne Westwood uses the 'Westwood orb' logo to identify her work and promote the business. She designed this logo in the mid-1980s when she was working on a royalty-themed fashion collection. This very successful logo has reinforced the image of her business over many years. The Westwood orb is not only used to identify and promote the Vivienne Westwood brand, but is also worn as jewellery by those interested in fashion.

## KEY POINTS

- Fashion and textile designs can be protected by copyright, design right, patents, trademarks and by registering designs.
- To copyright a work, a designer adds the © symbol, their name and the date.
- For design right, better protection is given by registering the design.
- A patent protects a new invention or how a new product works.
- A trademark is a new unique sign used to promote a brand, product or organisation.
- Logos are graphic symbols or designs.

## Check your knowledge and understanding

1 What is the difference between copyright and a patent?

2 How can fashion and textile designers protect their design work more effectively?

3 What is the difference between the following symbols: ©, ™, ® ?

4 Why are logos important?

5 Which is quicker to get: copyright or a patent?

# Further reading

Wiedemann, J. *Logo Design Hardcover*

Wilcox, C. (2015). *Vivienne Westwood* V&A Publishing

Government information on intellectual property: www.gov.uk/browse/business/intellectual-property

Burberry: www.burberryplc.com/en/company/history.hml

# 1.11 Design for manufacturing, maintenance, repair and disposal

## LEARNING OUTCOMES

By the end of this section you should have developed a knowledge and understanding of:

- the responsibilities of designers in ensuring that textile products have minimum impact on the environment
- how the choice of materials can affect the use, care and disposal of the end product
- the relationship between fibre and fabric properties, and recommended care.

If you are studying at A-level you should also have developed a knowledge and understanding of:

- how reducing manufacturing processes is beneficial for the environment
- how the correct care of textile products can extend their life.

This chapter overlaps with the knowledge and outcomes of the following chapters:

**1.2** Performance characteristics of materials
**2.3** How technology and cultural changes can impact the work of designers
**2.8** Responsible design
**2.9** Design for manufacture and project management.

Designing is a very creative activity, but as well as being innovative in their thinking, designers are expected to have knowledge of how products are manufactured and the working characteristics of fabrics and components. Cost is always an important consideration when designing new products, and designers must make sure that they work within the constraints of the budgets set.

There is increasing concern about how textile products and their manufacture affect the environment. Responsible designers and manufacturers think about how their products might affect the lives of other people, whether it is those involved in the manufacture or those who use the products. Consumers are becoming increasingly aware of environmental and ethical issues, and are starting to demand high standards of responsible, sustainable design and manufacture when choosing textile products. Designers of textile products are well placed to influence environmental and social responsibility by raising awareness of the issues throughout the industry.

## Manufacture, repair, maintenance and disposal

Textiles manufacture is a major industry, and uses a lot of the world's resources. It is one of the most polluting and waste-generating industries in the world.

Many retailers have made high fashion affordable for millions of customers, who are encouraged to buy more and more new clothes every season. Fashion has become a throwaway commodity, with garments often worn just a few times before being discarded. In addition, with new fashions available at low cost, consumers are more likely to buy new rather than repair items they already have.

Cheap fashion, however, has a cost – especially in relation to its disposal. Although many companies are keen to promote their 'green' credentials, these are mostly in relation to their sourcing and manufacture of textile products; disposing of unwanted textile products in landfill remains a major problem worldwide.

**Figure 1.11.1** Raw cotton is baled and sent to factories ready for cleaning and processing.

### Reducing the number of manufacturing processes

A-level only

**Efficiency** in manufacture is not just about saving time and materials. Making a fashion or textiles product involves many different stages and processes including:

- producing raw materials to make yarns and fabric
- cutting and sewing the product
- packaging and delivery to the retailer.

These processes use a variety of raw materials, chemicals, water and energy, all of which can be financially costly and have a negative effect on the environment. Careful planning – including the use of computerised systems – can help ensure that manufacture is efficient in terms of time and use of energy.

**Figure 1.11.2** Synthetic yarns such as polyamide are naturally white and clean when manufactured.

#### The raw materials

Natural fibres such as cotton, linen and wool require much more processing than synthetic fibres. They need to be cleaned and sorted before use, whereas synthetic fibres are naturally white and clean, because they are manufactured. Converting the fibres into yarn and fabric requires energy to work the machines.

Most fabrics are coloured in some way. Traditional dyeing methods use up large quantities of water and produce toxic waste, which must be treated before disposal. Synthetic fibres can have colour put into the spinning solution so the fabric does not need to be dyed afterwards. There have been some developments in the growing of already-coloured cotton fibres.

**Figure 1.11.3** Dyeing jeans uses a lot of chemical dyestuff, water and energy.

Special finishes are frequently added to fabrics to make them more functional, for example crease-, shrink- and water-resistant finishes. Although these are an additional process, they mean that a product may last longer and require less maintenance. A designer often has to strike a balance between using a finish and the aftercare of the product.

### Cutting and sewing the product

The design and style of a fashion product can have a big impact on its subsequent manufacture. The type of fabric selected will affect how it is cut and the amount of waste produced. For example, a garment cut on the bias will require far more fabric than one cut on the straight grain, and a lot will be wasted. Garments with a one-way design, nap or check will use more fabric therefore more will be wasted because of the need to match patterns.

**Figure 1.11.4** Storing and transporting clothes on moveable rails reduces the need for packaging.

The style of a product will affect the number of manufacturing processes required to make it. If it is possible to reduce the number of sewing processes then energy, time and thread can be saved. Placing a pattern on a fold line rather than including a seam, having an efficient order of manufacture so products do not need to be transported, using fewer components or decorative processes can all help to save thread and other materials, as well as energy. When manufacturing thousands of products, these small changes can help to make significant savings. The increasing use of CAM and automated manufacture means that products are made with less waste created by inefficient cutting and faulty products.

**Figure 1.11.5** Some clothes come with excessive – and therefore unnecessary – packaging.

### Packaging and delivery to the retailer

Textile products need to be packaged so that they arrive at the shop in good condition, and to keep them together in batches as an order ready to be delivered. However, packaging of textile products creates a lot of waste, uses energy (and materials) to make and transport the packaging and adds to the bulk and weight for transporting the goods. A modern transport system where garments are stored on hangers in warehouses and transported on moveable rails reduces the need for individual packaging, and means that energy does not have to be used to iron garments before they go on display in a shop. Using packaging effectively and keeping it to a minimum can help reduce the effect on the environment. As consumers, do we really need to have a 'designer' carrier bag, multiple layers of tissue paper, plastic bags and fabric ribbons to take purchases home?

## How the choice of materials affects the use, care and disposal of products

**Figure 1.11.6** Delicate fabrics need extra care when handled.

Thinking about the intended use and aftercare of textile products is an important part of textiles design and manufacture. Fabrics and components must be chosen carefully so that they meet the consumer's requirements and the expected use of the product. Delicate fabrics such as satins, chiffon, lace, fabrics that pill easily and pile fabrics such as velvet need careful handling, and will not last long in garments that are expected to be worn regularly. Many of these fabrics will require extra care when being laundered so that they are not damaged.

Woven fabrics are usually more stable than knitted fabrics, and will retain their shape better. Fabrics made from synthetic fibres tend to be stronger

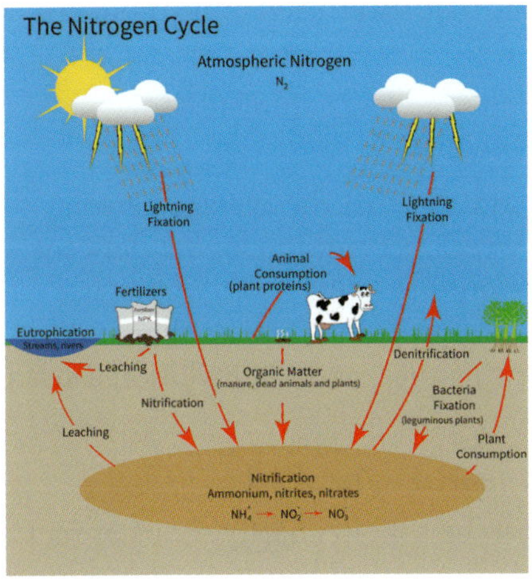


**Figure 1.11.7** The process of eutrophication is caused by the phosphates found in laundry detergents as well as fertilisers used on plants.

www.alamy.com - EKK518

**Figure 1.11.8** Detergents and laundry aids contain chemicals that can damage the environment.

than those made from natural fibres, but are less absorbent and do not biodegrade as easily. Fabrics intended for products that will be subjected to regular and prolonged use may benefit from an applied finish to keep them in good condition for longer, for example the use of a stain repellent on children's schoolwear or sofa cushions, or a crease-resistant finish on workwear garments. Such finishes may also reduce the need for repeated cleaning and ironing, reducing the amount of detergent and energy used in their upkeep.

Cleaning of textile products requires the use of water, detergents, cleaning fluids and energy to power washing and drying machines. Laundry detergents are made from chemicals including phosphorus, which cause eutrophication in the lakes and rivers where they end up as sewage waste. Phosphorus from detergents causes aquatic plants to grow faster than normal, and when they die and eventually rot, they use up the oxygen dissolved in the water. Fish in the lakes and rivers die from oxygen starvation, and eventually the water is displaced by the plants as they continue to grow. When this happens, the lake becomes a bog and eventually dry land.

Fabric softeners and dry-cleaning fluids contain many different chemicals that can affect people's health and the environment. Fabrics that can be washed and ironed at lower temperatures can save a lot of electricity. Fabrics with low absorbency use less energy for drying than those that are very absorbent, and may also absorb water-borne stains less easily.

Most textile materials can be recycled, however, products made from mixed fibres such as polyester and cotton can be more problematic because it is difficult to separate them out for reuse. New fibres have been developed to be more environmentally friendly, for example lyocell, and these are increasingly used to replace some of the cotton content in many fashion products.

Some fibres such as cotton and linen will eventually biodegrade and rot in landfill, but synthetic fibres do not. Some dyes and finishing chemicals break down in landfill sites and give off poisonous chemicals, which can seep out into nearby waterways.

### Advisory labelling

A-level only

You can read more about advisory labelling in Chapter 1.9. Many manufacturers encourage consumers to care for textile products using lower washing temperatures, and give other advice about the use and care which could extend the life of the product.

## The six Rs of sustainability

When designing and manufacturing products, it is important to consider the **six Rs of sustainability**:

### Reduce

Think about the design of the product, and the materials and manufacturing processes used. Some parts such as trims, fastenings and added decoration may not be essential, therefore it may be possible to use less fabric by making a small adjustment to the design. Simplifying the design or manufacture can also contribute to savings of energy and materials.

Designing products for a longer life means that fewer need to be produced, saving valuable resources.

Figure 1.11.9 Cotton products can be broken down and the fibres re-spun to make new yarns.

## Recycle

The Environmental Protection Agency estimates that the average person throws away 70 pounds of clothing every year, accounting for 5.2 per cent of the waste in landfills. Recycling textile products cuts down on the use of natural resources such as water and petroleum, and reduces the need for chemicals used in the manufacture of new textiles, and the pollution caused by manufacturing processes.

All textiles and their components can be reused or recycled:

- Products that are in good condition can be sold in charity shops or sent to developing countries.
- Products that are not in good condition can be turned into wiping cloths, which are used in a variety of industries.
- Textiles can be broken down into fibres and used to make new products such as yarns, insulation materials and paper.
- Metal components such as rivets can be sent to metal recyclers.

Recycling of non-textile materials can also be used to create new fabrics. For example, plastic bottles can be recycled to make fabrics such as Patagonia fleece and those used to make some school uniform items.

Figure 1.11.10 A tree sculpture made from recycled fabrics.

## Reuse

Many small and craft manufacturers are showing increased interest in upcycling, and reusing fabrics and components to make new products that are manufactured in small batches, making them more individual. Some retailers such as H&M and Marks and Spencer encourage consumers to return their unwanted clothing so that they can be turned into new products.

Figure 1.11.11 These dresses are made by reusing denim and other fabrics.

## Rethink

Rethinking the design of a product to see if it could be made using fewer materials – or ones which have a reduced impact on the environment – can help to ensure that textile products are sustainable.

Fabrics made from fibres such as lyocell, ramie, banana leaf, corn and soya fibres are considered to be more sustainable than others such as cotton. Polyester fibres are the most commonly used synthetic fibres, and are often considered to be unsustainable. However, as their manufacture uses very little of the world's petroleum supply, and does not require land and copious amounts of water for growth, polyester fibres can be considered to have less impact on the environment than cotton and other cellulosic fibres. In addition, clothing made from synthetic fibres requires less energy use for drying and ironing.

Selecting different techniques that use less energy and considering where fabrics and components are bought is important; if fabrics have to travel a long way to the factory, more fuel will be needed for the planes, boats and lorries used to deliver them, and more exhaust fumes will be released into the atmosphere. There is also more damage to the road system and a greater risk of traffic accidents.

### Repair

It can be difficult to repair a badly damaged textile product, but some components are easy to replace, and some minor repairs can extend the life of a textile product. Most manufacturers provide a replacement button, and some give extra trims such as beads as well as a short length of matching thread.

**Figure 1.11.12** An appliqué patch used to cover a hole can be an additional feature on some garments.

It is good practice to get into the habit of checking garments and other products so that buttons can be re-attached before they fall off, small holes can be caught before they become too big to mend and hems re-stitched when they have fallen down. It is easy to buy a new set of buttons if the original ones are lost. Many dry cleaners provide zip replacement services, and can re-line products such as jackets to extend their useful life.

Some clothing items can have patches put over holes, and these can sometimes be used as an additional feature of the product, especially on children's clothing.

### Refuse

As consumers, it is easy to be lured into buying new clothes and to fall for the marketing ploys used by retailers, who offer enticements such as special offers to persuade us to continually buy more products. We should stop to consider whether it is really necessary to buy yet another fashion product, as reducing our consumption can help cut down on textile manufacturing activity.

Responsible consumers are beginning to question the way in which their clothes are made, and the working conditions of those who are employed to make them. Refusing to buy clothes that have been made by workers who are treated unfairly can help make clothing manufacture more sustainable.

**ACTIVITY**

Design a textile product to be made from recycled textile materials.

Reuse discarded textiles to make samples of some of the techniques that could be used in the manufacture of the product you have designed.

## Maintenance

Looking after textile products correctly helps to prolong their life, and reduces the amount of waste sent to landfill. Caring for products by following the care labels attached is one way to look after them, and information about care is given below. Repairing products can also give them a longer life.

## Care and maintenance of products

Textile products need to be cared for to keep them in good condition, and to maximise their useful life. This usually means that they must be cleaned and stored in a way that is appropriate for the fabric and product, and does not cause damage.

Textile products usually have **care labels** attached to them. Care labels use a set of recognised symbols to tell the consumer the best way to wash, dry and iron the product, as well as other relevant information. The symbols are owned by a company called GINETEX, and are a registered trademark.

There are five basic symbols to cover the main areas of cleaning care, and additional information is encoded within each symbol. The basic

**Figure 1.11.13** The five basic care symbols are internationally recognised. The washtub refers to machine or hand washing. The triangle refers to chlorine bleaching. The iron refers to the iron temperature. The circle refers to dry cleaning. The circle in a square refers to tumble drying.

symbols are shown in Figure 1.11.13. A cross through any of these symbols means 'do not'.

The wash tub symbol (Figure 1.11.14) has a number inside the shape – this number refers to the maximum temperature of the washing water in °C. There may also be one or more bars under the wash tub, and these indicate the washing conditions in terms of the amount of agitation recommended; one bar is reduced agitation, two bars indicate much reduced agitation.

A hand in the wash tub (Figure 1.11.15) means that the product should only be washed by hand, usually because the fabric is delicate or may shrink if subjected to anything but the gentlest agitation.

**Figure 1.11.14** This example of a wash symbol indicates a maximum water temperature of 40 °C with much reduced agitation. It is used on machine washable wool products.

**Figure 1.11.15** The hand wash only symbol.

Chlorine bleach can remove colour from fabrics, and can weaken and yellow others.

Fluorescent whitening agents are commonly used to whiten all fibre types during fabric manufacture, especially where a very white fabric is required. These are colourless dyes that cause the fabric to reflect an ultraviolet light, which makes it appear to be whiter and brighter. These fluorescent dyes will be broken down by the bleaches commonly used in home laundering, and this is the reason why consumers are sometimes advised not to bleach white cotton fabrics.

**Figure 1.11.16** An iron with two dots means a warm iron can be used.

The iron symbol (Figure 1.11.16) contains one, two or three dots that indicate the ironing temperature – the more dots, the hotter the iron can be. The use of an iron that is too hot can damage fabrics, especially those made from synthetic fibres because they are thermoplastic and will soften and melt with excessive heat.

The **dry-cleaning** circle may contain a letter to tell the cleaner which solvent and process to use.

**Figure 1.11.17** The dry-cleaning process does not involve the use of water.

Dry cleaning uses solvents instead of water to dissolve soiling and stains. Because water is not used, cellulosic fibres do not swell so do not shrink. The lack of heat and moisture means that wool and other delicate fibres are not damaged by the process.

The tumble dry symbol (Figure 1.11.18) indicates that the product can be tumble dried, unless there is a cross through it. It may also contain one or two dots – these refer to the drying temperature.

**Figure 1.11.18** The tumble dry symbol with one dot means a low heat-setting; two dots refer to a high heat-setting.

The recommended care for a textile product is linked to the fibre type used to make the fabric. Some fibres – such as cotton and linen – can withstand high temperatures and agitation without being damaged, while wool fabrics that do not have a shrink resistant finish will felt and shrink.

Care labels recommend the washing of fabrics containing thermoplastic fibres at 40 °C or less. If the wash temperature is any higher, there is a risk that the fabric may be heat-set into unwanted creases that will be difficult to remove. This is also the reason why these fabrics are not ironed with a hot iron or put in a tumble drier on full heat – it is not because they might shrink.

Other factors that influence the care recommendations include the fabric structure – for example knitted or loosely woven, the use of applied finishes – for example crease resistance or flame resistance, and the way the product is constructed – for example the inclusion of linings, shoulder pads and trims that need specific care.

The type of detergent used will affect the product; some detergents are very alkaline and will damage certain fibres such as wool and silk. Some detergents contain enzymes that can cause bright colours to fade, and can damage protein fibres such as wool. There is a wide range of detergents and laundry products available, and some are specially made to be used with delicate fabrics.

When not in use, textile products should be stored carefully to keep them in good condition. Wool fabrics can be attacked by moths, white wool and polyamide are yellowed by sunlight and cellulosic fibres such as cotton and linen will become mildewed if stored when damp.

### ACTIVITY

Collect a range of textile products made from as many different fibre and fabric types as possible. Analyse how the recommended care relates to:

- the fibre content
- the fabric structure
- the way the product is made.

### KEY TERMS

**Sustainability:** the reduction of all aspects of design and manufacturing activity that have a negative impact on the environment or the lives of humans.

**Efficiency:** the use of materials, energy, time and effort with minimal wastage.

**Care label:** a label that contains internationally recognised symbols that tell the consumer how to cleanse, dry and iron textile products.

**Dry cleaning:** a cleaning process that uses solvents and not water.

**Detergent:** a soap-based or synthetic cleaning agent made from chemicals, and sold in powder or liquid form.

### KEY POINTS

- Responsible design and manufacture considers the impact of a product on the environment and on people's lives.
- Disposing of unwanted textile products poses a huge environmental challenge, so they should be recycled and reused rather than sent to landfill.
- Consumers as well as designers and manufacturers have a responsibility to choose and use textile products wisely.
- The recommended care for a textile product is based on the characteristics of the fibres and fabrics it is made from, as well as the structure of the product.
- Storing textile products carefully and repairing them when needed can prolong their life, which will help increase their sustainability.

## Check your knowledge and understanding

1 Give three ways in which the manufacture of textile products can affect the environment.

2 The following care advice relates to a product made from 100 per cent wool:
- Wash in cool water (40 °C).
- Dry flat.
- Do not tumble dry.
- Do not use biological detergents.

Explain why this care is recommended.

3 Look at the trouser suit shown below in Figure 1.11.19.
- The trousers and jacket are both made from a woven fabric made from a blend of 74 per cent cotton, 15 per cent viscose and 11 per cent polyester.
- The jacket is dry clean only and the trousers are machine washable.

Explain the reasons for the different care advice.

4 Giving examples, discuss the impact that the aftercare of textile products can have on their durability.

5 What are the issues that are likely to affect the environment when disposing of textile products? Suggest ways in which the impact might be reduced.

**Figure 1.11.19** Trouser suit.

## Further reading

The following YouTube videos:
- *How textile recycling works*: https://youtu.be/URokpcF4Nfo
- *How it's made – recycled clothes*: https://youtu.be/xnutURokix0

Article on polyester fibres and their ecological impact: qz.com/414223/if-your-clothes-arent-aleady-made-out-of-plastic-they-will-be/

Hallett, C., Johnston, A. and King, L. *Fabric for Fashion: The Complete guide*

Information about the 6Rs: www.fashionrevolution.org

Information about the meaning of care labels and advice about caring for textile products: www.care-labelling.co.uk

# 1.12 Feasibility studies

A-level only

**This topic is for A-level only. If you are studying at AS Level, you do not need to cover the content in this section.**

**LEARNING OUTCOMES**

By the end of this section you should have developed a knowledge and understanding of:

- the use of feasibility studies to access the practicability of proposed designs for production
- the testing of prototypes with potential consumers.

Feasibility studies involve analysis and evaluation of the design ideas, design **prototypes** and plans for making. It is important to check whether the proposed design is going to work and whether it meets the needs of the target market. Businesses need to assess whether a fashion or textile design is viable, or whether alternative ideas should be considered instead. Feasibility studies inform the development team about possible modifications and improvements that could be made to the prototype in order to make a successful final design.

## Producing and testing prototypes

Textile and fashion designers develop and improve their design ideas by making prototype products and garments to test and evaluate the success of the design. In Figure 1.12.1, a product development team are meeting to assess prototype garments, and to make decisions on whether to develop them further. A standard sized model is wearing a prototype skirt to check for fit, length and ease of movement.

**Figure 1.12.1** Meeting in fashion retail studio to assess prototype garments.

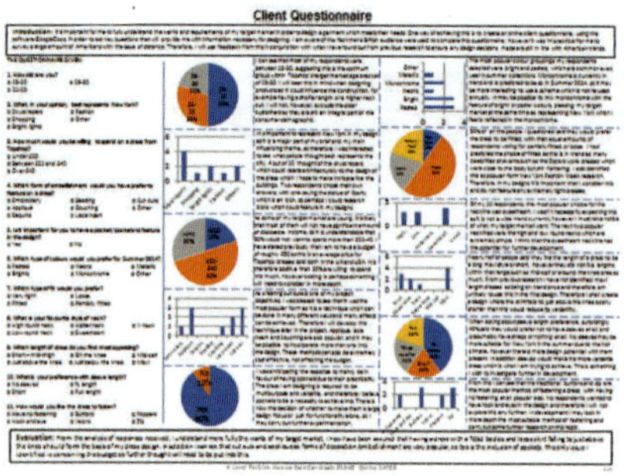

**Figure 1.12.2** Student example of questionnaire analysis using charts and graphs.

Some prototype products might be tested by showing them to people who would be likely to buy the new design, and asking their opinion. One-to-one interviews could be used to collect opinions, or a **focus group** could be consulted to get feedback. One example of this is a mother and baby group, who could be asked to trial a new baby change bag design. Mums could be asked about:

- how well the product performs in use
- whether the bag is easy and comfortable to carry
- ease of cleaning
- whether pockets for storage are the right size
- how much they would pay for the bag
- what improvements to the design they would recommend.

The results from the focus group could give the bag designer important information about how the design could be modified, to make it more useful and appealing to the target market.

## Analysing consumer feedback

Market researchers collect data about potential consumers and what they would prefer to buy. In the student example above (Figure 1.12.2), a questionnaire has been used to collect information about consumer preferences in garments such as colour, pocket design and jean length. The student makes pie charts and graphs to analyse the information, and uses them to evaluate the requirements for the jean design.

### MATHS LINK

**Interpreting statistical analyses to determine user needs and preferences**

A popular online brand of jeans has launched a new range of jeans which consists of six different new styles. The product developer analyses the sales data from over the first 7 days after launching the range to determine the appeal of the different styles to the target market. The figure below shows the histogram drawn to analyse the results.

What does it tell us about the popularity of the different styles of jeans in the new range?

**Answer**

- Super skinny fit, mid wash is the most popular style
- High-waisted, embroidered is the least popular style
- Sales of high-waisted, embroidered and skinny fit with rips are low but fairly consistent across each day.
- Cropped with frayed hem and ripped knee, gem studded increased in popularity each day
- The popularity of supper skinny fit, mid wash and slim fit, dark indigo fluctuated each day
- More jeans were sold on days 6 and 7; fewer jeans were sold on day 1

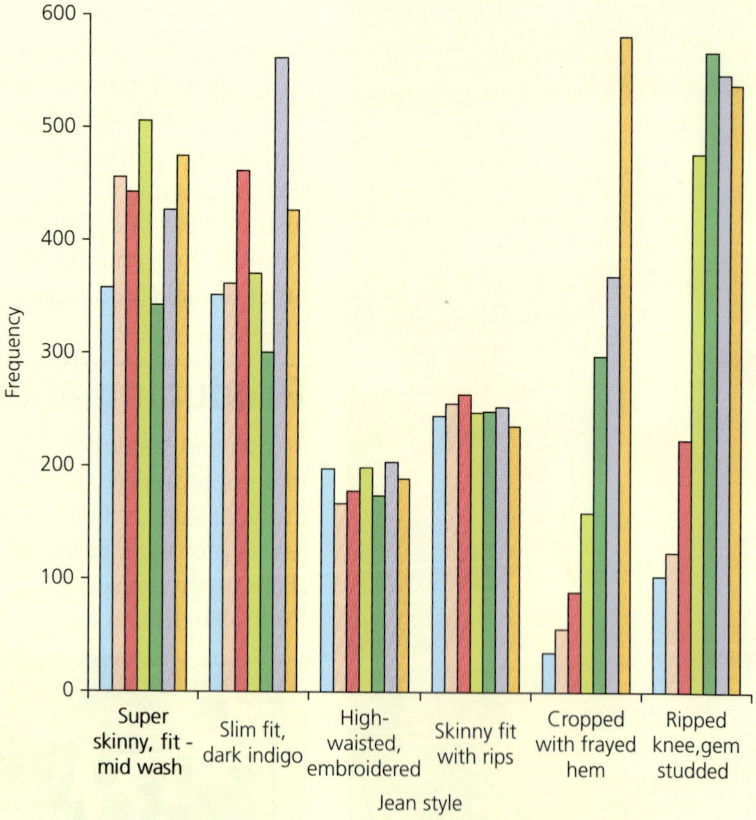


**Figure 1.12.3** Histogram based on the data below.

| Jean style | Day 1 | Day 2 | Day 3 | Day 4 | Day 5 | Day 6 | Day 7 |
|---|---|---|---|---|---|---|---|
| Super skinny, fit-mid wash | 358 | 456 | 443 | 506 | 343 | 427 | 475 |
| Slim fit, dark indigo | 352 | 362 | 462 | 371 | 301 | 562 | 427 |
| High-waisted, embroidered | 198 | 167 | 178 | 199 | 174 | 204 | 189 |
| Skinny fit with rips | 245 | 256 | 264 | 248 | 249 | 253 | 236 |
| Cropped with frayed hem | 35 | 56 | 89 | 159 | 298 | 369 | 582 |
| Ripped knee, gem studded | 103 | 124 | 224 | 478 | 568 | 548 | 539 |

## Product scale and dimensions

The relationship between dress styles and cost of materials would be examined by a business as part of feasibility studies. Product developers need to consider how lengthening the dress will impact the product costs. For example, a time series graph could be made to show the length of dresses and sleeves, compared to the cost of materials over a 5-year period. (Refer to Chapter 1.14 for an example of a time series graph.)

The standard measurements of the average human body are recorded in chart form, to guide designers and product developers when they are planning the scale and size of garments to fit the body. These measurements are known as **anthropometrics**. There are differences in these standard measurements between countries across the world. Measurements are taken using different units of measurement – such as centimetres and inches – and the standard measurements differ between populations. Designers and product developers need to consider where they intend to sell the clothes, in order to size the garments appropriately.

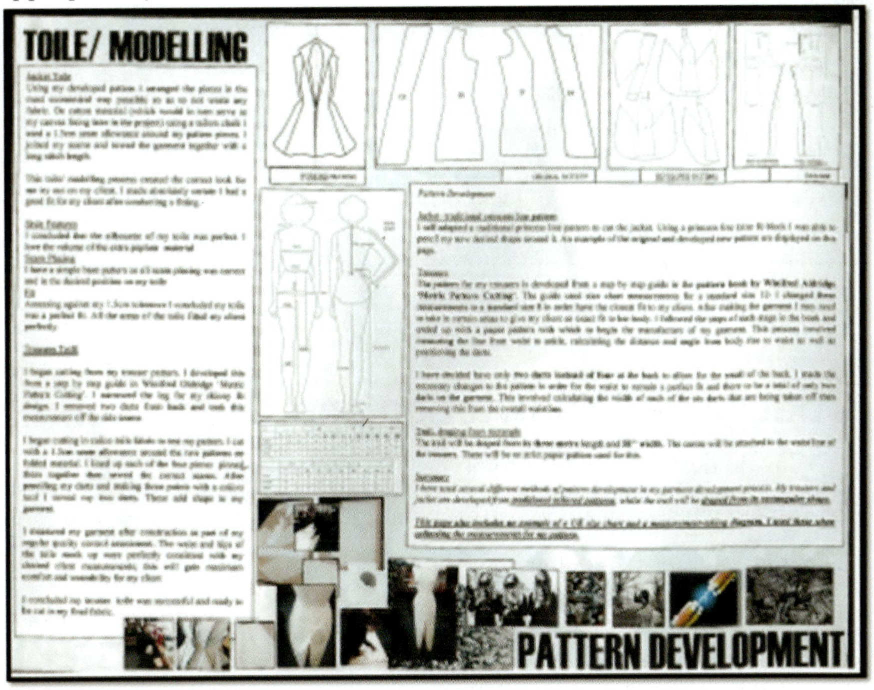


**Figure 1.12.4** Student example of pattern development using anthropometrics.

### KEY TERMS

**Prototype:** the first version of a design to see it if works as intended, and to find out if improvements are necessary.

**Focus group:** a panel of consumers who rate the product and feed back their opinions.

**Anthropometrics:** measurements of the human body.

**Pattern grader:** someone who scans or traces the design pattern and marks additional measurements at key points. These are used to adjust the pattern's proportions, to give a range of different sizes for the same pattern.

Sizes are described differently across the globe, for example a UK size 10 in women's clothing is equivalent to:

- US size 8
- Japan size 9–11
- France, Spain and Portugal size 38
- Germany and Scandinavia size 36
- Italy size 42
- Australia and New Zealand size 10.

In the student example above (Figure 1.12.4), anthropometrics are used to inform the modelling and development of a toile and pattern. The student uses the chart to find out about the standard measurements for a size 8. For example, the measurement between the waist and the knee guides the student to decide the length of the dress from waistline to hemline.

## ACTIVITY

1 Take measurements of your body and use the chart below to find out your UK, US and European size.

2 Take some more measurements of your body that would help a designer to decide the dimensions of a shirt.

3 Make a chart to show your full body measurements.

| Size | Inch | cm | Inch | cm | Inch | cm | Inch | Cm |
|---|---|---|---|---|---|---|---|---|
| Bust | 32 ½ –33 ½ | 82–85 | 34 ½ –35 ½ | 88–90 | 37 ½ –28 ½ | 94–98 | 40–42 | 102–107 |
| Waist | 24 ½ –25 ½ | 62–65 | 26 ½ –27 ½ | 67–70 | 29–30 ½ | 75–77 | 32–34 | 81–86 |
| Hip | 35–36 | 89–91 | 37–38 | 94–97 | 39 ½ –41 | 100–104 | 42 ½ –44 ½ | 108–113 |

**Figure 1.12.7** Anthropometric size chart.

## KEY POINTS

- Feasibility studies are carried out to analyse and evaluate the viability of a design proposal.
- The results from feasibility studies indicate possible modifications and improvements that could be made to the design.
- Questionnaire results can be analysed and evaluated using charts to present the collected data.
- Anthropometric data is used to guide the scale and proportion of fashion and textile designs.

## Check your knowledge and understanding

1 Why do designers make prototypes?

2 Explain what is meant by anthropometrics, and give some examples.

3 Why are graphs and charts used to present data?

4 What is meant by grading a pattern?

## Further reading

Cooklin, G. *Pattern Grading for Women's Clothes: The Technology of Sizing*

Virtual prototyping: www.clothierdesignsource.com/virtual-prototyping/

# 1.13 Enterprise and marketing in the development of products

## LEARNING OUTCOMES

By the end of this section you should have developed a knowledge and understanding of:

- the importance of marketing and brand identity, including customer identification, labelling, packaging and corporate identification.

If you are studying at A-level you should also have developed a knowledge and understanding of:

- the concept of global marketing: the promotion and advertisement of products including the use of new technologies, for example social media, viral marketing
- product costing and profit
- the role of entrepreneurs
- the collaborative working of designers in the development of new and innovative fashion, clothing and textile products
- factors affecting product price, including costs, profit margin, target market and budget
- the sales and marketing cycles for specific product groups, including fad, classic and standard products
- the impact of fashion on trend and the development of design products, including retro, vintage, industrial and traditional products
- industry development cycles, including colour trends, fibre trends, predictions and the importance of trade fairs
- the influence of trend and changes in lifestyle on fashion, clothing and textile products.

## Enterprise and marketing

An **enterprise** is a business that sells products or services to make a profit. The word is often used to describe a business that has been set up by someone who has seen a business opportunity and is prepared to take a risk with an innovative idea. Funding for a business is essential for its set up and day-to-day running, and those who have an enterprise are able to secure investment in their business and get it established.

In fashion and textiles, enterprises are often:

- new start-up companies in their first few years of trading, for example those set up by fashion graduates

**Figure 1.13.1** Designer pop-up store open for only a few months in an empty commercial space.

**ACTIVITY**

Investigate new technological developments in sportswear and outdoor leisurewear fabrics by researching sportwear brands on the internet. Find out which new fabrics they are promoting and the advantages of wearing the latest clothing designs. How do brands engage the audience on their websites?

pop-up shops in temporary shop premises, selling a limited range of products for a short length of time, for example T-shirts featuring handmade screen-printed artwork
- online businesses that provide niche products, for example digitally printed leggings with offbeat print designs
- project businesses set up by celebrities which may be in collaboration with other businesses, for example where a pop star brings out a fashion collection that they have helped to design
- community projects for recycling, **customising** and mending clothing, for example **co-ops** (co-operatives – businesses owned by their members).

Marketing is about developing a product for an identified market and promoting it to the consumer. The product needs to appeal to the target market, be priced at the right level and be readily available for the consumer to purchase.

In fashion and textiles, marketing is used to advertise new products and the latest fashions, and to create a demand for them. New fibres and fabrics for sports and outdoor leisure wear are marketed on shopping websites, in sales literature and on **swing tickets** attached to products in shops. This makes consumers aware of new technological developments, and tells them why they should buy the new products. People who want up-to-date fashion clothing are also receptive to marketing techniques such as fashion articles in magazines, and they are inspired to buy new clothing, accessories and home furnishing products that are described as the latest 'must have' items.

## Marketing and brand identity

Market research is carried out to identify the opportunities to develop a product that will meet the requirements of consumers and be attractive to buy. In fashion, retail businesses' analysis of sales data is part of market research, and it directs product development. It is essential to build on past successes in order to bring to market a product that is likely to be popular with shoppers.

**Figure 1.13.2** Fashion advertising in shopping areas.

Advertising and promotion is targeted at those who are likely to buy the products. In the photograph above, a fashion brand is advertised in a major shopping area. There is a wide range of methods to reach the consumer, and those marketing the product need to consider which channel of communication is the most effective way to promote and advertise the particular product:

- websites selling the products: they promote the products and company values, they can also offer lifestyle articles promoting the products and newsletters. They can give advice to consumers about buying and using the product, and encourage further purchases to extend the consumers' wardrobe
- shop front and instore promotional displays and literature; sales staff wearing the clothes from the latest collections
- promotional events including fashion shows, launch parties and sales events aimed at both loyal and new customers
- packaging to promote the brand
- online fashion blogs and product reviews to validate buying the product
- online vlogs (video blogs) to show the product in use
- use of social media such as Facebook and Instagram to show influential people wearing the fashion products, and to promote a lifestyle that encourages brand loyalty

- online pop up adverts
- newspaper and magazine articles and adverts
- TV and radio adverts
- billboard posters, digital display boards and adverts on buses and at bus stops.

**Brand identity** is determined by the set of principles guiding the business or company. The values and style of the brand are seen in the product design, and conveyed to the consumer through how they conduct their business and how they publicise it. A **strapline** is often used when promoting the business and brand identity. It is a short phrase that summarises the principles of the business, the type of product they are selling and the kind of person they are aiming their product at. For example, the strapline 'Evans, created for curves', promotes the fashion retailer Evans' plus size clothes for women, and gives a clear message about the brand identity.

**Figure 1.13.3** Former pop star promotes her fashion brand.

In Figure 1.13.3, Myleene Klass promotes her business enterprise with the retailer Mothercare. She holds up a baby-changing bag, part of her 'My K' range of children's wear, accessories, nursery furniture, bedding and buggies designed for Mothercare. Myleene Klass is a former pop star, a TV and radio presenter, model and writer about pregnancy and parenting, who also designs products for children. Her brand identity is fashionable clothing for children in black and monochrome colourways. It is represented by a simple black logo that reflects the frequent use of black in her designs.

## Customer identification

Knowing and understanding who buys products is essential to marketing and success in business. Finding out about the age, gender, location, interests, lifestyle and friends of customers can make product development and product promotion more focused and efficient.

In the student example below (Figure 1.13.4), a client profile is compiled to identify the type of person who would be interested in the product being developed, and their requirements for a dress. The student includes an introduction, to explain why they are writing the client profile and how it will help them to understand the needs of the target market. Details of the client's name, age, height, marital status, location, occupation, interests and hobbies and possible design requirements are given, and images are presented to reflect the personality and lifestyle of the client. The student evaluates the client profile, to explain what has been learnt from building a picture of the type of person that would buy the dress they are going to design. They have decided that the client requires a garment that is:

**Figure 1.13.4** Student example of client profile.

- easy-care to complement their busy life
- versatile to suit a range of occasions
- a reasonable price
- durable.

The student example is an effective client profile because it is detailed, focused, concise and clearly presented. The information is communicated using written notes and images, the purpose of the research is made clear in the introduction and the findings are evaluated.

Small independent shops can make personal contact with customers to understand who their customers are by talking to them in the shop. Larger businesses can carry out surveys and questionnaires to build up customer profiles.

Modern technology online is used to collect data to make a customer profile, and to build up information about customer shopping. Online shops ask the customer to create an account and sign in each time they browse the website or make a purchase. To get customers to do this, they may offer discounts such as free postage and packaging for new customers who create an account. This enables businesses to capture and store information about who is interested in their products, and to track website activity. Product promotion and advertising can then be channelled to connect to the appropriate potential customers. Having a system in place to build customer profiles and make use of them is known as customer identity and access management (CIAM).

**Figure 1.13.5** Superdry brand labelling.

## Labelling

Labelling of products is important because it identifies the product brand and promotes the business. Figure 1.13.5, a Superdry jumper has a prominent fabric label stitched onto the inside back, which is visible in-store and every time the product is used. This is a classic style of product so the main brand label is on the inside of the garment. However, a more discreet, embroidered Superdry logo on the front of the garment is just visible at the bottom right corner of the photograph. A separate card swing ticket is attached to promote the jumper on the shop floor. It is called a swing ticket because they are attached to products by a ribbon, cord or plastic thread, and they move or swing to attract attention. This encourages the shopper to handle the swing ticket to find out the price, and also carries the stock details for the retailer.

**Figure 1.13.6** Brand packaging.

## Packaging

Product packaging is important because it protects the product on its journey from manufacturer to consumer, and also provides an opportunity to promote the product and business. The style of packaging can help build brand loyalty, for example shops sometimes wrap fashion and textile products in colour co-ordinated tissue paper, and present it in an attractive bag with stickers and promotional leaflets included. This adds value to the product; it reinforces the idea that the product is special – like a gift that has been individually wrapped. In the photograph below (Figure 1.13.6), the paper carrier bags advertise the shops with distinctive and identifiable colours and logos.

**ACTIVITY**

Make a collection of fashion and textile product labels and company trademarks by researching online or collecting swing tickets and packaging materials. What makes a distinctive and memorable corporate identity?

## Corporate identity

**Corporate identity** is the visual image of the business seen in their logos, **trademarks**, signage, outlet design, uniforms, company stationery and packaging. Corporate identity is expressed using colour, font style, logos and images that best convey the aims and values of the brand. A strong corporate identity will mean that customers, investors and employees understand what type of products are sold, and the principles by which the company trades. It also sets them apart from their competitors.

**Figure 1.13.7** London Fashion Week promotes the work of Indian fashion designers.

**Figure 1.13.8** Textile factory in India manufacturing Fairtrade cotton bags for a discount supermarket in Europe.

## Global marketing

A-level only

Global marketing takes place when products are sold internationally or worldwide. Products made in one country are exported and sold around the world. Trade agreements within groups of countries – for example EU countries – mean that there are no taxes paid when importing or exporting textile materials or products within the group; this benefits the participating countries by encouraging trade and business growth. However, individual governments may prefer to agree high import taxes to reduce imports and benefit their own industry. This is because high import taxes would put up the price of the imported goods; it would protect employment by encouraging manufacturing in their own country.

In the fashion world, consumers in many culturally diverse countries have an appetite for western-styled products and fashion designers, and fashion retailers sell their collections globally. The rising affluence of some emerging countries such as India has seen an increase in the demand for such western fashion, but has also seen the rise of new talented designers from within India and a growth of Indian businesses. In Figure 1.13.7, the work of designers such as Rocky S, Lanacherry, and Bhumika & Jyoti is being promoted in London.

Textile products from developing countries such as India are popular in more economically developed countries such as the UK; they are often inexpensive as the cost of manufacturing is low. However, if there is a tariff or tax on importing such goods from developing countries, they are less affordable to those in more economically developed countries.

In the photograph below (Figure 1.13.8), Fairtrade bags are being manufactured in India for a discount supermarket in Europe.

Fairtrade artisan enterprises provide much needed income for households and communities across developing countries. Traditional handicraft skills are incorporated in ethical fashion and textile products, and sold to more wealthy countries, enabling consumers to afford handmade decorative textiles.

## The promotion and advertisement of products including the use of social media and viral marketing

Promoting and advertising products on social media sites is less expensive than more conventional methods, and can reach a global audience instantly. Social media can be used to build a community of potential customers who are interested in fashion and textile products; it targets people who are likely to buy the products.

Social media sites such as Facebook, Twitter, YouTube, Snapchat, Instagram and Pinterest engage with people online who can be encouraged to interact with businesses. For example, a Facebook page can be set up to promote a product and consumers can 'like', 'follow' and add comments and reviews about the product. Links between social media sites and the business website encourage consumers to buy products. Customers can be further engaged by special discounts, surveys, competitions, blogs, lifestyle articles and reviews from brand advocates or ambassadors. The brand advocates may be previously unknown people who present a street fashion image

**Figure 1.13.9** Fashion blogger Chiara Ferragni.

wearing the brand clothing. Many people are now influenced by what these fashion-conscious individuals are wearing, rather than by celebrity endorsements.

In Figure 1.13.9 Chiara Ferragni – a 27-year-old Italian fashion blogger – is arriving at a New York fashion show. She started by sharing her own fashion photographs on Instagram, and now her business TheBlondeSalad.com collaborates with major fashion houses and designer brands. She has more than 3 million global Instagram followers and is one of the most influential personalities of the international fashion world.

Viral marketing is where advertising and promotional messages are spread very quickly to others over a short period of time. The message might be a video clip promoting a product, an image of a celebrity wearing a fashion brand or a discount coupon to encourage sales. It is passed on via email or through posting on social media. Viral videos posted on YouTube are often very humorous and reach a huge audience. Fashion marketing campaigns exploit people's interest in watching these very popular videos by posting their own to sell their brand.

### Product costing and profit

During product development, the retail fashion buyer negotiates with suppliers and manufacturers to develop a new range of products. This is to ensure that the products will be priced at the right level to compete successfully with other businesses and appeal to the target market. The costs of making a garment, accessory or home furnishing item needs to be balanced with the price of the item in the shops, to ensure that those involved in supplying and selling the product make sufficient profit to run their businesses.

### The role of entrepreneurs

Fashion **entrepreneurs** look for opportunities to set up small businesses. They network with others, and may collaborate with other people in business or education by running joint projects. Entrepreneurs are interested in new, creative ideas and innovative products. As their businesses expand, they look for new opportunities. They also remain flexible in their approach to raising finance, marketing and product development. Fashion entrepreneurs inspire and mentor others; they often win awards for their work in the fashion industry and perhaps for giving back to society through charity work and links with education.

## Collaborative working of designers

Collaborative working is where two or more designers or brands work together to produce a limited-edition range of fashion or textile products. Designers work together in collaborative partnerships or collectives to build on individual success by bringing creative ideas together in a new product. Collaborative working is not a new idea, however it is one that has recently become more popular.

Creative people work collaboratively to:

- expand business customer base
- develop brand identity

**Figure 1.13.10** Motel fashion clothing designed in collaboration with Grace Neutral.

- reduce business costs
- combine skills and experience
- share workspace, facilities and specialist machinery
- give emerging designers support while benefiting from the next generation's ideas
- generate creativity and encourage innovation.

Collaborations are also formed with creative people such as artists, social influencers, photographers, celebrities and musicians. In the example below (Figure 1.13.10), the fashion brand Motel collaborated with Grace Neutral, a tattoo artist and social media star, to create a capsule range of clothing featuring a tattoo-inspired print.

## Factors affecting product price

A-level only

Product price must cover the cost of running the business and producing the product, and include profit. Product price is influenced by competitors' pricing and by the demand for the product. If cost per unit decreases as more products are made, the price per unit can be less for a large quantity than for a small quantity. For fashion products, the price is discounted over time as fashions change and the original product becomes less popular. When setting the price, some allowance needs to be made for future price cuts, and to cover the costs of unsold stock.

Price is also determined by the route from producer to consumer. When selling directly to the consumer, the price can be lower than when wholesalers or agents are involved. If there are shop premises to account for, the price will need to be set higher than for goods sold only online. If you are selling your product through traders, your trade or wholesale price will be your costs to produce the product plus profit. The recommended retail price (RRP) is higher than the trade price, and allows for the retailer to make sufficient money to pay for their own costs in running their business plus profit.

### Costs

To work out the costs of producing a product, the following need to be considered:

- business overheads such as rent, business rates, utilities (electric, water rates), insurance, phones
- the cost of materials used to make the product
- marketing costs
- administration costs
- packaging and transport costs
- contingency for mistakes and unpredictable costs.

The costs can be calculated and used to work out the cost per product, by considering how long it takes to make the product and the hourly rate of pay for those producing the product.

### Profit margin

Profit margin is the amount of income gained from product sales once the costs of making the product and running the business are deducted. It is written as a percentage, and is a measure of how much money is kept after all costs have been taken away. For example, a 30 per cent profit margin is when a business has a net income of 30 pence for every £1 of total earnings. A low profit margin indicates that costs are too high or the price is too low.

## Target market

The target market is the group of people who are likely to buy a product. It could be a broad or narrow range of potential customers. The target market can be described by age, gender, interests, location and level of disposable income. It is important for businesses to know their target market so that they can develop products that are relevant to their interests.

### MATHS LINK

**Interpretation of market research data.**

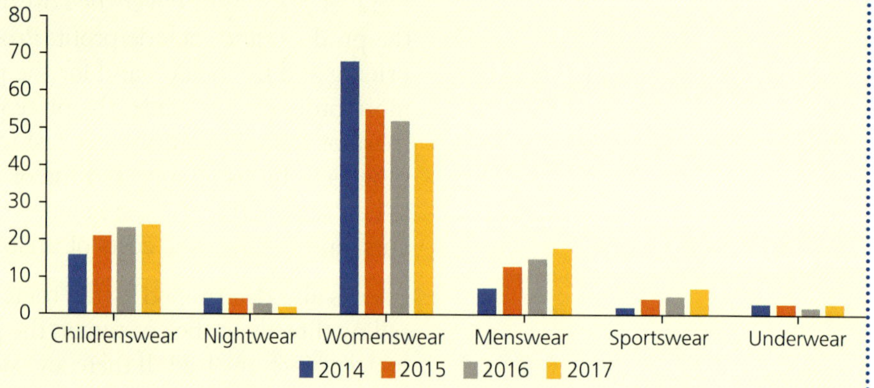


**Figure 1.13.11** Chart of spending on fashion and textiles products.

The chart above concerns spending on fashion and textiles products over a four-year period.

Analysis shows that there is little spending on underwear and night wear compared to other areas. Spending on underwear is fairly consistent. The spending on childrenswear, menswear and sportswear has increased over the four-year period, while spending on womenswear has decreased over the same time period.

Businesses can use this data to plan product ranges and areas in which to develop new products. The rise in demand will influence product design.

## Budget

A budget is the fixed amount of money designated to fund a project, development of a product or the production of a product. Budgets can be worked out according to income and expenses. They must be realistic to include all costs involved in completing work.

**MATHS LINK**

Calculating costs and profit for a fashion accessory.

Costs and considerations:

- £10,000 overheads per year
- 50 per cent of time spent making products, 40 per cent on admin, sales and despatch
- 46 weeks each year are worked, 40 hours per week
- £20,000 salary
- 2 hours to make each product
- £25 materials cost per product, including contingency for mistakes
- designer maker sells fashion accessory for £180.00.

Cost of a product = (overheads/hour + wages/hour) × length of time required to make product + materials cost/product

Work out:

overheads/hour:

time spent making each year = 46 × 40 × 50 per cent = 920 hours/year

overheads/hour = 10,000 ÷ 920 = £10.87

wages/hour:

salary of £20,000

wages/hour= 20,000 ÷ 920 = £21.74

hourly rate:

overheads/hour + wages/hour = £10.87 + £21.74 = £32.61

rate per product:

£32.61 × 2 hours to make product = £65.22

total cost per product:

£65.22 + £25 materials = £90.22

profit:

£180.00 - £90.22 = £89.78

The profit margin is almost 50 per cent.

Work out the profit if the designer makers salary is £18,000 and it takes 3 hours 45 minutes to make the fashion accessory.

## Fashion cycles

A-level only

A new fashion is initially worn by a few trendsetters. It then becomes increasing popular for a period, and it reaches a peak of fashion before declining and then disappearing. The **fashion cycle** for a particular style of clothing may be repeated over time as new generations discover a taste for a past fashion. An example of this is black leggings. These have become fashionable a number of times over the last three decades. In the photographs on the next page, black leggings are worn by fashionable women from two different periods of time.

Figure 1.13.12 Grace Jones wearing black leggings in 1985.

Figure 1.13.13 Black leggings worn by a fashionable woman in 2012.

Figure 1.13.14 1955 fashion photograph of a classic cardigan.

Figure 1.13.15 Today's classic cardigan.

## Sales and marketing cycles

For businesses to be successful they need to attract customers, engage with them and get them to buy products. This is known as a marketing and sales cycle. Advertising and promotional activities will communicate what the business is offering, and this needs to be reinforced through contact with potential shoppers, therefore giving them the confidence to buy the products. What they buy has to satisfy their needs in order for them to make repeat purchases. Fashion and textile businesses operate in this way to promote and sell fashionable products.

### Fad

A fad is a temporary craze to buy a particular fashion. It rapidly becomes the 'must have' item that fashionable people rush to get hold of as they want to be seen wearing or using the product. Businesses can find it difficult to supply sufficient quantities of a fad fashion before it passes and something else is the latest craze.

### Classic

Fashionable styles of clothing that remain popular over many years are known as classics. Certain garments – for example fine wool button-up cardigans – are worn every year and never seem to go out of fashion. Classic colours such as navy and red are always available to buy, in contrast to fashion colours which last only a season.

### Standard

Standard fashions have a longer popularity than fad fashions, but shorter than classic. For example, the standard fashion for flared fit trousers called 'flares' lasted over several years during 1970s, but since then they have not been fashionable. Standard fashions become obsolete at the end of the fashion cycle and may not become fashionable again for some time, unlike classic fashions, which are always popular to some extent.

**Figure 1.13.16** Vintage clothing shop.

**Figure 1.13.17** 2015 industrial fashion.

**Figure 1.13.18** Faux tweed fitted jacket and mini skirt fashionable office wear in 2004.

## The impact of fashion on trend and the development of design products

Extreme fashions (or those for particular groups in society) often influence more mainstream fashions, which appear on the high street for a much broader range of shoppers. For example, the handmade punk fashions of the 1970s included rips and tears in the clothing and offensive slogans. These two elements still influence commercial fashions today, such as jeans made from stonewashed denim and fashion tops that feature humorous slogans.

### Retro

Retro fashions are retrospective, which means that designers look to the past and reinvent or reinterpret past fashions. Nostalgic past designs become popular with the next generation of shoppers, and are manufactured again to be sold as fashionable items. Most people agree that retro style concerns bringing back past designs from the second half of the twentieth century.

### Vintage

Vintage fashion and textile products are actual items from the past. People interested in vintage fashion appreciate the colours, patterns and fabrics from past eras, and the craftsmanship evident in many of the authentic designer label pieces. The appeal is often the uniqueness of each piece compared to standard fashions available on every high street.

### Industrial

Industrial fashion first emerged in the late-1980s in mostly black clothing with a military influence. It has a tough anti-establishment, post apocalypse or sci-fi mood with hints of punk, goth, steampunk and fetish wear.

The influence of industrial fashion is seen in more mainstream fashion where products have a distressed look and feature buckles and straps, faux black leather, and perhaps body revealing styles.

### Traditional

Traditional styles and fabrics such as kilts and riding jackets made from tartan and tweed are often seen in fashions for the masses. Harris tweed, a very traditional fabric produced in the Scottish Isles, was made popular by the designer Vivienne Westwood. Her Harris Tweed collection of autumn/winter 1987 inspired a trend for traditional fashion which often appears in the fashion cycle.

**ACTIVITY**

Make a theme board of retro, vintage or industrial fashion and textiles designs. Use your theme board to create a range of fashion colours.

## Industry development cycles

It takes between 18–24 months to develop seasonal fashion ranges from fibre to fashion products for sale in shops. This long lead time enables designers and product developers to research, design, plan and manufacture fashion products. Traditionally there are two seasons in the fashion industry: spring/summer and autumn/winter. However, there is now a tendency to bring mid-season mini collections into shops, in addition to the seasonal ranges. This is because consumers are demanding fresh designs with increasingly fast changes in what is available to buy.

**Fast fashion** is often inexpensive and disposable. It has a much shorter development time than seasonal fashion, and is based on updating current trends using stock fabrics. Popular designs are very quickly reproduced by high street shops, and there is little originality or difference between those of competing high street brands.

## Colour trends

**Figure 1.13.19** Fabric colour swatches in a fashion studio.

Companies buy **trend forecasts** to make sure their fashion ranges fit the future trends. Trend forecasts include written reports about the predicted themes, styles, colours, fabrics and direction that fashion will take. Mood boards with images, colour and fabric swatches along with video presentations convey the design concepts and fashions of the future season.

Fashion colours are those that change from season to season. In Figure 1.3.19, the designer includes specific colours in their designs. These colours are based on colour charts supplied by trend forecasters, or provided by fabric suppliers who have based their fabric colour ranges on trend forecasts.

## Fibre trends

New developments in fibres are incorporated into the fabric ranges that fabric suppliers offer to fashion designers and product developers. The latest fibres are more aesthetically interesting or have better performance characteristics than previous developments. Marketing the new fibres to consumers increases the demand for them. Fabric that is more easy-care, more stain resistant and has better moisture management appeals to those wanting more advanced fashion products.

There is a trend for environmentally friendly fibres such as recycled polyester, and for those that can be grown sustainably such as lyocell (from eucalyptus trees), hemp and bamboo. Increasing numbers of people want to buy organic fibres such as organic cotton and organic wool (wool produced from humanely treated sheep, and that has not been dipped in toxic insecticides and fungicides).

## Predictions

Trend predictions are important to businesses because they need to make sure their products will be popular and profit is maximised. The predictions include catwalk analysis, and provide summaries of the most up-to-date fashion directions, which enable fashion businesses to plan ahead with more confidence and get the right looks on the shop floor. The predictions include alternative suggestions for themes and cover different market areas, so designers and product developers can pick out which ideas best suit their business. For example, menswear companies will select predictions that relate to the style of clothing for a specific fashion collection such as casual or formal, sporty or classic. Fashion colours, patterns, styles and fabrics will be suggested for each of these categories.

**ACTIVITY**

Research trend predictions at www.trendstop.com or www.trendtablet.com. Collect some inspiration and design a garment that would be a best seller in the future.

**Figure 1.13.20** Pure London fashion trade show.

## Trade fairs

Trade fairs are international exhibitions or shows where those working in the fashion and textile industry can research the latest trends in materials and technological developments. They can meet up, shop for supplies and arrange business contracts.

Figure 1.13.20 shows trade fair exhibition stands at Pure London Summer/Spring 2017 – a fashion trade show that takes place twice a year in London Olympia. Tradeshows that exhibit fashion clothing are visited by fashion buyers and range planners looking to stock retail outlets such as boutiques.

Fashion designers and product developers travel to the main fashion and textile trade fairs and exhibitions that relate to the type of product they make. Suppliers of fabrics and trims display their goods and look for business. For fashion designers and product developers, it is a chance to get new ideas, find new suppliers and network with others. Materials are sourced and deals negotiated to get best prices.

The most important trade shows include:

- Heimtextil in Frankfurt
- Premiere Vision in Paris
- Texworld in New York.

## The influence of trend and changes in lifestyle on fashion, clothing and textile products

Trends and changes in lifestyle influence the style of clothing and textile products, what they are made from and the performance characteristics required in the products.

**Figure 1.13.21** Comfortable lounge wear for home workers.

For example:

- Work clothing for many people has become less formal as some work places encourage dressing down, and more people work from home. This has meant that fashion clothing for work has become more casual, and the loungewear market has expanded to include comfortable homework wear.
- Health and fitness has become an increasingly popular leisure time interest, and there has been an increase in fashionable active wear. There has been an increase in breathable clothing using elastane fabric blends with fashionable prints and trims.
- New technology has meant that many people use smart phones and computers all through the day. Therefore the design of bags, hats and jackets has been modified to include earphones, speakers and channels for wiring and solar panels for charging equipment.
- The cult of the individual – where fashion is seen as personal style and people are free to dress eclectically to create individual looks – has influenced attitudes to following fashion trends. People are customising clothing, and special-order items such as monogrammed fashion accessories are more popular. Shoppers are tending to mix brands within one outfit and include vintage clothing.
- Internet access and social media has given people the opportunity to communicate fashions more quickly, and to follow trends set by social influencers.

**Figure 1.13.22** New technology included in bag design.

- An increase in people taking mini breaks and going on long haul holidays means that a broader range of clothing needs to be available to consumers. Holiday wear is available in shops all year round. Those travelling to more extreme climates can buy specialist clothing such as shirts, socks and trousers impregnated with insect repellent.

In Figure 1.13.22, photovoltaic solar cells are included on the bag for charging electrical devices and mobile phones – a useful feature for those with a busy lifestyle and a need for access to electrical power while on the go.

## KEY TERMS

**Enterprise:** a business that sells products or services to make a profit.

**Customising:** individualising fashion and textile products with unique embellishments, or to suit a particular person. This can be done by a business or by the consumer.

**Co-ops:** short for co-operatives, these are businesses that are owned and democratically controlled by their members.

**Swing tickets**: the card label attached to products by a thread to draw attention from shoppers.

**Brand identity:** the distinctive and memorable style, ethos and values of a business.

**Strapline:** (also referred to as a tagline, catchphrase or slogan) a short memorable summary in a few words, which tells the customer what the brand stands for.

**Corporate identity:** the visual representation of the business.

**Trademark:** the logo that is designed to express the brand identity and label the business; it is used to protect others from copying the brand products.

**Entrepreneurs:** enterprising business people.

**Fashion cycle:** the journey a fashion product makes: from its first launch onto the market to its peak of popularity and then to no longer being fashionable.

**Fast fashion:** affordable fashion designs seen on the catwalk, which are then quickly manufactured and sold in shops within a very short timescale.

**Trend forecasts:** predictions for future fashions produced by forecasting businesses and sold to fashion design companies.

## KEY POINTS

- An enterprise is a business that has been set up by someone who has seen an opportunity and is prepared to take a risk with an innovative idea.
- Marketing is about developing a product for an identified market and promoting it to the consumer.
- Brand identity is the values and style seen in the product design, and is conveyed to the consumer through the way in which brands conduct their business and how they publicise it.
- Knowing and understanding the target market is essential to marketing, product development and success in business.
- Labelling of products is important because it identifies the product brand and promotes the business.
- Corporate identity is expressed using colour, font style, logos and images that best convey the aims and values of the brand.
- Global marketing takes place when products made in one country are sold internationally or worldwide.
- Social media can be used to build a community of potential customers who are interested in fashion and textile products; it enables companies to target people who are likely to buy the products.
- Collaborative working is where two or more designers or brands work together to produce a limited edition range of fashion or textile products.
- Product price must cover the cost of running the business and producing the product, and include profit.

- Fast fashion is often inexpensive and disposable with a much shorter development time, and is based on updating current trends using stock fabrics.
- Trend predictions are important to businesses because they need to make sure their products will be popular and profit is maximised.
- Trends and changes in lifestyle influence the style of clothing and textile products, what they are made from and the performance characteristics required in the products.

## Check your knowledge and understanding

1. What are the characteristics of an entrepreneur who has a business enterprise?
2. Why is marketing important?
3. Can you give an example of a brand identity and how it is conveyed to the target market?
4. How can social media be used to market fashion?
5. What is the difference between fad and classic fashions?

## Further reading

Harris, C. *The Fundamentals of Digital Fashion Marketing*

Jeffrey, M. *Costing for the Fashion Industry*

www.thedesigntrust.co.uk

www.connect.lycra.com

www.trendstop.com

www.trendtablet.com

# 1.14 Design communication

**LEARNING OUTCOMES**

By the end of this section you should have developed a knowledge and understanding of:

- a range of communication and presentation techniques for conveying design proposals to clients, potential users and manufacturers.

Information about design ideas can be presented using a wide variety of techniques and methods. Some aspects are best communicated visually, while other points can be described in more detail through written reports, especially where some evaluation is required. Designers combine presentation techniques to include design aesthetics, technical aspects, manufacturing details, numeric data and written material in their design presentations.

In the student example below, a variety of techniques are used to present the final design prototype. A written summary of modifications is displayed alongside technical drawings and photographic evidence; these are presented on a board, which has been enhanced with paper collages.

**Figure 1.14.1** Student example of communicating design prototype evaluation.

## Report writing

Written reports set out and explain the detailed information concerning fashion and textile product design. Design ideas and final developments are described, analysed and evaluated in extended pieces of writing, which can be shared with co-workers or presented to clients. Final design written reports are formal documents to put forward the design proposal, and summarise the findings of testing and evaluating the final design.

When writing a final design report, you need to consider who will be reading it and write in a clear, succinct way in a style that is direct and suited to your audience. For clarity, a report needs to follow a conventional structure and cover the following aspects:

- initial statement known as an abstract, which summarises the objective, contents, results and conclusions of the report as briefly as possible
- short introduction to explain the context, design task and objectives of the project, to outline what you set out to design
- reference to the key research activities that you undertook to investigate the task and the design brief
- section explaining how ideas were tested and refined during development
- final prototype description to highlight main design features
- note of any relevant safety issues or hazards concerned with the design or manufacture of the product
- reference to costs associated with product design, including possible modifications to design
- section to consider the impact of the design on the environment, with reference to sustainability and possible modifications to design, including sourcing of materials and methods of production
- section about the manufacturability of the design, including possible modifications and improvements
- summary of findings from comparison of final design to existing products already for sale commercially
- summary of results from testing final design against design criteria, trialling final prototype and customer feedback concerning usability and value
- conclusion to highlight strengths of design, and suggestions for further development
- appendix to provide any further details of data referred to in the report
- bibliography to reference any sources of information used when researching or writing the report.

## The use of graphs

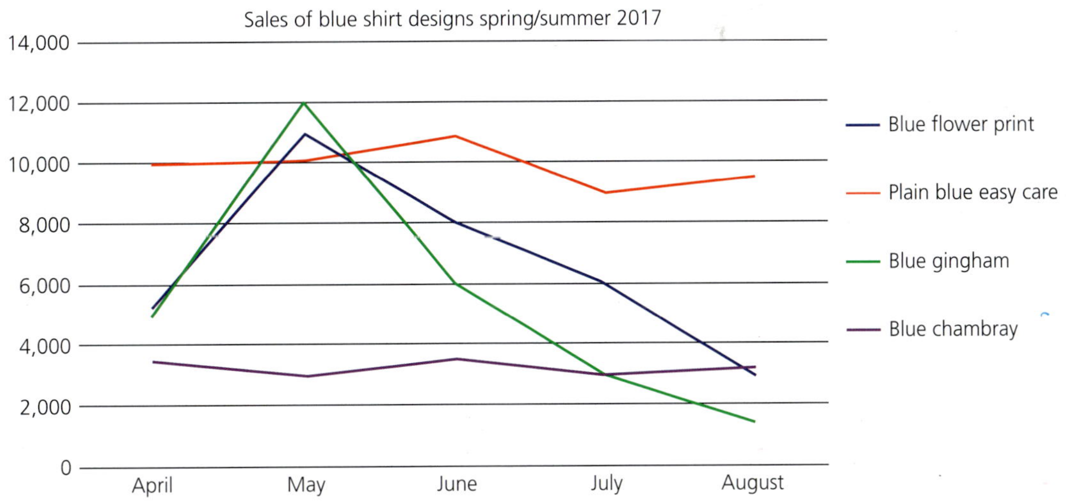


**Figure 1.14.2** Line graph to show sales of blue shirt designs over a 5 month period.

**Graphs** represent numerical data in a visual form. This means that changes in the data can be seen clearly, and trends over time can be analysed. Graphs have X and Y axes, with the unit of measure on the left side (Y axis) and the timeline along the bottom of the graph (X axis). Once data is plotted, the graph can be filled in using columns or bars, or by joining points with lines.

The graph in the example above (Figure 1.14.2), provides a visual display to show how many shirts were sold over 2017 spring and summer months. The information is clear, and the graph can be analysed to conclude that:

- blue gingham and flower print shirts are bought in the largest numbers in May, after which time there is a decline in sales
- sales of plain blue easy-care shirts and those made from blue chambray fabric are consistently sold at the same level during the spring and summer months
- there is less demand for blue chambray shirts compared to the other blue shirt designs
- demand for plain blue easy-care shirts is consistently high throughout the season
- in comparison to other blue shirt designs, gingham shirts were the best seller in May and the worst seller in August.

This kind of sales data could be used to help predict trends in future years. It could also be used to propose a wider range of print and woven pattern designs in spring and summer shirt collections. It is clearly important to note that May is a prime month for selling blue shirts, and this has implications for stock control on shop floors.

**Figure 1.14.3** Student example of a table to record testing and evaluation of final made piece.

## Tables and charts

Tables are used to organise data in a clear and ordered way using rows and columns. The table in Figure1.14.3 shows a comparison between a dress designed and made by a student and a commercial design. Both designs are evaluated against the design criteria. The advantage of using a table as opposed to a piece of extended writing is that each point of comparison is clearly defined and can be located quickly in the table format. Photographs of both designs appear alongside the table so that comparison is immediate; the table is displayed on a theme-related board to enhance the presentation.

Charts are used to show facts and statistics collected during research and testing; the information is presented in a visual form. There are a wide variety of different formats of chart including **bar charts**, **pie charts**, **scatter diagrams** and **radar charts**. It is important to select the type of chart that best displays the particular information you need to communicate. Professional charts can be drawn using a computer program such as Microsoft Excel. This method of presenting data to clients provides clear analysis of results, which can be referred to in final evaluations. The following charts show the difference between these formats using the same data presented in a variety of ways.

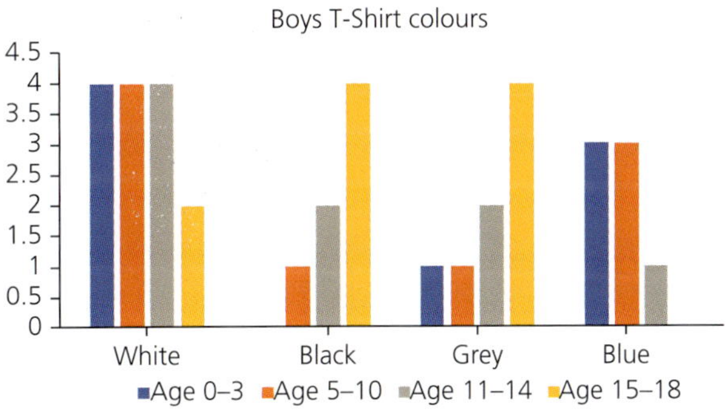


**Figure 1.14.4** Microsoft Excel bar chart to show the number of white, black, grey and blue T-shirts owned in different age ranges of boys.

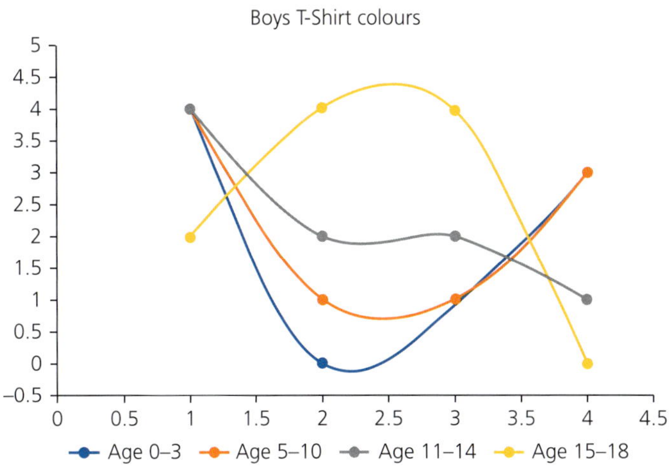


**Figure 1.14.6** A Microsoft Excel scatter diagram using the same data as above, where the X axis shows colours numbered from one to four.

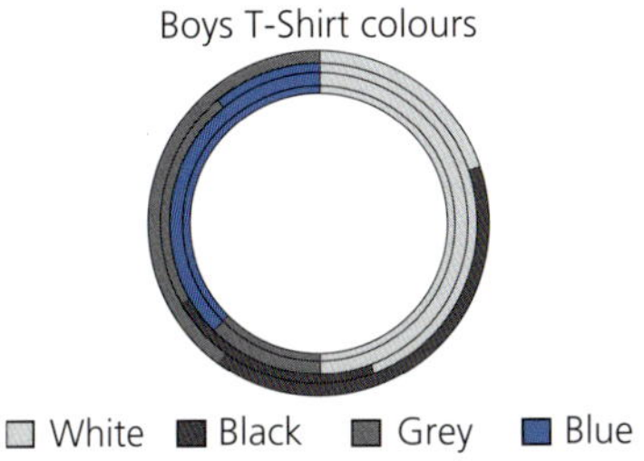


**Figure 1.14.5** A version of a Microsoft Excel pie chart called a 'donut' chart, where the outer ring gives the data for the oldest age range, and the inner ring for the youngest age range.

**Histograms** can also be used to show the boys T-shirt colours for different age ranges. This type of chart has bars of different heights – similar to a bar chart – but where the X axis gives ranges rather than single units, and the area of each bar represents the frequency. For the example in Figure 1.14.8, the X axis would be the age range of the boys.

In the student example below (Figure 1.14.9), a more creative approach is used to draw a chart. The bar chart gives a clear indication of the most popular design idea.

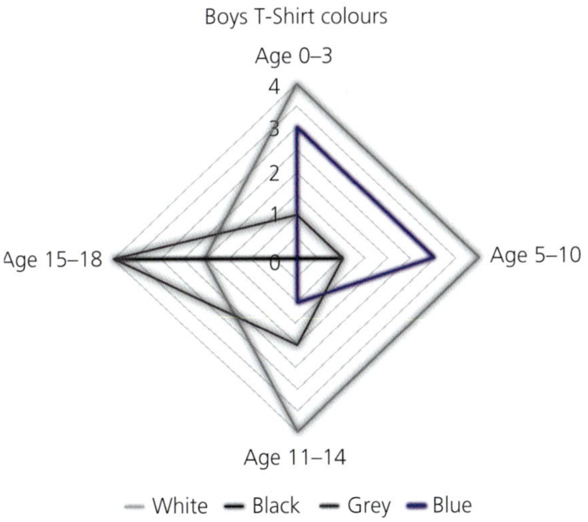


**Figure 1.14.7** Data presented in a Microsoft Excel radar chart.

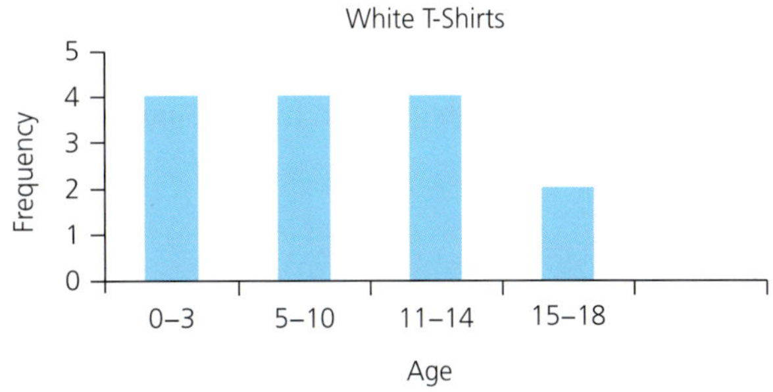


**Figure 1.14.8** Data presented in a Microsoft Excel histogram.

**Figure 1.14.9** Student example of a bar chart.

## MATHS LINK

**Using market data to make a pie chart.**

The table and pie chart below present the market data, user preferences and outcomes of market research. Calculate:

**a)** the fraction of sales for each shirt design

**b)** the percentage of sales, for each shirt design

**c)** how many degrees each section of the pie chart should have.

**Table 1.14.1** Market data to show blue shirt design sales in April 2017.

| Shirt design | Sales figures April 2017 | Fraction of sales | Percentage sales | Degrees |
|---|---|---|---|---|
| Blue flower print | 5,300 | 0.22 | 22% | 79 |
| Plain blue easy-care | 10,000 | 0.42 | 42% | 151 |
| Blue gingham | 5,000 | 0.21 | 21% | 76 |
| Blue chambray | 3,500 | 0.15 | 15% | 54 |

Total sold = 23,800 shirts

To find out the fraction of sales for each shirt design, divide number of each type of blue shirt sold by total number of blue shirts sold. For example, for blue flower print:

5,300 ÷ 23,800 = 0.22

To get the percentage of sales, take the fraction and times by 100, work to the nearest whole number. For example:

5,300 ÷ 23,800 = 22 per cent

To find out how many degrees each section of the pie chart should have, multiply each fraction by 360 degrees. For example:

0.22 × 360 = 79 degrees

**Figure 1.14.10** Using market data to make a Microsoft Excel pie chart to show blue shirt design sales in April 2017.

The pie chart shows in a clear visual form that:

- plain blue easy-care shirts sold in the greatest numbers during April 2017
- blue flower print and blue gingham shirts sold in almost equal numbers
- lowest sales were for blue chambray fabric shirts.

In the student example below (Figure 1.14.11), the findings from a target market questionnaire were analysed using bar and pie charts. The charts represent the results in a visual format, and show at a glance the preferences of the target market. The analysis of the findings and subsequent evaluation of results provide the direction for designing and the requirements for the design criteria; the representation of data is used to inform design decisions for the style of the dress.

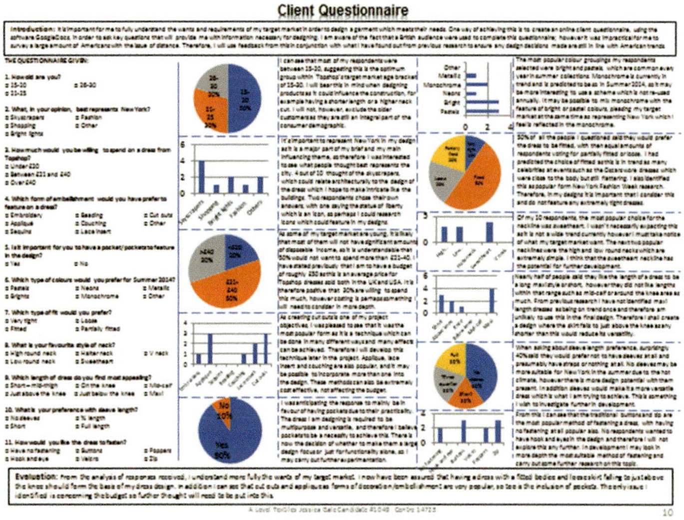


**Figure 1.14.11** Student example of using bar charts and pie charts to analyse research findings.

## 2D/3D sketching

Theme boards and mood boards are compiled by the design team to show the influences and inspiration for fashion and textile products, and to convey the mood or context for designing. The images, samples, text and colour swatches are also used to communicate the information in support of the design proposals, during presentation of the final designs to clients. (See Chapter 2.4 for further information.)

Designers draw design ideas to communicate design proposals to other members of the creative team, and to those concerned with product development, costing and production. Initial ideas are quick sketches, which might only focus on certain design features. Developed ideas are drawn in more detail as concepts take shape, and ideas are focused on particular aspects of the product.

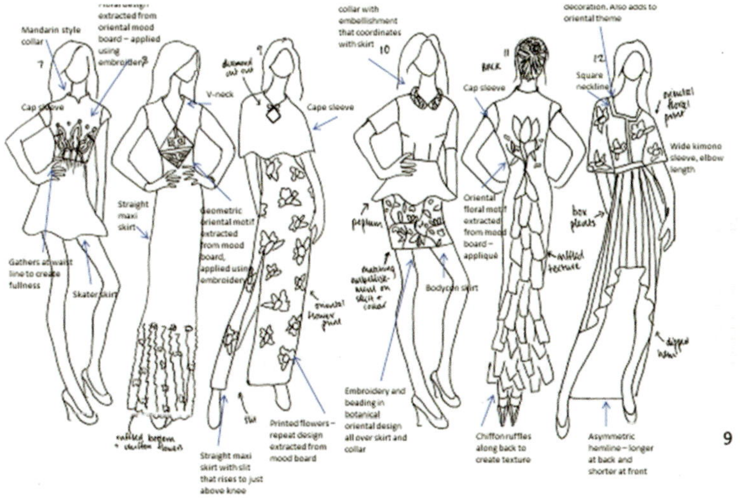


**Figure 1.14.12** Student example of initial design idea drawings.

It is essential to visualise the shape, style, patterns, colours, textures and product details being put forward by the designer, because using words alone is insufficient to convey the actual elements of the design. For example, the exact style needs to be shown in a sketch rather than just describing it in words so as to prevent time from being wasted developing incorrect samples. Two or more people talking about a new design must literally have a shared vision in the form of a sketch.

A system of classifying and numbering colours – called the **pantone colour matching system** – is used by designers to identify and communicate exact colours. This method of defining colours is successful because it is recognised worldwide, and provides a clear reference point for every colour. This enables the choice of colour to be understood by everyone working to design and manufacture the product. For example, matching colours of different components is possible between distant work places and suppliers.

Fashion illustrations are created to market designs to potential users. The illustration communicates the design of the fashion or textile product to the consumer, and conveys the style and mood of the piece.

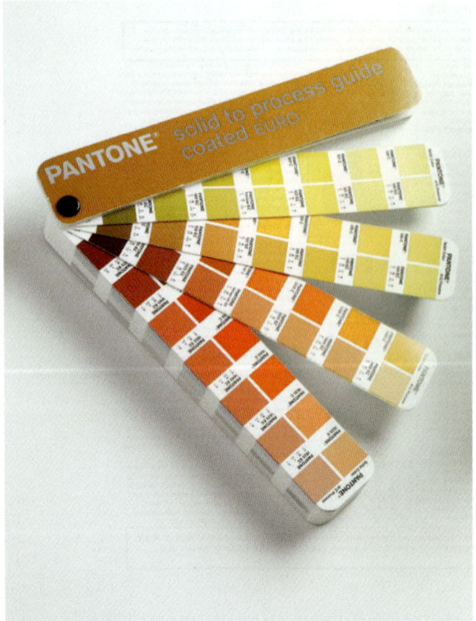


**Figure 1.14.13** Pantone colour swatches.

**Figure 1.14.14** Fashion designer working on technical drawings.

**KEY TERMS**

**Pantone colour matching system:** a standardised colour referencing system where each different colour has a code number to identify it. Pantone is the name of the company that developed and sells the system.

**Media:** art materials that are applied to a base. Singular version of media is an art medium.

**Rendering:** adding colour, texture and tone to drawings.

## The use of mixed media and rendering to enhance drawings

An art medium is a material that can be used to add marks and colours to a base. Materials might include pencil, paint, chalks, charcoal and crayon, while bases could be any type of paper or card. **Media** such as watercolour paints and coloured pencil crayons can be used together to add colour and texture to sketches. Paper can be painted or printed, and this can then be cut or torn into pieces to use in collage work, where the fragments of paper are pasted together to create a new surface pattern. Working in mixed media or using collage as a technique are creative ways to explore design ideas, and to trial different ways of representing them in visual presentations.

**Rendering** means to add colour, shading and texture to a sketch. Different media such as paint, coloured pens or chalks could be used to create different shades or tints of colours with various tonal effects. When you use tone in drawings to give lighter and darker areas, a 3D effect can be given to shapes. Texture can be added to suggest use of different types of fabrics in the design. For example, parallel marks made by a pen or pencil could convey the texture of corduroy fabric, or groups of diagonal lines in alternate directions could conjure up a Harris tweed.

Design drawings can be done by hand or using computer programs such as Adobe Illustrator, Adobe Photoshop and CorelDRAW. There are also some programs specifically developed for use in the fashion industry. Using these programs, existing designs can be adapted quickly, stored easily and can be shared instantly to anyone around the world. A design might start with a hand-drawn sketch which is scanned and further enhanced on the computer. Different colour options can be quickly trialled, drawings scaled and images viewed in 3D. Textures of fabrics can be scanned and incorporated in fashion sketches to show how fabrics could be used to make the garment.

In the student example below, a collage effect is created using images of corals to indicate pleats and gathers in fabric.

**Figure 1.14.15** Student example of presentation of design ideas.

## Dimensioning and details for manufacture

**Working drawings**, fashion flats or flats are accurate drawings of the product that include product dimensions. These technical drawings communicate the design of the product to those manufacturing it. The length, width and depth of each part of the product is shown on the drawing. This documents the product, and provides a standard against which the manufactured sample and samples from the production run can be checked for accuracy.

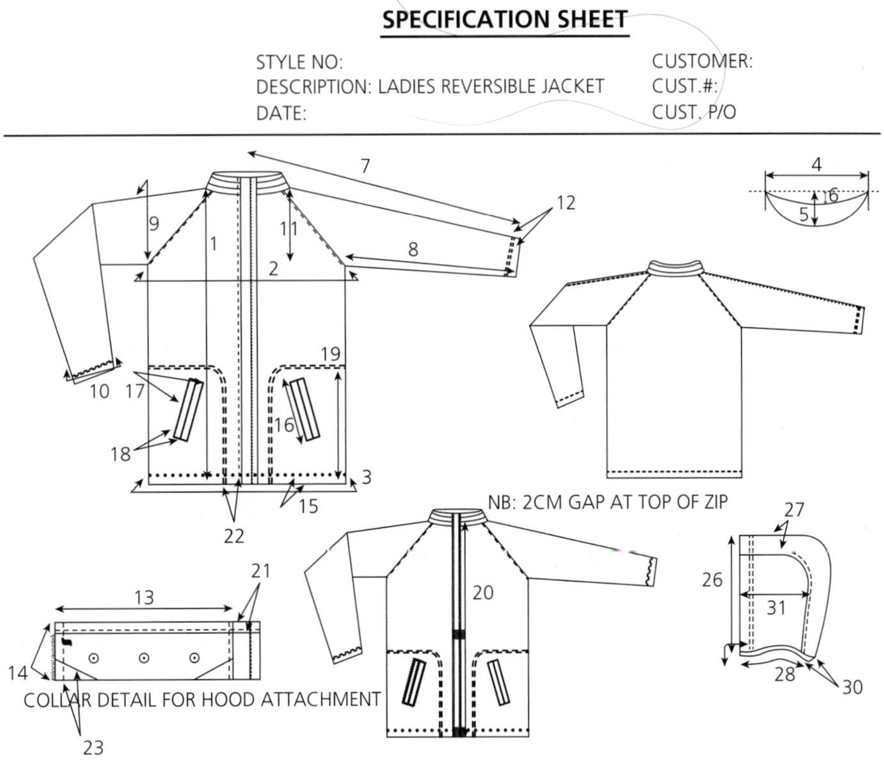


**Figure 1.14.16** Technical specification sheet created on Adobe Illustrator.

### KEY TERMS

**Graph:** a visual representation of numerical data plotted against a time scale.

**Bar chart:** columns or bars arranged in a chart to represent numerical data.

**Pie chart:** a circular diagram with wedge shaped slices that represent a proportion of the whole numerical data.

**Scatter diagram:** data points are plotted along the X and Y axes to show the relationship between two sets of data. Also known as a scattergram or scatterplot.

**Radar charts:** a chart with a central point and radiating arms to display multiple sets of data on a single chart. Also known as a spider chart.

**Histogram:** a chart with bars of different heights. It is similar to a bar chart but the X axis gives ranges rather than single units, and the area of each bar represents the frequency. For example, the X axis could be an age range for a target market.

> **KEY TERMS**
>
> **Geometry:** mathematics that is concerned with points, lines, shapes and space.
>
> **Datum point:** the base point or point of reference when measuring. For example, the waist is a datum point when measuring the length of a skirt.
>
> **Working drawings:** a set of technical drawings to show different viewpoints of a product. In addition to the overall product, design features can also be drawn close-up to show fine detail. Dimensions are included on the drawings for each part of the design, and all aspects such as position of pockets, fastenings, stitching and trims are included.

**Geometry** is the area of mathematics that is concerned with points, lines, shapes and space. Geometry is a feature of many fashion and textile product designs, for example 'V' necks, skirt gores (trapezoid panels of fabric), asymmetric styles and geometric print designs. Geometry should be understood and used in designing to create accurate shapes, and to work out requirements for product development.

Geometry is used to plan and demonstrate pattern dimensions. In the student example below, geometry has been used to work out the shape of the flat template for the 3D flounce around a skirt. The student first experiments with different methods of creating a flared-out skirt shape using a small-scale model and fabric test samples. They consider adding a gathered strip of fabric and using triangular panels to create the flared-out shape. From the investigations, the student decides to add a flounce to the skirt.

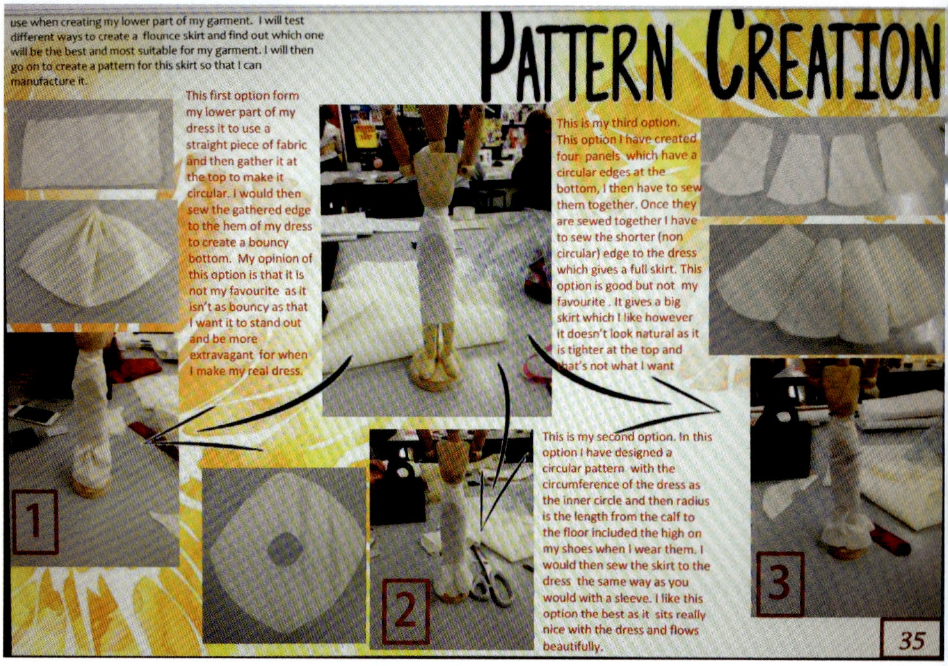


**Figure 1.14.17** Student example of using a small-scale model to test ideas.

**Figure 1.14.18** Student example of use of geometry and datum points.

## MATHS LINK

**Using geometry to calculate measurements and calculating percentage waste**

A diamond patchwork logo is made out of two equilateral triangles sewn together at the centre.

1 How much material is needed to produce one diamond logo?

2 12 logos are cut from a piece of fabric measuring 0.5m by 54cm. How much waste material will there be?

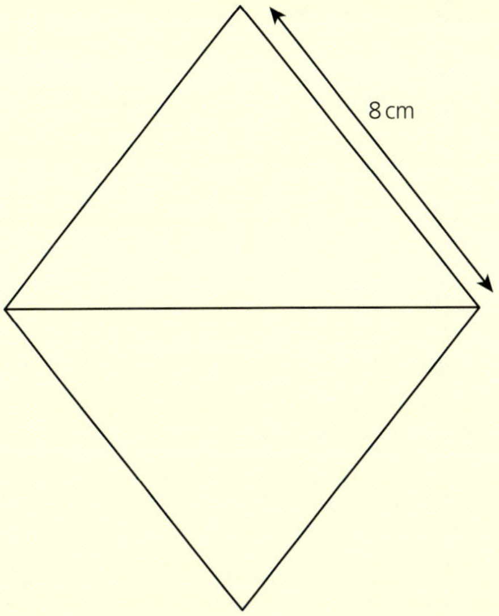


**Answer**

1 In the equilateral triangles all sides of the triangle are equal.
Dividing a triangle in half produces two identical right-angled triangles:

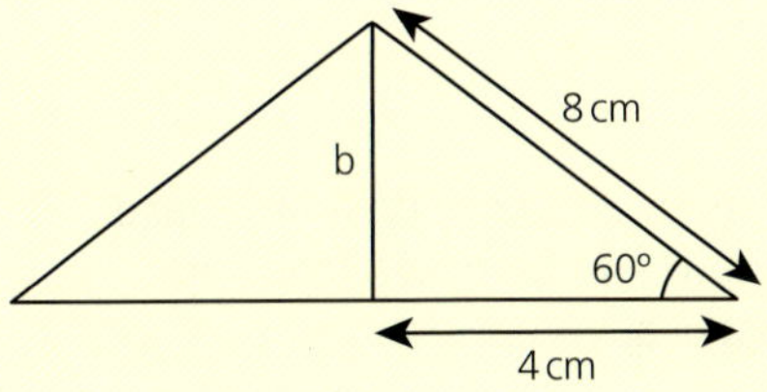


Using Pythagoras:

$a^2 + b^2 = c^2$

$b^2 = 8^2 - 4^2$

$b^2 = 64 - 16$

$b^2 = 48$

$b = \sqrt{48}$

$b = 6.93$cm

Area of the triangle = ½ × base × height

= ½ × 8 × 6.93

= 27.72cm$^2$

Area of the diamond = 27.72 × 2 = 55.44 cm$^2$

2 Fabric needed for 12 logos = 55.44 × 12 = 665.28cm$^2$ or 6.65m$^2$

Area of the fabric = 500 × 54 = 2700cm$^2$ or 27m$^2$

Once the diamond logos are cut, wasted material = 27 – 6.65 = 20.35m$^2$

### ACTIVITY

Carry out a survey to find out how your peers rate your design ideas from 1–10, where a score of one indicates an unappealing design and ten indicates a very appealing design. Add up the scores for each design idea.

Organise your collected data in a table similar to Figure 1.14.1. Instead of using sales figures, input the final score for each design idea. Complete the table to show percentages and degrees.

Draw a circle and use a protractor to measure the degrees for each design idea. Colour each section of the pie chart. Label each section and make a title for the pie chart.

What conclusions can you make from your pie chart?

### KEY POINTS

- Final design written reports are formal documents to put forward the design proposal, and summarise the findings of testing and evaluating the final design.
- Graphs have X and Y axes, with the unit of measure on the left side (Y axis) and the timeline along the bottom of the graph (X axis). They represent numerical data in a visual form.
- It is important to select the type of chart that best displays the particular information you need to communicate.
- Designers draw design ideas to communicate design proposals to other members of the creative team and to those concerned with product development, costing and production.
- Two or more people talking about a new design must literally have a shared vision in the form of a sketch, so that there is no misunderstanding about the design.
- Working drawings document the product, and provide a standard against which the manufactured sample and samples from the production run can be checked for accuracy.

## Check your knowledge and understanding

1 What points should be covered in a final design report?

2 What are the differences between graphs, tables and charts?

3 Why are design ideas sketched?

4 Give some examples of how use of mixed media can add colour, shade and texture to drawings.

5 What are working drawings also known as?

## Further reading

Tallon, K. *Digital Fashion Illustration*

www.bbc.co.uk/education/clips/z893cdm

# Section 2

In this section you will learn about the following:

- **2.1** Design methods and processes
- **2.2** Design theory
- **2.3** How technology and cultural changes can impact the work of designers
- **2.4** Design processes
- **2.5** Critical analysis and evaluation
- **2.6** Selecting appropriate tools, equipment and processes
- **2.7** Accuracy in design and manufacture
- **2.8** Responsible design
- **2.9** Design for manufacture and project management
- **2.10** National and international standards in product design (A-level)

# 2.1 Design methods and processes

**LEARNING OUTCOMES**

By the end of this section you should have developed a knowledge and understanding of:

- different approaches to user centred design (UCD) including designing to meet a need
- the use of primary and secondary data to inform design decisions
- the use of anthropometric data and percentiles, as well as ergonomic data, when designing products
- development of a design proposal
- the planning and manufacture of a prototype solution
- the evaluation of a prototype solution to inform further development.

When fashion and textile designers and product developers work on new designs, they need to consider the purpose of the design and who will use it. Initially they need to be sure that they are creating a desirable product for customers to buy, and that there is a potential demand for the product. During development, there are issues that will influence the form that the design takes, as well as how it will be manufactured. At each stage of the design process, the work is tested and evaluated to ensure the final prototype meets the requirements of the brief. A series of investigations and further developments takes place, and a number of prototypes (or test pieces) are made, before the design challenge is met with a final outcome that is ready for production. This route through designing is referred to as an **iterative design process**. (You can read in more detail about this process in Chapter 2.4.)

## Iterative design processes: user centred design

**User centred design (UCD)** is about developing a new product according to what the consumers need or want. During its development, the design of the product is frequently checked with the likely users to ensure it is still relevant to them. For this reason, it is also referred to as user driven development (UDD).

UCD involves:

- identifying the target market and how, when and under what conditions they will use the product
- understanding the requirements for a successful design

- creating design ideas, samples and prototypes
- testing and evaluating design ideas, developments, final design and manufactured product.

The new product is tested at every stage – from first concept based on user requirements, through all developments, to tests on the final commercial product in use. This approach to designing, developing and producing a product is an iterative process; one design proposal can be explored, modelled, tested, evaluated and modified several times before the final version is complete.

UCD is focused on finding out the real opinions of the likely user. Product developers need to know if the design proposal is desirable, useful, performs well and satisfies the customer. If the product is only tested by those involved in developing the product, they would miss issues raised in feedback from a first-time user of the product. By showing potential consumers initial concepts and storyboards through to working prototypes and observing the final product in use, they can gather invaluable feedback.

## Designing to meet a need

In fashion and textiles, the demand for a new product might be driven by the need to find a solution to a problem, or by the desire to have the latest fashion trend or designer piece. There are different types of need:

- A gap in the market might be identified and a textile product developed to fulfil the needs of the consumer, for example a textile product or piece of clothing for a new trend in leisure activities.
- New high street fashion products are developed according to a predicted trend; this desire to have the latest fashion item is fuelled by advertising and marketing.
- For top designer products, the demand is created by those seeking something innovative, different and exclusive. The final designs are presented on the catwalk and orders are taken for bespoke garments that can be further modified to meet the individual needs of clients.

## Investigations to inform the use of primary and secondary data

**Primary data** is gathered directly by businesses. Alternatively, businesses can pay someone else to research and present the data about the potential for product development. New data can be collected using:

- questionnaires
- shop surveys including observing consumer behaviour
- social media surveys
- telephone, online or face-to-face interviews
- **focus group** meetings
- **consumer panels**.

In the student example below (Figure 2.1.1), the research plan shows the primary research activities that will be carried out. The sheet is effective because the student states the purpose of planning the research in the introduction and evaluation. Each type of primary research is listed and described, and the student is clear about what they hope to find out from the research. These investigations will provide the market research information that will help the student justify decisions they will make later in the project.

### KEY TERMS

**Iterative design process:** a cycle of sampling, testing, analysing and refining a design until the final design is created.

**User centred design (UCD):** developing a new product according to what the consumers need or want. Sometimes referred to as user driven development (UDD).

**Primary data:** information collected from research activities.

**Focus group:** a one-off discussion group with participants from the target market, who rate ideas for a new product and feed back their opinions.

**Demographics:** the study of a population or groups within it to find out statistical information such as age, gender, marital status, income and occupation.

**Customer panels:** a group of potential customers who are regularly consulted on their opinions about a new product design at different stages of its development.

**Research Plan**

**Introduction:** I am now able to see what I need to do in order to gain sufficient research for my project which will help me justify decisions I make later in the project, and help me understand the brief in more detail and what will be expected of me. I will now create a moodboard which be my first point of inspiration.

| RESEARCH | HOW? | WHY? |
|---|---|---|
| **Moodboard** | Using all pictures that I took myself on a recent trip to New York, I will choose a range which I believe best represents the many aspects of the city and present them in a collage form. This will then show the most iconic features, allowing me to be inspired. | As the brief states that the dress must be inspired by the city of New York, by creating a moodboard of pictures from the location I will enhance my understanding of it. This will therefore allow me to be more informed when I decide on design aspects and be able to reflect New York as the main theme and create colour palettes to use when designing. |
| **Client Profile** | I will create a montage of pictures, some of which will be my own, which I believe represent the typical person who would buy the dress I am creating. I will also produce a small summary of their life which will further bring them to life and aid me when considering design requirements. | It will make me understand the needs of my target market more fully and I can use it as a point of reference when struggling to make a decision regarding whether people would like what I am considering. |
| **Fashion Research: How trends differ in London and New York** | I will look at the UK and US versions of websites for two high street chains which are present in both countries and see how their main lines differ in terms of which trends are present. I will then look at a British and American blogger and see how their styles are different, taking them to be a representation of their country. | As my brief specifically states this is for the American branch of Topshop, I need to understand how their taste, requirements, trends and view of fashion is different from British peoples and my own. If I were not to do this, the dress may not be suitable or popular for the target market; resulting in poor sales and ultimately an unsuccessful project. |
| **Shop Report** | I will go into a Topshop store and take photos of dresses they currently have in their range as this is the brand specifically noted in my brief. I will then analyse the dresses and identify if there are any common techniques used which I could consider for my final design. Lastly, I will create sketches which were inspired by those dresses when I saw them. | I will be able to understand in more detail the way in which Topshop make their dresses, materials they use, which styles are common within ranges and what my design will need to be like in order to fit into their collections. By visiting other shops, I will be able to compare these factors and take away aspects which I may transfer into my designs. |
| **Product Analysis** | I will take pictures of the product to show all the small details, including blow ups, and then analyse the negative and positive points of the design. From this I will then list modifications which could be made, and determine whether it would be suitable for my target market. | By deeply analysing an existing product which would also suit my brief, I am able to see the strengths in it which I may wish to transfer into my designs but also see the flaws. This will allow me to make decisions as to ensure that my garment meets all of the requirements for it success. |
| **New York Fashion Week trend board** | I am going to choose pictures of dresses from the runway at New York Fashion Week 2013 which I find to be inspirational and annotate them with thoughts and how they are applicable to my project. | This will give me inspiration for my designs and further educate me on the spring/summer 2014 trends which will guide me on the style of my dress. |
| **Client questionnaire** | I will create a survey online using GoogleDocs and, after this, ask a selection of people to complete it within the target market ages of 15 to 30. I will then analyse the results and produce charts and graphs to display the results, as well as writing my thoughts as to how they will influence the design of the dress. | This will give me invaluable research which will help me with decision making during the process, for example what requirements the target market will have and how the dress can be made a success. It will also ensure that the design of the dress is suitable for its intended purpose. |

**Evaluation:** I now have a detailed plan of the research to carry out, clearly focused on what I aim to achieve from each piece. The ideas of areas to research came from carrying out the design task analysis with the purpose of helping me understand my target market better and critically identifying the difference between US and UK fashion trends. I believe that I will learn a great deal about these key areas by completing the research I planned.

A Level Textiles Jessica Gale Candidate #1049 Centre 14723 17

**Figure 2.1.1** Student example of planning primary research.

**Secondary data** can be gathered free of charge from printed publications or online, or purchased from specialist market research companies. Secondary data includes:

- trend forecasts
- sales and company reports
- government publications
- media sources such as magazines and newspapers
- internet research, for example product reviews
- industry and trade association publications
- educational institution reports such as articles and university dissertations.

## Market research

Market research consists of collecting data to determine whether there is a need or desire for a particular product, and to find out about the target market, competitors and market trends.

- **Quantitative data** is the factual information gathered from market research. It is often in numerical form and can be collected by measuring 'how many'. The question is usually a closed question with a 'tick the box' choice of answer or a 'yes/no' response to the question. The data is sorted into rank order or into categories, and statistically analysed.
- **Qualitative data** is the opinions of people, or observations of their behaviour collected through market research. It is often data about human behaviour gathered from open questions, which encourage descriptive answers explaining their point of view.

Market research helps a business to decide whether to continue developing an idea or product design before money has been spent on the full development or manufacturing of the product.

### KEY TERMS

**Quantitative data:** the factual information gathered from market research. It is often in numerical form and can be collected by measuring 'how many'. Research-gathering questions are usually closed questions, and data is sorted into rank order or categories and then statistically analysed.

**Qualitative data:** consists of opinions, behaviours and viewpoints. It is data about human behaviour collected from open questions that encourage descriptive answers.

**Secondary data:** information gathered from existing sources of researched data.

### Interviews

Interviews with the target market can be face to face or over the telephone. If face to face, body language can be observed in addition to recording the spoken responses, and product prototypes can be tried out to get feedback about usability and product appeal. Quantitative interviews – where facts and brief answers are collected – may take the form of pre-scripted questions which are read out, whereas qualitative in-depth interviews may feature indirect or open questions based on a topic guide; this allows the interviewee to fully explain their point of view. The results from telephone quantitative interviews can be instantly put into a computer system for analysis, using a computer aided telephone interviewing (CATI) system.

## ACTIVITY

**Representation of data used to inform design decisions and evaluation of outcomes.**

A variety of different tables, charts and graphs can be used to represent data and analyse market research findings. Displaying the data in a visual form clearly communicates the information that will influence design decisions during product development. The data collected from testing during product development and testing of the final prototype can also be presented and analysed using these techniques.

An online questionnaire was used to carry out market research to find out the preference of the target market for women's travel wear gilets and there were 80 respondents.

The following results were collected:

**Table 2.1.1** Table showing findings from market research.

| Age range | Preferred length of gilet | Preferred gilet colour | Most essential feature in gilet |
|---|---|---|---|
| 15–17 | Short 72/Medium 7/Long 1 | Most: white<br>Least: mushroom | Streamlined style |
| 18–24 | Short 60/Medium 17/Long 3 | Most: blue<br>Least: white | Designed to accommodate electrical devices |
| 25–34 | Short 10/Medium 65/Long 5 | Most: black<br>Least: white | Multiple secure pockets |
| 35–54 | Short 2/Medium 70/ Long 8 | Most: navy<br>Least: black | Light weight |
| 55+ | Short 0/Medium 35/Long 45 | Most: mushroom<br>Least: blue | Insect repellent |

1 What kind of graphs or charts could be used to represent the data in the table above? Explain how the graphs or charts could help you to evaluate the research findings.

2 Draw a graph to represent the data or the preferred length of a gilet.

### Human factors

When designing products for use by people, **anthropometrics** and **ergonomics** need to be considered so that the design will fit the size of the person it is intended for, and so that it works as planned. (See Anthropometric data and percentiles and Ergonomic data (pages 182-3) for further information.)

### Focus groups

Focus groups are set up by market researchers to find out the opinions of the target market. An initial questionnaire is used to screen participants. This ensures that the focus group is made up of those likely to buy the products being tested, and so that there is a good spread of demographics in the group. This means there will be variety within the target market of different ages, gender and any other appropriate characteristics. There are usually between five and ten participants in a focus group – a number that is small enough to promote discussion yet large enough to give a range of opinions.

Once recruited, the discussion group is brought together in a one-off meeting lasting one or two hours, to respond to a set of pre-planned questions. A facilitator or moderator guides the structured discussion, and actively encourages each individual to express their thoughts, so that the conversation is open ended and not dominated by any particular member of the group. The participants may be asked to consider design concepts or to examine a product prototype. The discussion points are recorded to analyse comments afterwards, and the group may also be observed to pick up on body language and reactions to issues covered.

> **KEY TERMS**
>
> **Anthropometrics:** the standard measurements of the size and shape of the human body.
>
> **Ergonomics:** the relationship between people and the products they use.
>
> **Pattern grading:** to scan or trace the pattern and mark additional measurements at key points. These are used to adjust the pattern's proportions to give a range of different sizes for the same pattern.
>
> **Percentiles:** a method of grouping statistical data based on percentages.

Focus groups that meet regularly to feed back on each stage of product development are known as **customer panels**. In the student example below, a group of people likely to buy the parka-style coat is consulted to find out the positive and negative points about the design ideas.

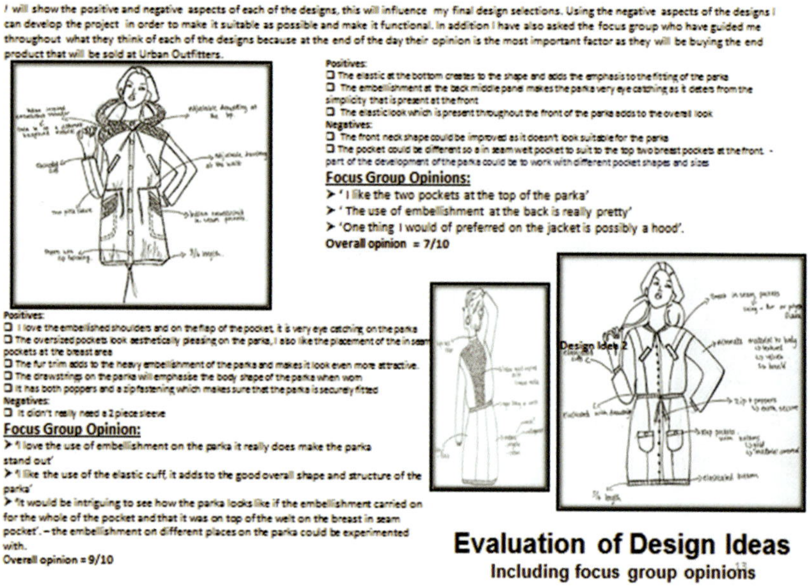


**Figure 2.1.2** Student example of testing and evaluating using focus group opinions.

## Product analysis and evaluation

Researchers and designers carry out investigations to find out what is already on the market and what their competitors are selling. They consider what already appeals to the target market, and determine the successful aspects of other products. The research data is used to inform their design decisions when developing their own products. (You can read in more detail about product analysis and evaluation in Chapter 1.8.)

## Anthropometric data and percentiles

Anthropometry tables give the standard measurements of the average human body. Measurements such as height, chest and waist are shown for each standard size of person. The data is used by designers to guide decisions about dimensions of the products they are designing, so that they meet the target market requirements. Pattern graders use the anthropometric data to gauge the differences in the pattern pieces for each different standard size. Designers, product developers, manufacturers and

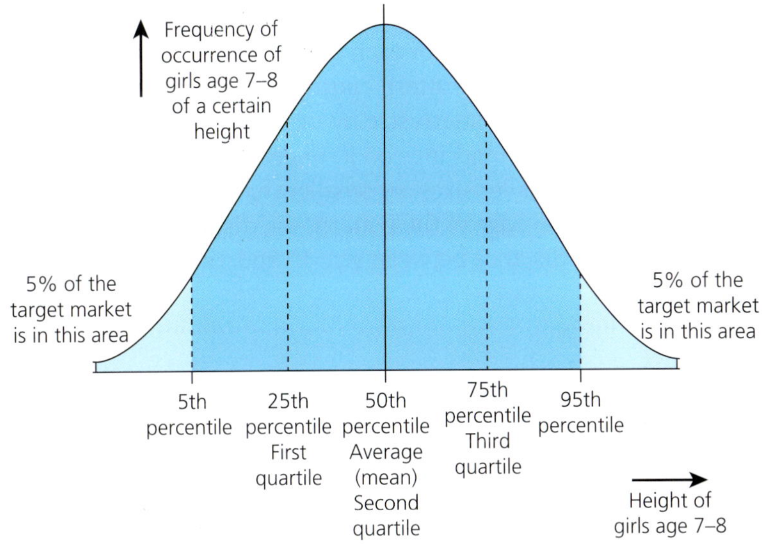


**Figure 2.1.3** Use of anthropometric data as part of research and designing.

retailers use standardised size charts to ensure that products are uniform in size and meet customer expectations.

The average or mean measurement is shown in the anthropometric data, however, within the target market there will be a great deal of variation in body size and shape. For example, when measuring the height of girls between the ages of seven and eight, there will be some very short and very tall girls, but most will be somewhere in between the two extremes. The designer needs to consider whether they are just designing for the average human body, or if the product style could be designed to suit a broader range of measurements. For example, elastic could be used in a skirt waistband to accommodate a range of different waist sizes.

The graph below shows how the variation in height of girls between the ages of seven and eight can be plotted. Percentiles are used in the measurement of statistics to indicate how a range of measurements can be grouped based on percentages. For example, in Figure 2.1.3, the average height is marked as the 50th percentile. This is the highest point of the graph, and the most frequently occurring height of girls in this age range. The 5th percentile shows that 5 per cent of girls (or 1 in 20) are at this height or shorter. The 95th percentile shows that 5 per cent (or 1 in 20) are at this height or taller. The 25th percentile is referred to as the first quartile, the 50th percentile as the second quartile and the 75th percentile as the third quartile.

When a designer is using anthropometric data to inform design decisions, they need to be clear about whether they are making the product to fit only the average size (at the 50th percentile), or whether they will make it work for a much broader range of people – for example from the 5th to the 95th percentile.

## Ergonomic data

**Ergonomics** concerns the way that people and products interact. Data can be collected from the study of how humans move and how they complete physical tasks. For example, by finding out how the body shape changes during walking, bending and stretching, the amount of stretch required in fabric or the volume of fabric required in a garment can be decided. A successful fashion and textile design will take into consideration the comfort, ease of fit and usability of the product. It is essential that a garment can be put on and taken off without too much difficulty.

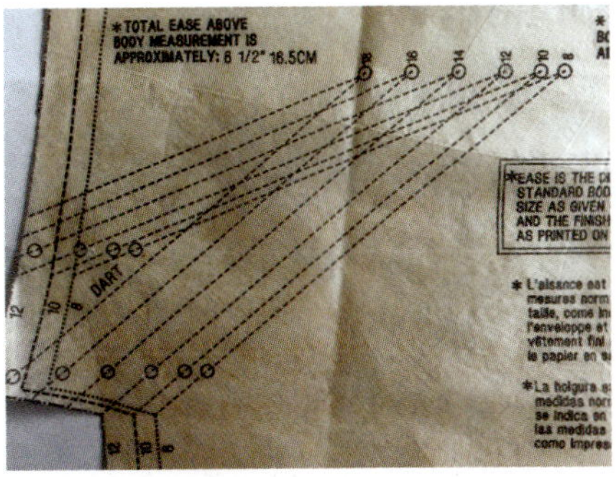


**Figure 2.1.4** Commercial pattern with pattern grading for sizes 8 to 18.

Pattern designers use anthropometric and ergonomic data when drafting patterns for clothing, and when **grading patterns** for different sizes of the same design. When designing the pattern, the size and shape of each pattern piece is developed to style the garment as the designer intended, and to fit the standard size of body with an allowance for ease of fit and movement in use.

The sample size pattern is the base for increasing or decreasing the pattern dimensions for larger and smaller sizes of the original pattern. For example, a fashion garment may be produced in a range of sizes from size 8 to size 18, and therefore requires a graded pattern for each of the different sizes. The pattern is altered using computerised pattern cutting software, which applies standard grading rules to alter the pattern size by increments. Figure 2.1.4 shows a commercial pattern with markings on it, to give the different sizes. The increments between the smaller sizes are smaller than those between the larger sizes. For example, at the edge of the pattern, the distance between size 8 and 10 is smaller than the distance between size 10 and 12.

### MATHS LINK

**The use of ergonomic and anthropometric data when designing products**

**Example**

A pattern grader is working out the increments for changing a size 10 pattern into a size 8 and a size 12.

The length of the pattern piece for a size 10 is 26cm.

**a)** If the size 8 length is 1.5% shorter than the size 10, work out the new pattern piece length for size 8.

**b)** If the size 12 length is 1.75% longer than the size 10, work out the new pattern piece length for size 12.

**Answer**

The size 10 length of 26cm is 100%.

**a)** The size 8 length is 1.5% shorter than the size 10 length: 100 – 1.5 = 98.5% of the size 10 length.

1% of 26cm = 0.26cm

0.5% of 26cm = 0.13cm

98.5% of 26cm = (0.26 × 98) + 0.13 = 25.61cm

**The size 8 length is 25.61cm.**

**b)** The size 12 length is 1.75% larger than the size 10 length: 100 + 1.75 = 101.75% of the size 10 length.

1% of 26cm = 0.26cm

0.75% of 26cm = 0.195cm

101.75% of 26cm = (0.26 × 101) + 0.195 = 26.455cm

**The size 12 length is 26.46cm.**

## Development of a design proposal

You can read about development of a design proposal in Chapter 1.8.

## Planning and manufacture of a prototype solution

The final prototype is made by the sample machinist, who makes it using the same machinery, techniques and processes that full production would employ. This allows designers to see whether further modifications are required to make the product design suitable for manufacturing using cost effective processes. Planning for manufacture is also an essential aspect of quality assurance, to make sure that proposed techniques will result in an acceptable quality of finish, and that standards can be met.

## Evaluation of a prototype solution to inform further development

Iterative design involves cycles of developing samples – testing and evaluating the samples and further developing them, then testing those developed samples to see how further modifications and improvements can be made.

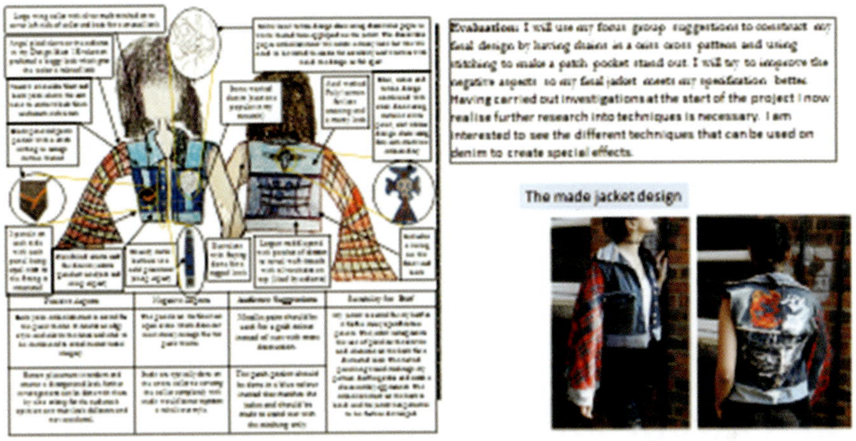


**Figure 2.1.5** Student example of an iterative design process testing and evaluating a prototype denim jacket.

In the student example above, the prototype denim jacket is tested and evaluated. These investigations suggest the need for further research to find out how different techniques can be used to create special effects on denim. In the student example below, the student continues with the design process to research a wide variety of techniques. They use secondary research sources on the internet, and primary research is performed to find out how to create special effects on denim.

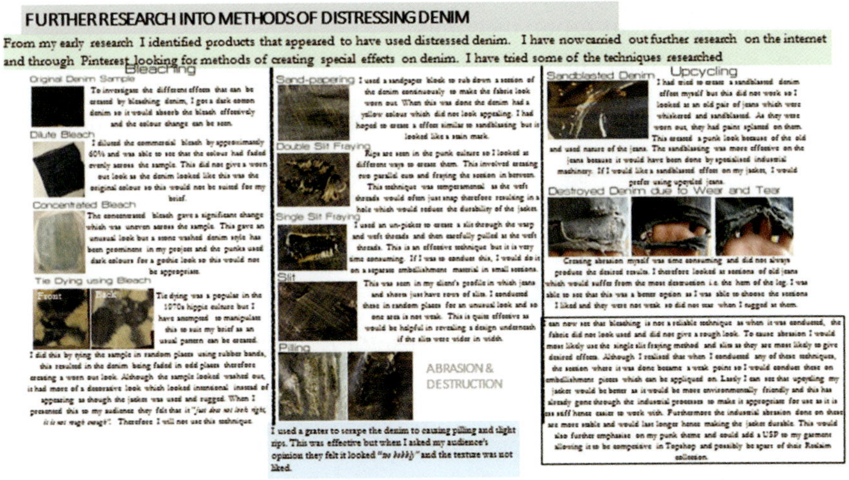


**Figure 2.1.6** Student example of further research in an iterative design process.

> **ACTIVITY**
>
> Secondary market research: Imagine that you are a fashion accessory designer working for a sportswear brand, and you have been asked to design a gym bag for women. Use the internet to search for existing information about products made by competing companies.
>
> Read existing product reviews to find out some opinions that the target market has. How could you present your findings?

## KEY POINTS

- UCD is about developing a new product according to what the consumers need or want. During its development, the design is frequently checked with the likely users to ensure the product is still relevant to them.
- Market research concerns collecting data to determine whether there is a need or desire for a particular product, and to find out about the target market, competitors and market trends.
- Focus groups and customer panels are set up by market researchers to find out the opinions of the target market.
- Product analysis and evaluation is completed to find out what already appeals to the target market, and to determine the successful aspects of other products.
- Anthropometric and ergonomic data is used by designers to guide decisions about the dimensions of the products they are designing. This ensures they meet the target market's requirements.

## Check your knowledge and understanding

1. What is meant by the term user centred design?
2. If UCD stands for user centred design, what does UDD stand for?
3. Which one of the following is **not** a technique for gathering primary research data?
   - **A** writing questionnaires
   - **B** carrying out shop surveys, including observing consumer behaviour
   - **C** setting up social media surveys
   - **D** searching for existing data in media sources such as magazines and newspapers
   - **E** carrying out telephone, online or face-to-face interviews
   - **F** holding focus group meetings
   - **G** questioning consumer panels.
4. What is the difference between anthropometrics and ergonomics?
5. Give two other ways to describe the 50th percentile.

## Further reading

Hyman, M. and Sierra, J. *Market Research Kit For Dummies*

www.ergonomics4schools.com/lzone/anthropometry.htm

www.mathsisfun.com/data/percentiles

# 2.2 Design theory

**LEARNING OUTCOMES**

By the end of this section you should have developed a knowledge and understanding of:

- how key historical design styles, design movements and influential designers helped to shape fashion and textile design and manufacture
- Art Nouveau, Art Deco, pop art, Minimalism and punk design styles and movements
- the work of Chanel, Dior, Vivienne Westwood and Alexander McQueen, and how the work of these influential designers represents the principles of different design movements.

If you are studying at A-level you should also have developed a knowledge and understanding of:

- the work of Paul Poiret, Mary Quant, Yves St Laurent and Pierre Cardin.

## Design influences

New aesthetic ideas and styles are prompted by social and cultural changes, and by new technological advances in machinery and materials. Economic and political developments influence the aspirations of each new generation and give rise to new ways of thinking. Design movements of the twentieth century were greatly influenced by the two world wars, the changes in attitude to women's role in society and cycles of austerity and prosperity. Fashion and textiles are generally flamboyant and colourful in times of plenty, whereas during wartime and economic depressions, colours become muted and styling has less volume, using fewer materials.

New production techniques, for example of knitted fabrics in the twentieth century, influence the design of fashion and textiles products. New technologies in textile manufacturing are exploited to produce innovative designs. Developments in modern materials – for example synthetic materials – influence the design of fashion and textiles products by offering new fabrics with more aesthetic appeal, better performance and recently, increased sustainability. (For more information, please refer to Chapter 2.3 How technology and cultural changes can impact the work of designers.)

Artists working in different areas of art inspire each other, and the cross-over between the visual arts, music, theatre and dance have influenced both individual fashion and textile designers as well as design styles and movements. An example of this is the Yves Saint Laurent Mondrian dress

(Figure 2.2.22). This particular dress, based on Piet Mondrian's block colour painting from 1930, became an iconic 1960s dress. Please see the Yves Saint Laurent section below for more information about the link between art and fashion.

## Design styles and movements

The work of key fashion and textiles designers has been at the forefront of cultural shifts in artistic ideals and styles. When a group of artists and designers share the same approach to style during a particular period of time, it is known as an art or design movement. Some of the important historical design styles and movements of the twentieth century are described below.

### Art Nouveau

**Art Nouveau**, meaning 'new art' in French, was a decorative art form popular in Europe between 1890 and 1910. It featured organic flowing lines in stylised designs inspired by nature, especially plant forms. Art Nouveau influenced paintings, fashion and textiles, interior design, architecture, metal work, jewellery, ceramics, posters and illustration.

Liberty of London is a long-established textiles company that is well known for its high quality printed floral designs for fine fashion and accessories. The original 1900s print design, features organic shapes and patterns inspired by violets; the olive green and rust brown colours are typical of Art Nouveau designs.

Young, graceful women with flowing dresses and flowers were popular subjects for paintings and posters. The decorative border and halo design around the woman's head in the Alphonse Mucha art work below were frequent motifs in Art Nouveau designs.

**Figure 2.2.1** Fashion illustration by Alphonse Mucha.

Some of the most well-known examples of Art Nouveau include:

- Liberty fabric prints
- Charles Rennie Mackintosh's textiles
- Aubrey Beardsley's drawings
- Alphonse Mucha's poster designs
- Gustav Klimt's paintings
- Antoni Gaudi's architecture
- Metro station entrances in Paris with ornate metalwork.

### Art Deco

**Art Deco** was named after the Exposition Internationale des Arts Décoratifs et Industriels Modernes, an international exhibition of modern decorative and industrial arts held in Paris in 1925. The style was most popular in the 1920s and 1930s; it influenced the design of buildings, fashion and textiles, interior design, transport, jewellery and many everyday objects such as radios.

Art Deco designs were very modern, often geometric, colourful and bold with sleek lines, reflecting the forms and energy of the 'machine age'. Luxurious travel for the elegant rich included streamlined Art Deco cars, trains and ocean liners. The style was influenced by contemporary modern art such as Cubism and Fauvism, and exotic cultures such as

**Figure 2.2.2** Art Deco fashion illustration 1925 by George Barbier.

**Figure 2.2.3** Simultaneous dresses 1925 by Sonia Delaunay.

that of ancient Egypt and the Orient. Sergei Diaghilev's Ballets Russes – a touring ballet company that brought talented artists and designers together in productions based on Russian folklore – was a major influence on Art Deco. The ballet company brought great artists and designers together to put on stunning productions; the stage sets and costumes inspired audiences to want new fashions.

New technology for printing posters and fashion illustrations made it possible to reproduce very colourful images. The use of fine materials and high-quality craftmanship made Art Deco a glamorous style. High-end fashion often featured opulent, colourful, rich materials such as silks and velvets with expensive beadwork.

Art Deco fashions included the cloche hat that hugged the shape of the head, shorter hair styles known as the 'bob' and much shorter more practical hemlines that revealed women's legs. Tight, restrictive corsets were no longer fashionable; clothing was more practical to reflect the needs of modern women who had active lifestyles, were working, playing sports, swimming, going to the movies and dancing to jazz music. Trousers started to be worn by women. The fashion silhouette was less curvy, with a flattening of the chest to give a more boyish figure. This silhouette was known as the **'garçonne' look** which featured a dropped waistline. Some of the modern dresses were tubular, with pleats, gathers or slits at the knees to allow movement, as seen in the fashion illustration above (Figure 2.2.2). This style of dress was known as a 'flapper' dress, and was worn by modern, young women.

Sonia Delaunay was a painter and a fashion, textiles and costume designer whose colourful, geometric designs decorated fabrics, interiors and even car paint work. The dresses in the fashion illustration in Figure 2.2.3 are called 'simultaneous dresses' because the colourful flat pattern designs could be used across artforms – from paintings to fabric prints and embroideries, or to give colour and pattern to any other product design.

## Pop art

In the 1950s and 1960s in Britain and America, everyday images from popular culture were made into an art form known as **pop art**. Bold, bright colours and images seen in food packaging, comics, adverts, pop music and Hollywood movies were featured in this art movement's paintings.

The art pieces were about art for a young audience, who typically wanted something of the modern times that had gimmicky mass appeal to the consumer society, but only for a short time before the next popular artwork replaced it. Lichtenstein's comic book painting 'Ohh...alright...' is created using dots of colour to represent the printing techniques of the mass media comics.

The 'Souper Dress' is a pop art fashion piece designed by Andy Warhol. This colourful, iconic 1960s design was mass produced, inexpensive, appealed to the young and was disposable. The repeating pattern of tins of Campbell's soup made the wearer part of the commercial culture of the times.

The bright primary colours of pop art influenced the fashion colour trends in the 1960s. High-volume production of fashionable clothes – often made

**Figure 2.2.4** Yohji Yamamoto fall/winter 2012/2013 collection.

from new synthetic fabrics such as shiny, wet-look PVC, easy-care acrylics and polyesters – made popular fashions affordable for the youth market.

## Minimalism

**Minimalism** in art concerns simple and pared down abstract shapes and forms seen in paintings in the 1960s. Minimalist paintings consisted of simple geometric shapes or sometimes a seemingly single coloured canvas, such as the 'Monochrome White Painting' painted by Li Yuan-Chia, or the 'black' canvases painted by Reinhardt, which feature extremely muted shades of black.

In fashion and textiles, the popularity of pared down clothing in neutral muted tones with clean and sculptural shapes is often a reaction against excessive decoration, feminine frills and flounces in current fashions. New fashions reflect changes in society, and when times become austere, minimalist fashion is seen as an antidote to the excesses and complexity of colour, pattern and ornamentation seen in fashions of more affluent times. Minimalist fashion eliminates non-essentials and has a refinement of form and styling.

The use of new technologies and modern materials to sculpt dramatic yet simple shapes create a fresh and modern direction in clothing. Fastenings are discrete, and clothing appears to be gender neutral and functional. Minimalist clothing is considered to be sustainable because it is made from quality fabrics, is durable, versatile and outlasts other fashion trends. It became popular in the 1990s as a reaction to the glamourous 1980s fashions, and is sometimes referred to as 'urban chic'. In the photograph above, Yohji Yamamoto's dress in monochrome black and white drapes over the body in a sculptural form.

## Punk

**Punk** rock music developed in the early to mid-1970s in the United States, United Kingdom and Australia, and was initially popular with dispirited, unemployed youngsters. Punk bands were anti-establishment, and political in their song lyrics and appearance. Punk music is fast paced with counter rhythms that whip the audience into disturbing dance moves such as 'the pogo', which is constant jumping on the spot, named after the 'pogo stick'.

Punk clothing was androgynous and deliberately offensive, with slogans and controversial images on T-shirts, vests and jackets, which were often customised by the wearer. Black leather, jeans, metal studs and safety pins, ripped clothing, Dr Marten boots and tartan skirts were worn by the punk bands and their fans. Bondage-style trousers joined together at the back with loose, dangling straps were also worn. Bodies were adorned with tattoos and piercings, and hair was shaved, spiked and dyed bright, startling colours. The Mohawk hairstyle inspired by native Americans was popular, and was worn mainly by punk fans in the early 1980s.

Figure 2.2.6 on page 191 is from a record made by one of the best-known punk bands – the Sex Pistols. The song was released during Queen Elizabeth II's Silver Jubilee in 1977, and is a criticism of the Government's treatment of the working class in England in the 1970s. Malcolm McLaren – the manager of the Sex Pistols – and his partner Vivienne Westwood opened

**Figure 2.2.5** Black dress inspired by punk, known as 'That Dress' 1994 designed by Versace.

a shop in London's Kings Road where they sold punk inspired clothing. To many people, the punk fashions were deliberately ugly and made the wearers unnecessarily unattractive. However, elements of punk clothing inspired fashion designers in the 1980s such as ripped and distressed denim and slogan T-shirts, and black became a prime fashion colour.

**Figure 2.2.6** Sex Pistols publicity image.

The black dress in Figure 2.2.5 is punk inspired. It was designed by Versace and worn by the actress Elizabeth Hurley at a film premiere. The silk and Lycra dress was held together by several oversized gold safety pins at the side seams, and it caught much public attention and influenced other designers.

## ACTIVITY

Search the internet to find top designer collections inspired by historical art movements or design styles.

Research next season's top designer fashion collections.

Read the fashion reports to find out what inspires the top designers. View the fashion slides for top designer fashion collections. Look out for design influences such as historical art movements and design styles. Collect images of the designs. For example, in Figure 2.2.7 the monochrome black and white dress design is influenced by 1960s minimalism.

See Further Reading below for the Vogue and Harper's Bazaar websites, which provide useful information about top designers' fashion collections.

**Figure 2.2.7** Sportmax Spring/Summer 2016.

## Designers and their work

Some notable fashion and textiles designers have changed the course of fashion. Their innovative ideas challenged current ideals, and reflected and embodied social and cultural changes. Some of the most influential designers are described below.

### Paul Poiret

**A-level only**

**Figure 2.3.8** Fashion illustration showing evening wear by Paul Poiret.

The French fashion designer Paul Poiret was most prolific from 1900 to 1920. He liberated women from corsets and layered petticoats by creating a new look that concerned draping fabric across the body using simple rectangular panels of fabric, rather than tailored, shaped pattern pieces.

Poiret's innovative designs included:

- 'hobble' skirts, which had such narrow hems it made it necessary to take very small steps when walking
- 'harem' pantaloons – a full Turkish-style trouser with narrow ankles
- 'lampshade' tunics which were held out in a full circle at the hemline using boning, and worn over hobble skirts
- oriental-styled turban hats with stand-up feathers at the front.

Poiret was inspired by exotic and oriental clothing such as the kimono and kaftan, and influenced by the stage costumes of the Ballets Russes; there was little distinction between fashion design, art and costume design in his modern fashion collections. Poiret often used very bright colours and exotic, decorative embellishments; his fashions were considered by some as outrageous. In some of his clothing, he incorporated printed textile designs by the artist Raoul Dufy, whose graphic prints were well suited to his draped constructions.

The marketing of his designs was also very modern. Top fashion illustrators drew his designs for fashion journals, and Poiret had his fashions artistically photographed for publicity, which was a new media for fashion marketing. He was famous for publicising his designs by throwing parties and staging performances. The oriental themed costume worn by his wife at 'The Thousand and Second Night' party which was the basis for his fashion designs at this time. The colour and drama of Poiret's creative designs was superseded by the restrained and refined elegance of Coco Chanel's fashion styles.

### Chanel

**Figure 2.2.9** French fashion designer Coco Chanel, modelling her own clothes and costume jewellery in 1928.

Coco Chanel was a French fashion designer and business woman, who first became successful in 1915 during the First World War. Her simple chemise dress was a move away from corseted styles, and her design focus was on a more casual elegance, with sporty influence.

Post-war modern women were leading a much more active lifestyle both in work and leisure. Many women enjoyed tennis, swimming, golf, riding bicycles, yachting and horse riding, and needed practical clothing for such activities. This need for functional clothing influenced the styling of Chanel's fashion designs, for example hemlines were higher and skirts had pleats to allow ease of movement. Also, after the war there was a demand for clothing in high society that did not need the assistance of servants for dressing.

**Figure 2.2.10** Classic Chanel suit.

Chanel was also innovative in her use of jersey fabric. This had previously been used for underwear, but the machine-knitted wool fabric draped well and was readily available after the war, unlike some of the more exclusive fabrics such as silk. Chanel ordered the jersey fabric in neutral colours and used it to make elegant clothes with a fine finish, as if it were a luxurious fabric.

The Chanel tweed suit is well-known for its comfort and plain styling. The style is ever popular and has become one of Chanel's classic designs which was reinvented in different forms throughout her long career. The 1960s Chanel suit in Figure 2.2.10 has a nipped-in waist, but retains the original boxy shape, practical pockets and plain neckline.

In 1926 Coco Chanel used the colour black when designing one of her dresses. At the time, society considered black as a colour reserved for mourning. The simple, elegant style was embodied in the **'Little Black Dress'** by Chanel. The design concept has remained popular over time, and today is referred to as the 'LBD'.

## Dior

**Figure 2.2.11** Christian Dior 'New Look' 1947.

The French fashion designer Christian Dior is best known for his **'New Look' fashion**. In 1947, he launched a fashion collection that had a new and different fashion silhouette which challenged expectations. Dior's 'New Look' featured nipped in waists and had longer full skirts, which created a very feminine, curvy shape by extravagant use of fabric. The style required special bras to lift the breasts, boned corselettes – called 'waspies' – to minimalise the waist and petticoats to hold the full shape of the skirt. This was a post-war period when rationing of food and goods was still affecting society, and there was hostile reaction to this fashion from those who were still enduring rationing and poverty.

The 'New Look' was fresh and very feminine though, and it appealed to those keen to move on from the restrictions of war time; it influenced other fashion designers and remained popular through the 1950s.

## Mary Quant

A-level only

The British designer Mary Quant opened her first shop, Bazaar, on Kings Road in London in 1955 to sell affordable clothes to teenagers. She soon turned to designing her own stock for the shop, rather than buying it from suppliers. In Figure 2.2.12, Mary Quant is with the winner of a teen magazine competition. The Mary Quant simple black flower trademark can be seen in the background.

**Figure 2.2.12** Mary Quant, on the right, at her Knightsbridge boutique Bazaar in 1966.

Her fun fashions were for young people. They were easy to wear and made from the latest inexpensive synthetic materials such as Tricel, Crimplene and PVC. She is often credited as the designer of the 1960s **miniskirt**, naming it after the Mini car, although other designers of this time also claim to be the original miniskirt designer. Her clothing was for young, confident women with bright, block colours and simple tubular or slightly flared shift shapes. In the late-1960s, she introduced hot pants – by then London was the centre of the 'Swinging 60s' and fashions were focused on the youth market. Hot pants, as seen in Figure 2.2.13, were very brief shorts with a bib at the top.

**Figure 2.2.13** Lulu UK pop singer wearing hot pants in 1967.

**Figure 2.2.14** Vintage YSL 'Le Smoking' tuxedo suit worn to a fashion awards ceremony in 2008.

## Yves Saint Laurent

A-level only

The French fashion designer Yves Saint Laurent's first job was working for Dior; he was so talented that he became head designer at the age of 21. His work was particularly influential in the 1960s and 1970s.

**Figure 2.2.15** 'Robe Mondrian', by Yves Saint Laurent, fall/winter collection 1965/1966.

**Figure 2.2.16** Painting by Piet Mondrian, 1930.

Yves Saint Laurent was influential because his business was one of the first fashion houses to open a boutique, selling 'prêt-à-porter' or 'ready-to-wear' fashion lines. This range of clothing was much more affordable than exclusive bespoke haute couture fashion. His designs have been described as 'street chic' because he often turned everyday styles such as the parka and trench coat into elegant upmarket classics.

In 1966, he launched the **'Le Smoking'** tuxedo suit for women. This was inspired by men's tuxedos, but Saint Laurent made the shape more feminine by tailoring the jacket to fit the female body and styling the trousers to elongate the leg. His trouser suit became a classic fashion, although initially the public was reluctant to accept such an androgynous look.

Figure 2.2.15 shows Yves Saint Laurent's famous shift dress of 1965, based on a painting by Mondrian.

The sleeveless, knee length shift dresses of the 1960s were suited to the hip and arm movements of 'the twist', a dance craze of the times. It was quickly copied by manufacturers, who made cheap copies for the mass market.

## Pierre Cardin

A-level only

Pierre Cardin, an Italian-born French fashion designer, is best known for his 1950s and 1960s futuristic space age designs, in modern materials such as knitted and heat moulded synthetics. Space travel and science fiction were key inspirations for the use of metallic and plastic fabrics in his designs. Block colours and bold designs with 3D geometric forms such as discs and flounces were features of his designs, as well as metal rings, oversized buttons, visible zips and fabric helmets.

**Figure 2.2.17** Space age-style outfits by Pierre Cardin 1966.

**Figure 2.2.18** Space-themed dress by Pierre Cardin 2011.

His 'bubble dress', launched in 1954, came in at the waist before forming a full bubble of fabric that was then nipped in at the knees. The bubble theme inspired the design of his own villa 'the bubble house' in the south east of France. The bubble dress shape influenced other designers, and is still popular today.

Pierre Cardin, like Yves Saint Laurent, was also one of the first fashion businesses to launch 'prêt-à-porter' or 'ready-to-wear' fashion lines. He instigated designer logos on garments as part of brand marketing. He also produced industrial designs for colourful, patterned car interiors.

The space themed dress in Figure 2.2.17 is part of Cardin's 2011 collection, and his designs still look experimental, radical and unorthodox today.

## Vivienne Westwood

In the 1970s, Vivienne Westwood and her partner Malcolm McLaren (manager of the punk rock band Sex Pistols) opened their first shop on London's Kings Road, where they sold unisex punk-inspired street style clothing to young people. Typically, this included:

- T-shirts with political slogans and offensive images
- black leather clothing accessorised with spikes, chains and safety pins
- ripped and distressed denim clothing
- loose knitted vests and jumpers
- red tartan skirts
- clothing with straps and buckles.

In the 1980s, the British fashion designer moved away from punk and was inspired by historical costume. She launched the Pirate collection, which celebrated the romantic age of piracy and highwaymen. Colourful breeches and floppy shirts with pirate hats and sashes were key pieces in this collection. This was in keeping with the New Romantic movement in pop music. Vivienne Westwood's following collections were inspired by the ethnic patterns of native Americans, New York graffiti artwork and Rococo ball gowns.

Vivienne Westwood is known for:

- taking ideas from historical designs and bringing ideas from the past into the future
- the 'mini-crini', which combined the tutu with a shorter form of the Victorian crinoline to give a fairly short, structured full skirt shaped with plastic boning
- her use of traditional British fabrics such as Harris Tweed and Tartan. She has influenced other designers by reviving interest in Harris Tweed, the woollen fabric hand-woven in the western Isles of Scotland
- the idea of 'underwear as outerwear', when she suggested bras should be worn over the top of jumpers
- sexually liberating and empowering feminine designs, for example focusing styles on erotic zones as in the padded busts and metal cage bustles of her 1995 collection
- self-taught tailoring skills involving curved seams and dynamic folding of fabric panels to give pockets or folds of fabric in garment construction
- her T-shirt slogans publicising political causes such as the Campaign for Nuclear Disarmament, climate change and civil rights groups.

**Figure 2.2.19** Voluptuous folds of fabric in Vivienne Westwood Dress 1999.

**Figure 2.2.20** Vivienne Westwood Dress in traditional British fabric 1999.

## Alexander McQueen

The British fashion designer Alexander McQueen was one of the most influential designers of the 1990s and 2000s. He trained as an apprentice on Saville Row, during which time he became very skilled at tailoring; afterwards he gained a Master's degree in Fashion at Central Saint Martin's College of Art and Design.

His work was extremely creative and highly original with impeccable tailoring. His ideas were often very shocking and provocative, for example through some of his fashion designs he commented on brutality towards women.

His fashion shows were always spectacular. He made use of new technologies, for example using a holographic image of Kate Moss in a pyramid in 2006. In 1999, he used robots to spray yellow and black paint onto a model wearing a white dress, using her as a human canvas while she rotated slowly on a section of the catwalk. In 1998, he drenched the models in rain on the catwalk, and in 2003, he walked models through a wind tunnel to billow out capes which were made from metres of fabric. His theatrical fashion shows were a form of art; they thrilled and perplexed audiences.

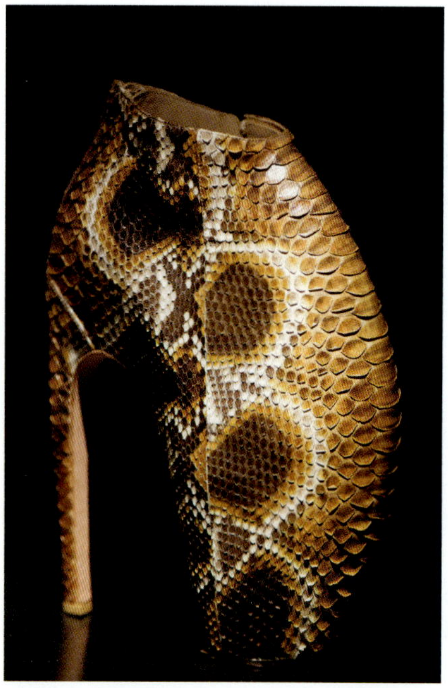

**Figure 2.2.21** Armadillo shoes of Alexander McQueen's 2010 Atlantis collection.

Alexander McQueen is also known for:

- his Highland Rape collection of 1995–1996, which featured ripped bodices and hems, and chains connecting the back and front of the skirts, worn by models with tangled hair. The theme was not about rape of women but of the Scottish culture
- Union Jack frock coat made for David Bowie for a stage costume in 1996
- using a skull image in his designs
- his 'bumster' low-rise trousers of the 1996 spring/summer collection, which influenced the cut of jeans worldwide
- using tartan fabric and black lace, and fine extravagant embroidery in his designs
- featuring intricately carved, wooden prosthetic legs on Aimee Mullins, a double amputee athlete, actress and model on the catwalk in 1999

## ACTIVITY

Design a dress based on:

- elements from one of the design styles or movements described
- one of the fashion silhouettes seen in the work of the influential fashion designers.

- contorting and altering the shape of women's bodies to create extreme fashion silhouettes using corsetry and boned, structural forms
- taking inspiration from nature, for example using feathers and taxidermy of birds in his fashion collections. The rainbow coloured feather chiffon dress in his 2008 collection is one notable example
- the 10-inch Armadillo shoes of the 2010 Atlantis collection, worn by Lady Gaga, whose song 'Bad Romance' was released as part of Alexander McQueen's fashion show. The shape of the shoes contorts the body to form part of the fashion silhouette.

## KEY TERMS

**Design movement:** a group of artists and designers who share the same approach and philosophy to design style during a particular period of time.

**Art Nouveau:** a style of art and design, popular from 1890 to 1910, inspired by natural forms and structures such as curvaceous plants and flowers.

**Art Deco:** a style of art and design, popular in the 1920s and 1930s, featuring bold and streamlined geometric shapes.

**The 'garconne' look:** a boyish, flat-chested fashion silhouette of the 1920s.

**Pop art:** an art movement of the 1950s and 1960s, featuring bold bright colours and images seen in food packaging, comics, adverts, pop music and Hollywood movies.

**Minimalism:** an art movement of the 1960s with simple and pared down abstract shapes and forms.

**Punk:** a style of music which was anti-establishment and political in its song lyrics, and the fashions and appearance of the punk bands and their fans.

**Little Black Dress:** a simple, elegant style of black dress first designed by Chanel.

**'New Look' fashion:** a fashion silhouette of 1947 that featured a nipped-in waist and full skirt, which created a very feminine curvy shape.

**Miniskirt:** an iconic 1960s simple, very short skirt for young women.

**'Le Smoking':** a tuxedo trouser suit for women by Yves Saint Laurent, designed in 1966.

## KEY POINTS

- Collaboration between artists working in different areas of the visual arts, music, theatre and dance influences both individual fashion and textile designers, and design movements and styles.
- The Art Nouveau fashion silhouette was restricted by corsets which shaped the female body into an 'S-shaped' curve, with a low full chest and curvy hips.
- The Art Deco fashion silhouette reflected the needs of modern women who had active lifestyles, working, playing sports, swimming, going to the movies and dancing to Jazz.
- 1960s fashion design was colourful, fun, mass produced, inexpensive and designed for the young.
- Minimalist fashion features neutral muted tones with clean and sculptural shapes and is sometimes referred to as 'urban chic'.
- Punk clothing was androgynous and deliberately offensive with T-shirts, vests and jackets ripped and customised by the wearer, with metal studs and safety pins, slogans and controversial images.

## Check your knowledge and understanding

1 Describe three innovative fashion styles introduced by Poiret between 1900 and 1920.
2 What type of fabric did Chanel use in an innovative way in her fashion designs?
3 Why was Dior's 'New Look' fashion controversial?
4 What does the Mary Quant trademark look like? Can you draw it?
5 Why are Yves Saint Laurent's fashion designs referred to as 'street chic'?
6 Use three words to describe the fashion designs of Pierre Cardin.
7 What features on Vivienne Westwood T-shirt designs?
8 What style of trouser is Alexander McQueen best known for?

## Further reading

Werle, S. *50 Fashion Designers you should know*

Design Museum Enterprise Limited *Fifty Dresses that changed the world*

Mendes, V. and Dela Hay, A. *20th Century Fashion*

www.tate.org.uk/art/art-terms

www.vam.ac.uk/content/articles/v/vivienne-westwood-designs

www.glamourdaze.com/history-of-womens-fashion

www.bykoket.com/blog/top-50-fashion-designers

www.vogue.com/fashion-shows

www.harpersbazaar.com

www.katedaviesdesigns.com/2015/02/09/sonia-delaunay-the-dress-of-the-future/

# 2.3 How technology and cultural changes can impact the work of designers

**LEARNING OUTCOMES**

By the end of this section you should have developed a knowledge and understanding of:

- how changes in society can affect fashions in clothing and interiors
- the main changes in fashion from 1900
- how women's changing role in society has had a major impact on the clothing styles worn today
- how worldwide events can change the direction of fashion
- how developments in fabric and manufacturing technology can affect fashions.

If you are studying at A-level you should also have developed a knowledge and understanding of:

- the product life cycle assessment
- how social, moral and ethical issues are shaping the future of textiles.

Fashion is about the clothes and styles that make up the diversity shown in dress across different generations, countries, genders and socio-economic groups. Two world wars, scientific and technological revolutions and the rapid social changes that took place during the twentieth century have had more impact on the way people dress than in any other comparable period in history.

The twentieth century saw many extremes in clothing – at the start of the century, women's skirts were trailing the streets, but by the 1960s, they were so short they barely covered the bottom. Breasts were exaggerated during the Edwardian period, and bound to make the chest as flat as possible in the 1920s. Shoulders were padded out in the 1980s, and at other times – in the 1950s for example – were sloped like bottle tops. Men dressed to look affluent and reliable during Edwardian times, yet in the 1950s and 1970s it was fashionable to appear deliberately poor and ragged. Suede shoes were thought effeminate when worn by men in the 1950s, yet pink shirts, velvet trousers and shoulder-length curls were seen as masculine – a fashion adopted by many men including construction workers – in the 1970s.

Figure 2.3.1 Elaborate Edwardian clothing with trailing hems and exaggerated breasts was worn by upper-class women at the start of the twentieth century.

Figure 2.3.2 By contrast, the 1920s fashions had a flat-chested boyish silhouette.

Fashion in clothing is like fashion in literature, humour and music – it is a social reflection of the time. Clothes suit the period when they are worn and look right at the time. There are also fashions in other aspects of life – interior decoration, architecture, theatre, dance, food, medicine, technology and philosophy – all of which are in vogue for a while until they are replaced by a different fashion.

Since 1900, fashions have been influenced by:

- the changing roles of women
- the widening gap between different generations and the rise of youth culture
- technological developments
- sport and leisure activities
- what royalty and celebrities are seen wearing
- social identity and membership of different cultural, political and religious groups.

Figure 2.3.3 Eighteenth century fashions were set by the aristocracy who showed their wealth and status through their elaborate and impractical clothes.

## Socio-economic influences

Socio-economic influences define lifestyle, attitudes and expectations, and have an important effect on how people live, what they wear and how they behave. At the beginning of the twentieth century, it was easy to distinguish people's social class by the way they dressed. The classes led very different lifestyles and there were big differences in wealth and standards of living. Dress was a very clear indicator of wealth and social class, with wealthy upper-class people following fashion rigidly or facing social ridicule.

Throughout the 20th and 21st centuries, these socio-economic situations have changed, and this has had a major impact on the fashions of the time. The fashions and influences for each decade are described in some detail on the pages that follow. Many different socio-economic influences are intertwined with each other, and have helped to shape the fashions; each decade has its own unique characteristics.

## Trends

Fashions extend beyond clothing into every aspect of a person's lifestyle – how we spend our leisure time, decorate our homes, travel and live our lives. Designers need to understand evolving trends so that they know what to design for their specific market, and so that their ideas fit within the current standards of fashion and taste of the times. Failing to get trends right – particularly in relation to colour – can be very expensive.

Two reasons for wearing a particular fashion of clothes are for personal self-esteem and individuality, and to keep up with the current fashions as a statement of our awareness of the modern world. Fashion designers need to be aware of world events and developments within the microcosm of their target market. Many use trend forecasting companies, who predict what will happen to particular market sectors in the future. The trend companies use information from many different sources including current fashion and haute couture, arts and sciences, economy, music and media, demographics and street culture. Design companies usually align the information bought from trend companies to their own in-house predictions, to make sure that their designs will be on trend and desired by the target market.

Some companies such as Topshop and River Island do not want to follow trends, and instead see themselves as trendsetters, developing their own concepts and predictions.

Further information about trends and fashion development cycles can be found in Chapter 1.13 of this book.

# Major developments in fashion design and manufacture

**Figure 2.3.4** Extravagant dress styles of 1900.

## 1900–1910

The 1900s is sometimes called La Belle Epoch or the Age of Opulence. It was the last decade of opulent living and entertaining on a grand scale by the upper class, which had been established over the past few centuries. People continued to show their success and wealth through luxurious and extravagant dress, particularly women. The impractical styles of the Edwardian period did not allow for a busy domestic or business life, and the time and labour needed to look after the fashionable woman's wide range of outfits including undergarments, shoes and gloves, was easy at a time when cheap domestic help was available. Upper-class women required many different outfits for their formal social lives and changed their clothes several times a day, often needing servants to help them dress.

Men were very clothes-conscious during the 1900s, and it was important to be correctly dressed. Although Paris led women's fashions, London set the styles of men's clothes. Men also needed many outfits for different occasions and times of day, and a servant to look after them. The basic outfit for men that was established in Victorian times – trousers, shirt and jacket –has changed little since the start of the twentieth century, and changes were

**Figure 2.3.5** Dress from 1901 showing the S-bend silhouette.

**Figure 2.3.6** This tight-fitting corset gave women's bodies the popular S-bend silhouette.

**Figure 2.3.7** Upper-class children's clothes were miniature versions of those worn by adults.

limited to variations in the cut of jackets and trousers, the height of shirt collars or the shape of hats.

By 1900, there had been very limited success in emancipating women and reforming their dress. They still did not have the vote and were discriminated against in social attitudes, the law, education and certain professions. In upper- and middle-class families, wives and daughters were not expected to work as this would have cast doubt on the husband's ability to provide for his family. These privileged women wore highly impractical styles of dress, which showed their traditional role as ornaments in a man's world.

Edwardian society aligned itself with the King's personal demands – everything was larger than life and fashion suited the mature figure. Edwardian women wore tight corsets that pushed their bust forward and hips back so that their bodies took on the fashionable S-bend shape. The highly ornate dresses were made from light-coloured delicate fabrics, with long trailing skirts that were lined with taffeta to give a coveted rustle when the lady walked. They were worn with several petticoats, very large hats and gloves to meet the strict code of etiquette based on Victorian ideas of respectability. This basic silhouette remained unchanged for most of the decade.

While the wealthy upper classes wore fashionable clothes, many people had to wear whatever they could get; poor people were shabbily dressed, and it was common to see children without shoes. The middle classes copied the upper-class styles only in a modified form, and the idea of the masses following fashion had not yet begun. Clothes worn by children of the upper classes were miniature versions of those worn by adults.

During the 1900s, new technical developments began to affect everyday life; telephones and electric lights were more commonplace, motor transport was increasing every year therefore people could travel more, and the pace of everyday life began to speed up. These changes helped to introduce a more practical style of dress.

Social changes that had been developing since the nineteenth century became more obvious, with more women going to universities and colleges, entering professions and taking part in active sports. They supported the suffragettes who were campaigning for women to be allowed to vote, and their new attitudes were shown in their more practical and less fussy dress styles. Masculine-styled tailored jackets became very popular, and a version of this style has been fashionable for women ever since. The 2-piece suit or costume – called a **tailor-made** – became classic wear for the country, sports, travel and town wear.

Although women had been taking part in a range of active sports since the 1880s, they had worn their normal clothes for these activities. By the end of the 1900s, sports clothes were more relaxed, although still very unsuitable by today's standards.

Liberal attitudes to life were spreading in the artistic and intellectual worlds, and this was reflected in dress. More forward-thinking women wore looser dresses with flowing lines that did not require stiff corsets. Many women thought these new styles too extreme or arty, and were unable to accept a concept of dress that was different from the tight-laced, corseted and covered up styles.

**Figure 2.3.8** A tennis outfit of 1909 with the skirt about 5 cm off the ground.

From 1907, the S-bend silhouette started to change, becoming slimmer and straighter, while hats got larger and larger. By 1908 and 1909, hats had become amazing in size and decoration, making it one of the most hat-conscious periods. These large hats – on top of the straight body-line – gave the silhouette a T-shape rather than the S-shape. By 1908, there was an important change in fashion started by Paul Poiret, a ground-breaking French fashion designer who thought that women's shape should be more natural. More information about Poiret's work can be found in Chapter 2.2 of this book.

## 1910–1920

The start of the 1910s was a very fashion-conscious era, with new changes starting to appear – many of them based on Poiret's ideas. The newer styles were better suited to a younger figure than the mature woman of the Edwardian period, and were more appropriate for the changing type of life they were leading. The difference between the generations was becoming more marked; the younger generation was very energetic and wanted to fill their lives with as many activities as possible, and for this they needed easier fitting clothes. The new styles had simple round or V-necks, breasts were less emphasised and waists were freer and looser fitting. Legs became the focal point.

Between 1912 and 1914, there were striking changes in the silhouette of younger women's clothes, and these changes shocked the older generation. The introduction of the V-neckline in 1913 was regarded as akin to indecent exposure, and doctors warned that it was a danger to health.

**Figure 2.3.9** A tango outfit from 1910 consisting of full culottes worn with an over tunic.

Some forward-thinking young women cut their hair very short and straight, in a 'Dutch bob' style. Dancing became very popular – especially the tango, which was seen as dramatic and erotic, and ragtime music – the basis of many of the new dance crazes. The energetic dances needed looser fitting dresses with long slits that enabled women to move freely, and dresses with transparent bodices were worn over trousers. Revealing evening and dance dresses were often heavily trimmed with fringing and beads, and calves and flashes of knee were visible on the dance floor, much to the disgust of the older generation. The dance dresses had a big influence on daywear clothes, causing hemlines to rise, and by 1914, the new fashions introduced at the start of the decade influenced the clothes worn by most women, leading to a slimmer silhouette.

Wealthy women still had their clothes individually made by dressmakers, but new department stores were beginning to be an alternative source of fashion for middle-class women. The stores had workrooms where high-quality clothes were made to individual customers' measurements. This encouraged the selling of a design and not just an individual garment, which helped to spread fashions designed for the affluent members of society to the less wealthy as ready-to-wear garments. Class distinction through dress was becoming less obvious than it had been at the start of the century.

The First World War (1914–1918) had a significant influence on fashion. By 1915 shorter, fuller skirts were worn by many women, and as the war progressed they became slightly shorter and therefore more practical. At the start of the war, many women who had worked in traditional female jobs such as dressmaking and millinery lost their jobs, as it was thought unpatriotic to waste time and money on new clothes and hats. As the war progressed, women began to play a very important role in employment and the voluntary services. Many women of all social classes joined the armed forces, trained as nurses or undertook some kind of war work, requiring them to wear more practical clothes. All women wore the same clothes when on duty in the services or working in the factories, and this blurred class distinctions in dress, forcing women of all ages and social classes to adopt a simpler and more practical style of dressing.

By 1916, many young men had been sent to fight, and this created more opportunities for women's employment, including the armed services and farming. Many worked in the dangerous munitions factories where they were well paid, allowing them to buy better quality food and have money left over for fashionable clothes.

Men's fashions remained largely unchanged in the early 1910s, as the conformist styles became more established. Burberry's of London produced the famous trench coat based on those worn by soldiers in the trenches, and men and women continued to wear this style of raincoat after the war. The trench coat is a raincoat that is traditionally double-breasted with storm flaps, raglan sleeves with wrist straps, wide lapels, buttoned pockets and a belted waist. Apart from minor changes in cut and length, the basic style of the trench coat has remained the same and is still a bestseller today.

**Figure 2.3.10** Easier fitting children's clothes in 1910.

Children's fashion followed the change towards simpler, easy-fitting clothes, and there was more scope for teenage dressing as the fashions were more suitable for younger people than the Edwardian styles. Teenage girls were often called 'flappers' – a term that was applied to all modern looking women. Boys' clothes also became less formal, and they wore home knitted pullovers, scarves and socks for many occasions instead of the earlier formal suits. There were few fashions for teenage boys, as most were in uniform by their late teens.

Music halls were still popular sources of entertainment, but the cinema was developing rapidly. Film stars became well-known and wicked, sultry-looking ladies called 'vamps' – with heavily outlined eyes, draped headbands, and smoking through long cigarette holders – were thought to be the height of sophistication. Film stars were beginning to be an important influence on women's looks and fashions.

After the war, everyday fashions continued to feature easy, feature styles. Evening dress was the area where affluent, fashion-conscious women indulged in new outfits in the latest styles. The post-war atmosphere of freedom presented many opportunities to wear evening dresses and dancing was more popular than ever. Ragtime developed into jazz, and young people danced to the bands in the new dance halls. A more sophisticated night life in clubs became established in the major cities of Europe and America.

This decade saw major social and political changes and, together with the First World War, forced a simpler, more practical style of dressing onto women of all ages and classes, and set the character of the twentieth century.

## 1920–1930

The 1920s are often referred to as the 'Roaring Twenties', and are usually thought of as a period of positivity, with jazz, dancing, wild parties and looser morals – but this was largely just the middle and upper classes. Social changes brought on by the war spread more slowly among the rest of the population, and for a lot of people, the 1920s were far from fun. Many men returned from the war mentally or physically disabled, and many did not return at all. Most women had little social or economic freedom because they were expected to return to their pre-war roles as full-time wives and mothers, and it was not until 1928 that the vote was given to all women. A shortage of men meant that many women now had to provide for themselves. While many were forced to find poorly paid work in employment traditionally seen as women's work, new jobs were created in developing industries such as insurance, banking and electrical engineering factories, causing a move away from the pre-war employment of young women in domestic service.

The post-war boom in industry was short-lived, with a slump in the worldwide demand for products like coal, textiles and ships on which Britain had built its wealth. This industrial decline and unrest led to prolonged periods of large-scale unemployment. Life was hard for many, with little money for basic clothes let alone clothes that followed the latest fashions.

At the beginning of the decade, some designers tried to recreate more elaborate, romantic-styled fashions based on period costume; Lanvin's mother-and-daughter dresses were a classic example of this style. The more modern garçonne (boyish) or jeune fille (young girl) look dominated 1920s' fashions however, as these simpler styles were more in line with the faster pace of life, as well as women's continued drive for emancipation. Only the elderly continued to wear the more elaborate styles from the early part of the century.

**Figure 2.3.11** Dress from 1926 showing the short skirt and straight, androgynous look.

The 1920s silhouette for fashion-conscious young women was short and straight, giving a youthful adolescent figure. Young women adopted new mannerisms and poses – the pelvis pushed slightly forward, the shoulders hunched and one hand rested on the hip, which gave a slightly concave look to the chest and torso. Women wanted a completely flat, boyish shape and wore foundation garments that were designed to deliberately flatten the breasts – a few women even bound their breasts. Short hairstyles worn under bell-shaped, felt cloche hats completed this androgynous look.

The chemise line dress became the main style for day and evening wear; garments hung straight from the shoulders and the waistline dropped to hip level. The simple styles were made from very decorative fabrics, especially evening wear. The discovery of Tutankhamen's tomb in 1922 created interest in Egyptian style embroideries, and motifs were used on dresses, jackets and cloaks, and there was a craze for chinoiserie (Far East Asian) inspired fabrics and motifs. Shawls were a popular accessory, adding to the straight silhouette and providing warmth over the skimpy dresses. Low heeled T-bar shoes and silk stockings completed the look.

Skirts became shorter until the end of 1924, when they were about 5 cm below the knee; these short skirts caused a sensation as women had never shown so much bare leg before. Young women were also using

**Figure 2.3.12** Chanel jersey suit worn with multi-rows of pearls, 1929.

**Figure 2.3.13** A velvet dress from 1925. Worn by flappers, the short, fringed skirt allowed movement when dancing the Charleston.

cosmetics on a daily basis, which was previously looked on as immoral in Victorian times.

The very simple shapes allowed many women to make their own dresses, and in the difficult economic circumstances experienced by many families, home dressmaking was the only way many could afford to dress themselves. Wealthy women had clothes made by professional tailors, or bought ready-made from fashion departments of the big stores. The quality and availability of moderately-priced, mass-produced clothes was improving, especially in America where the clothing industry was more established. However, class distinction through clothing was still noticeable.

Elegant understatement became synonymous with being well dressed and a more discreet way of showing affluence, while poor people still looked poor, with shabby clothes in low-quality fabrics.

The more casual styles had the greatest impact on clothes worn for the growing popularity of active leisure pursuits such as golf and tennis. Motorbikes were also becoming increasingly popular for men and women, and riders needed protective clothing.

During the 1920s it became fashionable to have a suntan, and affluent people started to go to Mediterranean resorts in the summer, rather than just in the winter and spring – which had been the fashionable seasons before the First World War. Sunbathing and skiing became popular, along with special resort clothes which included trousers, shorts and sleeveless tops. Sportswear was an important factor in women's dress reform during the early twentieth century, especially after the First World War. Young women expected the socially liberating time of the war to continue, along with its greater equality. As they became more competitive in sports, women wanted clothes that allowed them move freely for their more strenuous activities.

Men were also keen to forget the horrors of war, and their changing attitudes to life saw a move away from formal dress to more casual clothes. Young men moved away from the narrow leg trousers that were worn at the beginning of the 1920s and started to wear easier, baggy trousers. Towards the middle of the decade, Oxford undergraduates started wearing exaggeratedly wide flapping trousers known as 'Oxford bags', and although these had a limited success, they led to trousers having a looser cut with wide legs and pleats at the waist – a style that lasted for a long time.

The cinema grew in popularity, with film stars depicting amorous and sometimes sexually immoral characters. This raised concern about declining moral standards among the older generation. The cinema was beginning to be a major influence on how women and men should look and behave. Mass entertainment was more widespread than ever, with increasing numbers of radios and gramophones being sold – an industry of producing and promoting popular dance music developed quickly. Dance dresses with low-waisted fringed or glitter embroidered bodices were perfect for the new dance crazes including the Charleston.

Fashion and music are social reflections of the time, and often express a change of mood ahead of the changing times. By the late 1920s, music and clothes were softening as if they knew of the difficult and more serious times to come. By the end of 1927 the hard, angular silhouette was becoming softer, and a more feminine look began to develop.

**Figure 2.3.14** A 1930s backless evening dress by Worth.

**Figure 2.3.15** Foxes and fur were very fashionable trimmings in the 1930s.

**Figure 2.3.16** Beach pyjamas from 1931.

## 1930–1940

At the beginning of the 1930s, clothes started to became more elegant and ladylike again, and the more mature figure was fashionable again; the girlish flappers of the 1920s were no longer the fashion ideal. The Wall Street crash in October 1929 triggered an economic slump called the Great Depression, which meant that many women could simply not afford clothes. Colours and fabrics reflected the subdued mood – black, navy and grey were basic everyday colours. While skirt lengths stayed at a practical length for daytime, floor-length evening dresses were worn again by wealthier women for the first time since the 1910s. Interest moved from the legs to the back, and backless evening dresses were a daring new fashion in the early 1930s – the back was cut almost to the waistline and skirts usually cut on the bias, so that they clung to the body.

Many people were badly affected by the economic situation; women learned to alter existing clothes, and home dressmaking became more popular than ever. Home knitting was also popular, and knitted items helped to brighten up outfits. The quality of mass-produced clothes continued to improve, but many women had little money for new items. By the mid-1930s, the fashionable cut was a more fitted cut, with emphasis on the width of the shoulder for the first time since the beginning of the century, giving a slight military look. Fur trimming was very fashionable, and a fox (or pair of foxes) was frequently worn as an accessory by those who could afford it.

Couture fashion houses were still the most exclusive place for wealthy women to buy clothes, but as the American-style mass-produced garment industry grew, chain stores and department stores became popular places to buy clothes. The Depression brought the basic styles of clothing worn by the different classes closer together. A new process of clothes design helped to bring the creations of the famous Paris fashion houses within the reach of nearly every woman. Before 1930, buyers would purchase several copies of each selected design shown in Paris and then sell them on to wealthy clients. After the Depression, the American authorities put a tax of up to 90 per cent on the cost of the original model. As toiles were allowed in duty free, buyers bought them instead and copied them, making it possible to sell a simplified version of the original garment very cheaply.

Active sportswear was designed for the needs of the sport; swimwear had a better fit and a more modern appearance and two-piece costumes began to appear. Women did not generally wear trousers but wealthy people wore specially designed holiday and cruise wear, and there was a craze for loose fitting beach pyjamas in the early 1930s. An obsession with sunlight and fresh air gave rise to more revealing clothes such as shorts and bare-back sundresses. Underwear became lighter, and decreased in quantity as boned corsets were replaced by lighter corsets and suspender belts. Younger women wore briefs or bias-cut cami-knickers, and slips made from rayon or silk fabric with embroidered and lace inserts.

Mass media – especially radio and the cinema – was at the height of its popularity during the mid to late 1930s and the clothes worn in American films had a strong influence on the way people dressed. Film created a

**Figure 2.3.17** Children's clothes were simpler and easier fitting.

**Figure 2.3.18** A broader male silhouette became fashionable during the 1930s.

**Figure 2.3.19** Women's military uniforms 1939-1945.

**Figure 2.3.20** The CC41 label.

form of hero worship for the film stars and the 'tough guys' in the popular films of the time, although the glamorous fashions were out of reach for most women. Greta Garbo and Marlene Dietrich were two of the biggest superstars of the 1930s, and women today still wear trench coats with dark glasses in the style made famous by Garbo.

The economic situation gradually improved during the second half of the decade despite the growing threat of war, and the new fashionable silhouette was less elongated with more emphasis on the natural curves of the body, a broader shoulder line and shorter skirts.

Children's clothes had easy fitting simple lines and girls' outfits looked less like miniature versions of women's fashions. Dresses like a long button-through shirt became a basic style, and have remained so right up to the present day.

The looser styles worn by young men in the 1920s developed into the lines of all men's clothes during the 1930s, and a broader built, more athletic silhouette that gave a bold and masculine appearance was fashionable. The Duke of Windsor, formerly King Edward VIII, was considered to be an international leader of men's fashions, and wore brightly coloured and bold patterned fabrics, as well as trousers with belts rather than the traditional braces.

By the end of the 1930s, new fashion designs based on an hour-glass figure with a pulled-in waist, seemed to be going back to Edwardian and Victorian times but they were worn by only the most fashion-conscious women. As high-fashion designers were showing impractical ideas, more functional clothes were developing in the background, so that by 1939 most women were wearing skirts of just below knee length – the practical clothes in the basic styles that women wore until the end of the Second World War.

## 1940–1950

The Second World War affected civilian life far more than the First World War; food, clothing and consumer goods were scarce and often severely rationed. Fashion slowed down and most women had to adapt their way of dressing to the changed circumstances. More women were in uniform than ever before, and women who were not in the services went to work in plain, functional civilian clothes which had a drab appearance. The effects of the war made fashion less exclusive and clothes became more democratic, catering for a much wider market. By the end of June 1940, France had been defeated and Paris – the international centre of fashion – had closed. Clothes and fabrics were rationed from 1941 until 1949, and everyone was issued with an annual number of coupons to be used when buying clothing.

Women took great care of their clothes, repairing them when necessary so that they would last, and many made their own clothes. The government's 'make do and mend' campaign encouraged women to re-make older garments into new ones. The government also introduced regulations that limited the quality and amount of material allowed for every type of garment, including the number of pockets and buttons. These garments were called utility clothes, and had a special symbol (CC41 – Clothing Control 1941) stitched into them.

**Figure 2.3.21** A Poster from the Make-do and Mend propaganda in 1943.

To make sure that clothes were affordable for most people, and to stop profiteering, prices were controlled. British couture designers such as Norman Hartnell were commissioned to design special ranges of utility clothes – this was the beginning of famous designers producing ideas for the mass market.

The silhouette of women during the war was plain and square – padded shoulders gave a square, severe outline while skirts were straight and narrow. Many skirts were cut on the bias to make them seem fuller, and pleats and trimmings were rarely seen. Everyday life was constantly interrupted by air raids, and women of all ages and classes wore trouser outfits as well as all-in-one boiler suits called 'siren suits', which were worn in the air raid shelters.

As in the First World War, women replaced the men who had gone to war, and women from all sections of society worked in occupations such as farming, medicine, munitions and engineering, or volunteered for the Women's Auxiliary Forces. This meant that they needed to wear more functional clothing.

**Figure 2.3.23** Female ambulance drivers in 1940.

**Figure 2.3.22** Standard wartime fashion with short skirt, boxy, wide-shouldered jacket and sensible shoes.

America did not have the restrictions caused by the war in Europe, and New York became the new international fashion centre. American designers developed many of their own styles, which influenced European fashions for many years after the war. American fashions were based on practical, interchangeable separates that catered for the more relaxed American lifestyle.

American fashions influenced menswear throughout the 1940s. The fashionable male silhouette was a wedge-shaped line: wide brimmed trilby hats, jackets and coats that hung loosely from heavily padded shoulders and wide, straight cut trousers. When men were demobilised at the end of the war, they were given a civilian outfit – a suit, shirt, tie, shoes and a raincoat. These 'Demob suits' were made from poor-quality fabrics and lacked style, but many men were glad to receive them and wore them for many years.

In the spring of 1947, Dior launched his 'New Look', which brought a new luxuriousness to fashion and changed the female silhouette from head to toe. Breasts were more exaggerated than they had been since the early 1900s and, together with a small waist and full skirt, they gave a more feminine, rounded silhouette. The New Look produced shocked and hostile reactions, especially as the early months of 1947 had seen some of the coldest weather ever known, and rationing and shortages had never been so severe. Despite all of the angry reactions, women wanted the new styles, and the influence of the New Look lasted for many years, therefore helping to re-establish Paris as the creative fashion centre of the world. More information about Dior's work can be found in Chapter 2.2 of this book.

The effects of war removed many class divisions, and the younger generation in their late teens and early twenties followed fashion in a more casual way. American-style casual T-shirts and brightly patterned or checked sports shirts were popular new styles for boys, while girls wore tops and skirts that were either very full or very narrow. Special fashions for teenagers that started in America during the 1930s became more important during the 1940s, and have since become a permanent part of modern fashion.

**Figure 2.3.24** Well-fitting swimwear was popular with young people.

Many young men – especially students – wore clothing from their old service kit, or bought them from army surplus stores. In particular, duffle coats and sheepskin-lined flying jackets were very popular. Worn during the First and the Second World War by the British Royal Navy, the duffle coat was named after the coarse thick woollen fabric from which it was made, and is still popular today. The knee-length coats have a hood, two large patch pockets with covering flaps and three or four wooden or horn toggle fastenings with rope or leather loops – these were easy to fasten while wearing gloves in cold conditions at sea.

Cycling was a common form of transport, and girls began to wear American-style trousers called 'pedal pushers'. By the end of the war, trousers were accepted as casual fashion-wear but not as an everyday town style, as they were associated with the war and factory workers.

Clothing manufacturers began to realise the potential of the youth market, and started to produce young looking, inexpensive dresses – especially for summer. Swimwear was also popular with young people, and well-fitting one- and two-piece suits helped show off their figures. The bikini, designed by Louis Réard and named after the atomic bomb test at Bikini Atoll, appeared in 1946.

**Figure 2.3.25** Nylon was used instead of silk to make stockings.

From the outbreak of the Second World War until the New Look of 1947, the fashion industry underwent massive changes to accommodate the need for mass-produced, affordable clothes. The expanding world clothing industry was led by America, with mass-produced clothes giving more people access to the latest fashions than ever before.

Technological developments in the form of new synthetic fibres (primarily nylon) also affected fashion. Nylon had been discovered in 1929, but was not commercially available until 1940 when it was used for nylon stockings, replacing silk that was needed to make parachutes. Lingerie was often made from nylon from the 1940s onwards, becoming even more popular than natural fibres although a mixture was often used.

## 1950–1960

The 1950s saw the beginning of a new and prosperous era, as living standards improved steadily for many people. High levels of employment meant that more people had money for consumer goods, and there was

**Figure 2.3.26** Dior's new Look influenced fashions throughout the 1950s.

**Figure 2.3.27** Fitted suits were a staple in many women's wardrobes.

an ever-growing market for fashionable clothes at all price levels. This was the beginning of a new era when the working classes set their own fashion rather than following those of the upper classes, and this new trend developed strongly during the following decades. Life after the Second World War was taken more seriously than after the First World War. The reconstruction of industry and improvements in living standards took place during the Cold War and with new threats from nuclear weapons, therefore unlike the 1920s, this was not a time for daring fashions and frivolous behaviour.

The clothing worn by the British Royal family was not particularly fashionable, but they attended fashion events, which helped to create interest in British designers such as Norman Hartnell and Hardy Amies.

There was a mood of moderate conservatism and nostalgia in the first half of the 1950s, and the fashionable ideal was once again the mature, elegant woman. Women went back to figure constraining clothes set by Paris designers – especially Dior and Balenciaga, whose designs were modified and simplified by wholesale clothing manufacturers. Dior's New Look continued to influence very feminine styles, with small waists and extravagantly full skirts. This appeared to send out messages that women should return to the home-making after their wartime efforts.

The conservative attitudes gave rise to the tailored clothes that became important basics in many women's wardrobes. Darted or seamed suit jackets gave a fitted or semi-fitted look, and matching skirts were nearly always narrow, gripping the hips and tapering in at the hem.

Fabrics were mostly made from natural fibres as most synthetic fibres were still at the development stage. One exception to this was rayon, which had been available before the war and was sometimes used for summer suits and dresses. In 1952, Dior designed an unbelted 'sheath dress' – a style that was popular for many years. Complicated, uncomfortable underwear was essential under these closely fitted dresses, and for most women this meant a bra and roll-on or suspender belt, or an all-in-one corselet. Breasts had to appear prominent and large in size, and this was achieved by a bra with cone-shaped cups that were stiffened with circles of stitching.

Well-fitting, tapered trousers in wool tartan and twill fabrics became basic garments for many women, especially younger women – although they were only accepted as casual wear and never worn in offices or fashionable restaurants.

Menswear was inspired by British tailoring, and suits were precisely tailored with short fitted, single-breasted jackets that had narrow lapels and slightly curved cut-away fronts. Trousers were fitted at the hip and tapered down the legs to narrow bottoms. This style was known as the Edwardian look.

Young working-class men liked the styles, but did not want to look like Edwardian gentlemen. These teenagers benefited from full employment and had money to spend on clothes, so they adapted the Edwardian styled garments form their own fashions. They exaggerated the jackets into longer, looser shapes and wore them with a very thin slim jim or bootlace tie. Trousers fitted the legs tightly and were known as drainpipes, finishing just above the ankle to show brightly coloured socks and chunky lace-up shoes (brothel creepers) with thick crêpe soles. These streetwise young men were known as Teddy boys.

**Figure 2.3.28** The close-fitting sheath dress required constricting underwear to achieve the demanding silhouette.

**Figure 2.3.29** Teddy boy.

In the mid-1950s, the new rock and roll music began to revolutionise pop music, and rock stars began to replace film stars as the new idols. Elvis Presley, James Dean and Marlon Brando portrayed a more macho type of young man, and made a big impression on the younger generation who began to form biker clubs. Their style of dressing included leather motorbike jackets, T-shirts, blue jeans and boots, and members of these clubs became known as Ton-up boys.

Many disaffected young people began to reject their parents' conformist attitudes and to develop their own styles. Some were concerned about the materialistic developments in society and the risk of mass destruction in a possible nuclear war – Ban the Bomb marches became a feature of the late 1950s. Anti-establishment views were often held by the more style-conscious beatniks (beats), who developed a deliberately scruffy and unkempt appearance. The beatnik style for girls was loosely arranged backcombed hair, a pale face with heavily emphasised eyes and oversized pullovers called sloppy joes worn over cropped, skin-tight jeans or short, tight skirts in dark colours. The beat style for men was comparatively short hair, black pullovers and sombre flannel shirts with grey denim or cord jeans, and black leather jackets or waistcoats. Although fairly tame by today's standards, the beatnik style was seen by the older generations as disrespectful to the conventional way of life.

By the end of the decade, young cult fashions were being adapted by some designers such as Yves Saint Laurent, and the idea of lower-class fashions being refined for upper-class wear was unique in the history of fashion. The cycle of youth-oriented fads changed the structure of fashion for the remainder of the twentieth century.

Synthetic fibres such as Terylene, Acrilan, Bri-nylon and Orlon were beginning to be used by the late 1950s, and were popular with consumers. Reinforced nylon socks reduced the need for darning, and the shape-retaining qualities of the new children's clothes meant that they could be washed more easily. Materials for underwear became more lightweight and firmer, although still using latex elastic because Lycra was not invented until 1959.

## 1960–1970

The 1960s was the most prosperous of all the decades of the twentieth century; family incomes were spent on home improvements and consumer goods, and wealthy families sometimes took two or three holidays a year. The Swinging Sixties and the Roaring Twenties are marked out as the fun periods of the twentieth century. In many ways they were similar to each other, as both experienced economic and industrial expansion, major social changes, daring young fashions and new styles in popular music and dancing. The post-war baby boomers were teenagers, and becoming an important demographic group with disposable income to spend on fashion, music and leisure activities. The themes of youth, science and technology, women's position in society, space travel and new materials had strong influences on the fashions of the 1960s and 1970s.

The 1944 Education Act had been especially beneficial for girls, and by the 1960s, many more girls stayed on in the sixth form and went onto further and higher education. Manufacturing industries were in decline in Britain, but jobs in teaching and service industries such as banking were growing. Women, including married women, could find employment very easily.

Full employment meant that young people had their own money and were not dependent on their parents; many lived away from home and the term 'bachelor girl' was used to describe the growing number of young women who lived independent lives in bedsits and flats. The contraceptive pill was developed in the mid-1960s, and the reform of the abortion laws at the end of the decade meant that women had greater sexual freedom. However, women were still discriminated against in the workplace, education, law and socially. Equal pay and opportunities began to be the focus of some newly formed women's groups in the late 1960s. There were some attempts to develop gender-free styles of clothing, and these influenced many new fashions for women.

Fashions had become much younger looking and more relaxed during the late 1950s, but clothes at the beginning of the 1960s still looked conventional and mature when compared with the designs at the end of the 1960s. The youth-oriented styles of the 1960s were part of an international movement towards a new approach in dressing which started in the mid-1950s. Jacqueline Kennedy – America's first lady – became a fashion leader in the early 1960s, starting many new trends including pillbox hats, sleeveless A-line dresses, bouffant hairstyles and low-heeled court shoes.

Young women increasingly wore casual interchangeable separates, but tailored clothes still formed the basic wardrobe of many women, and the most successful new suit style of the time was the Chanel suit (see Chapter 2.2, figure 2.2.14). Easy, unfitted dress shapes became more popular, and the new shift dress was a slightly more shaped version of the late 1950s sack dress. These sleeveless, knee length shift dresses suited the hip and arm movements of the twist – a dance craze of 1961 (see Yves Saint Laurent's Mondrian dress, Chapter 2.2, Figure 2.2.19).

**Figure 2.3.30** Mary Quant designs from 1967.

Many new British designers started work in the 1960s including Mary Quant, who wanted to sell clothes to young people but was disheartened by the middle-aged styles that were available. She produced simple garments in slightly flared shift shapes, and tubular lines using jersey T-shirt shapes with blocks of strong colour and vibrant stripes. Most importantly, she shortened skirt lengths to make the famous miniskirt. The new young designers had a big influence on styles for the developing younger fashion market. More information about Quant's work can be found in Chapter 2.2 of this book.

Trousers and trouser suits became popular, and there were new fashions in trouser shapes and styles. Narrow, tapered trousers were still popular but more fashionable hipster styles sat on top of the hips rather than the waist. Flared, bell-bottom trousers were also introduced. Hipsters were often made in denim and worn with denim shirts; the Western look has been a recurring fashion theme since. Skin-tight jeans were also popular in the early 1960s, and were often so tight that they could only be zipped up by lying on the floor. Stretch trousers made from wool and Helanca (a new elastane fibre) or wool and Bri-nylon became stylish, often with a stirrup at the bottom to emphasise the slim leg line.

**Figure 2.3.31** Courrèges' designs, 1965.

**Figure 2.3.32** Cardin's 'Cosmocorps' collection 1965.

**Figure 2.3.33** Childlike Dolly dress.

André Courrèges, a young French designer, was inspired by space exploration in the 1960s. His autumn 1964 collection caused a sensation and his ideas were the most dramatic since Dior's New Look. The designs were stark and modern but also exciting. Courrèges is considered by some to be the inventor of the miniskirt –the most important fashion development of the decade.

Pierre Cardin, another young French designer, developed very futuristic ideas based on clean architectural lines. More information about Cardin's work can be found in Chapter 2.2 of this book.

During 1965 and 1966, skirts got shorter and shorter, and even older women shortened their skirts slightly each year. Trouser suits were worn as an alternative to miniskirts and dresses, but were still not considered appropriate for smart restaurants or the office. Classic blazers and Courrèges-inspired double-breasted reefer jackets in flannel and gabardine became fashionable. By 1966, the mature figure was no longer fashionable, and the new designs catered exclusively for the young. Jean Shrimpton and Twiggy became two of the best-known fashion models in the mid-1960s, and they were photographed in some of the latest trends for upmarket fashion magazines.

There were two popular ways of dressing: a boyish sporty look as symbolised by Twiggy, and a dolly girl style. Neat, short hair styles were part of the boyish look, and very simple, T-shaped dresses made in knitted stripes or strong plain colours with a contrasting collar and short front opening like a football shirt. Other styles were collarless, long sleeved in the winter and short-sleeved or sleeveless in the summer. As the popularity of the miniskirt grew, tights had replaced stockings, and they were often textured with ribs and fancy patterns. Cream tights were often worn with dark clothes and shoes that were chunky with thicker low heels and rounded or squared toes.

Clothes for the dolly look were under-sized and looked childish. Pastel-coloured, ribbed pullovers called skinny ribs were worn as small and tight as possible. Dolly outfits were simply shaped and mini length, worn with pale lacy tights. Dresses were trimmed with frills, lace edgings and embroidered ribbons. Open-knit and crocheted tops were a popular, alternative style.

It became popular for men and women to wear trousers and shirts in the same fabrics and colours, and the media started to refer to them as unisex fashions. During the early 1960s, leather was used for many fashion garments – coats, cardigans, skirts, pinafore dresses and jackets were made in a wide range of colours, and became known as kinky leather gear. New synthetics were used to simulate real leather, and shiny PVC was used to make fashionable wet-look garments. The new fabrics were far less expensive than real leather, and were very popular for mass-produced garments.

One of the most significant developments in the 1960s was the change in menswear, sometimes referred to as the Peacock Revolution. Since 1800, clothing for men had been plain and dark in colour, and at the start of the decade, men's suits and jackets were similar in style to the late 1950s. In the 1960s, a new youth culture called the Mods (Modernists) began to dress differently from their fathers, and new and colourful elements were

**Figure 2.3.34** A wet-look raincoat, 1969.

**Figure 2.3.35** The collarless jacket designed by Pierre Cardin was very successful.

**Figure 2.3.36** A 1960s advertisement for a jumper made from Acrilan®, a newly developed acrylic fibre.

introduced into menswear. Frills and cravats came back into fashion, jacket lapels and trousers became exaggeratedly wide and vividly coloured, printed shirts were fashionable.

Op-art fashions became popular, and many garments for men and women had bold colour-contrasting sections, especially geometric patterns in black and white.

Music and media began to have a huge impact on what people wore, especially teenagers. England – and particularly London – had begun to enjoy an international reputation for its lively, young fashion designers and fashions. Many highly successful pop singers and groups, especially The Beatles, put Britain firmly on the map of international pop music. Apart from their music, people liked the way the Beatles looked, and boys quickly followed their style of slim fitting, high fastening, collarless jackets – originally designed by Pierre Cardin for John Steed, a leading character in the British TV series The Avengers. The jackets were worn with slim-fitting trousers and boots.

Photography had an important influence on fashion as new fashion magazines became available and photographers were given more artistic licence, changing attitudes to fashion and the way clothes were worn. Colour pictures were taken in exciting locations with girls seen running, jumping and appearing to fly through the air, which helped to create an impression of youth. Petticoat and Honey were two of the new magazines aimed at the teenage market.

Young, trendy boutiques selling the latest fads opened up everywhere, especially in London's famous Carnaby Street and King's Road in Chelsea, and large department stores opened young departments, or shops within shops. The buying of clothes changed in the 1960s when fashion became more important than quality. Garments became so cheap that it was common for a girl to buy a dress, wear it once and throw it away, especially as fashions were changing so quickly. Energetic pop music and unconventional, less class-conscious clothes had become a form of communication between the younger generation.

Separates in easy-care fabrics such as Crimplene and Trevira became everyday basic garments for many women, and trousers, tops, knitwear and shirts that could easily be put in the washing machine were the most popular commercially mass-produced clothes. Easy-care and washability became important sales features, and the producers of synthetic fibres spent large sums of money on advertising. Nearly all children's clothes were made from man-made fabrics. From the early 1960s, new weatherproof and water-repellent materials were widely used for raincoats, and waterproof nylon was very popular.

Styles in active sports clothes followed the freer, less formal way of dressing. Skiing holidays became less exclusively upper-class, and a wide variety of ski clothes developed for all price brackets. Anoraks replaced topcoats for all ages, and sunbathing had become more popular than ever, with bikinis becoming much skimpier.

By 1967, the mood of the 1960s had begun to change and many young people were anxious to move away from materialism and the cynical aggression shown in the complacent acceptance of the horrors of the

**Figure 2.3.37** Hippie style fashions of the late 1960s.



Vietnam War, which were constantly shown on the new colour televisions. Drug taking increased alarmingly while others turned to mysticism, cults and Eastern religions.

Hippies and flower-power was one of the most popular cult movements, and the hippie styles of dress became an important influence on mainstream fashions. Indian-made shirts and over-blouses made from cheesecloth and embroidered with flowers and beads were worn with loose tunics and waistcoats. Plain or patterned sheepskin-lined Afghan style jackets were popular in winter. Some girls wore loose floor-length kaftans edged with braiding and embroidery. Trousers were very tight, fitting over the hips, but were widely flared at the hem. Pop stars including the Beatles changed from their smart, clean-cut appearance and adopted the unisex hippie style. Some older people were uncomfortable with unisex dressing, and did not allow women to wear trousers in the workplace or men to have long hair.

The romantic look was a strong fashion trend in 1967 and 1968. Velvet fabrics were used for many day and evening clothes. Men and women's jackets had wide, floppy collars and revers and body-shaped lines that flared slightly over the hips. Frilly blouses and shirts with high cravat necklines and ruffles down the front and round the wrist were worn by both sexes.

Miniskirts were still very popular, but longer skirts were introduced as an extra style. Lower calf and ankle length fur-trimmed Zhivago coats, inspired by the successful Dr Zhivago film, fitted in with the romantic revival, and were usually worn over minis and boots. Mid-calf-length dresses and skirts called 'midis' were less successful as women were not yet ready to give up the mini altogether.

Choosing to wear obviously old clothes was a new trend during the late 1960s, and one that older people found hard to understand. Young people not only found a nostalgic charm in old, hand-made clothes, but also saw it as a reaction against materialistic society and mass-produced clothes made from synthetic fabrics.

## 1970–1980

At the start of the 1970s, high standards of living and prosperous consumer societies were firmly established in the developed world, and people enjoyed greater material wealth than in previous decades. The 1970s was a serious decade and fashion was less extroverted than it had been in the 1960s. Many of the restrained fashion styles were easy to make and did not demand particularly high standards of quality. In order to survive in the highly competitive fashion market, wholesalers and retailers looked for ways of cutting costs, and having clothes made in countries where the labour was cheap provided the answer. Clothing manufacture in India and the Far East had been increasing since the early 1960s but it developed rapidly in the 1970s, and before long, more expensive clothes were being made in developing countries.

The calf-length midi of the late 1960s was referred to as 'instant age' by the American media. Simply adding length without introducing new lines and altered proportions did not make women want to wear the midi length

**Figure 2.3.38** A typical silhouette of the early 1970s.

**Figure 2.3.39** Hot pants were a craze in the early 1970s.

**Figure 2.3.40** Men wearing Oxford bags, platform-sole shoes and patterned jumpers, 1973.

clothes. Most carried on wearing minis, leaving clothing manufacturers with huge stocks of unsold calf-length garments, and many went out of business. Women no longer accepted new designs unless they liked them, and the clothing industry was made to realise that it was women's independent attitudes and the mass market appeal of new styles that determined their success; the era of dictatorial designers had ended.

At the beginning of the decade, there were several fashionable looks on offer. Tight-fitting shorts called hot pants were worn under front-buttoned, calf-length skirts that were left open to the thigh. Satin hot pants caused a sensation when worn for disco dancing.

A brash style, based on 1940s fashion, which included tailored jackets and loose hip-length coats with heavily padded shoulders worn with knee length dresses or skirts was partly successful but many of the details were used in mainstream fashions. Satin fabrics were used for shirts, jackets and trousers, and broad-shouldered fox fur capes and coats – particularly originals from the late 1930s – were the prized possessions of the young. Shoe designs were the most heavily influenced by the 1940s, in the form of platform soles that were used on every kind of women's and men's shoes and boots. Footwear styles were more extreme than at any other time in the twentieth century.

Trouser suits with very wide trousers were an international fashion worn by stylish young women. The two most popular trouser styles were flares and bags. Men and women wore flares over high-heeled boots or shoes with raised soles, which made the leg look longer from the knee downwards. Bags were inspired by the loose trouser styles from the 1920s and 1930s, but these new versions fitted much more closely over the bottom and looked more elegant. In the early 1970s, fashions for men and women became more unisex than at any other time in the twentieth century.

Children's clothes were very similar to those worn by adults and as the children's market grew in importance, more parents were willing to buy the fast-changing styles than would have been the case with earlier generations.

Young men's fashions were the most foppish of the century with long hair styles and figure-hugging shirts with large collars in mauves, pinks and blues. These shirts were worn with wide kipper ties, or left open at the front to show loosely tied scarves or a variety of necklaces. Jackets, topcoats and raincoats with wide revers and narrow sleeves were shaped to the body, and jeans or velvet trousers were tucked into high leather boots. Jackets, topcoats and raincoats with wide revers and narrow sleeves were shaped to the body, and style-conscious young men tucked their jeans or velvet trousers into high leather boots. There was a noticeable difference between the styles worn by younger men and the older generation, and older men realised that the flamboyant styles were not for them.

Blue denim jeans became the 'uniform' of men, women and children of all ages. Jeans were worn as working trousers by American men since the middle of the nineteenth century, and their popularity spread quickly in the 1960s. Style-conscious men and women in their thirties and forties started wearing them at a time when a youthful image was important. By the 1970s jeans had become a way of life, and the anti-establishment, anti-fashion young wore them deliberately faded and shabby with ragged fringed hems – a second-hand pair

**Figure 2.3.41** Skinhead styles were in sharp contrast to the popular foppish styles in the early 1970s.

**Figure 2.3.42** Laura Ashley garments were made from cotton fabrics and based on historical styles.

often cost more than a new pair. Embroidered and patched jeans were also very fashionable, and many American designers such as Calvin Klein, Ralph Lauren and Perry Ellis produced designer jeans that quickly became status symbols.

People copy the clothes worn by the most powerful members of society. At the beginning of the twentieth century, the prosperous middle classes were at their most influential and the lower classes copied their styles. However, by the mid-1970s the workers' unions were showing power and strength, and their working clothes and uniforms were copied as fashion garments for the mass market.

Denim and the jean influence developed into other kinds of garments – dungarees and boiler suits became popular alternatives, especially for women and children. Jeans and denim garments became the mass selling clothes of the age, and denim was used to make many different types of garment and accessories. T-shirts also started life as basic workwear. They grew in popularity along with jeans so that by the 1970s, there were many different styles including ones with names, slogans and messages, and top-of-the-market boutique and couture designs.

The Vietnam War produced strong antiwar reactions among some younger people in the early 1970s, but in contradiction to some of these feelings, army-looking khaki and camouflage clothes became a very commercial young fashion fad.

However, trendy commercialised fashions were not admired by all the younger generation and in Britain, a new brutal cult style appeared. Some working-class boys cut their hair very short and wore plain, vest-like tops or dull looking shirts, sleeveless pullovers and baggy-seated trousers or jeans, which were often hitched up high with braces. The trousers were turned up above the ankle to show heavy laced boots known as bovver boots. Boys wearing this style were called skinheads or bovver boys.

Some women began to look for something more feminine than mass-produced jeans and the army look. Laura Ashley, who had been developing a following for the country style, captured this reactionary mood and became internationally known for her Victorian prints, pleated and tucked bodices, ankle-length skirts lightly gathered into the waistline and trimmings of lace, broderie anglaise and ribbons.

Film and pop music had a more generalised effect on fashion, and the new stars of the 1970s tended to exaggerate or endorse existing fashions rather than start new trends.

The Middle East war that began in the autumn of 1973 brought an end to the economic boom. As fuel prices escalated, inflation grew rapidly and world trade went into recession. Many people started to question the growing materialism and where it was leading, and how long it might be before the world's natural resources would start to run out.

A number of designers created easy-to-wear, fun clothing without fussy embellishments for the young. The Japanese designer Kenzo promoted new ethnic look fashions, and in 1973, was showing longer gathered or flared skirts and dresses. Fashions for summer 1974 were longer, more mature looking and based on nostalgic views of the 1920s and 1930s created by the popular film The Great Gatsby (1974, remade in 2013).

**Figure 2.3.43** The mid-1970s silhouette was layered and baggy.

**Figure 2.3.44** Sportswear styles began to influence casual fashions.

**Figure 2.3.45** Punk fashions were designed to be deliberately offensive and unattractive.

Until the mid-1970s, the trend for layered clothes with strong peasant influences continued, and were referred to as ethnic clothes. Baggy trousers were sometimes worn under the skirts instead of boots, making yet another layer. Thick woollen socks or leg warmers with Peruvian-style patterns were worn over the trouser legs, and the trend was for everything to be big and baggy.

As inflation caused living standards to fall, there was a political swing towards left-wing in many countries and traditional workwear clothes began to be a fashionable trend for men and women. Overalls and dungarees became everyday garments during the later 1970s as trend-setting manufacturers produced fitted boiler suits in a variety of fabrics. Some girls wore them for evening occasions as well as practical day clothes, especially as trouser styles were suitable for the athletic movements of the popular trend in disco-dancing.

In the second half of the decade, trousers became slimmer as narrow legged styles replaced flares, giving a more flattering line and a better proportion with boiler suits and dungarees. Knitwear shapes changed and the new silhouette for casual wear was bulky at the top and narrow in the legs. Tunics in quilted fabrics were adopted as all-purpose garments for everyday wear, especially by the middle and upper classes, and they became part of an identifiable set of clothes referred to as The Sloane Ranger look by Harper's Bazaar. A Sloane Ranger was used to describe a young, aristocratic woman – including Lady Diana Spencer, who lived round Sloane Square in London and wore practical, good-quality separates.

The 1970s was a very sports-conscious decade, and active sportswear improved and developed. Plain and striped knitwear and towelling tops were based on nautical themes that were emphasised with embroidered or embossed anchors and ship's wheels. Ski clothes developed a space-age look with padded anoraks and trousers, or all-in-one ski suits made in white, metallic silver or bright colours with a metallic finish. Boots in modernistic shapes and fastenings were called moon boots. In the late 1970s, active sports were an important part of keeping fit and jogging became popular. Special colourful and practical outfits were worn for keep fit activities, and the practical and comfortable styles were soon integrated into general casual or informal evening wear.

Italian influences on menswear became more pronounced during the late 1970s. Giorgio Armani was an influential designer, and his new shapes and styles influenced the direction of men's fashions. Skinny fit styles and long hair were completely out-of-date by the end of the decade, and were replaced with shorter hair and a bulkier, broader, more masculine style of clothing.

In the summer of 1976, a new youth culture began to develop as a reaction to commercialism, unemployment and the commercialism of youth. Punk fashions were initially adopted by unemployed lower-class youth. The styles were deliberately distasteful and threatening, often sexualised and including leather and chains. For more on punk style, see Chapter 2.2.

The fashion industry was quick to spot the new trend and adopted the punk styles, developing and refining some of the key elements of the new designs such as unstructured garments, boiler suits, superfluous zips and decorative safety pins and chains, so that by the end of the 1970s many mainstream fashions were punk inspired. The Italian shop, Fiorucci, was one of the many fashion retailers that sold punk-inspired clothing.

By the end of the decade, the overloaded silhouette had slimmed down and skirts were becoming slightly shorter. Britain had been affected by industrial problems and inflation more than many other countries; good quality clothes had become very expensive so women bought classic styles as investment pieces. Italy's economic problems were less severe than the ones in Britain, and Italian ready-to-wear clothes held their own in the international market. Italian knitwear was well known for its inventiveness, and Missoni produced some of the most artistic combinations of yarns, stitches and colours.

## 1980–1990

The 1980s saw a shift towards more expensive, ostentatious fashions, which reflected the money-obsessed, image-conscious era. It became smart to indicate wealth by wearing expensive designer clothes and accessories, and the right designer logo was an important part of this showiness. Finance was big news, and the lifestyles and huge salaries of young stockbrokers were admired; this competitive group of people became known as 'yuppies'. The mobile phone became a desirable accessory. Many new designers began to challenge the established ideas of fashion and dress, and presented radical and innovative alternative styles.

London was the centre of youth style again, and distinctions between designer and street fashions became blurred. Vivienne Westwood was an influential designer of the era and her use of historical costume as a source of inspiration was the start of the New Romantic image of pop stars such as David Bowie, Boy George and Adam Ant. More information about Westwood's work can be found in Chapter 2.2.

**Figure 2.3.46** Armani's relaxed silhouette for men was very popular at the start of the 1980s.

When Princess Diana married Prince Charles in 1981, her romantic full-skirted wedding dress with its tight bodice and long train – designed by Elizabeth and David Emanuel – was copied within hours of the ceremony and set a trend for crinoline style dresses and skirts. Princess Diana became one of the most powerful fashion icons of the 1980s and 1990s, and her style of dress had a huge influence on the British fashion industry.

The demand for designer menswear increased, and top designers began to include fashionable clothing for men in their collections. Armani designed his much-copied suits for men and women; the loosely tailored jackets had wide shoulders and long lapels, and fastened at the waist with just one button. They were softer and more relaxed, and were made from textured wool fabrics, often with contrasting yarns to add interest to the softer colours than those used for traditional city suits. Paul Smith was an important British designer of menswear who showed classic, highly wearable clothes with his distinctive hallmark twists such as quirky patterns and bold colours.

Greater numbers of women wanted careers rather than being just wives and mothers, and were more financially independent. Cohabitation and single parenthood became more socially acceptable as the marriage rate declined. The big-shouldered power suit became a symbol of women's success, representing efficiency and ambition. Margaret Thatcher, the first female UK Prime Minister, was seen on TV news daily and reflected the power-

**Figure 2.3.47** Joan Collins in Dynasty 1986.

**Figure 2.3.48** 'Post-nuclear chic' was the name given to Comme des Garçons' 1st Paris show in 1982.

**Figure 2.3.49** Yamamoto dress from 1988/89.

dressing styles in her suits, even wearing structured brocade evening suits rather than lighter dresses. Jackets were often double-breasted and usually worn with a skirt, although it was now becoming acceptable for women to wear trousers in the workplace. Armani developed a range of clothes for women that were based on men's traditional suits, and the elaborate outfits worn in the American soap operas Dallas and Dynasty exemplified the powerful shoulder line.

An alternative fashion scene began to develop in the mid-1980s and influenced many new designers including Alexander McQueen and Gareth Pugh. Many new skirt shapes based on historical costume were developed, including Westwood's *mini-crini* collection, tutus and ra-ra skirts, like those worn by Madonna and the band Bananarama. Historical research also influenced other designers including Karl Lagerfeld, Christian Lacroix and Franco Moschino.

Moschino was influenced by Surrealist art, and he designed clothes that made fun of high fashion and the consumer society; he wrote *For Fashion Victims Only* on a shirt with very long sleeves that crossed the body in strait-jacket style, and decorated a Chanel styled suit featuring the words *This is a Waste of Money.*

Other British designers based their ideas on fantasy and escapism, but others were confronting contemporary issues such as the environment and peace. These included Katherine Hamnett's autumn/winter 1983/1984 *Choose Life* collection, which included T-shirts with slogans such as *58% Don't Want Pershing*, a reference to public displeasure about a type of missile being based in the UK. Her decontamination-style body suits and fatigues in crumpled washable silk fabrics were very influential fashions of this period.

Japanese designers began to assume greater importance in the world of fashion; Yohji Yamamoto, Rei Kawakubo of Comme des Garçons, and Issey Miyake established a new school of fashion which promoted an intellectualism in 1980s' designs, and challenged established ideas of dress. Miyake developed innovative and modern new materials and garment forms, and is best known for his flowing organic garments made from circular and rectangular fabric shapes which do not follow the lines of the body, and combine comfort with practicality. Kawakubo's designs challenged the uniformity of mass-produced fashions, and often featured large square shapes cut dissymmetrically and with deliberately misshapen features, rips, tears and creases. Her work was frequently considered to be an expression of feminism.

Yamamoto – known for his radical approach to fashion and outstanding cutting skills – designed garments which blurred gender categories and made a feature of shapeless, asymmetrical styles. Many of his designs are in black and use experimental textiles. His first collection shown in Paris in 1981 was nicknamed Hiroshima Chic when he broke with established trends and dressed his models in black, asymmetrical garments worn with flat shoes and white make-up.

Jean-Paul Gaultier also began to challenge the traditional French designs with his radical and provocative ideas. He showed underwear as outerwear and bondage styles (Madonna's corset with conical cups in 1989), dressed men in women's clothes (skirts for men in 1985 and corsets for men in 1997), and designed menswear influenced by gay culture.

**Figure 2.3.50** Gaultier's Corset dress 1984.

American designers such as Donna Karan and Norma Kamali designed more relaxed clothes with an emphasis on comfort, and knitted fabrics as well as unstructured styles were very popular. Body image became an important factor in looking good, and sport and leisure activities had an important influence on fashion.

## 1990–2000

The stock market crash on 19 October 1987 – referred to as Black Monday – shook world economies and caused the recession of the early 1990s. This brought a financial downturn for the fashion trade, leading to a reaction against the brash, conspicuous consumption of the 1980s. Less became more. Smaller disposable incomes and more restrained social lives led to a fall in the sales of high fashion clothing. The Gulf War intensified the fall in the sales of fashion products as it prevented trade with the wealthy Arab Emirate countries.

With the advent of the internet, more people began working from home, and many offices relaxed their strict workplace dress codes, so fashion began to be less important than in previous decades. Dressing down spread to every area of life, and became the acceptable norm. As in the late 1960s, clothing design increasingly reflected an interest in spirituality and ecology, with traditional ethnic clothing and subcultural styles starting to have a major influence on fashions. The main push in fashion became individuality as people no longer slavishly followed the latest designer trends.

Broad-shouldered men's suits gave way to softer, more subtly tailored garments with a long, slimmer fit and single-breasted styles; the informal Nehru style became popular. As 'dress down Fridays' took off in the workplace, executives began to wear smart casual clothes instead of a suit on Fridays, leading to an overall relaxing of standards in many offices.

The influence of street styles that began in the 1970s had a greater effect in the early 1990s, when fashion began to be more heavily inspired by a variety of past and present subcultures. In 1993, the grunge look developed from a mix of punk and hippie styles, and was a colourful and scruffy fashion based on home-made and craft-based garments. Customised clothes worn in layers and ex-army boots were worn by both sexes, and the trend was especially successful in America where it was developed by Marc Jacobs and Anna Sui. Grunge only caught on with British teenagers for a very short period of time.

Rap culture was an important influence on men's fashion as Hip hop styles became part of mainstream street fashion. The look included half-mast jeans, baseball caps, undone shoe laces and very baggy, casual layered sportswear styles which created a menacing and oversized silhouette. Tommy Hilfiger, Ralph Lauren (Polo) and Karl Kani developed Hip hop fashion ranges.

Street style influences led to trainers that were originally worn for sports becoming high fashion footwear, and part of the anti-fashion culture. Timberland boots, Nike Air Jordans, Vans, Dunlop Green Flash, Adidas and Puma were popular brands of footwear throughout the 1990s and beyond. Sportswear styles continued to have a major impact on fashions, and clothes made from comfortable stretch fabric worn with trainers were popular items of leisure wear at all market levels.

**Figure 2.3.51** Hip hop styles of the early 1990s.

**Figure 2.3.52** Issey Miyake's Pleats Please design from 1993.

**Figure 2.3.53** The 1940s inspired Galaxy dress by Roland Mouret was introduced in 2005 and quickly became a favourite of A-list celebrities.

**Figure 2.3.54** In 2007, Anya Hindmarch designed the 'I'm not a plastic bag' canvas bag produced in collaboration with a movement campaigning for global social change.

Celebrities began to influence fashion trends, and the 1990s saw the rise of the supermodel. A group of five models including Naomi Campbell and Claudia Schiffer came to represent glamorous fantasy, and when three of them featured in advertisements for Versace jeans, they became a must-have item of clothing. Cindy Crawford's popularity made a curvy figure the desirable fashion silhouette of the decade. But before long, supermodels were viewed as overpaid and overexposed, and the money-led elitist fashion system was considered vulgar. Concern was raised that the very thin, waif-like models were leading to a rise in eating disorders among girls and young women.

Chinese and Japanese inspiration was used in the cut and decoration of clothing by many designers, including Alexander McQueen and John Galliano and Issey Miyake's 'Pleats Please' line was an instant success in 1993.

Many people adopted a minimalistic attitude towards fashion as they tried to fit into an increasingly aggressive urban society. Rifat Ozbek was an influential designer, whose work typified the anti-consumerism message of the 1990s and the growing links with green issues and spiritualism. His white and silver New Age collection of 1990 signalled the backlash against excessive consumerism – this excessiveness led many designers to develop fashions that were less about image and more about vintage and recycling. Other designers' work reflected the changing attitudes; Katherine Hamnett promoted the use of environmentally friendly fabrics and manufacturing processes, and Helen Storey showed her Second Life collection of recycled clothing.

Eco-fashion was exemplified by the use of natural fibres including hemp, cork-soled Birkenstock sandals, chunky walking boots and other footwear made from leather-substitute materials.

Concerns about personal welfare and safety, the destruction of urban life and world conflict were also legitimate influences on fashion developments. Lucy Orta's Refugee Wear collection of 1992 included multi-functional clothes that doubled as sleeping bags and tents. Technological developments led to cyber fashions that were inspired by science fiction, virtual reality, punk, rubber, PVC and leather from fetishism, as well as a new genre of adult comic characters. These fashions were made from materials that had not been used in fashion before – polar fleece, neoprene and high-performance microfibres.

Deconstruction style was another strong influence on 1990s' styles, and started with the Antwerp Six. Ann Demeulemeester, one of the original Antwerp Six, designed garments with unrefined and unfinished details that were the antithesis of consumerism.

The Asian financial crisis at the end of the 1990s led to a fall in the profits of many fashion houses, and consumers in the Far East were supporting their own fashion industries rather than those based in America and Europe. To win back this lucrative market, many designers began to concentrate on quality, value and wearability. By the end of the twentieth century, fashion – as at the end of the nineteenth century – reflected the socio-economic and technological developments of the time. The internet now gave immediate communication across the globe, as well as 24-hour shopping facilities. Exciting new developments in textiles technology – many of them inspired by sportswear – stretched the boundaries of fashion and high-quality fashion products were available to all, not just the wealthy few as was the case at the beginning of the century.

**Figure 2.3.55** Gary Harvey designed a dress made from 30 copies of the Financial Times.

**Figure 2.3.56** This dress by Christopher Kane uses digital printing to achieve the spectacular effect.

**Figure 2.3.57** Hussein Chalayan created an experimental series of robotic dresses in 2007.

## 2000 onwards

Developments in technology are a major influence on the fashions of the twenty-first century. Improvements in communication and especially the use of the internet have made the world a smaller place, and are helping people to be more aware of what is happening across the globe. Global trading arrangements and advances in manufacturing and distribution systems have made fashion faster-moving than in earlier times. Modern manufacturing systems are efficient and lean, and developments have allowed for improved design and manufacture to sit alongside value for money, so that high fashion can be available to all.

The changing nature of society means that fashion is now much more inclusive than ever before. New materials, finishes and methods of manufacture can create amazing effects, especially when electronics are integrated into textiles.

Celebrity continues to be interwoven with fashion. Concerns for the environment and the dilemma of those working in the fashion industries and living in poverty have also given rise to new attitudes, and ethical concerns are important to socially aware consumers.

The internet is changing the way people shop and how fashion products are marketed; most fashion retailers have a physical shop as well as a website where purchases can be made by the consumer. E-commerce is an important player in the fashion business, and some new retailers only sell via the internet, for example ASOS. Internet buying gives consumers access to retailers all over the world, and developments in virtual reality allow customers to try on clothes before they buy. E-commerce allows for mass customisation of fashion products, and for retailers to target their potential customers more effectively than more traditional methods of marketing.

Sustainability has become a driving force for fashion designers in the twenty-first century. Concern for the environment and rejection of the greedy over-consumption encouraged by capitalism is leading the textile industries to think about how environmental and ethical impacts can be reduced during the life cycle of garments. Some retailers, for example Marks and Spencer, are trying to educate consumers by providing information about their ethical strategies. The global financial crisis that started in 2008 has meant many people now have less disposable income for fashion purchases.

Vintage clothing has become a fashionable and acceptable alternative to brand new garments, and the ability to customise mass produced fashion products is a rising trend. These trends, encouraged by celebrities, are part of the rejection of the similar styles sold in the retail outlets that dominate the high street. Some designers are well known for their creative use of recycled materials and approach to sustainability.

New manufacturing technologies based on digital systems are giving rise to many new processes for decorating products, many of which would be impossible to achieve using hand techniques. For example, Erdem's layered floral print and embroidery patterns, and Christopher Kane's use of fabric enrichment using digital and manual techniques.

Seamless knitting technology allows garments to be made without seams, and is used in many sportswear and underwear applications. This gives garments a close body fit while reducing fabric and manufacturing processes. Issey Miyake's A-POC (a piece of cloth) system is based on a knitted tube of

**Figure 2.3.58** Nicolas Ghesquière used eco-friendly fabrics for his multi-function road warrior outfit of 2010.

fabric that includes the shape and pattern of an entire garment within the fabric. The wearer simply cuts the fabric to their own size.

New materials and the use of electronic components have opened up exciting possibilities for designers, especially in the field of performance sportswear and health applications. For example, Speedo's biomimetic Fastsuits introduced in 2000, Adidas trainers incorporating Wi-Fi and the Nike+ trainer that syncs performance data with a mobile phone. Many of these hi-tech innovations are used by fashion designers in sportswear-inspired ideas for body-con and casual garments.

Hussein Chalayan was one of the first designers to use electronics in garments, and his 2007 One Hundred and Eleven collection allowed parts of the garment to move according to preprogrammed sequences.

In addition to providing useful functions, electronic technology can have a more sinister side when used in clothing items. Surveillance of people in the UK by authorities is escalating, and when electronics are embedded in textile products, it becomes possible to record, store and transmit information about an individual's whereabouts and activities. The Embedded Theatre, a wearable electronic device by a company called CuteCircuit, can analyse information about a wearer's location. This can be used as a wearable GPS system or could help parents keep track of their children, but might also be used in less ethical ways to monitor people's lives. The use of minute radio frequency identification (RFID) chips that have a unique identity code for individual products can be embedded in fabric and used to track a garment's progress through different stages of manufacture. But these chips could also be linked to a customer's credit card details and would allow retailers of the garments to keep track of individual consumers.

**ACTIVITY**

As a class, make a wall chart to show the changes in women's fashions that have been influenced by their role in society from 1900 to the present day. Place images of dress styles on a timeline matched to key historical events.

Today's designers are influenced by world events, war, terrorism and religious conflict. Concern for the homeless – especially in the light of the worldwide escalating number of refugees caused by war and famine – has led some designers to explore ideas for garments that are multi-purpose and for other humanitarian products. Hussein Chalayan's Afterwords collection in 2000 showed models wearing clothes that were able to be transformed into furnishing items.

Cultural influences have also shaped the direction of twenty-first century fashion designs, particularly African designers. Lagos in Nigeria is now one of the most important fashion cities in Africa. Duro Olowu's acclaimed Duro dress is based on a traditional kaftan-style dress worn by West African women, and Paul Smith's 2010 menswear collection was based on suits worn by men in the Congo. Other designers are working to bring positive change to Africa by having products manufactured in socially responsible ways on the African continent.

## Major developments in technology

Advances in technology are shaping the world in which we live, especially in the development of new and smart textile materials. At the beginning of the twentieth century, textile products were made only from fabrics containing natural fibres. Many households spent a long time caring for clothes – often a whole day would be spent washing and drying, and the next day ironing.

Different ways of buying and paying for clothes have had an impact on the availability of fashions. Shopping via the internet is becoming more popular with consumers, leading to retailers on the high street having to re-consider the way in which they operate. Chain stores and department stores have had to move with the times, and many now work with designers to develop their own brands of fashion, as well as selling online. Major supermarkets now sell quality clothing at reasonable prices, and the consumer is encouraged to keep up with the latest trends by buying new garments each season.

## The introduction of regenerated and synthetic fibres during the twentieth century

Synthetic fibres developed during the 1930s and 1940s came into general use during the 1950s and 1960s. They have been important in the development of easy-care fabrics, and a range of smart and technical materials. The following fibres were developed during the twentieth century:

- **Viscose rayon:** the first man-made fibre, it was invented in the late Victorian era and was called artificial silk. First produced in the UK in 1905, it was used for clothing in the 1920s. Viscose started to become more popular during the 1980s when there was a consumer backlash against the use of synthetic fibres. It is a useful alternative to cotton, and the rising cost of cotton in 2010 led many manufacturers to use rayon fabrics for their newest designs.
- **High tenacity rayon** and **high wet-modulus rayon:** developed in the 1940s and 1950s, it gave improved strength to the fibre. The new generation lyocell fibres are stronger and do not shrink as much as ordinary viscose, and are increasingly used in blends or on their own because of their reduced impact on the environment.
- **Nylon:** the first synthetic fibre developed as an alternative to silk in 1935. It was used for many products after silk became scarce during the Second World War, for example nylon stockings in 1940, parachutes and other military applications.
- **Polyester:** developed in the 1940s, it was initially known as Terylene in the UK. Polyester fibres came into general use in the 1950s.
- **Acrylic:** first made by Du Pont in 1941 when it was known as Orlon and Acrilan. Dralon is a brand name still in use today.
- **Elastane fibres:** developed in America in 1959 and were called Spandex, which is an anagram of 'expands'. It is also known as Lycra. These fibres became very popular during the 1960s, and have revolutionised many areas of clothing, especially sportswear and underwear.
- **Microfibres:** developed in Japan during the 1960s, and Ultrasuede was one of the first uses in the 1970s. They began to be used for a wider variety of applications in the 1990s, including sportswear and underwear.
- **Aramid fibres:** for example Nomex, Kevlar and Cordura®, they are developed from polyamide and were introduced in the early 1970s. Kevlar is regarded as one of the most important technical fibres developed, especially the newer fibres, which are four times thinner than the original fibre. The fibres are used where strength, slash-resistance and lightweight properties are important, such as in protective garments worn by police and military personnel.

**Figure 2.3.59** Kevlar is used for body armour.

Concerns about the environment have led to the development of new fibres such as lyocells, recycled polyester, Ingeo® (from corn starch), soya protein fibre, spider silk, and the use of non-traditional fibres such as hemp, ramie and nettle. Many designers are becoming very innovative in the way they use materials.

## The development of fabric finishes, e-textiles and smart materials

**Figure 2.3.60** Tactel microfibres are used for sportswear.

Modern fabric finishes have allowed fabrics to be more suited to their end uses, and easier to care for. Many of the developments have been in relation to the use of chemical finishes and the inclusion of thermoplastic fibres, which give shrink and crease-resistant properties to many fabrics.

Modern water-repellent fabric finishes are based on the use of fluoro-carbons rather than the older wax treatments. New finishes mean that wool fabrics can be machine washed and tumbled dry without risk of shrinking.

Some fabrics were developed specifically for sportswear, including moisture management fibres such as Tactel (1983) and Coolmax (1986). Tyvek, developed in the 1960s, is a non-woven fabric that allows water vapour to pass through, but not water in liquid form. Smart materials and electronic textiles are developing all the time, and have a variety of health and well-being, sports, safety and fun applications.

Nano-fibres are being developed for a number of applications, including self-cleaning textiles and sportswear applications. Explorations in space, and the requirements of military personnel who work in extreme weather conditions and challenging situations, have led to the need for a new generation of textile materials. The modern textile industry is moving forwards at an unprecedented rate, particularly in the area of intelligent textiles that include electronic devices or smart materials, and this is where future developments lie. These materials are increasingly used in specialised clothing, especially those worn for safety or protection, and for everyday products to make life easier.

Interactive textiles include a microchip and a circuit, and may be used for garments that can generate power to:

- help keep a wearer warm
- operate lights for safety and novelty applications
- allow MP3, mobile phones, tracking devices and radios to be included in garments, for example, the O'Neill MP3 jacket
- monitor body functions for health and fitness purposes, e.g. the VivoMetrics® life shirt.

Phase-changing materials such as Outlast contain paraffin wax capsules, which can change from a solid to a liquid and vice versa. They can be micro-encapsulated into textiles, embedded into foam or used as a coating, and can make textile materials which can store heat and are thermo-regulating. These materials are used in some extreme sportswear for example, and as fillings for mattresses and duvets.

Impact-resistant textiles such as D3O® are used to make wearable, shock- and impact-resistant sportswear garments that can protect the body from injury, for example when motorcyclists are thrown off their bikes.

**Figure 2.3.61** The Lifesuit is tested by the US army.

Robotic textiles are being developed, and have many potential applications in safeguarding soldiers, rescue workers and construction workers in dangerous environments. The Lifesuit, which was invented in 1986, is a robotic skeleton worn under normal clothing, and is used to help seriously injured people walk again. In the twenty-first century, differences between types of textiles are becoming blurred, and it is not so easy to put them into specific categories.

Further information about fabric finishes and new materials can be found in Chapter 1.4 of this book.

## New methods of manufacturing clothing and textile materials

For clothing to be manufactured on a large scale, fabrics need to be produced quickly. Most of the developments in weaving, knitting, dyeing and printing machines took place during the Industrial Revolution, and by the end of the nineteenth century, fabrics were mass produced efficiently. However, the mass production of clothing has been slower to develop, and garments for the upper and middle classes were usually made by a dressmaker until the early twentieth century. Poorer people made their own clothes, often remaking old garments into new ones, or bought them second-hand at fairs and street markets such as Petticoat Lane in London or the Rag Fair in Manchester.

The manufacture of garments became easier after the invention of the sewing machine in the mid-nineteenth century, but the complex styles and an increase in demand for clothing by the newly established middle classes did little to increase the speed at which garments could be manufactured. Many processes such as buttonholes and sewing on buttons still had to be done by hand. Clothing factories began to be built in the mid-nineteenth century, but these mainly produced menswear and workers' garments.

At the start of the 20th century, there were no retailers selling mass manufactured garments, and no call for mass produced fashions. During the First World War, the need for millions of military uniforms that were of a standard quality and were the same style led to a growth in factory production and labour-saving machines. By the end of the First World War, the easier fitting simpler garments made in the cheaper new rayon fabrics were suited to factory production.

Technical manufacturing equipment and expertise came over to Britain from America, especially with regard to sizing and grading of garments and patterns. Electricity became an important source of power, and mass-produced consumer goods aimed at the working classes became more available, promoted by new forms of advertising including fashion articles in magazines such as Woman and Woman's Own.

During the 1930s, Marks and Spencer were instrumental in improving efficiency and quality in clothing manufacture. They began to work directly with manufacturers rather than buy textile goods from wholesalers, and encouraged the manufacturers to invest in the best technology as well as more efficient methods of manufacture. The company set up its own testing laboratory in 1931 and began to write manufacturing specifications to improve the quality of the products. In

1936, they set up a design department to keep them up to date with the latest styles and trends.

The mass production of clothing made fashion available to all. It was developed between the two world wars, but it was not until clothes rationing was introduced in 1941 that manufacturing methods became more efficient and streamlined. The shortages of materials meant that manufacturers had to produce clothes more efficiently and economically, while at the same time maintain standards of quality. By the 1950s, increasing numbers of women were buying their clothes from chain stores rather than having them made by a dressmaker.

During the 1980s, cheaper overseas manufacture led to a need to improve productivity and reduce manufacturing costs, so that companies could remain competitive in the world market. There was also consumer demand for a wider range of fashion products and better quality, leading to an increase in the development of CAD and CAM technologies. The biggest progress has been made in automated pattern cutting and grading systems, fabric cutting and the movement of materials between work stations. Since the 1990s, some large companies have made significant investments in automated pattern design and fabric cutting equipment, which is used to cut out large numbers of garments for many different manufacturers. Less progress has been made with the automation of sewing processes, and these are often done by smaller companies where the cost of labour is cheaper.

CAD technology was integrated into fabric and garment manufacture so that new fashions can be produced much more quickly and efficiently. The traditional fashion seasons now change much more quickly than in the past, as clothes can move from the drawing board to the finished product on the high street in a very short period of time.

Just as important are the computer integrated systems which can help plan and manage the manufacturing processes. This ensures that the right products in the right quantities are delivered on time. The development of JIT and EPOS systems in the 1990s has helped speed up manufacture, and allow for rapid response to market demands.

Throughout the 20th and 21st centuries, cross-cultural and historical influences have had a strong impact on fashion design. Styles from other cultures have become more accessible as improved travel and communications have allowed people to travel the world with relative ease, and designers are able to experience first-hand a wide variety of designs and materials. Developments in photographic and printing techniques have allowed them to be inspired by secondary sources such as lavishly illustrated books, magazines and journals.

Further information about manufacturing systems can be found in Chapters 1.6 and 1.7 of this book.

**Figure 2.3.62** Digital printing gives designers more scope for introducing pattern in fabric and garments.

## New decorative techniques

Fabric manufacture and decoration have also benefited from computer control, and many complex weaving and knitting patterns can easily be incorporated into exciting fabric effects. Digital printing, computerised embroidery and the use of lasers to produce decorative cut effects on fabrics have allowed for a greater variety of patterns to be used.

Further information about fabric finishes and new materials can be found in Chapter 1.4 of this book.

## Development in the care of textiles

The natural fibres used for textile products at the start of the twentieth century could be difficult to care for, and the complex structures of the garments – including many layers of undergarments – took a long time to wash, dry and iron, especially as there were no electric washing machines or instant hot water. The prosperous classes had the help of servants to take care of their many garments and accessories. Improvements in fabric technology and facilities for home laundering meant that it was much easier to wear the latest fashions, and to change them in line with the latest trends. This encouraged a more relaxed attitude to dress, including throwing clothes away when new fashions became available.

**Figure 2.3.63** Electric washing machine with wringers 1950s. The washing had to be rinsed separately.

The development of easy-care synthetic fibres and finishes since the 1950s has made the work of caring for textile products much quicker and easier. Fabrics containing polyamide or polyester fibres are lighter, quicker drying and do not crease so much as the natural fibres. Many modern fabrics have crease-resistant finishes that reduce or remove the need for ironing.

Electric washing machines became more available, particularly after the Second World War when labour-saving devices were more common in middle class homes. During the second half of the twentieth century, these machines developed from being just washing machines that required separate rinsing operations (usually done manually in a sink) to twin tub machines, with one tub to wash the clothes and a spin dryer next to it. These machines still needed the washing to be transferred manually from one side of the machine to the other. Now most homes in the UK have an automatic washing machine that can wash, rinse and spin-dry. Many homes also have a tumble dryer as people have become relatively better off and the price of the machines in real terms has fallen.

Detergents and other laundry aids have improved, and help to clean textile materials more efficiently than was the case in the past. At the start of the 1900s, soap was used for cleaning, and it often had to be grated off a large block to make soap flakes that would dissolve easily in water. Stains needed to be removed using a variety of techniques and chemicals, and cotton fabrics were starched to add stiffness in a separate operation. Modern detergents are produced as easy-to-use liquids or capsules, and many contain enzymes to remove stains during the wash without the need for separate and harsher treatments.

**ACTIVITY**

As a class, make a collection of images of fashion garments that include the use of new technologies, such as laser cutting and digital printing. How have these techniques made the garments more appealing to the consumer?

Some new fabrics based on nano-technology are hydrophobic, and are able to repel water-based stains. Self-cleaning clothes, such as those made from cotton fabrics coated with titanium dioxide, use sunlight to break down dirt and bacteria.

Further information about the care of textile products can be found in Chapter 1.11 of this book.

## Product life cycle

A-level only

A product fashion life cycle is the story of the acceptance of a specific fashion from its first introduction until the end of its life. The fashion cycle of a standard product is usually shown as a bell-shaped curve with five main stages, as shown in the chart in Figure 2.3.64.

### Design introduction

At the first stage in the cycle, the designer creates the new style which is made in small quantities, making it very expensive and exclusive. The new style is worn by models and celebrities, and shown to the media.

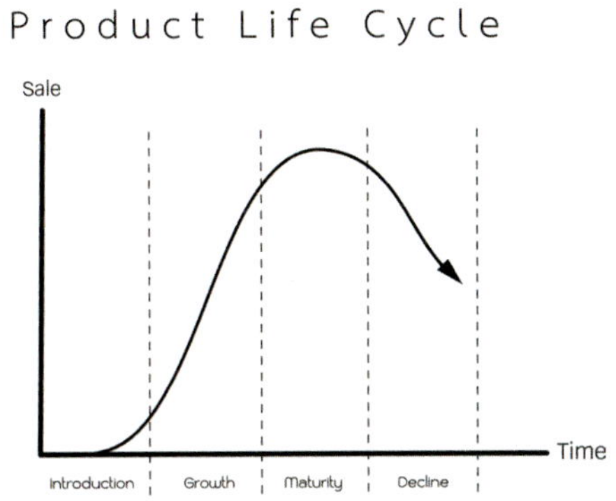


**Figure 2.3.64** The fashion cycle.

### Evolution

The style begins to rise in popularity as it becomes worn by people in the media and seen in fashion magazines, on TV and on social media sites on the internet. The style becomes available to others, but is still expensive and therefore out of most people's range.

### Growth and maturity

The design is modified and made using cheaper fabrics to be sold in high street shops at a lower price. There is no set time for this stage as the style can last for a season or many years depending on its popularity. Many other manufacturers may copy and develop the style, and it will be sold at many different price levels.

### Decline

People begin to become tired of the fashion and look for a new style. The garments are sold off at reduced prices in sales.

### Replacement

The style is obsolete and not available in the shops as consumers have moved on to a new fashion.

Further information about sales and marketing cycles can be found in Chapter 1.13 of this book.

**ACTIVITY**

Make a product fashion cycle analysis of a garment that was popular last year. Give specific dates for its launch, the height of its popularity and when the start of its decline was. Find media references to its popularity.

## Social, moral and ethical issues

A-level only

Social factors are things that affect our lifestyle, and include wealth, gender, family and religion. These can change over time as well as people's attitudes to them. Designers need to be aware of these changes to make sure that their products meet the changing needs of consumers. Today, our society is multicultural with people of many different religions and races, often with their own traditions, which will influence the type of products they will want.

Morals are concerned with the differences between proper and improper behaviour. They may be related to a code of conduct based on a person's religion or culture, or the standards of goodness expected within society.

Ethical factors concern things that are seen as the 'right thing to do', and morally correct. The way that a product is designed and made has an impact on the well-being, safety and comfort of all people who will be affected by the product.

Many social, moral and ethical issues are related to the environment and sustainability. Some people are concerned about animal welfare and therefore will not wear fabrics made from fur or leather. However, it is possible to use synthetic alternatives that resemble the real thing.

The manufacture and processing of fabrics and components can have many negative effects on the people and communities where they are made. Designers need to think about the impact of fast and disposable products, and whether it is ethically right for some people to be negatively affected by the desire to replace perfectly useable products in order to meet these constant changes.

How and where a textile product is made will impact society in terms of employment opportunities, and the effects of manufacturing activity on the local environment.

## Sustainable materials and ethical production methods

Today's fashions are tomorrow's rubbish, and an estimated 1 million tonnes of textile waste ends up in landfill every year. Many of these fabrics and components take decades to decompose, and give off methane gas as they decompose, as well as leeching heavy metals such as cadmium from components.

The world's natural resources are dwindling, and designers have a responsibility to use them carefully and to use recycled materials where possible. Manufacturers need to be aware of where materials come from, and to purchase them from ethical sources when possible.

Textiles can impact on the environment in many different ways. The growing of cotton plants uses fertilisers and pesticides which can pollute the atmosphere and waterways; synthetic fibres are made from chemicals from non-renewable sources. Using land to source raw materials means that less land may be available for growing food crops in parts of the world where people do not have enough to eat, for example India. Lots of land is needed for cotton plants, and this causes drastic changes to the landscape because of the intensive farming and deforestation.

Cotton needs vast amounts of water to grow, and diverting rivers and streams to irrigate crops has caused major ecological disasters such as the drying of the Aral Sea. In many countries where cotton is grown, such as Uzbekistan, there is not enough water for the people who live there to drink.

The pesticides and fertilisers used on cotton crops can have adverse effects on the health of farmers and other workers, including cancers and breathing problems. Chemicals from the pesticides and fertilisers can pollute water courses, poisoning drinking water.

Manufacturing activities can cause pollution of land and drinking water, which will affect the health of people living nearby. Manufacturing and finishing processes use chemicals such as those found in dyestuffs, and their effluent can be damaging. Water and energy are also necessary for these processes. Building factories and access roads may reduce the land available for housing and schools, and also contribute to pollution which affects people's health and well-being.

**Figure 2.3.65** Plastic bottles can be recycled to make polyester fleece fabric.

Many workers in the fashion industry – particularly those employed in less economically developed countries – are paid very little and forced to work long hours, often in hot, cramped and dangerous factories. Sometimes these workers are young children. Some unscrupulous manufacturers in the UK have been known to employ illegal immigrants to manufacture textile products for little pay in dangerous conditions. Many of the fashion textile products that are sold at low prices have been manufactured with no regard for the workers' health, safety or dignity.

Assessing a product's life cycle and considering its impact on the environment from 'cradle to grave' can help designers and manufacturers to use more sustainable methods of manufacturing. Cotton can be replaced by newer fibres such as Modal, which come from sustainable sources and use 'clean technology' in their manufacture. Ingeo, a new fibre designed to replace polyester, is made from plant starches and is fully bio-degradable. Recycling fabrics and making new fabrics from recycled materials can reduce waste; polyester fibres can be made by recycling plastic bottles – an example of this is Polartec® fleece fabric.

The cleaning, dyeing and application of additional finishes to fabrics during manufacture use many chemicals, and these are often disposed of in rivers in countries where the environmental laws are not as strict as those in the UK. A lot of water and energy is also needed for these processes. Using fewer dyes or developing fibres that are able to grow in different colours can reduce the need for dyeing. Synthetic fibres can have colour put into the spinning solution so that the fabric does not need to be dyed afterwards. Microfibres and dark colours use enormous amounts of dye and water to achieve the desired colour. Some modern printing techniques, for example digital printing, are cleaner than more traditional methods.

Making components such as zips and buttons also uses energy as well as plastics and metals, and this can have a toxic effect on the environment. Textile products are made all over the world before being sent to the country where they will be sold. When choosing materials, designers need to consider whether they can be sourced near to where the products will be made. Using more economic forms of transport – for example lorries that use biofuels and trains that can transport very large loads – can help reduce carbon emissions.

## Culturally acceptable products

Cultural factors are the values of an individual or a specific community that determine the way a person behaves. They have an important effect on the products that people buy, and a product acceptable in one culture may be perceived as offensive or less desirable in another. The use of colour and colour schemes are a good example of cultural influences on the design of fashion products. Red is associated with good luck in China but is the colour of mourning in South Africa, therefore red garments would be worn in different situations in these two countries.

**Figure 2.3.66** Red clothes are worn during Chinese New Year celebrations.

Today's society is multicultural, and designers of textile products need to consider the needs of the specific groups of people who will use the products. Clothing especially reflects the values of people and makes an important statement about the wearer - what we wear and when we wear it is part of our culture and socially learned way of life. It allows us to

**Figure 2.3.67** A prototype textile shelter developed by NASA could be put up quickly to provide temporary homes.

communicate who and what we are to others. The cultural group to which a person belongs will affect their choices, for example many young people are interested in music and the clothes worn often reflect those interests. Those who are members of a particular cultural group can recognise each other by the styles they wear. Peer pressure will also impact on clothing choices, along with the influence of what celebrities and fashion idols wear. The choice of colours, fabrics and components used for garments will be an important part of that culture.

## Products that are inclusive

Inclusive design is covered in Chapter 1.8 of this book.

## Products that could assist with social problems

Designers are increasingly using their skills to help meet humanitarian needs. Social problems such as poverty and homelessness mean that textile products need to be multifunctional, and able to operate in many different environments. Clothes will need to be functional and genderless as well as good quality, while remaining affordable. They should be able to protect people from extremes of weather, carry goods and children, function as flotation devices and transform into shelters and sleeping bags. Textile materials that are able to insulate are used for lightweight, transportable shelters, which could be used by those made homeless through natural or man-made disasters. For example, the inflatable lunar shelter developed by NASA and tested at the McMurdo station in Antarctica is a prototype shelter designed to protect people from extreme weather.

**Figure 2.3.68** These garments by Angela Luna were designed to meet the needs of migrants.

Medical textiles are able to monitor life functions such as heart rate, allowing people to go about their daily lives as normal while their health is constantly monitored, and without needing to spend as much time in hospital. BMS have created a new weaving technique which allows for the creation of more lifelike structures that imitate natural tendon and ligament performance – this complements its current tapering and bifurcation capabilities for very fine fabrics. You can read more about this at www.innovationintextiles.com/fibres-yarns-fabrics/new-class-of-textile-implant-solutions

## Fairtrade

Fairtrade is a trading partnership that works towards paying fair prices, and ensures good working conditions for farmers and workers who produce goods all around the world. Fairtrade methods of manufacture ensure that workers are not exploited and have decent working conditions. It is about supporting the development of communities and giving them a better chance of protecting the environment in which they live and work. Cotton products are typical Fairtrade items.

The Fairtrade mark is awarded to products that meet the international Fairtrade social, economic and environmental standards agreed by members of the scheme.

## The six Rs of sustainability

Please see Chapter 1.11 to learn about the six Rs of sustainability.

## Upcycling

Textile waste is produced when fabric products are disposed of by consumers, and this often ends up in landfill sites. Many unwanted textile products can be upcycled by changing them into new products. Upcycling is different to recycling because the product is reused, rather than broken down into the raw materials from which it is made.

Upcycling is not new – the 'make do and mend' campaign during the Second World War was all about reusing existing products, however the move towards more sustainable fashions has made it popular again. A number of designers and small companies are creating innovative and exciting new fashions by upcycling discarded clothing.

### ACTIVITY

Investigate how designers are using unwanted garments to create new fashions.

### KEY TERMS

**Socio-economic influences:** the social and economic factors that help to shape lifestyle, attitudes and expectations.

**Fashion trend:** a development in style that leads to new fashions being developed.

**The tailor-made:** a lady's two-piece suit with a masculine-styled tailored jacket, which became very popular at the beginning of the twentieth century and was a symbol of women's emancipation.

**Androgynous style:** a genderless style of dressing that does not put emphasis on women's natural curves, giving them a boyish silhouette.

**Life cycle assessment:** a method of assessing the environmental impact of the manufacture and use of materials and products.

**Sustainability:** the use of materials and manufacturing processes that do not harm the environment, communities or individual lifestyles.

**Upcycling:** the process of changing an unwanted product or materials into something new.

### KEY POINTS

- Women's evolving role in society had an important impact on the fashions of the twentieth century.
- Two world wars changed the established social patterns more than anything else, and this influenced the clothes that people wore.
- Developments in clothing manufacture helped to bring fashion within the reach of everyone.
- Cult fashions associated with young people started in the 1950s, when young people became disaffected with their parents' lifestyles and wanted their own fashions.
- The use of synthetic fibres from the 1960s onwards had an important impact on the care of fashion products.
- As the internet developed in the 1990s, the trend towards working from home led to more relaxed fashions.
- New developments in smart and technical textiles are having big impacts on everyday life, and on the lives of people living and working in extreme conditions.
- Sustainable design and manufacture considers how the materials, processes and disposal of textile products impacts the environment, and the health and well-being of all people who make or use the product.

# Check your knowledge and understanding

1 Who were the fashion leaders at the beginning of the twentieth century?

2 Name three fashion garments that have developed from workwear garments.

3 Explain how war influenced the styles of twentieth-century fashions.

4 Analyse the ways in which technical developments in textile materials have had an impact on sportswear since the 1950s.

5 Explain the difference between recycling and upcycling.

# Further reading

Jenkyn Jones, S. *Fashion Design* has many chapters about the principles of fashion design and the fashion industry.

Rouse, E. *Understanding Fashion* describes the influence of social change on fashion.

Quinn, B. *Textile Futures* includes information about many modern and smart textile materials.

Hibbert, R. *Textile Innovation* describes many new and innovative textile materials (www.textileinnovation.com).

O'Mahony, M. *Advanced Textiles for Health and Wellbeing* looks at how high-performance textile materials are used for non-traditional applications.

www.wgsn.com/en is a trend prediction company.

www.fashion-era.com has information about fashion history.

www.vam.ac.uk The V&A museum website has many articles about historical fashion.

www.cutecircuit.com has information about wearable technology.

www.innovationintextiles.com has information about new developments in textile materials.

# 2.4 Design processes

**LEARNING OUTCOMES**

By the end of this section you should have developed a knowledge and understanding of:

- a range of design processes including investigations and analysis, use of inspirational materials, ideas generation, illustration, modelling, planning, evaluating and testing
- development of a prototype from design proposals, using basic pattern/template drafting, block patterns and toiles.

If you are studying at A-level you should also have developed a knowledge and understanding of:

- the iterative design process in industrial or commercial contexts
- design methodologies in the corporate world, including collaborative working
- the cyclical nature of commercial design and manufacture.

## The design process

Designers work through the design process to create innovative and original design ideas, and to find the best way to make them into a prototype product. Designers gather information to inspire ideas and to establish criteria for the creation of new designs.

The design process can be outlined in the following stages:

- ideas investigated to explore possible design opportunities
- research carried out to find out about context, materials and techniques
- inspirational material collected and refined
- design brief details confirmed and agreed
- further research carried out
- design criteria established
- ideas generated
- ideas modelled and developed
- ideas tested and evaluated.

During investigations and designing it is helpful to plan, analyse, test and evaluate at intervals to:

- structure activities
- guide design thinking
- provide evidence to justify design decisions.

Designing is an **iterative** process – designs may be trialled and modified several times before finalising the prototype. It is not a linear step-by-step process because further research can be carried out as and when required, and design ideas created and developed at any point along the way. For example, critical evaluation of a design may suggest the need for further research, which in turn may generate more ideas for modelling and development.

## Investigations and analysis

In the early stages of the design process, the specific type of investigations carried out will depend on the context for exploring design opportunities. There may be a reason to look at specific needs of the target market, or to study cultural or historical influences. Particular experts may need to be interviewed and trend forecasts consulted. Designers will also consider what has already been designed and review existing products.

In this chapter, the stages of the design process are illustrated by student project examples. The first of these is based around the theme of mechanics, and we will revisit this project in a number of places later on in the chapter.

In the mechanics project example below, the student is going to design a garment with sculptural influences, inspired by classic Porsche cars. A variety of inspirational research is gathered and analysed, to consider the main elements that will influence design and development work:

- Historical research about classic Porsche cars highlights design features in the cars, which will influence the student's choice of techniques, fastenings, fabrics and finish in the final design.
- **Mood board** images of architecture, motor vehicles and mechanical parts inspire the choice of colour, pattern, techniques and materials for the design ideas.
- Existing design features seen in the work of a fashion designer inspire colours, textures and fastenings.

It is clear from the detailed analysis (Figure 2.4.1) that the investigations are relevant to the context, and establish a distinct and exciting basis for designing. The student states in the introduction that the reason for evaluating each piece of research is to help formulate the specification points. The sheet is laid out very clearly with tables to explain:

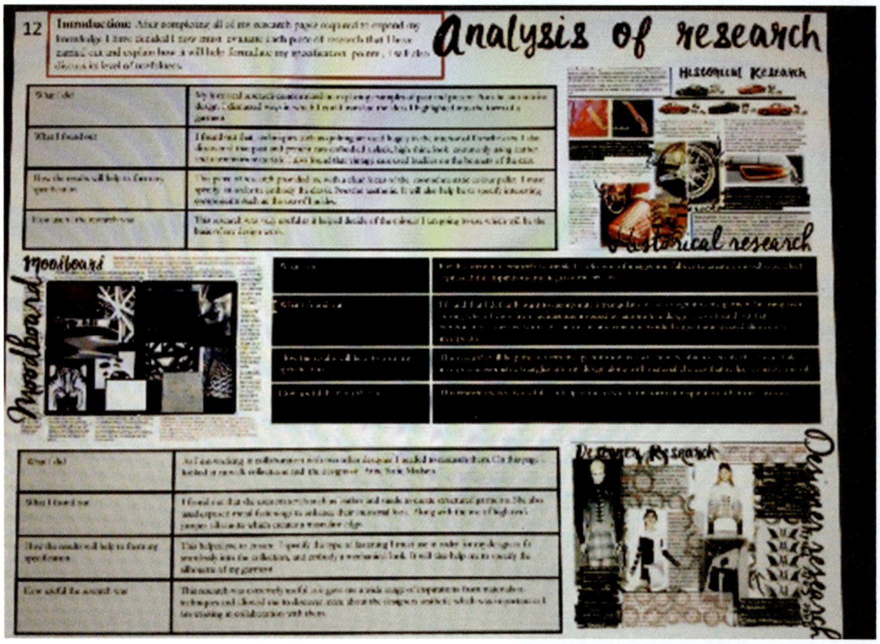


**Figure 2.4.1** Analysis of research.

- what research was carried out
- what results were found out
- how the results will help form specification points
- the usefulness of the research.

The student has researched the context for the project and analysed the findings. At this point they decide that further research is required (Figure 2.4.2) to find out about the level of finish in commercially produced garments. Therefore, they plan to analyse a shop-bought garment to find out about construction techniques, finish and accuracy. In the conclusion, the student also states that they need to find out how to laser-cut fabric, create honeycomb smocking and perform ruching techniques in order to meet the brief.

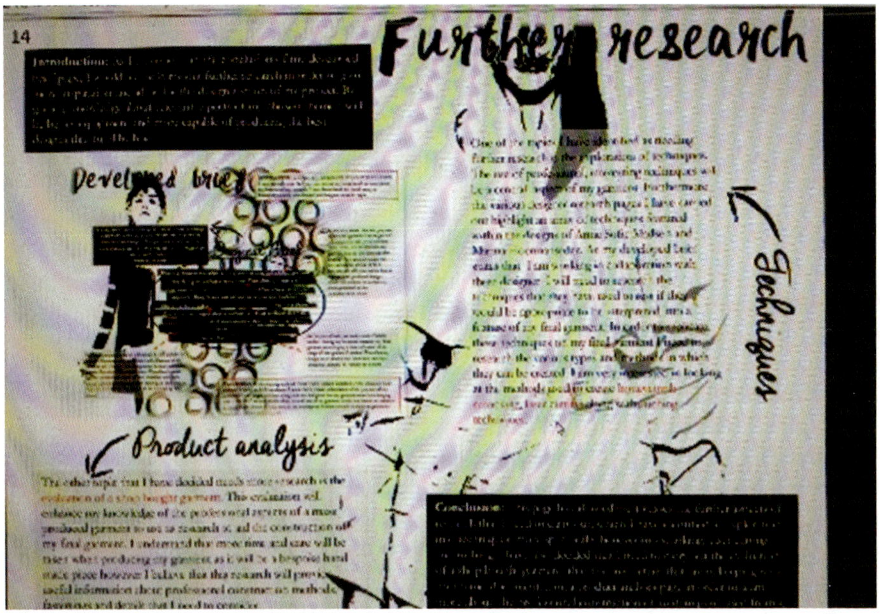


**Figure 2.4.2** Further research.

**Figure 2.4.3** Inspirational mood board.

## Using inspirational materials

Designers gather inspirational materials to give them ideas for unique and inventive design proposals. Visual references are sourced from internet searches and photographs, and the selected images are arranged on mood boards and **theme boards**. Drawings and fabric samples may be added to reflect the qualities in the images. The mood boards and theme boards are then analysed to pick out the most interesting elements.

In Figure 2.4.3, the student annotates the coastal mood board, using font colour to highlight the main points and key words to describe the mood. The mood board images in the centre of the sheet give the colours, textures, patterns, shapes and mood of the theme, while the surrounding annotation analyses and explains the images. Mood boards are also used by designers to communicate the design concepts to the client.

## Ideas generation

Through analysis, research findings become meaningful, and enable the designer to understand what is required and establish the design criteria. Once the design specification has been written, design ideas can be generated to meet the requirements.

Ideas can be explored through:

- quick outline sketches and experimental work in **mixed media** to investigate design possibilities
- more detailed drawings by hand or using drawing software combined with samples of fabrics and components, to experiment with colours and textures
- sampling of techniques to explore possible methods of working
- trialling the use of materials to find out what is possible and what is most effective
- modelling activities in paper, fabric or using CAD to investigate 3D shape, proportion and scale, and to lead into the development of the pattern for the product.

Designers need to be prepared to take design risks when designing and developing their ideas, in order to think 'outside of the box' and look into designing something new and different. However, reference to the design brief and specification throughout the designing and development of the design proposal is necessary to keep the design relevant.

In the mechanics project example below, a variety of media have been used to explore design ideas. A waxy, black pencil and watercolour paint are combined in the first idea (Figure 2.4.4) to show contrasting fabric textures. In the second idea (Figure 2.4.5), fabric swatches are put together in a collage to suggest a combination of materials in a geometric design.

In the student exemplar below, fabric choices and ideas for fabric printing, embellishment, embroidery and manipulation techniques have been inspired by images on the coastal mood board in Figure 2.4.3. The student includes peer opinion and picks out keywords when evaluating the two ideas.

### KEY TERMS

**Theme boards:** images on a display board selected to inspire design ideas based on a specific theme.

**Mood boards:** images, colour swatches, drawings, photographs and fabrics included on a display board to inspire the designer and create a feeling of the context for design.

## ACTIVITY

Generating ideas for a repeat pattern: Take a photograph of contrasting shapes, colours or tones, for example dark branches against the sky as in Figure 2.4.6.

Print multiple small coloured copies or copy and paste an area of the photograph using a programme such as Photoshop. Form a repeat pattern by positioning the copies of your photograph next to each other without any gaps between the copies, as in Figure 2.4.7.

Consider making different arrangements of the copies to create alternative repeat patterns. For example, reflected or rotated patterns. Alternatively, use an app on your smartphone such as Layout, to create a repeat pattern.

**Figure 2.4.6** Photograph of tree branches.

**Figure 2.4.7** Repeat pattern from a photograph.

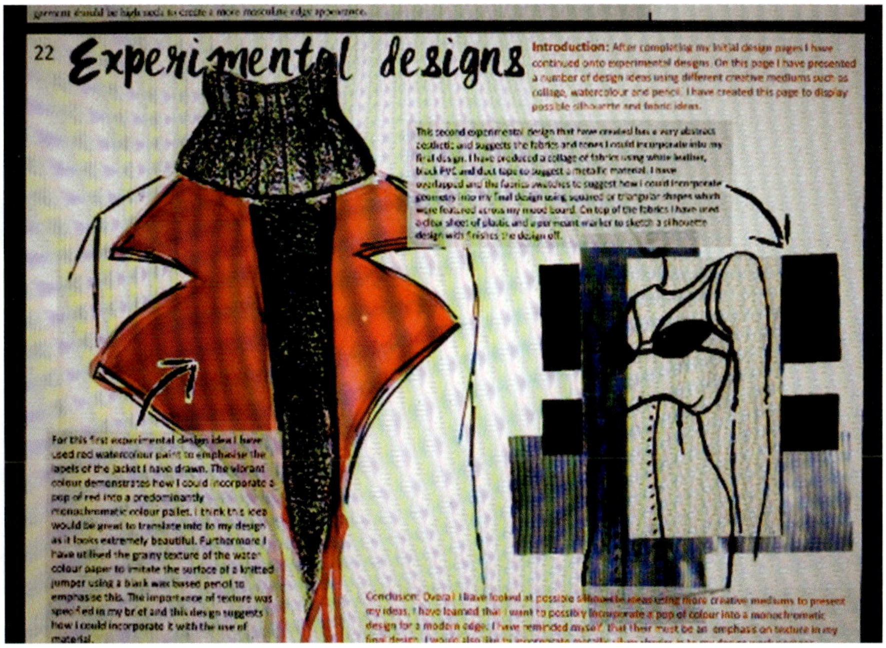


**Figure 2.4.4** Experimental ideas.

**Figure 2.4.5** Generating ideas from a mood board.

## Illustration

Design ideas are illustrated to make a record of the design concept and final design, and also to convey the mood and appearance of the design to others. The designer incorporates colour, style and textures, and indicates choice of fabrics and techniques. Illustrations can be sketches, drawings, paintings, collages and other media done by hand, or can be drawn using a programme such as Adobe Illustrator.

In Figure 2.4.8, butterflies and design ideas have been illustrated using a variety of different techniques to experiment with line, colour and shape. The student drew in pencil, coloured pencils and pen to explore qualities taken from the butterfly theme, and to analyse an existing design by

Alexander McQueen. Butterfly wing images were cut out and arranged in a mirrored pattern using a computer; this design was later developed further, sublimated onto fabric and used in the final prototype.

**Figure 2.4.8** Illustration of design ideas.

## Modelling

Modelling is about trying out ideas to help make decisions during design development. Designers choose modelling materials that are inexpensive, readily available and quick to use. Sometimes there is a need to model with more challenging materials that are being considered for use in the final prototype, to test how they work in the design. It may only be necessary to model part of a design, for example a design feature that may be unique in 3D shape or in decorative embellishment. Some modelling may be carried out to practise manufacturing skills so that the final prototype is accurately and skilfully made. If appropriate, models can be made to a smaller scale than the final piece.

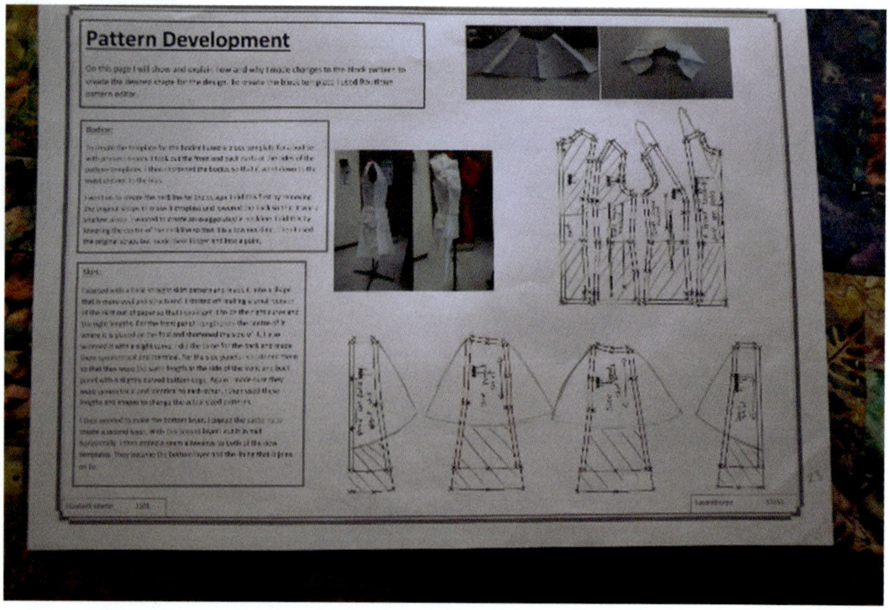


**Figure 2.4.9** Pattern development from modelling.

In Figure 2.4.9, the student tests a new skirt idea by making a smaller version out of paper and working out the proportions of the skirt, before making a full-scale pattern using pattern drawing software.

The use of metallic and quilted fabrics have been explored in Figure 2.4.10 to experiment with different ideas for layering materials. The student has investigated different fabrics, 3D shapes and techniques to develop the front panel of a skirt.

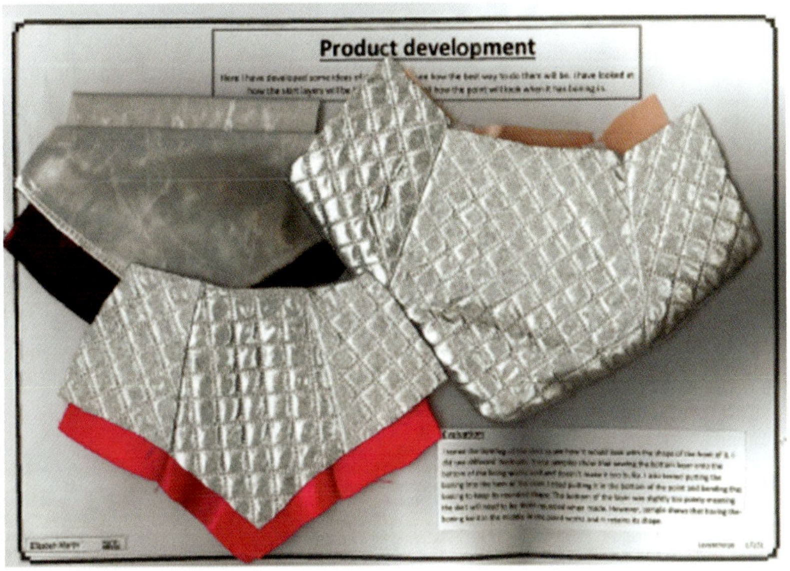


**Figure 2.4.10** Modelling in fabric.

## Planning

Design ideas are evaluated to make a judgement about which ideas should be further developed. It is important to keep in mind the design brief and design criteria so that further development is focused on requirements. The designer needs to work out which materials, components, techniques and processes could be used to build a successful design prototype, and needs a plan to outline areas for investigation.

A development plan sets out what needs to be done, and explains why the work is necessary. The student decides how the work will be carried out and which processes will be used. The student then writes an introductory section to explain that the plan will detail what they need to do, and why they will be carrying out the listed areas of development. They consider what needs developing, why they are going to develop it and how they will carry out the development work. A column in the table can be used to point out how they will provide evidence of the development work in such pieces as samples and photographs. They set out to develop the neckline, dress tail shape, embellishment techniques, colour, toile, fabric and component specifications. This action plan is an efficient way of mapping out the work to be completed in order to finalise the design.

## Evaluating and testing

Evaluating and testing is about finding out about the strengths and weaknesses of design proposals by collecting opinions and making judgements about:

- design ideas
- samples
- patterns and toiles
- proposed manufacturing methods.

Design proposals can be tested against the design criteria, and feedback can be sought from the client, fashion and textiles experts and those likely to wear or use the product. Critical reflection and evaluation of design ideas is necessary in order to take the best concepts through to development.

**Figure 2.4.11** Evaluating design ideas.

In Figure 2.4.11, peer assessment has been used to evaluate the design idea, and the student applies personal judgement to pick out the best features for design development.

# Prototype development

The prototype is made using a suitable commercial pattern, or by drafting a new pattern for the design.

## Basic pattern/template drafting

A pattern is a set of templates that can be used to give the shape of each part of a garment or textile product. The pattern pieces are laid out on the fabric, then either traced around and cut out, or cut out around the template. Pattern pieces have written notes and symbols on them to label each piece, and to direct how to use them to construct the fabric pieces into a product.

Existing commercial patterns for styles which are similar to the proposed design can be used as a starting point. The commercial patterns may only need minor adjustment to develop the pattern. For example, the length of the sleeve or the shape of the neckline could be altered.

Patterns can also be developed:

- from standard **block pattern** templates
- using pattern drawing software
- by tracing shapes from existing products
- using **moulage** techniques.

## Pattern notation and labelling

Agreed symbols and technical terms are used on pattern pieces. When you draft a pattern, you need to use the same language as the commercial **pattern notation** seen in Figures 2.4.12 and 2.4.13. However, the pattern you draft will be for a specific size and labelled in only one language.

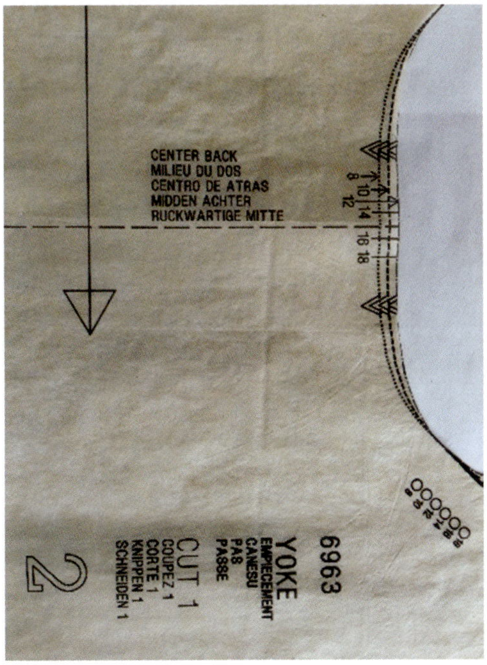


**Figure 2.4.12** Pattern notation on a commercial pattern.

## KEY TERMS

**Block pattern:** basic shaped templates for a garment pattern.

**Dart:** a folded and stitched area of fabric that allows flat fabric to form 3D shapes.

**Grainline:** the line parallel to the warp threads and selvedge of woven fabric.

**Selvedge:** the edge of a woven fabric with a higher density of warp threads which strengthen the edge and prevent it from unravelling.

**Notches or balance marks:** marks on a pattern that correspond to those on adjoining pattern pieces. They guide the placement of fabric pieces when stitching them together.

**Pattern notation:** the written and drawn instructions and labels on a pattern.

The following notation and labelling are common to most pattern pieces that you will come across:

- The pattern reference number and pattern piece name is written on each pattern piece. Figure 2.4.12 is a pattern piece for the yoke of a shirt. The yoke is labelled as pattern piece two.
- This pattern piece has been cut out for a size 12, which is shown using a dash-dot-dash cutting line indicated at the top of the yoke in the photograph above.
- The large arrow moving across the yoke shows the direction of the fabric **grainline**; the grainline arrow has an arrowhead at each end of the line. This shows the direction in which to line up the pattern piece on the fabric. For the yoke, the warp threads in woven fabric need to run across the shoulders because this is where the strength in the fabric is needed in use. The grainline is lined up with the warp threads, parallel to the fabric **selvedge**.
- The centre back is shown by the dashed line, and this is the line midway between the shoulders. Centre backs and centre fronts are always straight, vertical lines.
- The triangles at the top of this pattern piece are called **notches**. Triangles are cut in the fabric to help match up two fabric pieces accurately when stitching them together. On a sleeve, one notch indicates the front of the sleeve and a double notch indicates the back. The notches prevent you from putting in the sleeve backwards or on the wrong side.
- Notches are sometimes referred to as **balance marks** – they have the same purpose but are shown as short, straight lines pointing in the same direction as the notches.
- Two bold lines running parallel show the adjustment line. This is the best place on the pattern piece where the garment can be lengthened or shortened without changing the pattern shape.
- Some pattern pieces have a fold line – a double-headed arrow with two bent ends. This line needs to be lined up with the fold in a piece of folded fabric. When the pattern piece has been cut around and the cut-out piece of fabric is opened out, the shape of the fabric will be symmetrical along the fold.
- The seam allowance is usually 1.5 cm wide. This is the distance between the cutting line and the stitching line.
- The circles identified by size 8 to 18 markings (top right) show where to match up the yoke with the neckband. On other pattern pieces, they can be used to show where to place a pocket or match up points on a **dart** (Figure 2.4.13).
- Darts allow a flat piece of fabric to be shaped to fit the curves of a body. They are made by folding and stitching the fabric piece from the edge of the fabric to a point; the fabric then takes on a 3D shape to fit the body. For example, on a bodice the dart might start from the arm hole with the point at the apex of the bust. The wider the dart at the open end, the more accentuated the 3D shaping. A dart is shown on the pattern by two lines that meet at a point. The lines indicate where to fold and stitch the fabric. The dart positions are shown for the whole range of sizes in Figure 2.4.13.

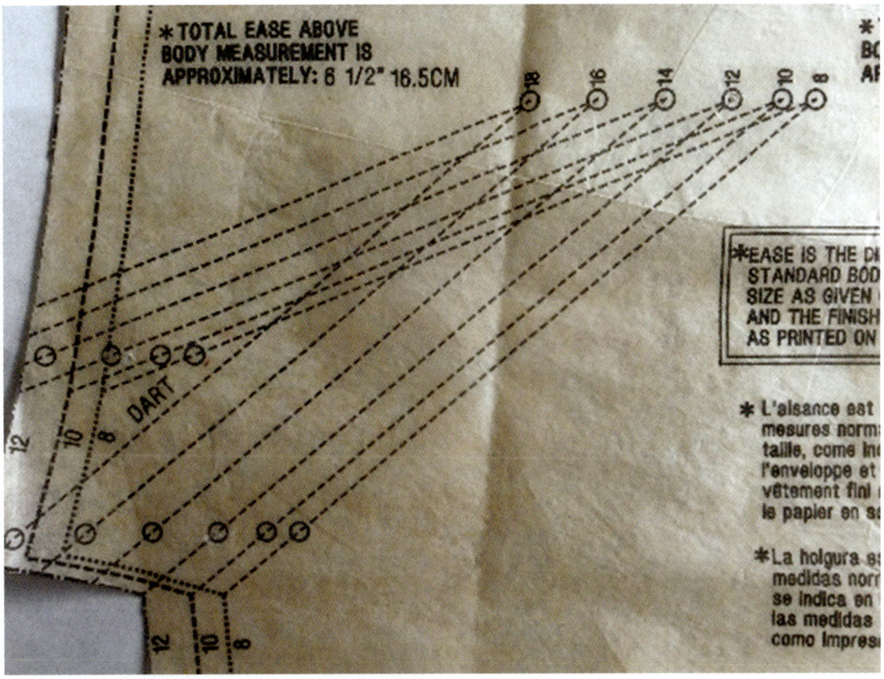


**Figure 2.4.13** Dart notation on a commercial pattern.

**ACTIVITY**

Make two samples of darts – one with a wide-open end and one with a narrow-open end. Present your samples in your file or notebook.

## Working from basic block patterns

**Figure 2.4.14** Block patterns.

If you are not using a commercial pattern, block patterns like those seen in Figure 2.4.14 can be used as a starting point for the prototype pattern. The block is selected for its general shape, for example a trouser leg front or skirt front. The block is traced onto paper and the shape is modified to build the pattern for the prototype. Changes can be made such as altering the shape of an armhole, the position of a dart or flaring out the bottom of the shape to add fullness to the resulting garment.

> **KEY TERMS**
>
> **Dot and cross paper:** paper for making patterns which has dots and crosses on it to guide straight lines when pattern drafting.

## Basic adaptations to create unique and individual styles

In the student example in Figure 2.4.15, a drawing programme called Pattern Master was used to print the basic block pattern pieces. These were then developed by extending them with **dot and cross paper**. The student tested the adapted pattern pieces on a mannequin, to check if sufficient volume had been created in the 3D shape of the garment. The student manipulated the basic templates to develop a pattern in the desired shape. Once the pattern had been modified, a toile was made in fabric to test the new pattern.

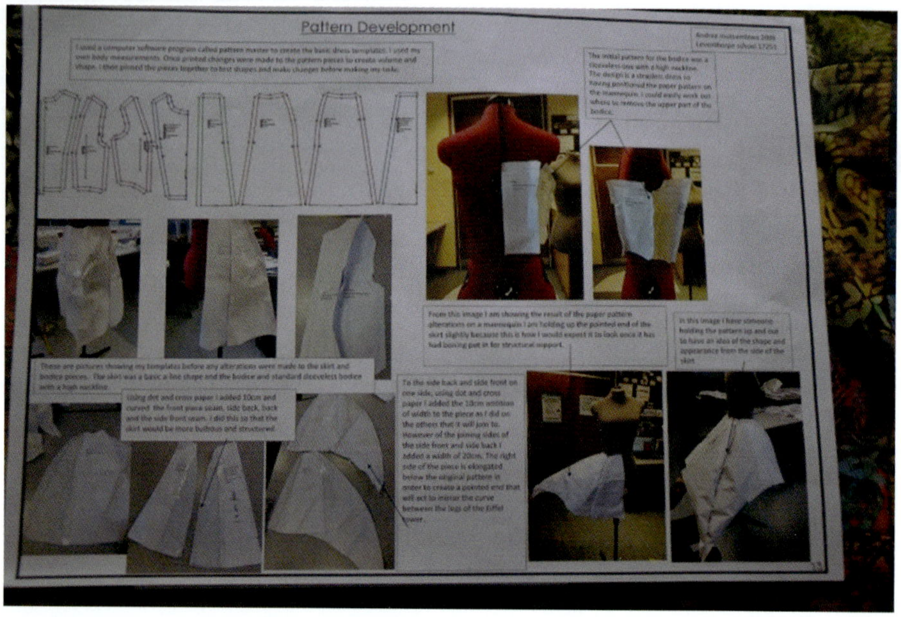


**Figure 2.4.15** Adapting the block pattern.

In the mechanics project example shown in Figures 2.4.16 and 2.4.17, a commercial pattern provides the basic shape for the bodice pattern pieces. The student adapts the pattern by first using it to make a toile, and then redrawing the desired shape of the bodice on the toile. The fabric toile is cut into the new shape, and this is used as a template from which to create the new pattern.

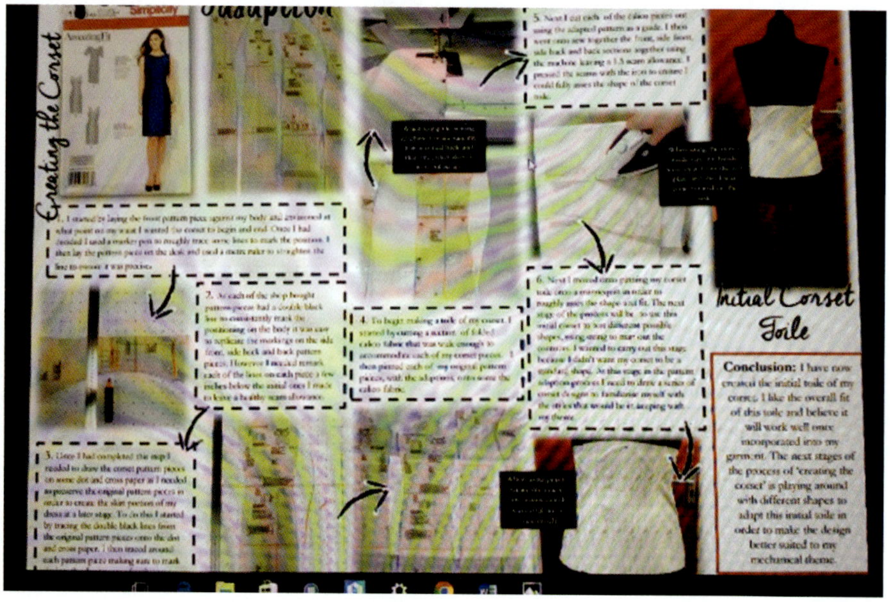


**Figure 2.4.16** Adapting a commercial pattern.

**Figure 2.4.17** Adapting a commercial pattern.

## Using existing products to develop patterns

Existing products can be laid out very flat on pattern paper and drawn around to trace simple shapes from sections of the actual garment. A seam allowance is required around each pattern piece, and this can be added using a piece of drawing equipment called a **pattern master**. Alternatively, if the existing product is no longer needed, it can be carefully taken apart. Each section can be ironed flat and then traced around to make the pattern pieces.

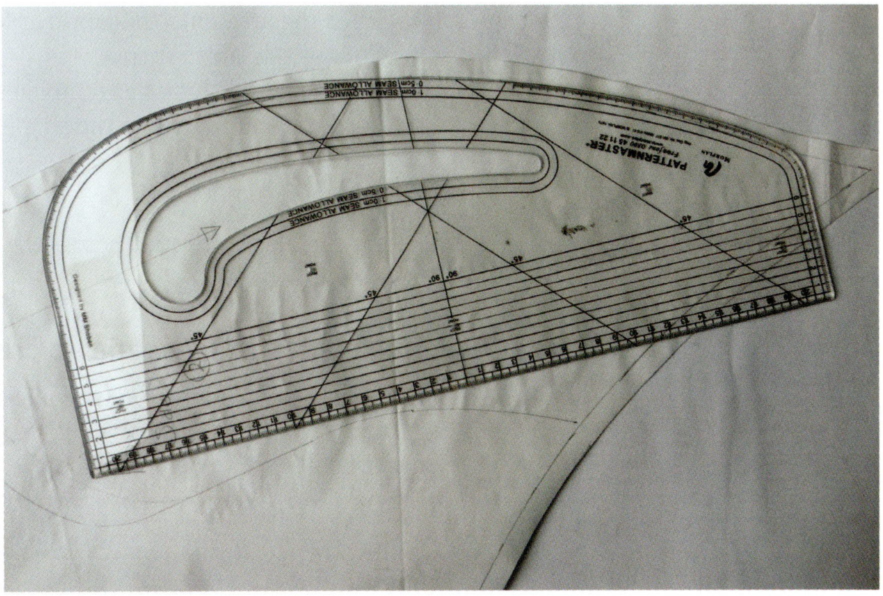


**Figure 2.4.18** Pattern master used to guide the drawing of curves, measure and add seam allowance.

The example in Figure 2.4.19 from the mechanics project shows how a basic sleeve pattern is made by tracing around the sleeve of a jumper. This forms the basis for further experimentation to create a unique sleeve design. A ruched or gathered sleeve is developed by pleating the sleeve fabric along the inside seam of the sleeve pattern, and manipulating the fabric into the desired shape.

Figure 2.4.19 Drafting a unique pattern from an existing product.

## Moulage

Moulage is a method of moulding fabric around a mannequin to develop a pattern. Pieces of fabric are draped across the mannequin and templates are made from the fabric pieces. It is done in the following stages:

- Mark out the seamlines and edges of the new garment design on a mannequin using fashion design tape.
- Lay a piece of fabric over the top of each section and mould the fabric around the shape of the mannequin.
- Trace the area onto the fabric to form the shape of each pattern piece.
- Cut out the fabric shapes.
- Use the fabric shapes as templates to make paper pattern pieces.
- Add seam allowance to the shape to make the pattern using a pattern master.
- Add pattern notation.

Fabric can also be draped across the body to work out how to manipulate folds and gathers.

> **KEY TERMS**
>
> **Moulage:** moulding fabric around a manikin to work out garment design and pattern pieces.
>
> **Pattern master:** a ruler with straight and curved edges for measuring shapes and seam allowances and drawing patterns.

### Moving darts and seams to create new fullness

Darts on a block pattern can be altered to change the shape of the garment. When tailoring a garment to an individual person, their body measurements can be taken and the pattern adjusted to make an exact fit: the position of darts can be moved and size of darts can be changed.

Figures 2.4.20, 2.4.21 and 2.4.22 show how a dart can be removed and the fabric fullness transferred to the waistline, in order to adjust the style of the garment. The pattern piece is adapted by cutting the pattern along the lower dart line towards the bust, and cutting a vertical line from the waistline towards the bust. The section of the pattern that is released is pivoted from the point of the bust, moving the lower dart line to line up with the upper dart line. An extra piece of cross and dot pattern paper is inserted into the gap to extend the pattern piece.

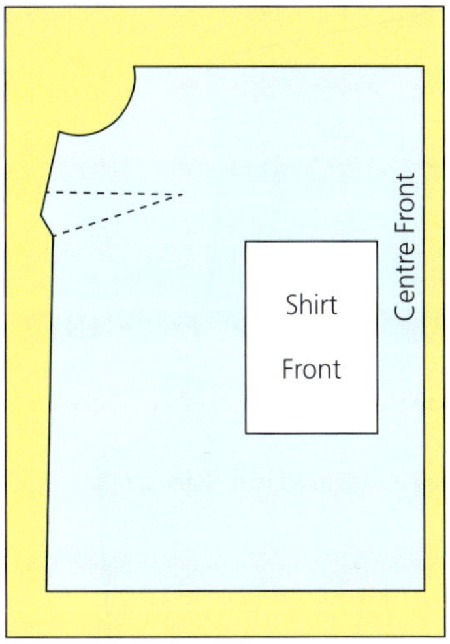


**Figure 2.4.20** Adapting pattern style.

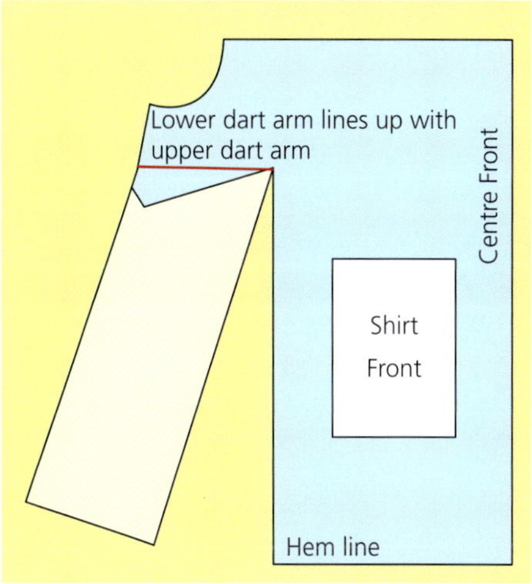


**Figure 2.4.21** Adapting pattern style.

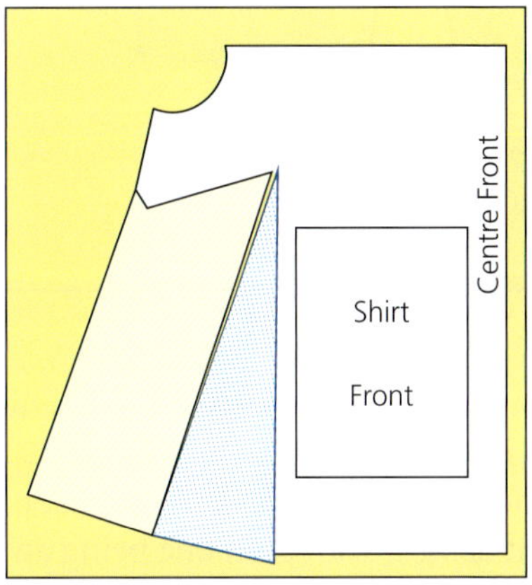


**Figure 2.4.22** Adapting pattern style.

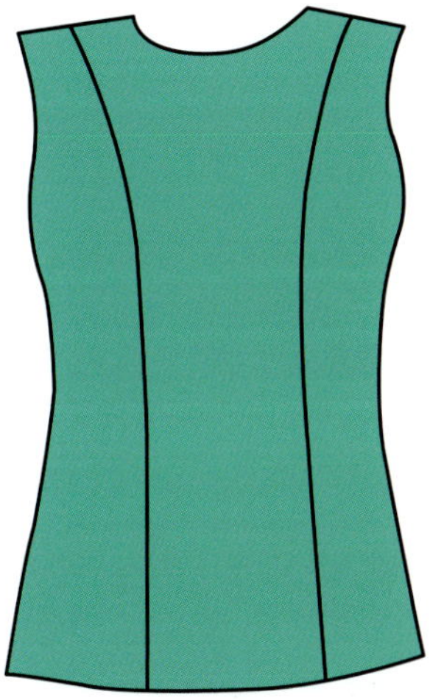

**Figure 2.4.23** Using curved seams to fit body shape.

Seams can be used instead of darts to shape the fabric around the curves of a body. In Figure 2.4.23, the curved seams – called princess seams – give a close-fitting style without the need for darts.

## Shaping or creating yokes

A yoke is a section of the pattern that fits around the neck and shoulders, or around the waist. The yoke supports the lower part of the garment, which may be gathered. A yoke across the shoulder and chest will replace the need for a dart at the bust because it can be shaped to follow the line of a curve, or can end above the bust line with gathered fabric below.

Figures 2.4.24, 2.4.25 and 2.4.26 show how the dart from bust to side seam can be replaced by a shaped yoke:

- A line is cut from bust to arm hole, and the dart is closed by pivoting the blue section in the diagram below, to join up the original dart lines.
- The pattern piece is redrawn into two sections to replace the original single pattern piece. Curved lines are drawn across the bust line and over the previous dart line, to make the shapes for the top and bottom pieces. The yoke is the top half.

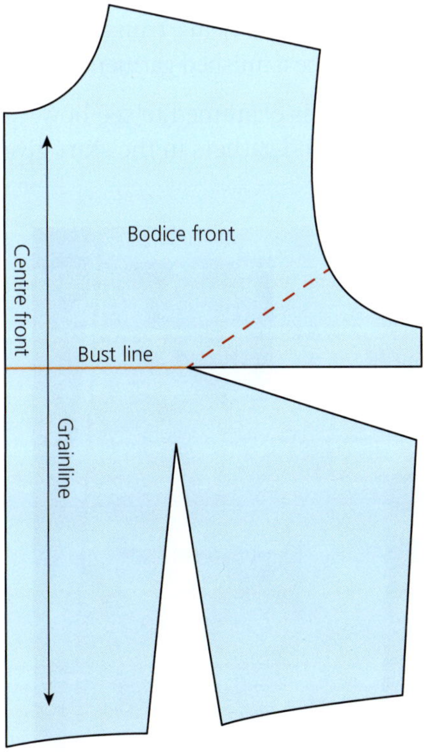


**Figure 2.4.24** Creating a yoke from a dart.

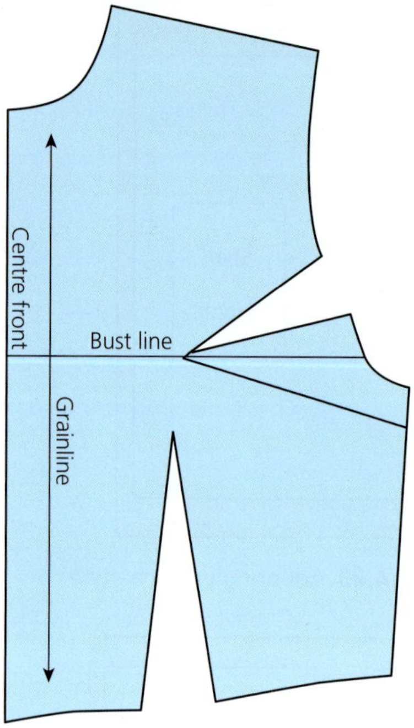


**Figure 2.4.25** Creating a yoke from a dart.

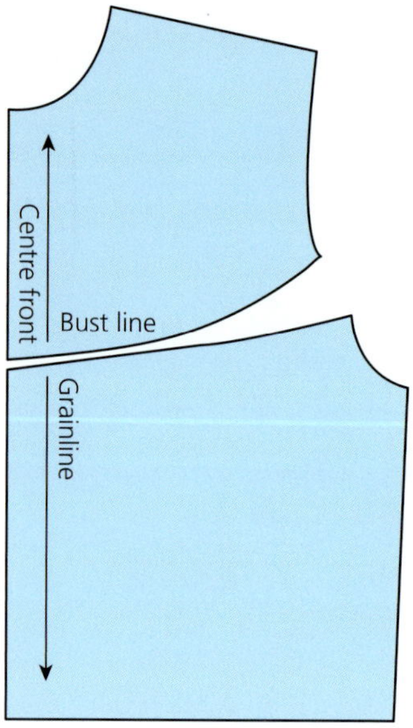


**Figure 2.4.26** Creating a yoke from a dart.

## Use of toiles

**Toiles** are made in fabric to test the pattern and enable the designer to see what further modifications may be necessary to adjust style, fit and how features work in use. Several toiles may be made during the development of a new garment design, with each one being an improvement on the previous. Toiles may be whole or part garments; only the necessary features will be included on the test garments. Fastenings may not be included and hems, trims and embellishments are not required; the toile will not be a finished garment.

The toile in the student example in Figure 2.4.27 is examined to see how the bodice collar works, and whether the pleats and gathers in the skirt give the desired volume and shaping.

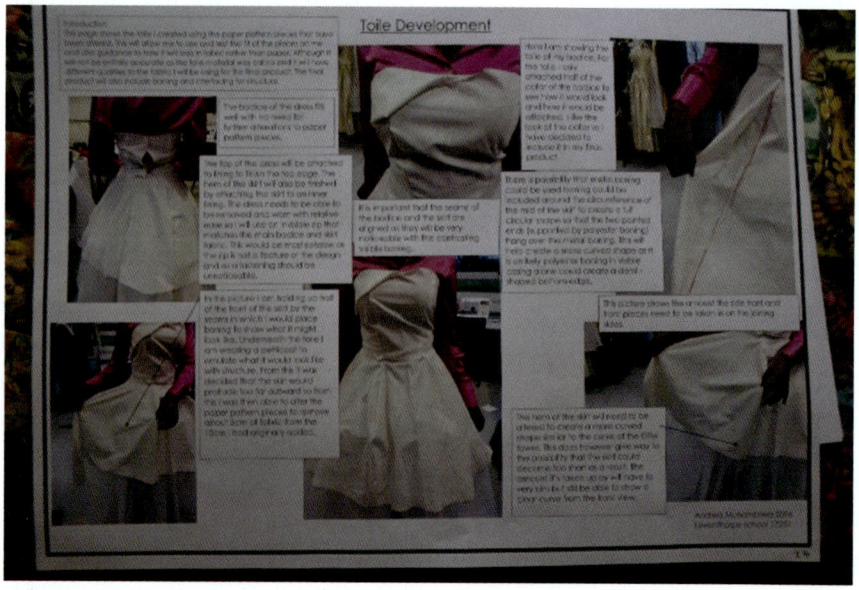


**Figure 2.4.27** Toile development

# The iterative process in industrial and commercial contexts

A-level only

In commercial practice, the design process is driven by the need to develop a product at the right price that will be fit for purpose and attractive to consumers. The designer will understand the requirements of the market for which the product is intended; high street retailers demand designs developed in response to sales figures and fashion trends, whereas designer labels require designs that are distinctly innovative.

In the process of researching and developing new products, designers will trial different samples, and repeat the development stages a number of times to improve the prototype. Each changed or developed design is an iteration. This continues until the design concept is realised in a final prototype that is ready for manufacturing.

## The use of different design methodologies when designing products

A variety of research methods are used to bring together information that will be used to generate design ideas, or to develop existing products to update them. Commercial trend forecasts are used to guide the designer as to what will be fashionable in the future. Trend forecasts set the trends by describing the colours, textures, patterns, motifs and techniques that will interest consumers.

### KEY TERMS

**Iterative design:** a cycle of sampling, testing, analysing and refining the design that is continued until the final design is created.

**Mixed media:** combining different drawing and colouring materials in one piece of work.

Fashion designs for mass market consumers will be influenced by catwalk and celebrity trends, and sales of existing current products will be used to inform design decisions for the next season's fashion. Designers visit trade shows to keep up to date and informed about fabrics, components, techniques and fashion styles; they read magazines and keep track of blogs, reviews and social media on the internet so that they can respond to consumers' interests. Designers use many different design methodologies when designing products, depending on such factors as the type of product, the target market, the client and the budget for designing.

## Collaborative working

There are many different aspects to the development of a new fashion or textile product for manufacturing. In industry, a group of people with a range of design and technical skills will work together in a team to create the final prototype:

- A freelance or in-house designer creates a design, illustrates it and outlines the requirements to make it.
- The design is shared with the product development team to work out the most appropriate method of manufacturing the design, and to trial suitable and available fabrics and components to meet the budget.
- The pattern designer or cutter takes the design and makes a pattern to interpret the drawing.
- The pattern grader develops the pattern to give a range of different sizes that are in proportion to the original pattern.
- The sample machinist sews the first made-up sample of the new garment design from the pattern, using manufacturing techniques and processes.
- The garment technologist or product developer co-ordinates the team to develop a garment that fits well, can be manufactured within budget and is approved by the client (Figure 2.4.28).

The team approach exploits the skills and expertise of a range of specialist employees. It also provides the opportunity for alternative ideas and points of view to be considered in the development of a product.

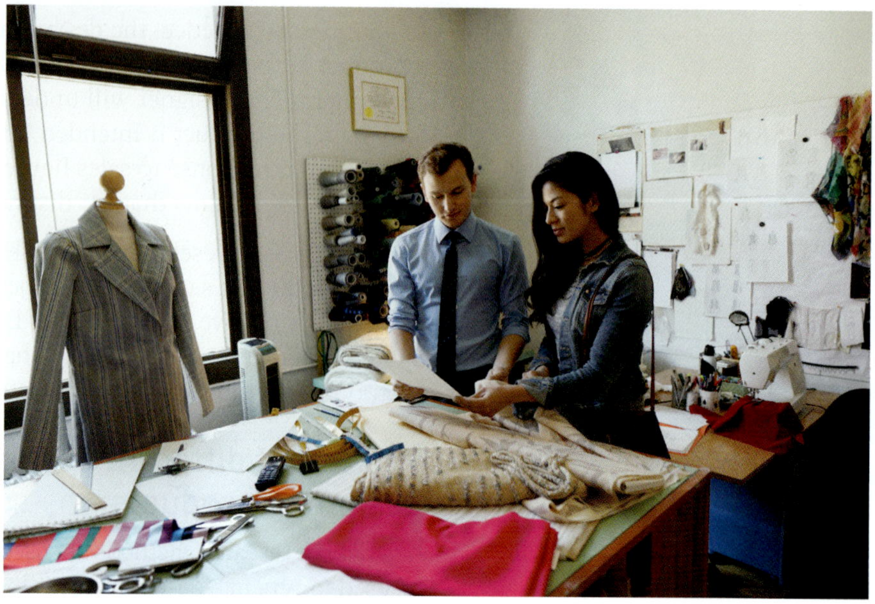

**Figure 2.4.28** The garment technologist works with the fashion designer to develop a prototype jacket.

## The cyclic nature of commercial design and manufacture

Prototype designs are developed through a series of activities researching, designing, evaluating and modifying the design. A cycle of development moves the design idea forward until a final prototype is ready for manufacturing.

During the cycle design, developers use a variety of testing methods such as:

- testing against the design criteria
- presenting ideas to the client
- asking potential consumers for feedback
- consulting fashion and textile experts
- presenting sample garments on the catwalk.

Commercial fashions are cyclic in the way that they are determined by the season. Fashion collections are conventionally produced for spring/summer and autumn/winter. There is a general pattern of including pastel and bright colours in light fabrics for spring/summer, and rich, earthy, darker colours in warmer fabrics for autumn/winter.

Fashion silhouettes are generally cyclic as shape and proportions change over time. For example, the length of hemlines varies from very short to very long, the emphasis on different parts of the body such as waist and bust varies over time. The variations move in a cycle – what may have been a popular silhouette last year may not be fashionable again for another decade. However, there is a trend for more individual fashions and for more rapid changes in fashion. This means a wider range of styles are in fashion.

There are also cycles with the seasonal collections where new products are introduced into the shops on a much quicker rotation. This is due to modern technology in sales analysis and manufacturing, which enables

## ACTIVITY

Find a pair of jeans and write down a list of ways that the jeans could be a starting point for a new product design.

Gather a group of design students together. Ask them to discuss ways that the jeans could be a starting point for a new product design.

Did the collaborative group come up with more ideas than one person on their own? How many ideas were the same as your original ones?

quick response to sales figures and consumer demand for the most up-to-date designs. Manufacturers can develop some products rapidly to fulfil a demand from shoppers.

Fashion is also cyclic in a broader sense because past designs are often recycled to form new products. Designers look to vintage or historical pieces to inspire modern interpretations of a previous fashion. Many consumers are interested in something fresh and different, and ideas for this can come from the fashions of past generations.

## KEY POINTS

- Designing is an iterative process during which ideas are explored to develop a prototype. This prototype may undergo several rounds of improvement before becoming the final version.
- Inspirational materials help designers to generate ideas that are innovative and creative.
- Modelling is used to trial ideas to help make decisions during design development.
- Critical evaluation of design ideas is necessary in order to take the best concepts through to development.
- Patterns can be developed from standard block patterns. Commercial patterns can be adjusted, and existing products and moulage can also be used to create new patterns.
- Pattern designers use technical terms and symbols to guide the use of pattern pieces.
- Toiles are made to test the pattern.
- Collaborative working in commercial practice brings together skilled specialists to develop the prototype within a product development team.
- Fashion design is cyclic, with new products being developed according to seasonal demand and fashion trends.

## Check your knowledge and understanding

1 Describe the stages in designing and developing a new product design.

2 Why do designers illustrate their ideas?

3 List some pattern notations.

4 Give three reasons why block patterns are used.

5 How do designers produce designs that appeal to those interested in buying fashionable clothing?

## Further reading

Gilewska, T. *Pattern-drafting for Fashion: The Basics.*

McKelvey, K. and Munslow, J. *Fashion Design: Process, Innovation and Practice*

www.clothingpatterns101.com

Pattern-making: www inthefolds.com

# 2.5 Critical analysis and evaluation

**LEARNING OUTCOMES**

By the end of this section you should have developed a knowledge and understanding of:

- critical analysis and evaluation of your own and of commercial products leading to possible improvements/modifications of the original idea
- how products are required to undergo rigorous testing, and the testing methods used before they become commercially available for sale
- the use of third party objective and unbiased feedback in the testing and evaluation process.

## Critical analysis and evaluation

When designing and developing fashion and textiles products, it is important to examine them carefully to find out whether the design is right and worth putting into production, or if further developments in the design are first required. In previous chapters, the value of testing and evaluating has been discussed; methods for the disassembly of existing products and for judging the success of prototypes have been described. (Please refer to Chapter 1.8 for further information about how the critical assessment of products can lead to the development of new designs.)

**SWOT analysis** is a method used to critically analyse and evaluate a product, project or person. In the context of product analysis and evaluation, it involves understanding the strengths and weaknesses of a product, looking for opportunities to develop the design further and identifying the possible threats to the success of the product. The structured approach enables product developers to analyse the following:

- Strengths: features of the product that give it a uniqueness or competitive advantage over other existing products. For example, it could be the use of materials, the styling, the decorative detail, the price or quality of the product.
- Weaknesses: features of the product that may be a disadvantage compared to other existing products. The product may not appeal to the target market in some way. There may be some aspect of how the product performs that is a weakness, such as fit or comfort.

**KEY TERMS**

**SWOT analysis:** a structured method of evaluating the strengths, weaknesses, opportunities and threats of a business venture, project or product.

**Prototype:** the first version of a design made to test the design, to see it if works as intended and to find out if improvements are necessary.

**Disassembly:** to take apart step-by-step or deconstruct.

- Opportunities: ideas for developments and modifications in the product design that could make it more successful and future fashion trends that might impact on design developments. New materials and technology might be available that could be exploited. The product design could be adapted to suit a new target market, a special event or a change in people's lifestyles or interests.
- Threats: issues that could cause difficulties in manufacturing, marketing or using the product. Competitors' products might be a threat. A change in social culture such as increased demand for sustainable products might be a threat to the current product design. There might be a limited life cycle for the product as the target market may be only temporarily interested in the product design, prior to a new fashion trend taking their attention.

The results of the analysis are written up in a report to guide further product developments and business decisions.

## Testing and evaluating industrial or commercial products

It is essential to make sure that fashion and textiles products are fit for purpose, and that they perform to the expected standards. Testing and evaluation takes place at each stage through the development of the design and of the final product. (Please refer to Chapter 1.12 for further information about the testing of prototypes with potential consumers.)

**Figure 2.5.1** Testing fabric density.

When the final prototype is complete, a commercial version of the product is made. The production sample is made using production line techniques and processes. Once approved, it can be used as 'the standard'. Samples taken off the production line during the production run can be tested against 'the standard' to make sure the garment meets the design specification and that quality is consistent throughout the batch.

Fashion garments are tested to make sure they fit as required by trying them on standard sized models, and making sure they can move around comfortably when wearing the clothing.

Garments designed for specific purposes, for example outdoor wear, are tested in appropriate conditions to see if they perform well. Fabric and garments are tested in the laboratory and outside in the environment for which they were designed.

In the laboratory, the fabric may be tested for:

- resistance to abrasion and pilling
- being waterproof or water repellent
- flammability
- strength
- stain resistance
- fade resistance
- resistance to creasing.

(For detailed information about fabric testing in industry and in the workshop, please refer to Chapter 1.1.)

**Figure 2.5.2** Testing technical outdoor clothing in the mountains

In the photograph above (Figure 2.5.1) the fabric sample is being subjected to air pressure to measure the density of the fabric. This test can be used to find out whether the outdoor clothing fabric is windproof.

The outdoor clothing may be tested to find out if the seams are waterproof by subjecting the whole garment to varying showers of water, and finding out if any water has seeped through to the inside of the clothing. The prototype can be tested to British and European Standards to consider the safety aspects of the product design. (Please refer to Chapter 2.10 for further information.)

For outdoor wear, companies need to know that the garments are strong, durable, hard wearing and can withstand the weather conditions stated in their promotional literature. In Figure 2.5.2, the outdoor top is being tested in use by wearing it to trek into the snowy mountains.

## Use of third party feedback in the testing and evaluation process

**KEY TERMS**

**Focus group:** a one-off discussion group with participants from the target market, who rate ideas for a new product and feed back their opinions.

**Customer panels:** a group of potential customers who are regularly consulted on their opinions about a new product design at different stages of its development. Also known as consumer panels.

**Quantitative interviews:** facts and brief answers are collected from the target market during face-to-face or telephone interviews; the conversation is in the form of pre-scripted questions which are read out.

**Qualitative interviews:** feature indirect or open questions based on a topic guide, to get the interviewee to fully explain their point of view.

**Third party opinion:** feedback comments from independent people who are not involved in the business of designing, making or marketing the product.

**Third party opinion** is of great interest to those developing products because the feedback is objective and concerns the opinions of potential customers. This type of feedback is essential at each stage of product design and development, to ensure that the product design is relevant to those who are likely to buy and use the product.

Sports and outdoor clothing brands often promote their products alongside magazine sports and lifestyle features. As part of their marketing, they encourage customers to interact with their website by writing product reviews or taking part in questionnaires and surveys in return for shopping discounts. For example, at the time of writing Columbia Sportswear – an American brand – is seeking a broad variety of outdoor athletes to test their footwear and clothing, and to provide constructive and candid feedback. The target market is invited to sign up to take part in testing and evaluating new products by trying them out. Social media such as Facebook and Twitter can be exploited by online companies by encouraging satisfied customers to promote products to their friends – they can post photographs of themselves using the products, and by advertising the products through product reviews and evaluative comments on Twitter.

Another technique to obtain feedback is to hold interviews with the target market to find out answers to brief questions (**quantitative interviews**), and more in-depth questions (**qualitative interviews**) concerning the product prototype. **Focus groups** and **customer panels** are also used to research opinions from the target market. In the case of a focus group, five to ten people from the target market are brought together to discuss prototype designs. Customer panels meet more than once to discuss faults, problems and further developments in the design of the product, thereby acting as consultants. (Please refer to Chapter 2.1 for further information about product analysis and evaluation.)

## KEY POINTS

- SWOT analysis involves understanding the strengths and weaknesses of a product, looking for opportunities to develop the design further and identifying the possible threats to the success of the product.
- Testing and evaluation takes place at each stage through the development of the design, and is carried out on the final product and on products made during production runs.
- Fabric and garments are tested in the laboratory, and outside in the environment for which they were designed.
- Third party opinion is essential at each stage of product design and development, to ensure that the product design is relevant to those who are likely to buy and use the product.
- Social media can be exploited by online companies, who encourage customers to post photographs of themselves testing out the products in return for discounts. Customers are also encouraged to post reviews in blogs and evaluative comments on Twitter, which are used to promote their products.
- Interviews, focus groups and customer panels are used to collect third party feedback.

## ACTIVITY

SWOT analysis of a denim jacket: examine a denim jacket or use the image below.

Consider:

- product styling
- colour and type of denim
- construction method
- range of components, including fastenings
- how well the product performs in use
- position and size of pockets
- ease of cleaning
- likely price of the jacket
- possible improvements, modifications or additions to the design.

Write a SWOT analysis report for the denim jacket.

**Figure 2.5.3** Denim jacket.

## Check your knowledge and understanding

1 What does SWOT stand for in SWOT analysis?

2 Why are samples taken off the production line during production?

3 Describe three fabric tests.

4 What is the difference between quantitative and qualitative interviews?

5 Focus groups and customer panels are the same thing. True or false?

## Further reading

www.gore-tex.co.uk/experience/quality/testing-outerwear
www.marketing91.com/swot-analysis-of-burberry
Testing and evaluating a prototype: www.technologystudent.com/despro_fish/evalintegr1.html

# 2.6 Selecting appropriate tools, equipment and processes

**LEARNING OUTCOMES**

By the end of this section you should have developed a knowledge and understanding of:

- the importance of using the correct tools and equipment
- workshop safety.

If you are studying at A-level you should also have developed a knowledge and understanding of:

- developing designs from a single prototype into mass-produced products
- the effects of batch and mass production on the manufacturing process
- how to select the most appropriate manufacturing process when realising design proposals
- the importance of health and safety in commercial settings.

## Using the correct tools and equipment

Using the correct tools and equipment for a specific process not only gives the best finished result to the end product, but is also more efficient and usually safer. There are many different tools for measuring, marking, cutting, sewing and finishing, and their use has been covered elsewhere in this book.

In industry, many specialised items of equipment are used at different stages of manufacture, so that multiple products can be made efficiently and to the same standard.

## Ensuring workshop safety

Revisit the information in Chapter 1.9 to remind yourself of the importance of health and safety when using tools and equipment.

## The effect of batch and mass production on the manufacturing process

**A-level only**

The scale of production of a textile product may affect the choice of manufacturing processes used in its construction. Mass production produces large quantities of identical products, and is used for products that do not change much, rather than for high fashion products. As a production line takes time to set up and is not very flexible in terms of workers' skills or machinery used, it will only be used when it is economical to do so, for example when making school shirts (which are essentially the same garment made in different sizes and colours) or white T-shirts that can be dyed to give the right fashion colours later in the process.

The work must keep moving along the production line therefore each stage of the manufacture must be planned carefully to make sure there are no hold ups; some processes that take longer to complete may require more workers and machines for that process, so that a steady supply of work can flow through all stages of the manufacture.

Batch production is more flexible because workers operate as teams and are more flexible in their working practices. This means that they can operate more flexibly as fashions change, or the type and number of garments being made changes.

More detailed information about batch and mass production systems can be found in Chapter 1.6 of this book.

## Selecting appropriate manufacturing processes

When planning the manufacture of a textiles product, it is important to take the following into account when selecting the most appropriate process:

- the style of the product and the techniques used, for example an embroidered panel may need to be made as a sub-assembly using specialist equipment
- the fabric that the product is made from – some fabrics require specialist handling or processes
- the components to be included – at what stage of manufacture do they need to be added and what equipment is required for their application? For example, piping needs to be stitched in when the seam is made – it is too late to add it afterwards; the zip needs to be inserted into trousers before the waistband is attached, so that the ends of the zip tape can be caught in the waistband seam
- the order of construction – it may not be possible to work on some aspects of construction if other processes are already completed or need to be finished first. For example, the cuff cannot be added until the sleeve seam is stitched.

## Health and safety in a commercial setting

Detailed information about safe working practices and safety in textile products and services to the consumer can be found in Chapter 1.9 of this book.

### Workforce training

There are many different jobs in the textile industry, for example designers, machine operatives, dyers and finishers, machine technicians, bespoke craftspeople, warehouse workers, supervisors and managers. The type and amount of training required for these jobs varies enormously; some jobs require a university degree and others learn their skills through on-the-job training, working alongside an experienced operative.

Many of the processes in textiles and fashion manufacture are automated, for example weaving, and there is a need for technicians to operate and maintain the machines. Garments are often assembled by machinists who will be trained to carry out specific operations. Training of new workers is often done by an experienced worker, who will start the new worker on simple tasks to learn how machines work. Once the new operator is confident in the use of the machine, they will be allowed to move on to more complex operations.

Whatever training or work a person does in the textiles industry, they must go through a health and safety induction process, so that they understand the dangers associated with the job and are aware of how to avoid accidents. A worker must be trained to use specific machines that they need to be able to operate efficiently and safely, so that they can do their job. It is the employer's responsibility to provide adequate training for all workers, whether they are new to the job or experienced workers working with new machines and equipment.

More detailed information about health and safety can be found in Chapter 1.9 of this book.

### National and international safety standards

Agreed national and international standards in relation to the design, manufacture and packaging of textile products is covered in Chapter 2.10.

**ACTIVITY**

Watch some of the video clips listed in the further reading section of this chapter.

Describe the different types of equipment and processes used, and explain how they help manufacturers to produce high-quality garments.

**KEY POINTS**

- Using the correct tools and equipment for a process increases safety, efficiency and quality in the work.
- Every worker is responsible for their own and other people's safety in the working environment, and must follow all rules and regulations set to increase safe working.
- There is a huge range of jobs within the textiles industry requiring many different skills and qualifications.
- Training in the operating of machines is an important part of a new worker's induction to the job, and in keeping experienced workers up to date with new machinery.

## Check your knowledge and understanding

1 Name two pieces of legislation designed to ensure safety in the workplace.

2 Name three items of PPE that might be used by an operative in a textiles factory.

## Further reading

The following YouTube videos show work inside clothing factories:

- A day in the life of a British clothing factory by Danny Cooke: https://youtu.be/9ctD5jjMeY8
- British clothing company – behind the scenes by Michael Folliett: https://youtu.be/2T3rteHTQ6U
- Process design – garment industry by Ehsan Sabet: https://youtu.be/uVoQJrz0sH8
- Clothing manufacturing and production by Satria Ngetis: https://youtu.be/F8Xx0-1C0F4

The following YouTube videos show a light-hearted look at safety in clothing factories:

- Raising awareness of occupational safety and health in garment manufacturing: https://www.youtube.com/watch?v=EqKwYZ1rYgo
- Raising awareness of occupational safety and health in garment manufacturing: https://www.youtube.com/watch?v=kO9Dy5-TNNO
- The POSH WORKER Episode 5 Garment Factory: https://www.youtube.com/watch?v=SNW9dSsulk

# 2.7 Accuracy in design and manufacture

## LEARNING OUTCOMES

By the end of this section you should have developed a knowledge and understanding of:

- how to work out quantities of materials
- the importance of measuring and marking out to achieve accuracy in manufacture
- how to use measuring aids to help with accuracy
- how testing can help to reduce errors in manufacture.

Efficient use of material is a very important factor to consider when producing both one-off prototypes and large-scale batches of a commercial product. The financial and environmental implications of efficient material management become more important as the scale of production increases; when calculating costs of manufacture, the waste material must be factored into the total cost of the product.

Accurate construction of a product is important to make sure that it looks and performs as intended and, in some cases, is safe to use. Manufacturers need to know how accurate the different parts of a product need to be, so that they will fit together. The level of accuracy required is known as the **tolerance** level. This is usually given as two numbers – an upper and a lower limit.

Very fine tolerances when working with textile materials are less important – and often more difficult to achieve – than with other materials. Woven and knitted structures have quite a lot of give in them, making it difficult to work to very fine tolerances, especially as soft and fluid fabrics change shape slightly during cutting and handling processes. If the angle of the cutting knife is not at a perfect 90° angle to the fabric, the under layers may be cut very slightly smaller or larger. Seams may not be exactly the same width all the way along, especially in commercial manufacture where many different machinists will be working on the same batch of products.

When bulk manufacturing clothing, there are often quite large and acceptable tolerances – usually between 5 mm and 20 mm – in the size of the finished garment. Since the size and shape of the human body varies so much even when people are a standard clothing size 8 or 16, it does not matter that the tolerances are so large, and it will not even be noticed that individual garments are slightly bigger or smaller. However, if a client were

**Figure 2.7.1** When cutting multiple layers of fabric, the angle at which the cutter holds the knife may make very small differences in the size of the pieces of the product.

to have a made-to-measure individual garment made, it would be expected that the tolerances would be smaller to give a precise fit. Furnishing products such as duvet covers and cushions are also manufactured to quite large tolerances because an exact size is not critical.

Different tolerances will apply to different types of textile product and these will be written into the manufacturing specification. However, individual parts of the product will need to be cut to the correct dimensions or they will not fit together as intended when the product is constructed. For example, for a collar to fit onto the body of a shirt, it must measure the same as the shirt neckline and be within a few millimetres; the front and back sections of trousers must be cut to the right size or they will not match up correctly when sewn together.

Certain textile techniques require smaller tolerances, for example patchwork and appliqué, which will not fit together accurately and that would spoil the aesthetics of the product being made.

## Measuring and marking out

Accurate measuring and marking out is essential if good-quality products are to be made. A range of measuring tools can be used when measuring fabrics and seam allowances, drafting patterns, checking and marking angles, such as a tape measure, metre ruler, set square, protractor and sewing gauge.

**Figure 2.7.2** Patchwork shapes need to be cut accurately so that they fit together to make the pattern.

There are many factors to consider when planning economic layouts for pattern templates and working out the amount of fabric needed for a product. Fabrics come in different widths; the most common are 115 cm, 140 cm and 150 cm. Many have one-way patterns and directional naps, which must be taken into account when planning layouts.

Wider fabrics may allow pattern pieces to be laid side by side, but when using narrower fabric, the pieces may need to be laid end to end. Sometimes it is possible to dovetail the pattern pieces to use the fabric more economically, but this will not work if the fabric has a directional nap or pattern.

Fabrics that have prominent patterns need special consideration to make sure that the pattern is used to best effect on the product – the pattern needs to be symmetrical and this is likely to require extra fabric, which will add to costs. Some fabric patterns such as checks and stripes should be matched across seams wherever possible, which is likely to make the layout less economical than on a plain fabric.

**Figure 2.7.3** A layout for this large busy pattern will need to be planned carefully so that it is balanced on the product.

To work out the amount of fabric required, the pattern layout will need to be planned carefully. If you are using a commercial pattern for your product, the layout will have been done for you; it is important to lay the pattern pieces as shown for the style and size you are making, so that you use the fabric economically and include all the pieces needed to make the product.

If you have developed your own templates, you will need to plan the layout yourself. Make sure that you have put a seam allowance on all the pieces, or that you allow for it when planning the layout. Otherwise, your product will not be the right size when sewn. A standard seam allowance is 15 mm on domestic patterns, but will be less on commercial patterns so that the pattern templates can be placed slightly closer together and fabric used as economically as possible. You may also need to include a hem allowance – this will vary from about 15 mm to 70 mm depending on the product.

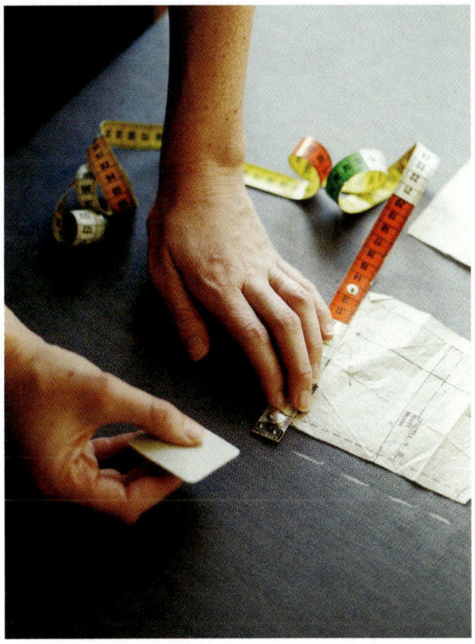

Figure 2.7.4 Use a tape measure to add seam and hem allowances to pattern pieces that you have made yourself.

The pattern templates should be laid out on a table or other large surface with the fabric width marked out – this can be done by placing one or more metre rulers at a set distance from the table edge. This allows you to try the pieces in different positions to find the most economical layout, and to calculate the length of fabric needed. Fabric for domestic use is usually sold in multiples of 10 cm, so you will need to work out the length and round it up to the nearest 10 cm. In industry, the exact length of fabric needed for a product is used when calculating the quantities.

Place the largest pattern pieces on the fabric first, making sure that they are placed on the correct grain line. Do not try to squeeze the templates into a smaller length by ignoring the grainline, otherwise the product will not hang well and patterns may be distorted. Place smaller pattern pieces in the spaces left, but take care not to overlap any. Once all the pattern templates are laid out in their correct position, the length of fabric needed can be measured.

When marking out a shape on a piece of fabric, you need to think how the design can be best placed on the fabric available. It is extremely wasteful to mark out a shape in the centre of a large piece of fabric when it will fit comfortably in a corner. Where possible, try to choose the smallest piece of fabric that is suitable for the relevant design, and if marking out several items, try to tessellate your designs as efficiently as possible. Tessellation involves dovetailing the shape to make best use of the fabric available; this may mean that the pattern has to be rotated so that more can fit onto the fabric.

Figure 2.7.5 Tailor's chalk and pencils or a special pen can be used to draw marks on fabrics.

In commercial manufacture, the most efficient layout will be planned using a computerised PDS. More information about computerised layouts can be found in Chapter 1.7 of this book.

When all of the pattern pieces have been cut out some of the pattern markings need to be transferred to the fabric to help make the product accurately. There are three ways to do this:

**Tailor's chalk** or a special marking pencil is used to draw on the fabric. This method marks only one side of the fabric, and can be easily rubbed off and the markings lost.

Figure 2.7.6 A tracing wheel.

When using a tracing wheel and tracing paper, the coloured side of the tracing paper is put next to the wrong side of the fabric, and the colour is transferred to the fabric using the tracing wheel. This leaves a line of fine dots on the fabric to show the pattern markings. Both sides of the fabric can be marked at once, but the marks can be difficult to remove from the fabric.

**Tailor's tacks** are made by stitching through the fabric and pattern with a double thread. This method marks both sides of the fabric at the same time, and the threads are easy to remove afterwards.

In commercial manufacture, a notcher will be used to make position marks at the edge of cut fabric pieces. A drill marker is used to make holes, for example to mark dart positions. A fluorescent dye can be used with a drill marker, so that the marks are only visible under an ultra-violet light.

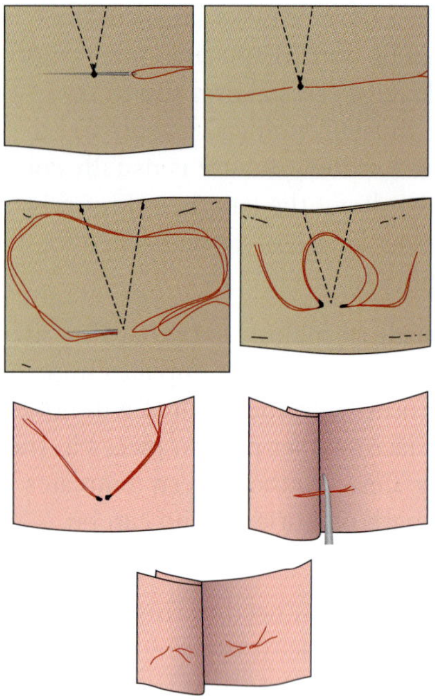

**Figure 2.7.7** How to work tailor's tacks.

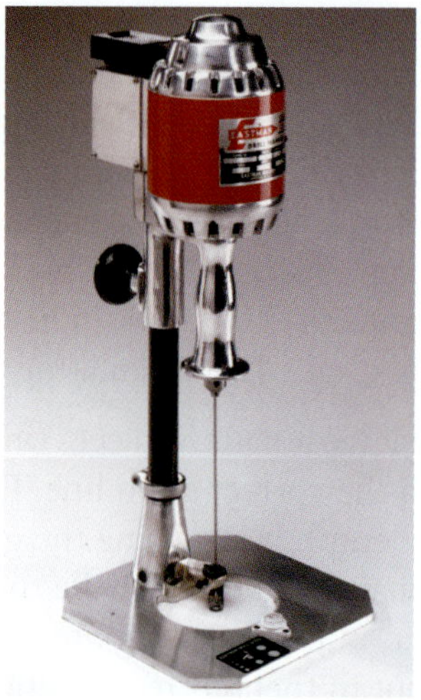

**Figure 2.7.8** A drill marker makes small holes through several layers of fabric.

**Figure 2.7.9** The hot notcher is used to make position marks at the edge of fabric pieces.

### MATHS LINK

**Determining quantities of materials**

A manufacturer has a choice of two different widths when making a dress:

- Fabric A is 115cm wide and costs £4.79 per metre.
- Fabric B is 160cm wide and costs £7.54 per metre.

The dress uses 3.60 metres of Fabric A and 1.80 metres of Fabric B.

**a)** Which fabric is the more economical when making 1500 dresses?

**b)** What is the percentage difference between the cost of the two fabrics?

**Answer**

**a)** 1500 dresses in Fabric A = 1500 × 3.60 = 5,400 metres

1500 dresses in Fabric B = 1500 × 1.80 = 2,700 metres

Cost of Fabric A for 1500 dresses = 5,400 × 4.79 = £25,866

Cost of Fabric B for 1500 dresses = 2,700 × 7.54 = £20,358

It is more economical to use Fabric B.

**b)** Percentage difference $= \frac{\text{difference in cost}}{\text{original cost}} \times 100$

$$= \frac{25866 - 20358}{25866} \times 100$$

$$= \frac{5508}{25866} \times 100$$

$$= 21.29\%$$

## Testing and the elimination of errors

It is likely that a number of prototypes will be made during the design stages of developing a new product, and these should help to make sure it is fit for manufacture, and form the basis of the product and manufacturing specifications. Further information about prototypes can be found in Chapter 1.8 of this book.

Commercial manufacturers need to make quality control checks at certain stages during production to ensure the products are of the agreed quality. These stages are built into the production specification. Checking at an appropriate stage is important, for example it may be too late to do anything about a pocket that is not made to the right size once it is sewn on the product.

One way to check the quality of products is to inspect each one. A quicker method is to inspect a sample of the products as they are made, and collect and analyse information about the samples. This is called feedback, and makes it possible to trace the reasons for any problems and make adjustments to the manufacturing, so that all products meet the agreed standards in future. For example, if a particular machine is faulty, it can be fixed before too many defective products are made, or if a machine operative is not producing the correct quality of work, that person can be identified and given training to improve the quality of their work.

## Using measuring aids

When laying out patterns or developing templates, it is often necessary to have a fixed reference point from which other measurements are calculated. This is called a **datum point**.

The fabric selvedge is an important datum point when laying out patterns; the straight grain line marked on the pattern template must always be parallel to the selvedge. This should be measured accurately using a tape measure, and not just guessed.

**Figure 2.7.11** French curves help to draw accurate and smooth curves.

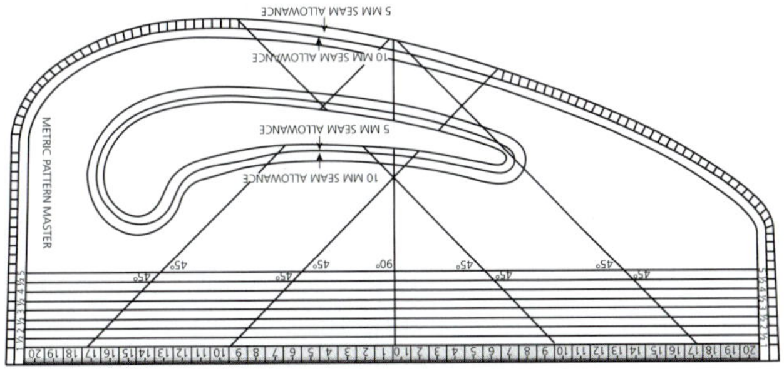


**Figure 2.7.10** A pattern master.

When working with checked fabrics, it is usually desirable to have the centre line of the check pattern running along the centre line of the product – these are datum points. Care must be taken to ensure that the pattern template is placed accurately with the centres matched, otherwise the checks may appear unbalanced or out of line on the finished product. It may also be necessary to consider where the check lines will fall at other edges of the product, especially when using fabrics with a large or uneven check pattern.

A pattern master makes it easy to draw curved and straight lines when making pattern templates. It is usually made from clear plastic, and has a straight edge and curved edges.

When working out angles for pattern templates, you should use a set square to draw and check that all angles that are meant to be square are at 90° to each other. Remember it is stitching lines that need to match, not cutting lines. A protractor will be needed when measuring other angles. Curved

**Figure 2.7.12** Templates are used for accuracy when cutting patchwork pieces.

shapes can be drawn accurately using a set of French curves, for example when drawing a neckline or armhole curve.

Templates are also available in shapes such as squares and hexagons, which are useful for marking out repeated shapes, for example those needed for patchwork or quilting.

### ACTIVITY

Select a pattern for a fashion top with a collar and sleeves. It can be a commercial pattern or one that you have drafted yourself. Develop pattern layouts for fabric that:

- is 115 cm wide
- is 150 cm wide
- is 150 cm wide and with a one-way printed pattern.

What impact does the fabric width and pattern have on the length of fabric needed to make the top?

### KEY TERMS

**Tolerance:** the acceptable variation in the size of a product or part of a product, usually given as an upper and a lower limit.

**Feedback:** information about the manufacturing process that leads to modifications and improvements in the manufacturing system.

**Tessellation:** dovetailing shapes so that they fit closely together.

**Datum point:** a fixed reference point from which other measurements are calculated.

### KEY POINTS

- Accuracy in manufacture is important if the products are to meet the expected standards of quality, fitness for purpose and safety.
- Tolerances will vary for different products and different parts of a product.
- Fabrics must be used economically to avoid unnecessary waste that adds to the overall costs of the product.
- Layouts must be planned carefully to make sure that any pattern on the fabric is used effectively.
- Seam and hem allowances need to be included on pattern templates.
- It is important to place the straight grain line of the pattern template parallel to the fabric selvedge.
- Establishing a datum point before making patterns or placing templates on fabric is essential for an accurate result.
- Using the correct measuring tool helps to ensure accuracy of manufacture.

## Check your knowledge and understanding

1 Explain why it is important to consider the fabric pattern when planning layouts.

2 Why is it important to follow the grain when laying patterns on fabric?

3 Name three different ways of transferring pattern markings to fabric.

4 Why is a datum point important when developing templates and placing patterns on fabric?

5 Explain why a manufacturing specification may have different tolerance levels for different parts of the same garment.

## Further reading

Smith, A. *The Sewing Book*

# 2.8 Responsible design

**LEARNING OUTCOMES**

By the end of this section you should have developed a knowledge and understanding of:

- the importance of environmental issues in design and manufacture
- the responsibilities of designers and manufacturers in ensuring products are made from sustainable materials and components
- the environmental impact of sourcing textile materials, their use, care and packaging
- conservation of energy and resources, and sustainable manufacturing
- the impact of waste in textiles manufacturing, minimising waste and cost implications of dealing with waste
- the impact of global manufacturing on product miles.

If you are studying at A-level you should also have developed a knowledge and understanding of:

- the concept of a circular economy and how products are designed to conserve energy, materials and components
- the impact of waste, surplus and by-products created in the process of textiles manufacture
- product lifecycle.

## Environmental issues

Fashion and textile products are made from natural resources or chemicals derived from them, and energy is used in their processing, manufacture, packaging and distribution. During use, fashion and textile products require cleaning, and at the end of their useful life, they are disposed of or recycled. It is important that environmental issues are taken into consideration when designing and manufacturing fashion and textile products because of the need to protect the environment and avoid depletion of finite resources. The major environmental impacts of the fashion and textile industry arise from the use of natural resources, water, energy and from the toxic chemicals used during fibre production and subsequent processing. Environmental issues concern the impact that textile production has on the environment, and on the lives of people involved in producing textile products.

## Sustainable materials and components

The following types of materials and components are **sustainable** due to their reduced impact on the environment:

**Table 2.8.1** Examples of sustainable materials and components.

| Reason for sustainability | Examples | |
|---|---|---|
| Recycled materials and components made from recycling waste or reclaiming fibres | • PET polyester is made from recycled plastic bottles or recycled polyester fabric, with a carbon footprint which is 75% lower than polyester made from **petrochemicals**.<br>• **Econyl®** is a type of nylon manufactured using a closed-loop system from recycled fishing nets and carpets. | <br>**Figure 2.8.1** Polyester fleece made from plastic bottles. |
| Organic fibres produced without the use of toxic chemicals | • **Organic cotton**<br>• **Organic wool** is produced by sustainable farming practices and without toxic chemical sheep dips. | <br><br>**Figure 2.8.2** Organic cotton. |
| Sustainably sourced materials and components | • Bamboo is from sustainably managed bamboo plantations.<br>• **Fairtrade** cotton is produced ethically without exploitation of the work force, and sold at a fair price.<br>• Fairtrade beads and buttons are made from carved wood by village communities in developing countries. | <br>**Figure 2.8.3** Socks made from bamboo. |
| Fibres produced in a closed-loop manufacturing system with recycled chemicals | • Lyocell<br>• Econyl is Nylon 6 and is made from 100% regenerated polyamide waste materials | |
| Modern fibre and fabric developments | • Coloured organic cotton that does not require dyeing.<br>• **Morphotex®** is a **biomimetic** fibre that does not require dyeing due to its microscopic structure which reflects light as colour.<br>• Stain resistant or self-cleaning fabric uses **nano-technology** or has an applied finish such as Teflon, which reduces the frequency of washing required.<br>• Deodorising fabric keeps fabric fresh, and reduces the need for frequent washing.<br>• Easy-care fabric allows faster drying with less ironing. | <br>**Figure 2.8.4** Coloured organic cotton that does not require dyeing. |

**Table 2.8.1** (Continued)

| | | |
|---|---|---|
| Biodegradable fibres | • **Ingeo** is a fibre made from corn plant starch, and is grown sustainably. | 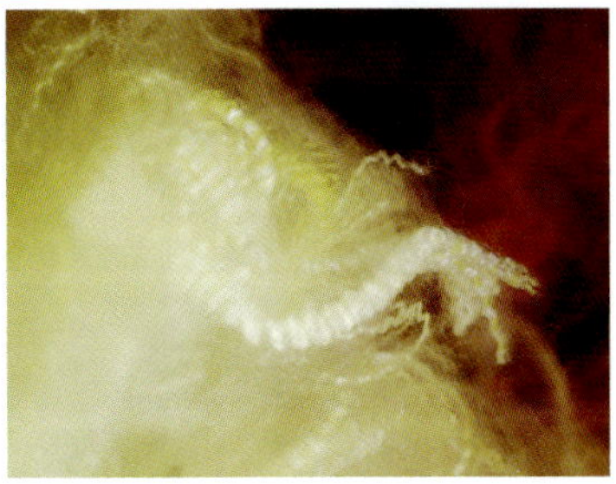<br>**Figure 2.8.5** Ingeo fibre from corn by-products. |
| Fibres produced with reduced water consumption | • **Hemp** is a natural plant fibre which is four times stronger than cotton, twice as resistant to abrasion, and more resistant to mildew, soiling, shrinkage and fading in the Sun. Hemp plants require much less water than cotton plants and less agricultural chemicals, and do not deplete soil nutrients. It is also easy to harvest. | <br>**Figure 2.8.6** Shirt made of 55% hemp and 45% organic cotton with bamboo buttons. |
| Fibres produced using renewable energy | • Textile factories use solar, wind or hydroelectric energy. | <br>**Figure 2.8.7** Wind turbine making renewable energy. |
| Humanely-processed fibres | • **Ahimsa** or peace silk is produced humanely by letting the moths hatch out of the silk cocoon before using it. The moths are not killed, but the silk is far more expensive due to the extra time allowed for the pupae to develop and hatch out. | <br>**Figure 2.8.8** Silk worm and cocoons. |

## Packaging textile products

Packaging of products can be wasteful of paper, card, plastics, printing inks and the energy used to produce and transport the packaging. Manufacturers and retailers need to ensure that packaging is bio-degradable and recyclable, and that the amount of packaging required is minimal. They can reduce the impact on the environment by manufacturing or buying packaging products nearer to the place where they will be required.

JIT distribution systems save on storage and stop packaged items from degrading over time, as stock can be ordered just in time for packaging textile products without prolonged storage. Modern storage and carrier systems allow garments to be stored and transported on hangers and moveable rails, so that they arrive at the shop ready to go on display;

this reduces the need to iron clothes, therefore saving energy. Vacuum packing allows more products to be transported at one time as volume of packaged goods is reduced, saving on fuel and unnecessary journeys.

KEY TERMS

**Petrochemicals:** chemical products derived from petroleum.

**Closed-loop system:** the solvent used in fibre production is recycled back into the start of the process.

**Organic cotton:** grown without the use of toxic chemicals.

**Organic wool:** wool from sheep farmed without the use of toxic chemicals.

**Lyocell:** a sustainable fabric, regenerated from wood cellulose.

**Fairtrade:** trade between companies in developed countries and producers in developing countries in which fair prices are paid to the producers following the principles of Fairtrade.

**Econyl:** Nylon 6 made from 100 per cent regenerated polyamide waste materials.

## Conservation of energy and resources

Efficient production and modern developments in fashion and textiles can reduce the amount of energy and resources required. For example, conventional fabric preparation and dyeing processes use up vast amounts of water, and a great deal of time and energy is required to heat up vats of dye, agitate the fabric in the dyebath, rinse the fabric, fix the dye and then dry the dyed fabric. The amount of water required, thermal energy needed and power to drive the machinery can be reduced by using more up-to-date technology to combine processes, or to make time and energy efficiencies at each stage of production.

**Figure 2.8.9** Nike's Morphotex dress mimics butterfly wing shimmer—without any dyes.

Alternatively, modern developments in fibres can eliminate the need for processes such as dyeing altogether, as in the example of **Morphotex** fabric, where the colour is integral to the fibre. The inspiration for this **biomimetic** fibre came from studying the wing surface structure of the blue morph butterfly – light refracted from the surface of the fabric is seen as a shimmering blue/violet colour, but the fabric itself is not dyed.

### How products are designed to conserve energy, materials and components

A-level only

Fashion and textile products are often designed to conserve energy and materials to cut costs to produce products within budget. However, the desire to do this is also driven by the need to design a sustainable product that will use up fewer resources.

Advances in technology have made it possible to make products more efficiently and sustainably. One such development is **seamless manufacture**. In conventional textile manufacturing, pieces of fabric are cut out for each part of the product and then joined together to make a 3D shape using seams. Seamless manufacture eliminates the need for seams,

## KEY TERMS

**Morphotex:** light refracted from the surface of this fabric is seen as a shimmering blue/violet colour but the fabric itself is not dyed.

**Biomimetic:** copying nature to get ideas for innovative designs.

**Ingeo:** a fibre made from corn plant starch, grown sustainably.

**Hemp:** a natural plant fibre.

**Ahimsa:** also known as peace silk, produced humanely by letting the silk moths hatch out of the silk cocoon rather than killing them.

**Seamless manufacture:** made without seams.

**Cradle to cradle clothing**: a regenerative cycle of fibre production, use and recycling for production.

**Slow fashion:** durable fashionable garments that have a long product life cycle.

**Returnity:**100 per cent recyclable polyester fibres, they are used in clothing that is designed to be reused with zero waste.

**Figure 2.8.10** Nike's Mercurial Superfly football boots

and therefore cuts down the number of processes required to make a textile item. It also makes a more streamlined and perhaps stronger product.

An example of this is seen in Nike's Flyknit trainers. They are sustainable because:

- computer controlled knitting is used to make a single piece of fabric for the trainer upper, rather than using several pieces that would need joining
- each section of the trainer upper is fully integrated into the single piece so it is an efficient way to make a 3D shape
- the single strand construction means that a variety of materials are not required; this simplifies stock purchasing and control
- a single piece shaped exactly to requirements eliminates waste, which makes it environmentally friendly
- a single operation is efficient to join shoe upper to sole as there is only one piece
- no multiple materials or layers, and no material cutting out is required so it is a quicker process.

(Please refer to Chapter 1.11 for further information about choice of raw material and cutting and sewing the product to conserve energy, materials and components.)

## The design of fashion, clothing and textiles for minimum impact on the environment

Fashion clothing is produced to satisfy a demand for the latest trend. Production and distribution is rapid, with shop stock quickly replenished in response to sales figures. This type of clothing – known as **fast fashion** – is only worn over a brief period before it is discarded in favour of the next new fashion. To reduce the impact on the environment, fast fashion items need to be designed for recycling, and consumers need to be encouraged to recycle. It is essential to prevent fashion and textile products from being thrown into landfill or incinerated; components should be reused and fibres reclaimed in a closed loop of fibre use. This is known as **cradle to cradle** clothing, where fibres are used and then reused. Used textiles can be shredded into loose fibres and then spun into new yarns and made into fabric; wool fibres can be reclaimed in this way. Fibre blends, for example polyester with cotton, can make reclaiming fibres more difficult, as can the need to separate contaminants such as dyes from the reclaimed fibres.

**Returnity**® and Infinity are 100 per cent recyclable polyester fibres. They are used in clothing that is designed to be reused with zero waste.

Infinity is promoted as a strong and comfortable polyester fibre, which is produced with 50 per cent of water use and 20 per cent of carbon dioxide emission compared to conventional cotton. It is used to make work wear that is collected back when it has reached the end of its useful life, to be recycled back into work wear.

Natural fibres are biodegradable, which means they will break down naturally if put into landfill. However, it is more desirable that the fibres are reused. (Please refer to Chapter 1.11 for further information about product design and the six Rs of sustainability.)

## Raw material extraction

Natural fibres are harvested from plants or taken from animals. Regenerated fibres are made from the cellulose found in wood or cotton waste, while synthetic fibres are made from fossil fuels. All raw textile material involves fibre production, so designers and manufacturers need to consider how to extract the fibres with as little impact as possible on the environment. Synthetic fibres are made from **petrochemicals**, which come from non-renewable sources, so it is important to recycle synthetic fibres to reduce the need for more raw material. Growing natural fibres such as cotton, and wood for regenerated fibres, can cause changes to the landscape because of intensive farming and deforestation. To lessen the impact on the environment, crops need to be managed and grown sustainably.

## Consumption

Consumers of fashion and textile products drive their production. Responsibility for conservation of resources lies not only with the producers but also with those buying and using the textiles. Textile waste is a significant problem because of 'fast fashion' – fashionable textiles are bought and then soon afterwards discarded because of rapidly changing fashion trends. Some consumers have little consideration of how this shopping behaviour impacts the environment. However, a growing number of people acknowledge that this type of consumer behaviour is not sustainable, and support the movement for '**slow fashion**'.

In order to conserve resources and lessen the impact on the environment of textile consumption, consumers are encouraged to:

- buy fewer, more durable, higher-quality garments and textile products
- hire clothes that would otherwise not be worn again, such as special occasion wear
- buy second-hand clothing and textiles
- repair clothing and textile products to extend their useful life, or upcycle and customise them to bring new life to products
- choose fashion and textile products made from organic fibres grown without toxic chemicals
- support Fairtrade companies who pay their employees a living wage, with reasonable working conditions and no child labour
- choose locally made products or those that have not been imported from countries across the globe, to reduce 'fashion miles' and carbon footprint
- buy fashion and textile products made from fibres such as hemp, which can be produced using less water, energy and toxic chemicals than cotton
- seek out biodegradable textile products
- choose products made from recycled materials
- wash clothes only when they are dirty, using eco-friendly detergents, at lower temperatures (30 °C), avoiding tumble drying and ironing to conserve energy and washing machines which are energy efficient and use less water. Wash a full load and not several smaller loads
- careful storage can extend a product's life, for example away from bright sunlight, moths and damp conditions
- recycle fashion and textile products for reuse or to reclaim fibres from unwanted textiles.

A website called 'Fashion revolution' has information about the global movement that calls for greater transparency, sustainability and ethics in the fashion industry (see Further Reading below).

## KEY TERMS

**Patching:** to apply a small piece of fabric over a hole or damaged area of fabric.

**Darning:** a stitch technique used for repairing holes or worn areas in fabric.

**Customise:** to alter the fashion or textile product to suit the needs of an individual person.

**Upcycle:** to convert an unwanted piece of clothing or textile product into something useful and creative.

## ACTIVITY

Find a favourite piece of clothing that has a hole in it and needs mending.

Repair the clothing by darning the hole. To find out how to do this, watch the following YouTube clip: www.youtube.com/watch?v=GtLj0iJnvqM.

### Ease of repair and maintenance

Designers have the responsibility to consider how the design of fashion and textiles products can incorporate ease of repair. The durability of a product is increased if it can be mended and made useful again by repairing or mending specific parts or replacing sections. Some clothing brands attach a small plastic bag to the clothing to provide not only spare buttons but also appropriate thread, embellishments and sometimes a small patch of the fabric for the consumer to mend the garment, if a minor repair is required. Mending garments includes **patching** and **darning** areas out of necessity, but this can also be done for decorative purposes to **customise** and **upcycle** fashion and textile products.

Fashion and textile products require cleaning. Over half of the energy used in the life cycle of a cotton T-shirt is put down to frequent washing and drying of the T-shirt at high temperatures. Energy requirements for washing, drying and ironing cotton garments are particularly high because cotton is very absorbent and creases easily. Care labels encourage consumers to wash at a lower temperature and avoid tumble drying in order to conserve energy. Caring for textile products requires the use of detergents, dry cleaning fluids, energy and water, which can have a detrimental effect on the environment and may harm those using the products. Many detergents are made from petrochemicals from non-renewable sources. (Please refer to Chapter 11.1 for further information about repair, care and maintenance of products.)

### Product life cycle

A **product life cycle** concerns all the stages in the life of a fashion or textile product – from sourcing fibres, production, distribution and use through to product disposal, to see how it affects the environment in a linear path of make, use and dispose – from 'cradle to grave'.

At the end of their useful life, fashion and textile products are often either incinerated – releasing toxic chemicals into the atmosphere, or sent to landfill sites. Fabrics and components can take many years to decompose in landfill sites, with the consequent methane production and leeching of heavy metals from components such as zips. End-of-life disposal has less impact on the environment if the product is biodegradable and can break down into the soil naturally, without leaving hazardous chemicals in its place. However, if chemical finishes are added to fabrics, it is more difficult to reclaim the fibres and they will pollute the soil if left to degrade.

Alternatively, the product life cycle can be continued through recycling or reclaiming fibres. This is known as a **circular economy**. Resources are kept in use for as long as possible, repairing the product and upcycling it until it has no further use. After this, materials are recovered through recycling and reclaiming, using the materials in the manufacture of a new product (see Returnity workwear above).

## Sustainable manufacturing

Sustainable manufacturing takes place when:

- resources such as water, energy and raw materials are conserved during fibre processing, yarn spinning, fabric production and garment manufacture
- materials and processing methods are non-toxic

**KEY TERMS**

**Product life cycle:** the sequence of stages in a product's existence from fibre, through its useful lifetime, to discarded and broken-down materials.

**Circular economy:** a continuous product life cycle through recycling or reclaiming fibres to make new products.

**Azo dyes and pigments:** bright chemical dyes used to colour textile materials.

**Natural dyes:** colourants for fabric derived from plants, invertebrates or minerals, such as vegetable dyes from plants.

- waste materials are kept to a minimum
- pollution of the environment is prevented
- local economies are supported by providing jobs in developing countries with fair payment, safe and decent working conditions, reasonable working hours and no use of child labour
- 'fashion miles' to transport items from production to market place are reduced.

Conventional methods of fabric preparation and dyeing use excessive amounts of water, energy and toxic chemicals, particularly in the cotton industry. Cleaning of fabrics made from natural fibres uses water and harsh detergents to remove dirt and natural oils, and to bleach the fabric prior to dyeing and printing, whereas fabrics made from synthetic fibres are naturally white and clean. However, microfibres and dark colours use enormous amounts of dye and water to achieve the desired colour. Water use can be reduced by dope dyeing synthetic fibres to add the colour before the fibre is spun.

Sustainable manufacturers use new technological developments to reduce requirements for water, energy and toxic chemicals or swap to alternative sustainable fibres. Sublimation printing reduces water use and effluent, as the colour goes directly onto the fabric. Modern low-impact dyes can be used in place of conventional dyes; they are still chemical-based dyes, but are low in salt, contain no metals and are free from **azo dyes and pigments**, some of which have been linked to causing cancers. Low impact dyes require much less water for the dyeing process. Alternatively, sunlight can be used to bleach natural fabrics combined with **natural dyes** from organic sources such as plant roots, berries, bark, leaves and wood.

**Figure 2.8.11** Sewage treatment plant for dyeing unit of cotton textile factory in India.

The impact of using toxic chemicals can be much reduced by putting closed loop processing systems or waste treatment systems into place. This prevents water and soil pollution around the factory location. Figure 2.8.11 shows the waste treatment plant at a cotton textile factory in India. Water is reused for dyeing and finishing processes. While part of the treated effluent is disposed of at a government appointed disposal site, the rest of it is used to prepare a fertiliser for local use.

## Using alternative energy

Using energy produced from renewable resources to power factories reduces the use of fossil fuels. Electricity generated from wind, solar power or hydroelectric power are used as sustainable sources of the energy needed to power machinery in textile factories.

## Minimising waste

Materials waste is reduced by use of:

- computer generated efficient lay plans
- automated manufacturing processes to improve quality and therefore reduce the number of inferior products made
- JIT systems to reduce over-ordering, stock degradation and subsequent waste of materials and energy by manufacturing unwanted products.

Where fabric waste occurs due to changes in fashion, production errors or over-ordering of fabric stock, a solution needs to be found for use of this resource. High street stores such as H&M are keen to promote recycling and to be recognised as sustainable businesses. H&M's 'Weekday's Remains' is a sustainable capsule collection made from waste materials such as leftover rolls of denim. The aim is to reduce the fabric waste that is buried in landfill.

Many retailers now encourage consumers to bring back clothing that is finished with, donate unwanted textiles to charities or reuse. Reclaiming fibres for making industrial wipes from the soft and absorbent used fabric or for making wall insulation material from the fibres is also encouraged. Clothing donated to charities is resold to other consumers locally or exported in bulk for sale in developing countries. Waste is also minimised by reselling fashion items on eBay or at car boot sales.

Other high street stores, for example Zara, are ordering smaller batches of stock to reduce surplus stock. They use an **EPOS** system to monitor shop sales, in order to fine tune how many garments to order for stock replenishment, or to guide the batch size for new lines of clothing. The changes in fashion have become more rapid, and retailers need to respond to this. By using more local manufacturers, transportation times are much reduced and consumers have the latest fashion in store as quickly as possible.

**Figure 2.8.12** Junky Styling's designer clothing made from surplus waste.

Turning textile waste and surplus into new fibres and fabrics can reduce the need for landfill and incineration. Junky Styling was a pioneering upcycling company which ran from 1997 to 2012. It was well known for its sustainable clothing made from high quality recycled pieces of suits and jackets. The clothing was taken apart, and sections were re-cut and redesigned into quirky innovative pieces. The clothing that was recycled was often stock that had failed to sell and would otherwise have been disposed of. In the Figure 2.8.12 the dress was made from the front section of a pinstripe jacket with a cowl collar made from the jacket sleeve.

By-products of the cotton industry include the cotton seeds, and cotton linters – the fuzzy fibres left over when separating the seeds from the cotton fibres. The cotton seeds are fed to cattle or pressed to extract cottonseed oil for human consumption. The linters are used to make cotton wool for cosmetic wipes and medical pads. Other parts of the cotton plant can be used for biodegradable packaging and soil mulch.

## The impact of waste, surplus and by-products created in the process of manufacture

Unless carefully managed, the impact on the environment of textile waste and by products can be extremely damaging to areas around textile factories. This is due to high volumes of waste – some of which is very toxic – and pollutants, which can end up discharged into local rivers or leeched into the soil.

The manufacture of synthetic fabrics requires large amounts of crude oil and energy to process the chemicals into fibres. Volatile organic compounds, particulate matter and acid gases such as hydrogen chloride are released into the air during production of fibres such as polyester, and these can trigger respiratory problems in the population; waste pollutants such as solvents can also be present in the waste water.

## Reusing material off-cuts

Material off-cuts are the pieces of fabric left over after cutting out the pattern pieces. Computer generated lay plans reduce off-cuts to as little waste as possible. Instead of throwing the off-cuts into landfill, the fabric can be used by other textile producers, or the fibres can be reclaimed by shredding up the off-cuts and re-spinning the reclaimed fibres into new yarns.

Some designers use off-cuts to make unique products from recycled waste. Precious scrap pieces of expensive materials such as silk, pure wool or linen fabrics can be patched together to make designer clothes or fashion accessories. Fashion and textile products made from these materials are described as having a 'pre-consumer recycled content'.

## Chemicals

Toxic chemicals are used in textiles production, for example in cotton growing, bleaching, dyeing, printing and finishing. Cotton production uses toxic chemicals such as fertilisers, pesticides and herbicides, which can pollute the atmosphere and waterways, and poison workers. Cotton grown organically – without the use of toxic fertilisers, pesticides or herbicides – would be a sustainable solution to this issue, although the cost of cotton produced in this way is increased.

**Figure 2.8.13** Fairtrade and organic cotton farming in India.

In organic farming, crop rotation maintains the nutrients in the soil, traps are used to catch pests, cow dung is used to fertilise crops and natural predators like birds and insects are exploited to promote cotton plant growth by controlling pests and weeds, which are competing with the cotton plants for water and soil nutrients.

Synthetic insecticides for cotton are associated with the poisoning and deaths of farm workers in producing countries, and some consumers of cotton products are concerned about toxic traces of chemicals used in production contaminating cotton clothing. There is evidence that some toxic chemicals used in textile production are carcinogenic.

## Heat and water

Fibre production and processing requires heat to melt solutions, air-dry synthetic and regenerated fibres, and to heat water for dyeing as well as steam for finishing processes. The textile industry also uses great quantities of water. If water is diverted from rivers and lakes to irrigate natural fibre crops or supply processing plants, the surrounding environment may become arid, exhausting local water supplies. There have been some recent developments in the textile industry using compressed and pressurised carbon dioxide as the agent to disperse dye within polyester fabric, rather than using water.

**Figure 2.8.14** High volume textile clothing production in China.

# Cost implications of dealing with waste

Responsible manufacturers need to factor in the costs of sustainable farming, processing and manufacturing of fashion and textiles products when they calculate the cost of producing products. Waste management is costly but essential to business, especially where there is a consumer-driven need for sustainably produced goods.

## The impact of global manufacturing on product miles

Clothing and textiles represent about seven per cent of world exports; products are moved around the world from fibre processer to fabric manufacturers to garment manufacturers, and then on to consumers. If donated to charity, the products can then move again across the globe from western countries to a less developed country. Globalisation has made it possible to produce clothing at increasingly lower prices, compared to the cost of clothing in previous decades. This has fuelled consumers' desire for inexpensive, almost disposable fast fashion. The impact of global manufacturing on product miles has been to drastically increase the distances that fashion clothing travels during its life cycle from raw material to the end of its useful life.

Countries in Asia such as China, Vietnam and Cambodia produce much of the clothing destined for western high streets, as seen in the photograph above. Recently though, eastern European countries such as Turkey and Bulgaria have competed with the Asian factories – they can respond to the demands of fast fashion with more flexibility, making smaller batches with shorter lead times.

Consumer-driven sustainable fashions see retailers using suppliers that are much closer to where the fashion clothing is sold, to reduce fashion miles. This is beneficial to the European and UK manufacturers, who until recently have found it difficult to compete with suppliers in Asia. Fluctuations in the value of the pound and import taxes also influence from where clothing is sourced.

### KEY POINTS

- Environmental issues are important because of the need to protect the environment and avoid depletion of finite resources.
- The major environmental impacts of the fashion and textile industry arise from the use of natural resources, water, energy and from the toxic chemicals used during fibre production and subsequent processing.
- Packaging should be used sparingly, and be biodegradable and recyclable.
- Efficient production and modern developments in fashion and textiles can reduce the amount of energy and resources required.
- To reduce the impact on the environment, fast fashion items need to be designed for recycling, and consumers encouraged to recycle.
- Used textiles can be shredded into loose fibres, then spun into new yarns and made into fabric.
- To lessen the impact on the environment, crops need to be managed and grown sustainably.
- Responsibility for conservation of resources lies not only with the producers but also with those buying and using the textiles.
- The impact of using toxic chemicals can be much reduced by putting closed loop processing systems into place.
- Using energy produced from renewable resources to power factories reduces the use of fossil fuels.
- Unless carefully managed, the impact on the environment of textile waste and by products can be extremely damaging to areas around textile factories.
- The impact of global manufacturing on product miles has been to drastically increase the distances that fashion clothing travels during its life cycle – from raw material to the end of its useful life.

## Check your knowledge and understanding

1 Name some sustainable fabrics. Can you explain why they are considered to be sustainable?
2 What makes Nike's Flyknit trainers sustainable?
3 How can consumers be encouraged to support the movement for slow fashion?
4 Which type of product life cycle is more sustainable – 'cradle to cradle' or 'cradle to grave'?
5 Clothing and textiles represent about seven per cent of world exports. True or false?

## Further reading


Farley Gorden, J. and Hill, C. *Sustainable Fashion Past, Present and Future*

www.ifm.eng.cam.ac.uk/uploads/Resources/Other_Reports/UK_textiles.pdf

www.patagonia.com/worn-wear.html#q13

www.ecouterre.com/morphotex-dress-mimics-butterfly-wing-shimmer-without-any-dyes/

www.circle-economy.com/textiles

www.coralrose.typepad.com/my_weblog/sustainable-textiles-definitions/

www.fairtrade.net/standards/our-standards/textile-standard.html

www.fashionrevolution.org/

# 2.9 Design for manufacture and project management

**LEARNING OUTCOMES**

By the end of this section you should have developed a knowledge and understanding of:

- planning for accuracy
- calculations based on economies of scale
- the impact of one-way designs, nap and pattern on fabric layouts
- quality control.

If you are studying at A-level you should also have developed a knowledge and understanding of:

- quality assurance systems including total quality management (TQM), critical path analysis, scrum or Six Sigma
- quality control, product sampling and quality circles
- labelling and quality assurance symbols
- BSI quality control standards and voluntary codes of practice.

When making prototypes for coursework, it is important to take into consideration how accuracy and efficiency can be achieved, so that a successful fashion or textile product can be made within financial restraints. In industry, it is essential that an order is completed within budget and to an agreed standard. To ensure this, there is a planned approach to accuracy and efficiency. **Quality assurance** systems are put into place to ensure that quality is integral to designing and manufacturing processes, and **quality control checks** are carried out during the production run to monitor quality.

## Planning for accuracy and efficiency

Please refer to Chapters 2.7 and 1.6 to find out about the efficiencies of the JIT stock control management system.

## The impact of one-way designs, nap and pattern on fabric layouts

Many fabrics are plain, and look and feel the same whichever way up they are held. However, some fabrics have a pattern or a surface texture that needs to appear a particular way up in the finished fashion or textile product. This is referred to as fabric with a **nap**.

For example, velvet has a pile with woven tufts that are not quite vertical. They lie in a particular direction which gives the fabric a slightly different shade of colour when viewed from different directions. The fabric surface texture can look and feel different according to which way up the fabric is held.

When calculating how much fabric is required for a fashion or textile product, if the fabric has a nap, a longer length of fabric will be required. The longer length will allow the pattern pieces to be laid out according to the nap of the fabric, however this will not be the most efficient way to group the pattern pieces and will result in extra fabric off-cuts or waste.

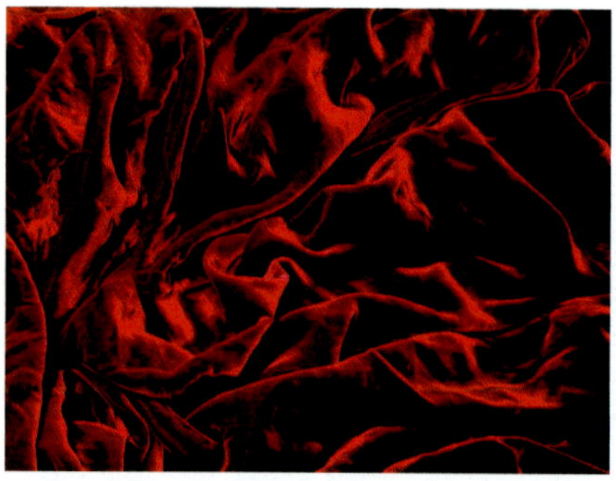

**Figure 2.9.1** Velvet – a fabric with a nap.

**Figure 2.9.2** One-way printed design on fabric.

If the fabric has a print or pattern that should be seen from a particular direction in the made product, this too will require extra fabric. The 'Thomas the Tank Engine' print fabric in Figure 2.9.2 above is a one-way design, because having all the trains upside down on children's pyjamas, for example, would not be right.

Pattern pieces for one-way fabric designs need to be correctly positioned along the length of the fabric to allow for the direction and repeat of the pattern. If the pattern repeat is large and the design of the fabric needs to be matched across two different sections of the finished item, there may be a significant amount of fabric wastage. This is because each pattern piece has to be placed on a particular part of the fabric pattern to ensure that the pattern falls correctly in the finished piece. The designer needs to understand the financial implications of selecting a one-way fabric, a fabric with a nap or with a large pattern repeat.

When using a commercial pattern, you need to know whether your selected fabric is with nap or without nap, so that you know how much fabric to buy; the fabric quantity required is given for both options on the back of the commercial pattern envelope.

**Figure 2.9.3** Checked shirt with matched pattern repeat.

## Quality assurance

A-level only

Quality assurance is about quality management – to ensure that manufactured products are guaranteed to be of the correct standard as defined in the product specification. Faulty or substandard work will not satisfy the customer; it will create waste and would be costly to rework or replace items, or to re-run production and compensate customers. Quality assurance is the responsibility of all those concerned in the designing, manufacturing and distribution of the product because every aspect and part of the process contributes to the quality of the end piece.

Quality is assured at every stage of designing and manufacturing by:

- following a clear brief
- carrying out appropriate research into target market needs and preferences
- evaluating design ideas against design criteria
- testing concepts and designs during development using models, samples and prototypes
- producing technical documents, including specifications, to provide clear and specific information about product design and manufacturing
- checking the quality of fabrics and other materials from suppliers
- training staff to follow correct procedures
- checking machinery is working properly, that work spaces are clean and safe working practices are followed
- checking production samples against the reference standard and specifications
- testing product against organisations' standards using testing laboratories
- carrying out quality control checks during production
- responding to recommendations from quality circles
- prompt delivery of orders to clients
- responding to feedback from customers, to make improvements in processes or carry out further staff training.

### KEY TERMS

**Quality assurance:** quality management to ensure that manufactured products are guaranteed to be of the correct standard as defined in the specification.

**Quality control checks:** an aspect of quality assurance which involves systematically checking that the product meets the required standard and matches the specification.

**Nap:** the fabric surface texture can look and feel different according to which way up the fabric is held.

**Total quality management (TQM):** a proactive approach followed by management and employees to ensure long-term customer satisfaction and customer loyalty.

**Critical path analysis:** a management tool to work out the most effective way of completing a task efficiently to meet deadlines.

### Total quality management

**Total quality management (TQM)** is a proactive approach followed by management and employees to ensure long-term customer satisfaction and loyalty. A culture of quality assurance is created through continual improvements in business practices, structures and systems throughout the company. It involves everyone in the workplace and includes every aspect of the business. Quality at all stages is planned for and monitored, to reduce the costs of wastage and defective goods. TQM aims to increase future business because customer expectations for quality are met and customers are confident to make repeat purchases. Every company employee has the responsibility to follow agreed methods of working to the set standard, and everyone's attitude to producing quality assured products counts.

### Critical path analysis

**Critical path analysis** is a management tool to work out the most effective way of completing a task efficiently to meet deadlines. For example, if a production run is being scrutinised, it is first separated into a list of all the separate processes involved in the production; this sequence of operations is referred to as the path. How long each separate activity takes is noted, so that the total amount of time required to complete the production run is understood. The information is displayed in a flow diagram. The critical path determines the shortest time possible to complete the production run. Any hold-up on the critical path directly impacts the planned production run completion date.

Critical path analysis is used to:

- aid production planning to meet schedules
- give an overview of complex production runs
- show how time is spent, so that efficiencies can be incorporated
- monitor completion of tasks along a timeline to highlight any delays or to gain time
- help manage costs, cash flow and budgets.

### Scrum

This term describes the framework put in place to encourage a teamwork approach to find the best way to manage quality; it promotes effective interaction between those working in different aspects of the business. Team members collaborate to ensure that business goals such as quality assurance are achieved. This is done by:

- planning for quality products
- finding out if there are any problems
- resolving any issues that will be detrimental to producing products of the correct quality
- working with other people who are not part of the immediate team to improve quality, such as suppliers of materials
- having a team responsibility to guarantee and improve quality.

**KEY TERMS**

**Six Sigma:** a teamwork approach to improving methods of eliminating waste, and increasing quality and efficiency in business.

**Quality circle:** a group of about 5–10 employees who volunteer to meet regularly to discuss issues with work, and to decide what changes would benefit the business.

### Six Sigma

**Six Sigma** is a business methodology used to improve quality management by making use of statistical analysis rather than intuition or guesswork. A business following the Six Sigma method creates a team of experts, who follow an agreed sequence of steps to make sure that quality and efficiency is improved. The aim is to reduce errors and defects, eliminate waste and lower costs. There is a clear target to increase customer satisfaction, reduce costs and to develop skills and knowledge to sustain improvements.

## Quality control

Quality control is an aspect of quality assurance which involves systematically checking that the product meets the required standard and matches the specification. Quality checks are made by testing samples of the manufactured product at intervals during the production schedule. The objective is to reduce or eliminate faults in the product and identify any errors that are being made during production. There may be defects in the sewing, construction, colour variations, sizing or garment details such as trims, fastenings, loose or pulled threads and fabric staining. It is important to check fashion and textile products during the production run, so that they are made accurately and consistently within the tolerances listed on the manufacturing specification.

**Figure 2.9.4** Operator stops garment transportation system to carry out random sampling.

## Product sampling

A-level only

A system is put in place to inspect samples from the production line to monitor and assure quality. Inspectors work to a plan to randomly sample a certain number of products in each batch. The number selected depends on the level of inspection and the size of the batch. The inspector is looking for defects in the products made which do not lie within the tolerances listed on the specification. The inspection plan might indicate a small sample to be carried out initially, but if defects are found, a more in-depth inspection is triggered. If the samples fail to meet the standard, the samples – and perhaps the whole batch – will be sent back to the factory floor to be reworked and corrected, and the reasons for the faulty products will be traced, in order to find out the cause of the error in production.

## Quality circles

A-level only

A **quality circle** is a group of about 5–10 employees who volunteer to meet regularly to discuss issues with work, and to decide what changes would benefit the business. The meetings are fairly formal, with an agenda and recorded minutes, and take place in paid working hours. The group is led by a facilitator, who helps to structure discussions and the approach to problem solving. Quality circles have been successful in making improvements in efficiency, and are an important part of quality assurance. They involve the workers who are best placed to identify where improvements can be made within the business and manufacturing operations, and they encourage employees to work together with senior management to develop and implement solutions to identified problems.

**Figure 2.9.5** Textile worker controls the quality of a fabric roll in garment factory and logs any faults.

## Automated equipment to check for faults in fabrics

The worker in Figure 2.9.5 below is looking at fabric as it scrolls over a light box, to check for faults in the fabric such as snapped threads, snags, holes, clumps of fibres, foreign bodies in the fabric construction, staining from processing machinery or uneven patches of fabric colour or texture. However, this is a labour-intensive operation, and the worker may not notice all of the faults. By using computers and automated machinery instead of a person, more accurate checks can be made with faster checking speeds possible and faults recorded automatically.

## Labelling and quality assurance symbols

Logos or marks are put on product labels and packaging to assure customers that they are buying a product of a genuine guaranteed quality. The Woolmark logo is a certification trademark to show that products labelled with it are 100 per cent pure new wool. The products have been tested at an independent authorised laboratory, and have been approved by The Woolmark Company.

**Figure 2.9.6** Woolmark on garment label.

The label in Figure 2.9.6 shows the bio-cotton logo, which states that no chemical fertilisers or pesticides were used in the production. Other cotton logos include the global organic textile standard (GOTS) label, pure cotton and non-GM cotton, which is a guarantee that cotton has not been sourced from genetically modified cotton plants.

**Figure 2.9.7** Bio-cotton logo.

**ACTIVITY**

As a class group activity, collect promotional packaging materials from purchased fashion and textiles products over a period of time, such as the swing tickets attached to items. Check through the packaging material to find examples of quality assurance symbols which guarantee safety and quality. Find out the full details of the symbols online and record the group's findings.

## Quality control standards and voluntary codes of practice

**A-level only**

Please refer to Chapter 2.10 for information about national and international standards in product design.

Some standards are mandatory, which means that it is a requirement of the law to follow the standard to produce, for example, children's nightwear. Other standards are voluntary, and many businesses choose to apply these standards to their own products in order to attract customers who are interested in buying quality assured products.

There are a great number of voluntary standards and codes of practice for businesses that wish to be known for following sustainable practices, and these businesses use recognised logos to label their products, to make customers aware of the principles they promote. For example, Figure 2.9.9 below shows the OEKO-TEX® Standard 100 logo, which certifies that there are no chemicals that are harmful or dangerous to human health in the product.

**Figure 2.9.8** Austrian version of the international OEKO-TEX Standard 100 logo to certify textile product is free from harmful chemicals.

## KEY POINTS

- Quality assurance systems are put into place to ensure that quality is integral to designing and manufacturing processes.
- Quality control checks are carried out during the production run to monitor quality.
- One-way fabrics or fabrics with a nap have a pattern or a surface texture that needs to appear a particular way up in the finished fashion or textile product.
- TQM aims to increase future business because customer expectations for quality are met and customers are confident to make repeat purchases.
- The critical path determines the shortest time possible to complete the production run, and any hold-up on the critical path directly impacts the planned production run completion date.
- Six Sigma is a business methodology used to improve quality management by making use of statistical analysis rather than intuition or guesswork.

## Check your knowledge and understanding

1. What is the difference between quality assurance and quality control?
2. Fabric with nap means that the fabric is damaged – true or false?
3. How are the results from critical path analysis written down?
4. What faults might occur in fashion and textile products?
5. What are the advantages of using automatic equipment to check for faults in fabric?

## Further reading

Martin, J. and Brenig-Jones, M. *Lean Six Sigma For Dummies*

www.fibre2fashion.com/industry-article/3055/quality-systems-for-garment-manufacture

www.standardsmap.org/identify?product=Textiles&

www.lenzing-fibers.com/en/tencel

www.chemours.com/Teflon_Fabric_Protector/en_US/benefits/how-teflon-textiles-work.html

# 2.10 National and international standards in product design

A-level only

**This topic is for A-level only. If you are studying at AS Level, you do not need to cover the content in this section.**

## LEARNING OUTCOMES

By the end of this section you should have developed a knowledge and understanding of:

- national and international standards as applied to textile products.

This chapter overlaps with the knowledge and outcomes of the following chapters:

- 1.9 Health and safety
- 1.11 Design for manufacturing, maintenance, repair and disposal.

A standard is a document containing a technical specification or precise criteria, so that it can be used as a rule, guideline or definition of goods or services to increase their reliability and effectiveness. For example, there are standard sizes for duvet covers so that they will fit the duvet.

Compliance with agreed standards marks a company's products as reliable, and differentiates them from cheaper alternatives that may be of a lower quality. Many major retailers specify that textile products supplied to them must meet specific performance criteria, and this often means that they must comply with a BSI, CEN or ISO Standard.

Standards are not the same as legislation, and there is no requirement for designers and manufacturers to follow them unless they are covered by legislation – for example the Nightwear Safety Regulations make specific reference to BS5722. However, the General Safety and Products Safety Directive makes it compulsory for manufacturers to make, suppliers to supply and retailers to sell a 'safe product'. This legislation applies to all products, not just clothing and textile products.

The CE (Conformitée Européenne) marking is the manufacturer's declaration that the product complies with the essential requirements of the relevant European health, safety and environmental protection laws. The products must have a technical file which explains how the production standards are maintained, and products with the mark are allowed to pass freely within the European Union (EU). The CE mark is not a measure of safety or quality however, just an indication that a product complies to certain requirements.

## Garment labelling

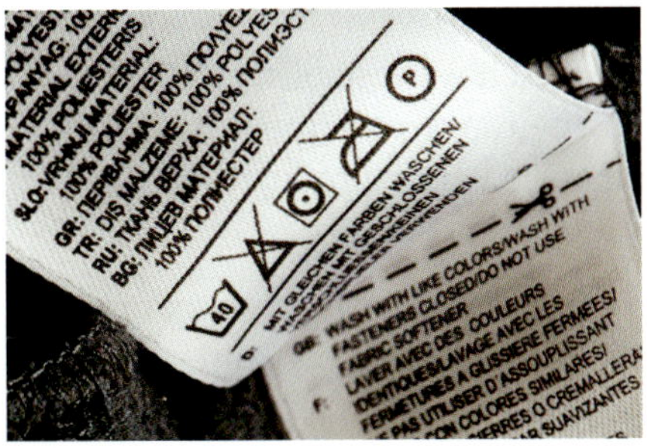


**Figure 2.10.1** Fibre content labelling must be understandable by consumers in the country where the product is sold.

The four key areas to be considered when labelling garments are:

- fibre content
- country of origin
- care instructions
- flammability.

### Fibre content

Fibre content labelling is mandatory in the UK as laid down in the Textile Products (Labelling and Fibre Composition) Regulations (2012). Labels must include information about the main fibres used and their percentages, and must be understandable for consumers in the market where the products are sold. For example, 67 per cent polyester/33 per cent viscose.

### Country of origin

As mentioned in Chapter 1.9, a country of origin label is only required where a consumer might be misled about where the garment was made.

### Care instructions

In the UK, it is not mandatory to include washing instructions but it is strongly encouraged. Information about care labels can be found in Chapter 1.11 of this book.

### Flammability

Information about flammability can be found in Chapter 1.9 of this book.

## British Standards Institute

The British Standards Institute (BSI) undertakes the process of standardisation in the UK. The BSI works in conjunction with Committee for Standardization (CEN), the European and the International Standards Organisation (ISO). Information about the work of the BSI can be found in Chapter 1.9 of this book.

## International Organisation for Standardisation

The International Organisation for Standardisation (ISO) is an independent non-government organisation, whose members are the standards organisations of the 162 member countries. The UK representative organisation is the BSI.

The ISO develops voluntary common standards between member nations, and is the biggest developer of standards in the world. Using the ISO standards helps companies to develop good quality products that are safe and reliable. It is easier to make direct comparisons between products from different markets, and helps the development of global trade on a fair basis. Consumers can also be confident that products meet the minimum agreed international standards.

**Figure 2.10.2** The European Ecolabel is awarded to products that meet tough environmental criteria.

## European Ecolabel

The European Ecolabel is a voluntary label which was established in 1992 to help identify products that have a reduced environmental impact throughout their life cycle. It is awarded to those companies whose products meet a tough set of environmental criteria set by a panel of experts.

The product life cycle covers the source of the raw materials (for example cotton) through production, packaging and transport, to consumer use and disposal.

The criteria vary from product to product, and focus on the lifecycle stages where there is the most environmental impact. For textiles, the biggest impact is at the bleaching, dyeing and printing stages where water pollution can occur, so the focus is on reducing damage at the manufacturing stage. Further information about pollution in manufacturing can be found in Chapter 1.11 of this book.

# Packaging directives

The EC Directive 94/62/EC on packaging and packaging waste came into force at the end of 1994. It placed a legal obligation on all EU member states to reduce the life cycle environmental impacts of packaging. The directive has the following specific objectives:

- to increase the recovery and recycling of packaging waste in a consistent way in all EU member states
- to reduce the amount of packaging used, and to encourage the reuse of packaging
- to limit the concentration levels of certain heavy metals used in packaging products in order to reduce the environmental impact of packaging products that are sent to landfill or incinerated.

**Figure 2.10.3** Fifty-five per cent of packaging waste must be recycled.

The directive sets mandatory recovery and recycling targets that member states must achieve, the first of which were required to be met in 2001.

The Packaging Directive was revised in 2004, and set new minimum recovery and recycling targets; 55 per cent by weight of all packaging waste is to be recycled. A further revision concerning the use of lightweight plastic carrier bags came into force on 29 April 2015 – large retailers are no longer allowed to give free plastic carrier bags to consumers.





### ACTIVITY

Use the internet to investigate false and misleading claims about the CE marking. Prepare an informative leaflet to warn consumers about false claims.

### KEY TERMS

**Standard:** an agreed and repeatable way of doing something, set out as a published document.

**Eco-label:** a mark awarded by the EU to producers who voluntarily employ verifiable measures that significantly reduce the harmful effects of their processes and products.

## KEY POINTS

- A standard is usually a voluntary agreement, and is not the same as legislation.
- Fibre content is the only labelling information that is mandatory in the UK.
- The BSI is the UK representative with CEN – the European Standards Body. The ISO is the International Standards Organisation.
- The European Ecolabel is awarded to products that have a reduced environmental impact throughout their life cycle.
- The EC Packaging Directive places a legal obligation on all EU Member States to reduce the life cycle environmental impacts of packaging.

## Check your knowledge and understanding

1 Name the four areas to be considered when labelling garments.

2 Explain how the work of the BSI makes sure that textile products are fit for purpose.

3 Explain why the criteria for the European Ecolabel focus on the bleaching, dyeing and printing stages in the manufacture of textile products.

## Further reading

www.care-labelling.co.uk

# Section 3

In this section you will learn about the following:

# 3.1 Non-exam assessment

**LEARNING OUTCOMES**

By the end of this section you should have developed a knowledge and understanding of:

- AS NEA: design, make and evaluate project
- A-level NEA: substantial design and make task.

The assessment criteria for both levels are the same – you will be designing, making and evaluating a textile product. In this section, you will see a variety of advanced work completed by students working at both levels. Study the exemplar work to give initial ideas, but always work independently and push yourself to produce the best you can.

The main difference between the two specifications is that at AS you are given a contextual challenge by AQA to work from. At A-level, however, you must identify and choose the context yourself, making sure you have the opportunity to challenge yourself as a designer.

## Introduction to the AS NEA design, make and evaluate project

In the AS NEA, you will be required to undertake a small-scale design, make and evaluate project in response to a realistic **context**.

The context of this task will be set by AQA. You must write a design brief which shows you have identified an opportunity to design and make a product that will meet the needs and desires of a user, client or market. You will need to ensure that the task you set yourself has an appropriate level of complexity or you will not be able to achieve marks in the higher bands.

### How will I be assessed at AS Level?

The NEA is worth 50 per cent of your total AS Level mark.

There are 80 marks available for the project. You will be marked against three assessment objectives (AOs) shown in the table below.

**Table 3.1.1** The assessment criteria mark weighting at AS Level.

| Assessment objective (AO) | Section | Criteria | Maximum marks |
|---|---|---|---|
| AO1 (24 marks)<br>Identify, investigate and outline design possibilities. | A | Identify and investigate design possibilities. | 16 |
| | B | Produce a design brief and specification. | 8 |
| AO2 (40 marks)<br>Design and make prototypes that are fit for purpose. | C | Develop a design proposal. | 20 |
| | D | Develop a design prototype(s). | 20 |
| AO3 (16 marks)<br>Analyse and evaluate. | E | Analyse and evaluate. | 16 |

# Introduction to the A-level NEA design, make and evaluate project

At A-level, you will be required to undertake a substantial design and make task, and produce a final prototype based on a context and design brief developed yourself.

A-level students are free to choose any design context and are not restricted to choosing one from those offered by AQA. However, the choice of context must be given careful consideration to ensure that you will be able to meet the assessment criteria for the NEA.

The brief must be of an appropriate level of complexity and contain a degree of uncertainty of the outcome. You will need to engage in an iterative process of designing, making, testing and evaluating. This means that you will go through a cyclic process which involves prototyping, testing, analysing and refining products and processes. Each time you pass through these stages, you should get closer to developing an original textile product.

## How will I be assessed at A-level?

The NEA is worth 50 per cent of your total A-level mark.

There are 100 marks available for the project. You will be marked against three assessment objectives (AOs) shown in the table below.

**Table 3.1.2** The assessment criteria mark weighting at A-level.

| Assessment objective (AO) | Section | Criteria | Maximum marks |
|---|---|---|---|
| AO1 (30 marks)<br>Identify, investigate and outline design possibilities. | A | Identify and investigate design possibilities. | 20 |
| | B | Produce a design brief and specification. | 10 |
| AO2 (50 marks)<br>Design and make prototypes that are fit for purpose. | C | Develop a design proposal(s). | 25 |
| | D | Develop a design prototype(s). | 25 |
| AO3 (20 marks)<br>Analyse and evaluate. | E | Analyse and evaluate. | 20 |

# AS and A-level assessment details

## When will the assessment task be completed?

At AS Level the contextual challenge will be released on or after 1 June in the year prior to the qualification being awarded.

At A-level, the decision about when to start the NEA will be left to the teacher's discretion. It is likely you will begin the preliminary investigations at the end of the first year.

## How long should I spend on the task?

Learning hours are not specified because the process of producing the design portfolio is iterative and undertaken independently, while the final prototype is manufactured under immediate guidance or supervision in school/college.

## How will you present the work for assessment?

You will create a design portfolio, which includes photographic evidence of processes, along with your final prototype.

- Your portfolio can be written or electronic.
- It is recommended at AS Level that you complete no more than 35 design sheets – although this will vary depending on whether you are using PowerPoint, a sketchbook or a flip folder.
- At A-level, the process of producing the design portfolio is iterative and undertaken independently, therefore it is difficult to specify a number of pages. It is not anticipated that you will complete more than 45 design sheets.

# How to approach the NEA

## Think as a fashion designer

The assessment criteria offer guidance as to the evidence you should be presenting in your portfolios, however, it is worth remembering that for these advanced specifications you should also enter the world of fashion design:

- be open to taking design risks and show innovation
- think creatively, innovatively and critically
- work collaboratively and use feedback from users, peers and expert practitioners
- consider the creative and manufacturing worlds
- be aware of the needs, wants and values of users and clients
- use your knowledge and experience of real world contexts
- learn new processes associated with the creation of exciting prototypes
- take a design idea forward and develop an original prototype with flair
- work safely and skilfully to produce high-quality prototypes
- understand cultural, economic, environmental, historical and social factors that will influence designing.

## Think about the advice AQA offer in the specification

- 'The brief must be of an appropriate level of complexity and contain a degree of uncertainty of the outcome, so that students can engage in an iterative process of designing, making, testing and evaluating.'

This means that if you write a simple brief, it will not give you sufficient scope for exploring the design potential and producing a product that is sufficiently complex to meet the assessment criteria at the highest level. Your final outcome – that is the garment you design and make – should not be something that you came up with originally. It must have started from an idea or inspiration, but then be revised and reinvented (iterations) so that it is the best version it can be.

- 'You must produce a written or digital design folder, clearly evidencing how the assessment criteria have been met. You should include an index, making it clear where the evidence for each criterion can be found. You must be appropriately focused on the demands of the task, and not include irrelevant information or activities. The coursework should be about quality and not quantity.'

Communication of your ideas and the presentation of your work are important. Your teacher and the moderator must be able to see your thinking clearly, and understand as you progress through the design and make process. You need to show you are focused on designing and making an original product, and you therefore only have the time to include relevant work, with each piece informing the next stage. To make it explicitly clear, include a detailed index showing where the evidence for each criterion can be found.

- 'This process is not linear, and you will move between the assessment criteria as and when it is appropriate. You may need to carry out research during development and evaluation when researching.'

The specification makes it clear that you must approach the work with an open mind and show your individuality. Our minds work in very different ways, but at every stage you must be prepared to say to yourself 'Is this working?', 'Perhaps I would do better to try it a different way?', 'If I do, I will need more research and then I may need to make another toile.', 'When I have made my best prototype, the client could well say they do not like it and ask me to modify the product'. This is called an iterative process of designing, making, testing and evaluating.

## Assessment Objective 1A and 1B

### The AS contextual challenges

You will be offered a range of contextual challenges by the examination board. These are intended to offer plenty of scope, not only to inspire you but also to give you the opportunity to show your knowledge, expertise and design and make ability.

Examples of possible contexts:

- Trends of the different decades continue to influence the design of outdoor wear.
- Different cultures of the world often inspire fashion designers when they design special occasion wear.

You are completing one piece of coursework worth 50 per cent of the total mark. Even though it is described as a small-scale design and make task, you have to meet the assessment criteria. You get one opportunity to show your skills, so make sure you choose wisely.

- Read and understand the assessment criteria.
- Have a look at an AQA exemplar project on their website.
- Read all of the context challenges carefully, highlighting key words.
- Be honest and consider what interests you the most.
- Think about your skills as a designer.
- Have a client or end user in mind, and make sure you have good access to them.
- Do you have the practical skills to make the outcome you are considering?

### Advice when identifying and choosing the context at A-level

Your ability to identify a context and write a challenging design brief is vital if you are to achieve success at this level.

- Read and make sure you understand the assessment criteria, because they make it clear what you must do.
- Choose a context that you can easily research. You must complete some primary research, so think about visits and whether they will be possible.
- You must identify client/user needs or wants, seeking out a niche in the market that would give you the opportunity to show some originality.
- Students tend to produce their best work when they choose a context that interests them.
- You will have certain strengths in the subject, so make sure your proposal will allow you to use them.
- Always have an end user in mind, and make sure you have good access to them.
- Think about your other A-level subjects and your future career hopes. For example, if you are planning a career working with young people who have specific disabilities, it would be a good opportunity for you to visit a learning centre, and perhaps make a product that would benefit their development. The jacket in Figure 3.1.1 is an interactive jacket for an autistic child designed and made by an A-level student.

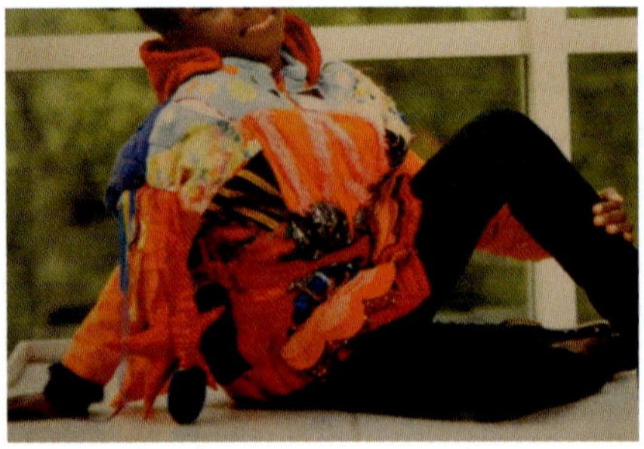

**Figure 3.1.1** An interactive jacket for an autistic child.

## Assessment Objective 1A: Identify and investigate design possibilities

### Understanding the assessment criteria

Your teacher will have given you a copy of the specification assessment criteria. You would be very wise to constantly refer to these as you complete the NEA.

This section accounts for 16 marks at AS Level and 20 marks at A-level, so detail and depth is required by both. However, you do need to be concise and only present relevant material, as time is short. At A-level, you must show a greater depth of understanding and knowledge. Your work will have greater content, be more extensive and contain prototypes that are significantly more complex and challenging in their development.

The assessment criteria are the same at both levels, and the evidence you present will reflect your level of ability. Please note that the exemplar work in this book is taken from a range of sources and levels, both AS and A-level. It is not intended to be a model for your own work, but as inspiration and ideas for the direction that your own work might take.

At A-level, it is very important that you explain your thinking and provide reasons for your choice of context. Explain your understanding of the constraints you might face when designing the product.

To meet this criterion, all students need to:

- plan and carry out extensive investigation into the context
- use primary and secondary methods of investigation
- carry out relevant, practical activities including experimentation, disassembly and modelling
- identify and thoroughly explore design opportunities
- relate the opportunities to the needs and wants of the end user
- use knowledge to make decisions which are fully explained
- analyse and show good understanding of information gathered
- reference in detail the constraints to be considered when coming up with a final idea for the prototype
- explore possible solutions by producing concept ideas
- present first concepts through a variety of methods and techniques
- present relevant and feasible ideas for further development.

## What might you include in the portfolio?

Tick off →

There is no right or wrong way to meet the assessment criteria. Here is a list of some of the activities you might carry out in order to meet this criterion:

- A plan for covering this criterion. Time is very limited on this project so do not spend too long on each of these activities. Be very focused.
- Initial analysis of the context. Show your understanding – create a thought shower or extended piece of writing. At A-level, there must be detailed reasoning behind your choice of context.
- Identify a client or user. Profile potential clients. You could set up a focus group that will evaluate throughout the project. Consider their needs and wants. When you have presented your concept ideas, get their feedback.
- Identify the inspirational theme and give reasons for your choice. You will need to research this theme, only presenting relevant material.
- List primary investigations into context. Relate these to a theme and client, for example visits, surveys and questionnaires. Museums, fashion shows, art galleries, shops and designer studios can also be visited. Attend events where the product might be worn, and talk to users. Set up a focus group.
- List secondary investigations into context. Relate these to a theme and client, for example internet, books, magazines or interviews. Consider existing designs, trends and shop reports.
- A disassembly activity related to your initial ideas for the product can be useful.
- Practical, experimental work related to context – this could be samples, models and sketches. Disassemble and reconstruct as experimental. Initial methods of colouring and product shapes. Use mood boards, and pattern and colour effects.

- Social, moral, environmental, health, sustainability issues – all must be related.
- List references.
- Analyse findings, list design opportunities and explain decisions.
- Concept ideas, initial thoughts – sketches and notes. These will be developed later. For now it is just asking for your first thoughts when you have analysed all this material.

Before you start the work, make sure you have read the advice on Choosing a context outlined above. At A-level, you have to identify the context, explain your reasons for choice and go on to develop a challenging design brief. Have a careful look at the four design sheets below, which were produced by a student working at a high level. They illustrate the process gone through in assessment objective 1A and how, following the initial investigations, they have been able to move forward and write an informed design brief for assessment objective 1B. The student has used an individual approach to analysing and presenting the work.

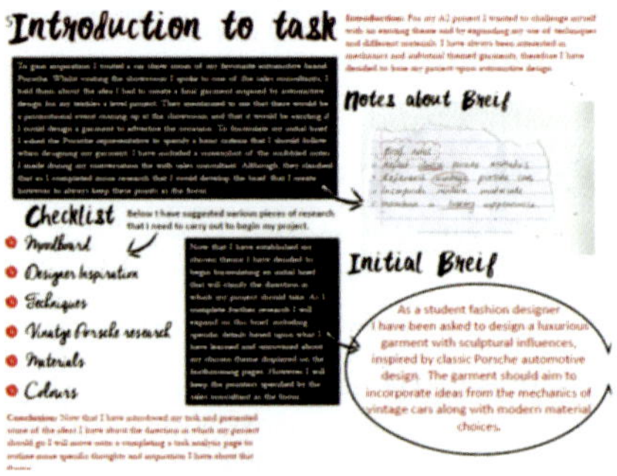


**Figure 3.1.2** This A-level student explains the context chosen for the NEA.

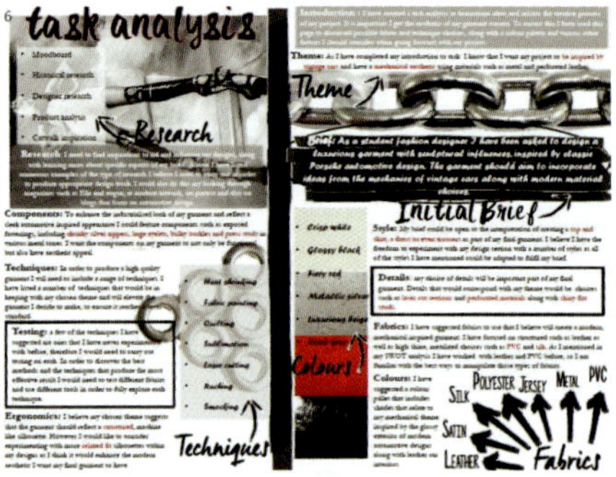


**Figure 3.1.3** The context and initial brief is analysed.

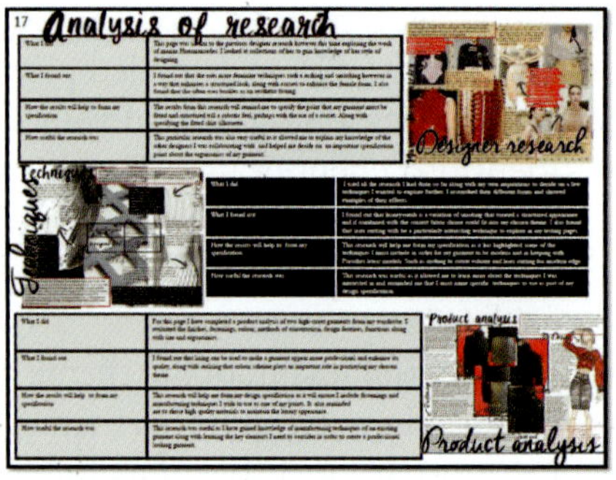


**Figure 3.1.4** The investigation work is analysed.

**Figure 3.1.5** The student has completed the investigation work for AO1A and is now in a position to write a developed design brief.

**Figure 3.1.6** Thought shower related to an AS context challenge.

When you carry out the analysis of the task, it will help you to identify the investigation work that needs to be done. Figure 3.1.6 is an example of early analysis through a thought shower. The student is faced with the challenge of designing rainwear, and needs to consider all aspects such as garment features, target market, financial constraints, trends, performance requirements and issues that need further investigation. You need to remember that not every thought has to be entirely relevant at this stage, and that much of the thinking may well disappear from the end product as a result of the iterative process. Whatever you decide to do, it must be concise and focused.

Figure 3.1.7 Analysing the context.

As this student analyses the task, ideas are beginning to form. This is good practice. You must remember to record your ideas every step of the way whenever they emerge, just put them to paper. Let the reader know what you are thinking. Notice how this student uses words, colour and images to convey thoughts and ideas.

It is advisable at the start of the project to identify a typical user of your product. See Figure 3.1.8 as you put together a profile, and possibly interview the user. Ideas may emerge when you consider what they like, what they might need or what they are most likely to desire.

Figure 3.1.8 Profile of intended product user.

At this stage, you might benefit from forming a focus group. Identify four or five people with a similar profile, and involve them at every stage as you develop and make your prototype.

In order to make your product different and original, you need to have chosen an inspirational theme that will provide you with colour, pattern, shape and texture, which you can use when developing your product. In most cases, the context will steer you towards the theme. When you make the decision, think about the user of your product. If it does not appeal to them, the product will not sell.

Inspiration can come from one or more sources with the following often popular:

- a fashion era
- different cultures
- the natural world
- the work of a specific fashion designer.

Figure 3.1.9 Mood board.

You can see from the high-quality boards below (Figures 3.1.9, 3.1.10 and 3.1.11) that these students have taken inspiration from images relating to personal interests and experiences.

Figure 3.1.9. is a good example of a board that is made up of carefully selected material that is likely to inspire designing. Some students prefer to look at current trends and present a board of related material, to ensure their ideas are modern and their products likely to sell.

The sheet in Figure 3.1.10 has been put together very well, with the student clearly identifying the fashion designers that they hope will inspire their design ideas for an original prototype.

In Figure 3.1.11, the learner has looked for material relevant to the Alaskan culture that is likely to inspire designing. The images presented proved to be invaluable when they went on to develop ideas.

Figure 3.1.10 Inspiration from the work of other designers.

Figure 3.1.11 Secondary research into the Alaskan culture.

Figure 3.1.12 Oriental mood board.

**Figure 3.1.13** Primary research – visiting an exhibition.

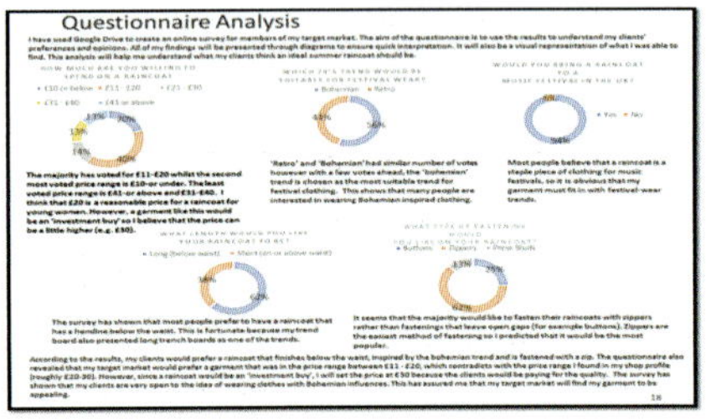


**Figure 3.1.14** Questionnaire.

**Figure 3.1.15** Shop report.

**Figure 3.1.16** Looking at the work of professional designers.

The A-level student who produced Figure 3.1.12 is working at a very high level, and not only selects inspirational images but also analyses their usefulness.

The assessment criteria state that you must carry out both primary and secondary research. You will need to do this to gather information about the theme, user and end product.

Examples of primary research include:

- visits – museums, holidays, art galleries, exhibitions, shops, design studios, work practice; while there, take lots of photographs
- surveys, questionnaires, interviews and focus group involvement
- disassembly activities.

Examples of secondary research include:

- internet, search engines
- TV channels
- books and magazines
- shop reports
- trends
- existing designs.

It is worth mentioning the importance of gathering information through visits and interviewing clients. For example, a student who designs clothing for children with specific disabilities should talk to the parents, visit the school and then try to arrange an interview with an expert. When you are carrying out your investigations, you must be on the lookout for any design opportunities.

The examples on this page show some of the activities that students have engaged in, to show they have met the assessment criteria for identifying and investigating design possibilities. Every portfolio will be different, so you must decide on the most relevant investigations for your project.

Following a visit to an exhibition, the student in Figure 3.1.13 went on to carry out practical investigations, to establish a way of embellishing the garment being designed and made.

When you complete a questionnaire, the questions need to be very focused and relevant. It is not just about the collection of data, but the analysis of the data and how it will inform designing. In Figure 3.1.14, the student has presented their analysis in a visual way. This is effective because it gives a quick interpretation of users' preferences of raincoat design. Try using charts, graphs and visual aids to analyse and present your data – choose the ones that will convey the essence of your data clearly.

It is good practice to combine internet searches with actual visits to the shops. Visiting a shop allows you hands-on access to garments, which can give you a better picture of garment construction, function and fabric choice, as well as the overall quality. Looking at fashion in a catalogue/online is very quick, but it does not allow close scrutiny of the details. In Figure 3.1.15, this student has recorded her findings particularly well.

The student in Figure 3.1.16 is looking to use recycled fabrics for her design, so has investigated the work of other designers who are concerned about the environment and share similar goals.

**Figure 3.1.17** Fabric choice.

The evidence you present in relation to fabric and component choice will depend on the context you have chosen to explore. The student in Figure 3.1.17 has done considerable and relevant research into fabric and component choice, considering sustainability in depth. It could well be that fabric choice for your product is limited because of the design context, and it would be more appropriate to consider fabrics as your designs develop. At whatever point in the process you present this work, the marks will be awarded accordingly.

You must guard against presenting cut and paste information that simply covers the issues criterion, as it will gain you no marks. You will find it helpful to highlight any social, moral, environmental, health and safety issues that are relevant to your product. You must make sure that any evidence you present is directly related to your product design. Figures 3.1.16 and 3.1.17 do this particularly well.

**Figure 3.1.18** Student exemplar.

Figures 3.1.18 and 3.1.19 are excellent examples of students working at a high level. Not only are existing products analysed in depth, but also there is evidence that the findings have been used directly, and new ideas are starting to emerge.

The criteria state that concept ideas must be relevant and provide genuine possibilities for further development. Show your individuality, use the research material you have gathered and then go on to use a variety of methods and techniques to show your original, first ideas. Not all of them will be suitable for developing, but you are being creative and moving towards finding that one spark of an idea which will result in the production of an innovative textile product. Figure 3.1.20 is a good example of a student doing this.

**Figure 3.1.19** A product analysis inspires a new design.

All learners will use different methods to help them come up with ideas. It is a difficult part of the process, so it is well worth the time studying exemplar projects on the e-AQA website, and perhaps trying some of the techniques that others have used.

This is an advanced specification, so you will be expected to use techniques that present more challenge than those you used at GCSE level. When you look at different methods of manipulating fabric, the textures you create can be used in product design. The student in Figure 3.1.21 has experimented with different ways of working with fabric to create textural effects. Shibori, batik, layering, burning and free machine embroidery have all been considered. Carrying out this work as part of the early investigations allows the student to eliminate those techniques that do not work. As product ideas are being developed, only the successful techniques are included, and further experimental work will take place at this stage.

**Figure 3.1.20** Experimental sketches using existing designs to inspire.

**Figure 3.1.21** Investigating fabric embellishment techniques.

**Figure 3.1.22** Experimental designs through collage work.

It is worth remembering that not all ideas emerge or are presented through sketching. The student in Figure 3.1.22 shows how collage work can also inspire ideas. When you take part in these activities, it serves to open your mind – you are looking for something that is original, and there is no better way of doing it than using your research material in as many imaginative ways as you can.

## Assessment Objective 1B: Produce a design brief and specification

### Understanding the assessment criteria

To meet this criterion, you need to produce a clearly stated and challenging design brief that addresses the context and meets the needs of the intended user(s).

You should formulate a fully detailed specification which is informed by your investigations. Statements in this specification need to be clear and unambiguous. There should be specific references to measurable outcomes as well as qualitative statements. However you present the specification, it must be a live and working document that you will constantly refer to throughout the process. It will guide your thinking as you develop ideas.

Remember your work must be concise and focused to meet the criteria, so only present a concise analysis of your investigations – clearly show the design opportunities, a detailed specification and a challenging design brief.

Have a look at these examples below written by students working at the advanced level.

Example 1: the student establishes the design opportunities, and then goes on to write a challenging brief.

**Design opportunity**

The current fashion market has seen a surging demand for formal fashion wear for younger men. It is at the height of fashion for nearly all occasions ranging from very formal evening wear to casual beach wear. Through my own personal experiences, I have found that it is hard to find a 'skinny-fit' suit which fits well for the younger man. Many suits are built for an older man's body, which is much broader and therefore 'drowns' a man in his twenties. I feel that there is a gap in the market for this cut of suit, especially for the growing market among younger people. I have been very influenced by the fine tailoring of Alexander McQueen and the Saville Row influence it brings, as well as the unique patterns and extravagant creations created by the house. I have also been influenced by the bold colours of Paul Smith, and the extreme modern and strange materials which are utilised by Mügler on the runway. I have also chosen to study the 1920s men's fashion with the jazz age and 'nipped-in waist' smoker jackets. Formal fashion was worn by nearly all men, and with this influence coming back, I want the outfit to be inspired from the generation in which this fashion was at its peak. Furthermore, I want the 1950s to be very influential in this style – suits from this period became very fitted; suit trousers became shorter outfits and more 'over the top'.

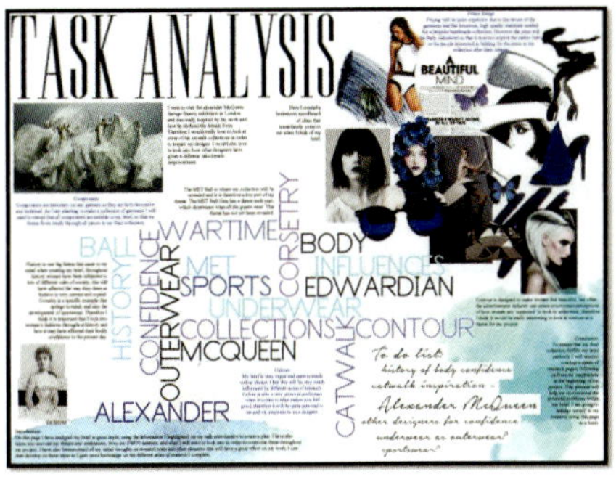


Figure 3.1.23 Analysing and identifying design opportunities for womenswear.

**Design brief**

I have been approached by a tailor who designs for a 'high-end' high street store. He has asked me to collaborate with him to design a skinny-fitting suit to go on sale for the autumn/winter '13 collection. As a tailor, he feels that there is a gap in the market in suits for younger men, and a garment that will fit them well. As a young man, he has approached me to help create the product, which must be reminiscent of old English styles of men's tailoring but also incorporate these trends to create a new and modern collection. While borrowing from older styles, I will use current trends from fashion houses and I will use production methods and modern fabrics to create a truly modern suit, which will target a young audience.

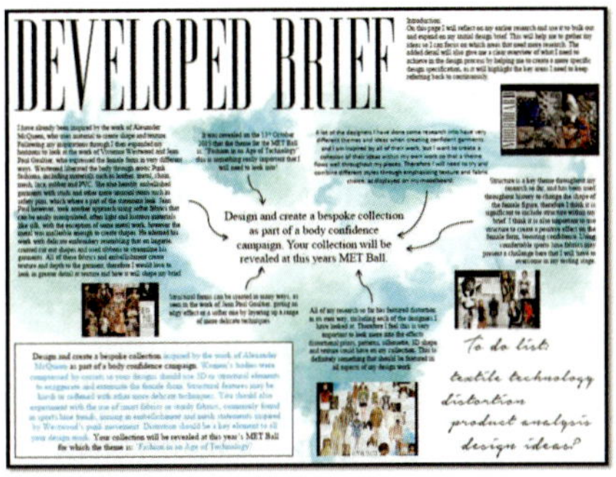


Figure 3.1.24 A developed design brief.

## Example two

In this second example, the student in Figure 3.1.23 and Figure 3.1.24 has identified a current issue regarding women's self-image and body confidence when choosing clothes. Following intensive investigation, she went on to write this challenging design brief.

## Example three

Design and create a bespoke collection inspired by the work of Alexander McQueen as part of a body confidence campaign. Women's bodies were compressed by corsets so your designs should use 3D or structural elements to exaggerate and extenuate the female form. Structural features may be harsh or softened with other more delicate techniques. You should also experiment with the use of smart fabrics or sturdy fabrics, commonly found in sports luxe trends, mixing in embellishment and mesh statements inspired by Westwood's Punk movement. Distortion should be a key element to all your design work. Your collection will be revealed at this year's MET Ball, for which the theme is 'Fashion in an age of technology'.

The analysis of your investigative work must show you have focused on the context and needs of the intended user. How you decide to present the information is up to you, but it should be an extended piece of writing that gives consideration to every aspect, and uses your analytical skills.

A simple table can be used to show what was established and then explain how this information would be used during the development of the end product. Some students choose to produce an extended piece of writing which fully explains what their investigations uncovered, and how these results would influence designing.

The specification pulls all of your findings together, and provides a list of criteria that must guide your thinking as you go on to develop design ideas. When you write the specification, you must name and describe the product. Do not be general – be focused, detailed and precise. This is a document that you will use throughout the rest of the process, so it needs to be useful.

When meeting the assessment criteria, you are likely to have done some investigating, designing, testing and evaluating. However, you are engaging in an iterative process, which means you are also likely to do more research, designing, prototyping, testing and evaluating as you work through the development of your ideas. Each time you pass through these stages, you are getting closer to developing an original textile product.

## Assessment Objective 2C: Development of design proposals

### Understanding the assessment criteria

The work you are completing at AS Level is described by the examination board as a small-scale design, make and evaluate project. At A-level, it is described as a substantial one. You have a limited amount of time to complete the work so all you do must be focused, with every stage informing the next.

You need to have a clear plan of the work you are going to carry out, with justification for each activity. To ensure their thinking is made clear, some students choose to explain the activity they are carrying out on every design sheet, along with a statement about any conclusions reached. Before you start developing your product, you need to study and understand what this assessment criterion is asking you to do. These notes may help to clarify what is being asked of you:

- Look back at your first concept ideas, have your design specification in front of you and read the brief you have written. All of these things should guide you during the development process.
- You must show clear evidence of originality, creativity and a confidence in taking risks with your designing.
- You may choose to spend some time putting your initial ideas on paper, and providing annotation to explain your thinking.
- You can present your ideas through a variety of different media, but whatever methods are chosen, they should be of a high quality and befitting this level of qualification.
- In the highest band, students should also demonstrate innovation by generating ideas that are different to the work of most of their peers.
- As you evaluate and explain this work, you must make constant reference to the design brief, specification and investigations carried out.
- Think about modelling techniques, high-quality drawings, sketches, annotations and notes. Modelling is a key element of this assessment criterion – whether this is part-modelling, practising manufacturing and finishing techniques, the production of scale models or material experimentation.
- As you make decisions and select possible designs, you will go on to develop all aspects through exploration and experimentation of different materials, techniques and processes.
- You will be expected to produce working drawings, plans and patterns to enable successful prototype manufacturing to take place. The use of CAD is encouraged, but this should not be the only form of design communication that is used.
- A comprehensive and fully detailed manufacturing specification with relevant quality control checks must be included.
- The prototype must be able to be made in realistic and achievable time, therefore some planning will be needed.

### Developing your ideas

You have considered the design brief in depth and your investigations will have resulted in some early ideas. Look back over your work and reconsider what you are being asked to do. Focus on the specification, be aware of the

**Figure 3.2.1** Mixed media presentation of initial ideas.

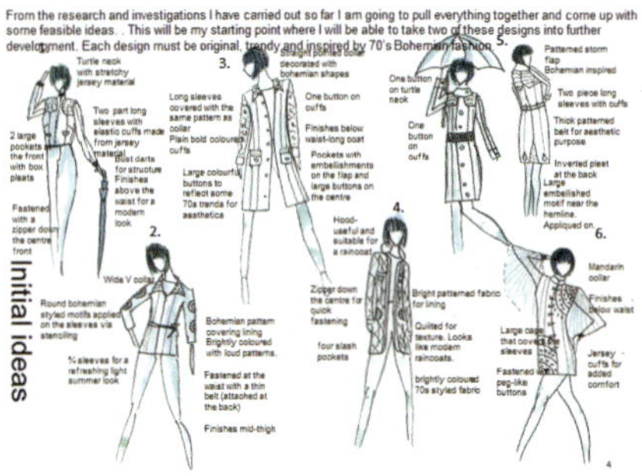

**Figure 3.2.2** Initial ideas for a coat design.

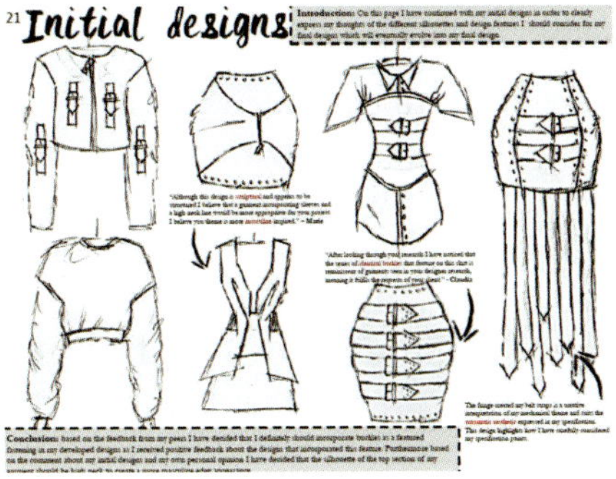


**Figure 3.2.3** Initial ideas for a garment inspired by the classic Porsche car design.

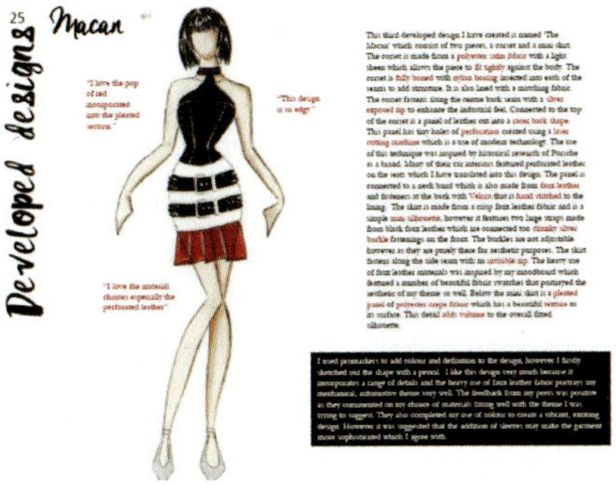


**Figure 3.2.4** A developed design for a garment inspired by the classic Porsche car design.

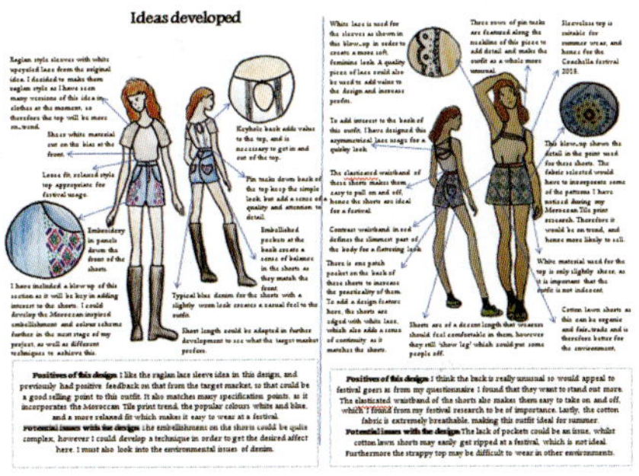


**Figure 3.2.5** Developed ideas for a pair of shorts and top design.

work of other designers and think about the type of product that the end user would buy.

There is no right or wrong way to present your ideas; you need to choose a method that works for you. This is just the starting point – you will continue to design, have ideas, develop them, carry out further research and then modify them, even after your prototype is made. Take risks and show your creativity – the ideas you present should be very different from your peers, and there must be a genuine attempt to be original if you are going to access the highest band of marks.

Have a look at the examples in Figure 3.2.1 and Figure 3.2.2. They show very different styles of presentation, with both learners displaying high levels of creativity. The student who produced Figure 3.2.1 should go into much more detail as the work develops, providing full annotation in relation to fabrics, techniques and the appeal to the end user. Evaluation with constant reference to the design brief, specification and investigations carried out is essential during the product development stage.

The student in Figure 3.2.3 has been inspired to design a one-off garment to be worn at the launch of a new Porsche vehicle. Concept ideas were produced to meet the requirements of assessment objective 1A, and these have been used as a basis for these initial, slightly more formal ideas. Figure 3.2.4 shows how the student then moved forward to present focused, developed and detailed ideas that would be feasible and meet the requirements of the specification.

The student in Figure 3.2.5 has moved their initial ideas forward, and is now very focused on the construction aspects of the garment. These are firm ideas ready for further development.

At this stage, you do need to plan your development activities carefully, as you only have a limited amount of time to complete the project and experimental work can easily consume vast amounts of time.

## Development activities

You will have established some of the key features of your product, in the work you have done so far. You must continue to be focused and only carry out relevant work. At this stage, it is a good idea to write down your thoughts about how you envisage the product developing to the final prototype. It must be clear that you have evaluated the ideas as they develop.

A realistic plan for further development activities could include:

- the making of a paper pattern and toile
- the choice of fabrics and components
- testing construction techniques and processes on the chosen fabric
- testing embellishment techniques
- consideration of costing, aftercare and environmental issues.

Remember there is no set plan or rules, and the development work you decide to do will very much depend on your design specification and the textile product you are making.

## Making paper patterns and toiles

To achieve marks in the highest band, there needs to be evidence of modelling techniques, high-quality drawings, annotations with all aspects developed through exploration and experimentation with different materials, techniques and processes. Not only must the product shape and style be established through modelling techniques, but you will also have to produce a paper pattern or template in order for a third party to make the product. In industry, a toile of the full product or part of it is made to help establish that it is functional. The students in Figure 3.2.7 and Figure 3.2.8 do this particularly well.

If you plan to add a pattern to your final garment, it is important that you experiment with methods that may achieve the best effect. Figure 3.2.9. shows the designed and made dress, which uses appliquéd blocks of colour to achieve the cityscape effect on the skirt border.

The students in Figures 3.2.7, 3.2.8 and 3.2.9 have worked with commercial and block patterns to develop the different features of their garments. Toiles have been made to establish if the pattern modifications work and whether they result in the most desirable product shape being achieved. Their thinking is made very clear through the excellent annotation, which explains how the features could be adapted to give better performance and a fashionable look.

When developing your ideas, it is not always necessary to make a toile of the full product. For example, if you are making a dress, and know the pattern for the skirt is accurate and will work well, you may choose to only make a toile of the bodice to establish if your idea is likely to work. A toile is a developmental piece and not a practice or test run of a commercial pattern. You need to show which features are working well by recording the activities through photographs and annotation. Designing original products is very time consuming, and the designer may well go through the process of making a final garment only to find that there are features the client does not like. This means you would have to return to the toile stage and make further developments. All modifications to commercial patterns should be clearly recorded.

**Figure 3.2.6** Dress design with a cityscape appliquéd border.

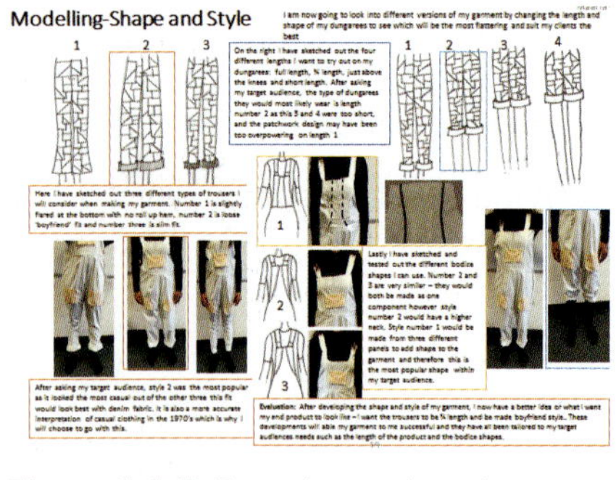


**Figure 3.2.7** Experimental work showing modelling techniques for the design of a pair of dungarees.

**Figure 3.2.8** Developing the style through pattern making and the use of part toiles.

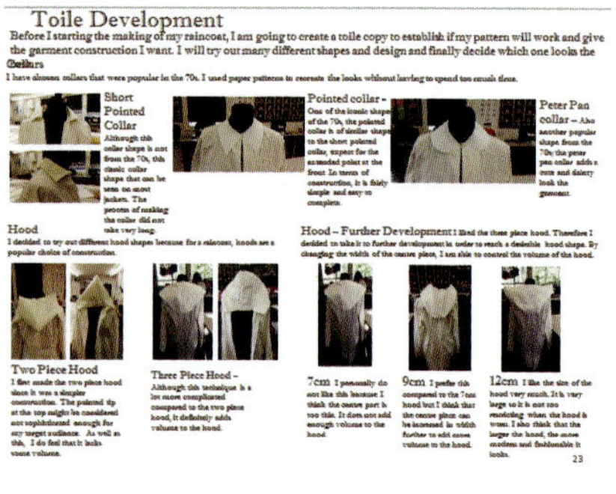


**Figure 3.2.9** Making the first prototype toile of collars and hoods.

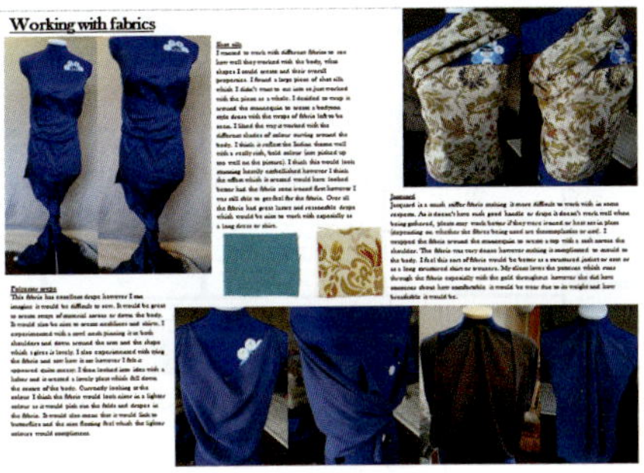


Figure 3.2.10 Fabric choice for a dress.

## Fabric and component choice

The fabric and components you choose must be carefully selected with regard for their working properties, as well as having high aesthetic appeal to the consumer. You should use your knowledge of fibres and fabrics, and make a preliminary choice. The student in Figure 3.2.10 has considered fabric drape and has explored particularly well, making their reasons for this choice clear. It is important to experiment with the fabrics – handling them to see if the features and special effects that you want are achievable. If you are not sure of the fabric composition and detailed specification when you buy the fabric, you would be wise to test it to establish whether it meets the requirements of the garment function. For example, if you are making clothing for children, you might consider such aspects as comfort, stain resistance and aftercare.

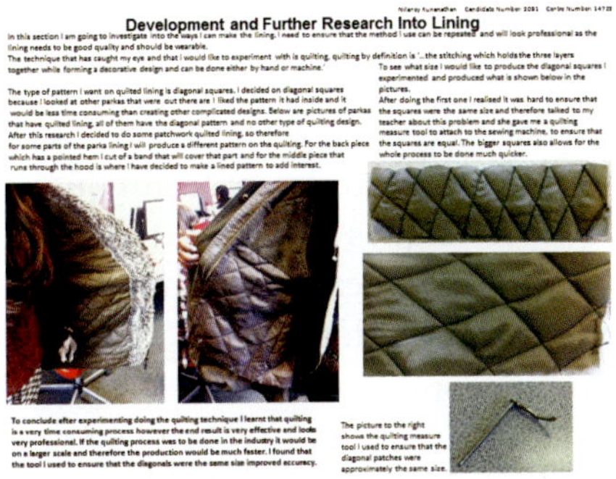


Figure 3.2.11 Techniques for lining a coat.

## Testing construction techniques and processes

Through making your toile and using your knowledge about techniques, you may decide it is unnecessary to test the construction processes by producing samples. However, it will be necessary to test your chosen fabric to see how it responds during stitching, and to establish ways of achieving the best results. You will need to consider the following:

- thread choice
- fabric stabilisation using interfacing
- sewing machine needle choice
- machine stitch tension
- stitch length
- tolerance levels
- iron temperature when pressing.

Refer to these aspects as you plan for making, and if possible, put technique samples in your portfolio.

The student in Figure 3.2.12 needed to establish if smocking would work on the chosen fabric and create a modern look. It was decided that the effect looked historical and did not reflect the desired theme, so it was not used in the final garment, however credit was given for testing.

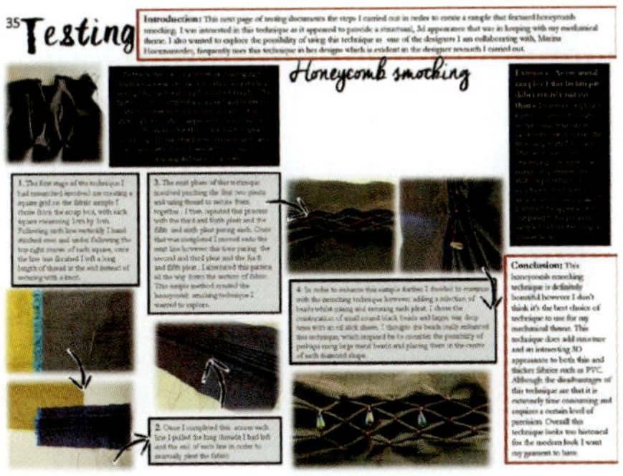


Figure 3.2.12 Sample smocking.

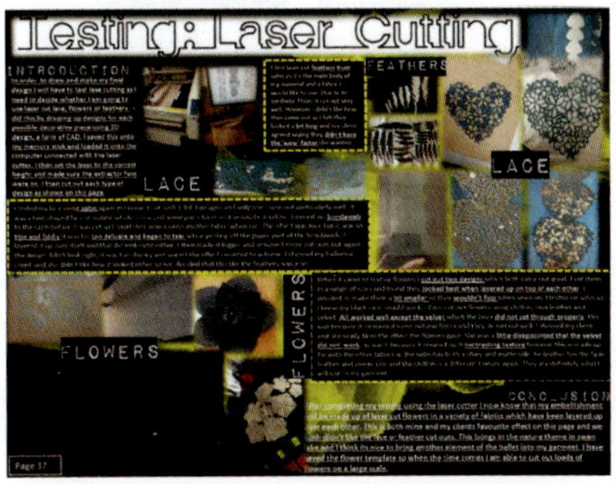


Figure 3.2.13 Working with the laser cutter to explore flower, feather and lace making.

Figure 3.2.14 Experimenting with Shibori to create a pebble effect.

Figure 3.2.15 Experimenting with quilting and appliqué.

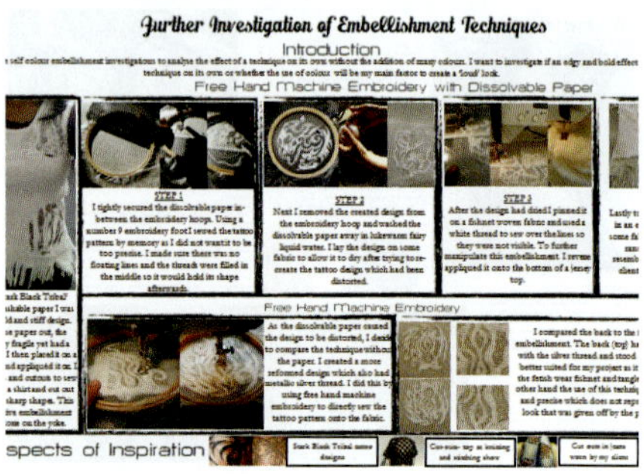


Figure 3.2.16 Experimenting with free machine embroidery.

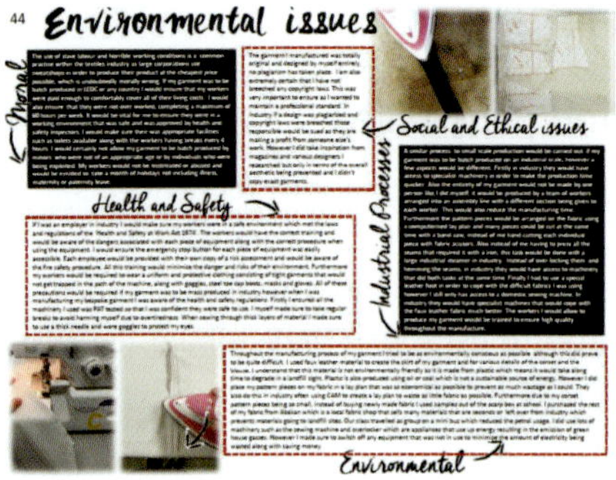


Figure 3.2.17 Consideration of the wider issues of garment design and production.

Figure 3.2.18 The dress design chosen to be manufactured.

## Experimenting with embellishment techniques

Many students find decorating or embellishing their product in some way the most exciting part. There are so many available components, techniques and modern technologies, and with imaginative use, they can guarantee that you are going to achieve originality. Make sure you use advanced techniques and that you experiment with layering the different techniques. This means that you might use three to four techniques to achieve the effect you want. Have a look at Chapter 1.5 for more ideas on methods of decorating your work. Here are a few ideas to get you started:

- colouring methods – batik, stencilling, dip dyeing
- processes – appliqué, trapunto quilting
- fabric manipulation techniques – folding, tucks, origami
- different textile marking media – fabric paints, sprays, foils, glitter
- technologies – sublimation printers, laser cutters
- stitching – hand or machine
- components – beads, buttons, shisha work, sequins.

The student in Figure 3.2.16 has experimented with free machine embroidery, and has shown where the inspiration came from. The work was successful because the student did not just test the technique – she focused on the theme and attempted to create a specific effect.

As a responsible designer, you need to consider how issues such as social, ethical, moral environmental and health and safety are relevant, as you present your ideas and plans for making a textile product. The student in Figure 3.2.17 has presented information concisely, and related it to the garment designed.

When you have developed your ideas fully, you will need to explain your thinking to account for the final choices you have made. At this stage, you must present an idea that you intend to make up into the final prototype.

It is clear from this learner's final design that development of the product has been thorough and all the key aspects established. Plans for making are ready to be drawn up, so that a third party could make the product.

## Planning the manufacture of the prototype

It is during the development stage that you plan for manufacture, and therefore you must take on the role of the project manager, ensuring the outcome is of a high quality and marketable. You will need to have a contingency plan to allow for further development in response to ongoing

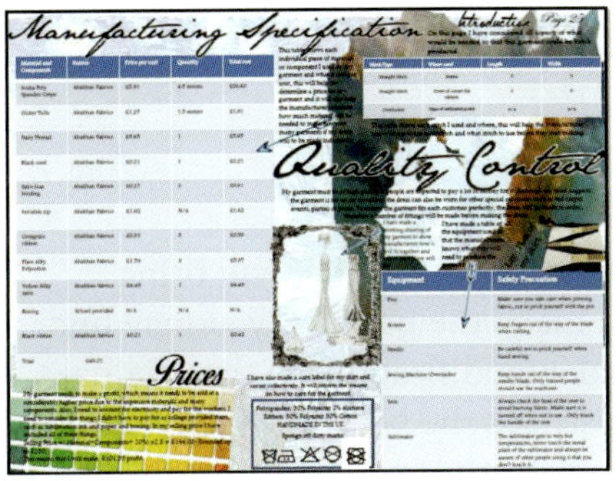


**Figure 3.2.19** Manufacturing specification for the production of a dress.

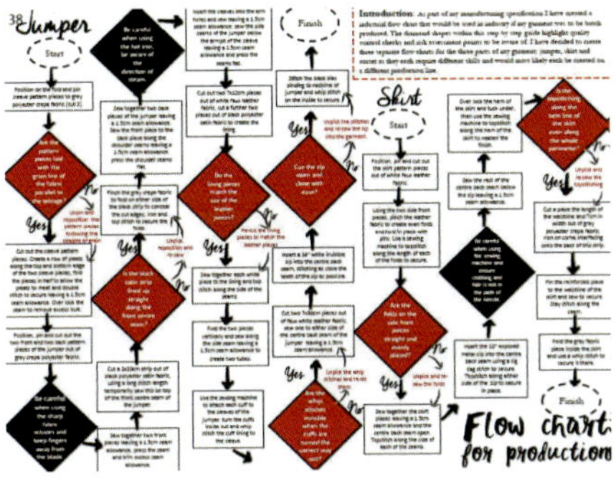


**Figure 3.2.20** A production flow chart.

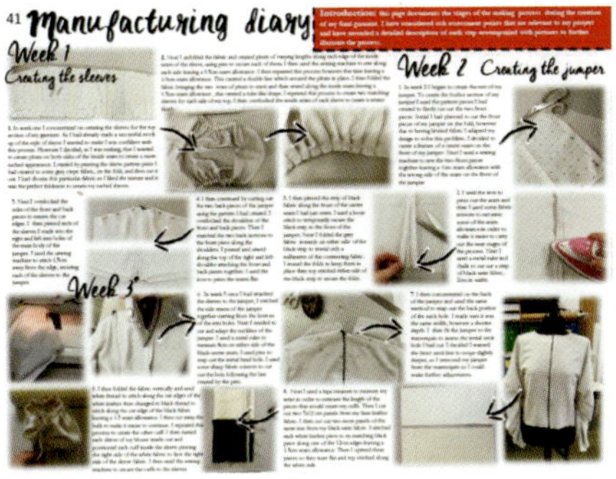


**Figure 3.2.21** A manufacturing diary.

evaluation and testing, and then put into place any changes that would improve the product.

As you plan and carry out this work, it is likely that you will make changes to try and perfect the garment and make it more suitable for the client. This is acceptable, but you should record every change and justify your actions. On occasions, be prepared to make another toile or carry out further research.

The assessment criteria require you to provide a comprehensive and fully detailed manufacturing specification, which refers to relevant quality control checks and allows fully accurate interpretation by a third party. A manufacturing specification gives details about the design, materials and order of making the product. In the fashion industry, they are used to ensure that each product is made to this set specification, and so it ensures that all are identical. Manufacturers will have their own style for presenting the manufacturing specification – one that suits their way of working. Here are some of the things you might consider including when planning for prototype manufacture:

- resources are identified and organised
- product name and description
- working flat drawing
- a photograph
- fabric and components listed
- pattern lay plan for fabric cutting
- flow diagram for the main stages of making
- quality control checks
- tolerance levels
- timings for meeting schedules.

Figure 3.2.19 is a good example of a manufacturing specification. The student went on to produce detailed production flow diagrams. The working drawing and lay plans are important to the third party making the product.

The student in Figure 3.2.20 has presented a concise flow chart, including the main stages of making, with the inclusion of quality checks.

To meet the assessment criteria, there needs to be evidence that you have considered quality control, industrial practice and health and safety issues. Sometimes students research these aspects and present their findings as a series of notes. However, be aware that you only gain credit if the information is related directly to your product. A simple table plan is one approach of presenting the most relevant information and include where quality checks could be made, how the process would be carried out in industry and any relevant health and safety issues. It is useful to include any modifications made during the process.

An alternative way to show evidence of your making skills (which also gives you the opportunity to include information about tolerance levels, safety issues and modifications) is by producing a photographic diary of the making process. To meet the requirements of moderation, you will need to include as much photographic evidence as possible to highlight the quality of your garment. You will need to show the inside of the product, along with close views of the seams, hems and special features. The manufacturing diary Figure 3.2.21 does this well.

**Figure 3.2.22** An example of an AS level made outcome.

**Figure 3.2.23** An example of an A-level made outcome.

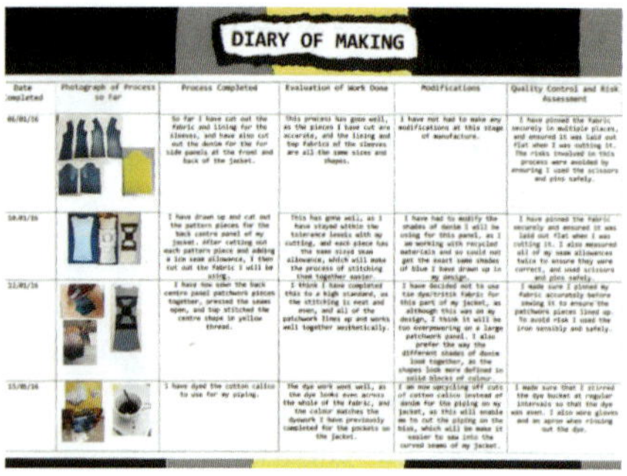

DIARY OF MAKING

| Date Completed | Photograph of Process so Far | Process Completed | Evaluation of Work Done | Modifications | Quality Control and Risk Assessment |
|---|---|---|---|---|---|
| [illegible] | | So far I have cut out the fabric and lining for the sleeves, and have also cut out the denim for the for side panels at the front and back of the jacket. | This process has gone well, as the pieces I have cut are accurate, and the lining and top fabrics of the sleeves are all the same sizes and shapes. | I have not had to make any modifications at this stage of manufacture. | I have pinned the fabric securely in multiple places, and ensured it was laid out flat when I was cutting it. The risks involved in this process were avoided by ensuring I used the scissors and pins safely. |
| [illegible] | | I have drawn up and cut out the pattern pieces for the back centre panel of my jacket. After cutting out each pattern piece and adding a 1cm seam allowance, I then cut out the fabric I will be using. | This has gone well, as I have stayed within the tolerance levels with my cutting, and each piece has the same sized seam allowance, which will make the process of stitching them together easier. | I have had to modify the shades of denim I will be using for this panel, as I am working with recycled materials and so could not get the exact same shades of blue I have drawn up in my design. | I have pinned the fabric securely and ensured it was laid out flat when I was cutting it. I also measured all of my seam allowances twice to ensure they were correct, and used scissors and pins safely. |
| [illegible] | | I have now sewn the back centre panel patchwork pieces together, pressed the seams open, and top stitched the centre shape in yellow thread. | I think I have completed this to a high standard, as the stitching is neat and even, and all of the patchwork lines up and works well together aesthetically. | I have decided not to use tie dye/tritik fabric for this part of my jacket, as although this was on my design, I think it will be too overpowering on a large patchwork panel. I also prefer the way the different shades of denim look together, as the shapes look more defined in solid blocks of colour. | I made sure I pinned my fabric accurately before sewing it to ensure the patchwork pieces lined up. To avoid risk I used the iron sensibly and safely. |
| [illegible] | | I have dyed the cotton calico to use for my piping. | The dye work went well, as the dye looks even across the whole of the fabric, and the colour matches the dyework I have previously completed for the pockets on the jacket. | I am now upcycling off cuts of cotton calico instead of denim for the piping on my jacket, as this will enable me to cut the piping on the bias, which will be make it easier to sew into the curved seams of my jacket. | I made sure that I stirred the dye bucket at regular intervals so that the dye was even. I also wore gloves and an apron when rinsing out the dye. |

**Figure 3.2.24** Manufacturing chart including photographs.





## Assessment Objective 2D: Development of design prototypes

### Understanding the assessment criteria

You are about to make a refined, considered prototype that will bring your ideas into fruition. However, as you make the product, you may find your design could be improved if you make modifications to the original plan. This is good practice because it illustrates the benefits of the iterative process. You should explain your thinking clearly, and show how to bring about improvements to your work.

To achieve high marks when making the prototype/product, you should show that you have:

- chosen to make prototypes that have significant complexity and challenge
- justified your choice of materials, components, techniques and processes
- an excellent understanding of material properties
- demonstrated excellent manufacturing skills, showing you understand the need for accuracy and finish
- chosen and used the right tools, machinery and equipment with skill, precision and accuracy
- made prototypes that meet the design brief specification, and recorded all modifications at every stage
- evaluated your work and used the feedback from others
- made modifications to the product in the light of earlier investigations and prototypes
- applied quality control checks to ensure a consistent quality of all aspects of the made outcome
- employed safe practices during the making process.

It is important to provide as much evidence as you can about the making of your prototype. Your teacher will have written a report to say how independently you worked, and if processes were carried out safely. There should be evidence of excellent quality, accuracy and finish. You should use photographs and annotation to show all aspects of the made outcome, including the product from all angles, inner seams, facings and fastenings. It would be wise to get someone to model garments to show that they are functioning as they should.

### Level of demand

The product you make should have challenge and sufficient complexity if you are to be awarded marks in the top band. The AS level project is described as 'a small-scale design, make and evaluate project'. Complexity is determined by many factors including:

- style and shape
- fabric and component choice
- construction techniques involved
- embellishments.

Have a look at the AS Level product in Figure 3.2.22. You can see that the product shown presents different challenges through the construction, choice of fabrics and embellishment techniques involved.

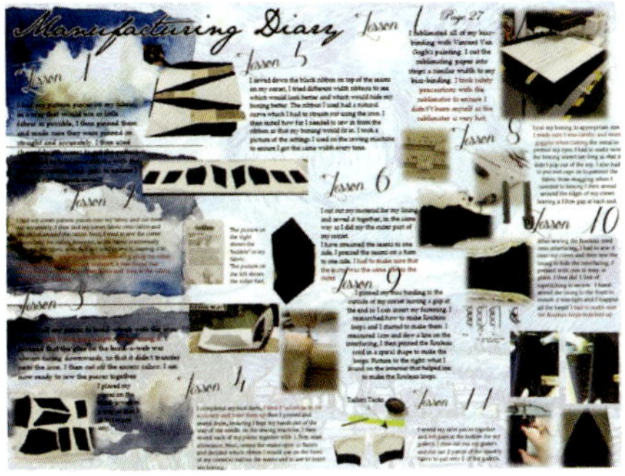


**Figure 3.2.25** A manufacturing journal including photographs.

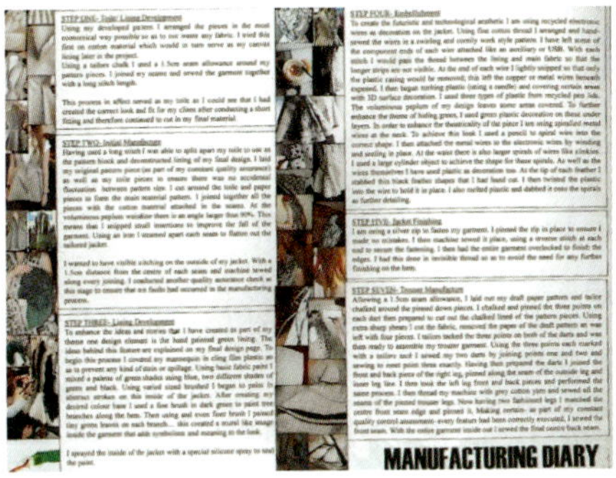


**Figure 3.2.26** A weekly manufacturing diary.

**4. I chose to use blue beading to fit in with the colour scheme of the dress, with the blue staying at the top. However, I chose a lighter, more turquoise, shade so that it would stand out on the deep, navy fabric. I placed beading central to the bust to draw attention to the dress and the performer. Despite the bold colouring, the positing is intricate and could be unsuitable for the purpose.**

**Figure 3.2.27** Further development.

When you study the A-level products shown in Figure 3.2.30, you can see a higher level of complexity. To make garments with this level of demand, it would be very challenging and form part of the substantial design and make activity.

## Manufacturing diaries

You need to show how the product was made. Completing a manufacturing diary can provide valuable evidence that you have met the requirements of the assessment criteria.

Have a look at the three different styles of presenting the manufacturing diaries below. How you carry out this activity is down to personal preference – just make sure that the information is accurate and recorded.

Figure 3.2.24 uses a chart with very clear headings that relate directly to the assessment criteria, whereas Figure 3.2.25 is a more of a journal. Figure 3.2.26 shows a slightly different approach and records the work on a weekly basis. When you present your work for assessment, it is important to make sure that the photographs you provide show clear evidence of the manufacturing process. It would have been more beneficial if the student in Figure 3.2.26 had spread the work over two pages.

When you are making the product, you might become aware that had you made changes to the original design, it could improve the overall quality. It is likely the changes will be minor because you will have developed the design very thoroughly. However, you can never truly anticipate what the product will look like until it is being made. Be prepared to have an open mind, record your thinking, and if necessary, present further developments.

The student in Figure 3.2.27 had made the stage costume dress but had second thoughts about where to place the beading. Further development was carried out and the most appropriate technique selected.

The assessment criteria specify that your prototype must fully address the design brief, satisfy all major points of the specification and also take into account any modifications to your original design proposal.

Have a look at the previous section and you will see examples of final proposals with full evaluations and modifications that have been made (Figure 3.2.17). The students have shown how the design meets the specification and would be suitable for the intended user. If you look at the making diaries, there are also examples of further modifications made.

In Figure 3.2.27, the student has a column devoted to modifications. It was the original intention to tie dye the fabric, but as manufacturing progressed there was a change of mind. The decision is explained.

During the designing and manufacturing of the product, you will have considered feedback from users and other third parties, and made modifications as necessary. You can make modifications at any stage but you need to explain and record your decisions.

Your final, manufactured product should now be subject to a range of testing strategies before final decisions about its manufacture are reached. It is at this testing and summative evaluation stage that you are likely to highlight even more improvements, and so meet the assessment criteria.

## Assessment Objective 2E: Analyse and evaluate

### Understanding the assessment criteria

You have been analysing your work and recording your thoughts as you have worked through this process, and your design thinking should have been very clear. You have also been evaluating your work, and this will have been informing the decision-making process, which brought about modifications to your design proposals and the development of the prototype.

Central to this, there should have been the regular involvement of the proposed client or user.

To meet the assessment criteria for this objective, you should show evidence that:

- analysis and evaluation has taken place throughout the process
- the end user/client has been involved at every stage
- testing of the final product is rigorous
- a well-reasoned critical analysis of the product has taken place
- you have shown the modifications required to improve the product
- you understand how the product can be further developed to make it suitable for different production methods.

Go through your portfolio before you submit the work, checking the thoroughness of your evaluations and making sure that you have made it clear how decisions have been reached. The work should flow, with each stage informing the next. Your thinking must be obvious to both the teacher and moderator when they mark this project.

Points to consider:

- At the start of the project, you wrote a design specification that was to guide your thinking. Explain how well your final product has met this specification.
- If you altered the specification at a later stage, explain why.
- Above all else, you must explain and justify how the product fulfils the design brief and why it would be suitable for the user.
- The evaluation must always be a critical analysis of the product and **not** of the process or your personal skills.
- Testing the final product must be rigorous; it must be user trialled to see how well it performs. Return to the group or visit the individual you worked with during your initial investigations. Their opinions are vital to this process. It is impossible to write an accurate product analysis report if the product has not been user trialled.
- Use a variety of other techniques when testing and evaluating, such as wearing it at a fashion show or comparing it with a similar product available in the shops.
- In light of this testing, you must explain how to improve your product further.
- Be honest when evaluating the product, highlighting strengths and weaknesses.
- With a limited amount of time, you must be concise.
- The assessment criteria require you to explain how the product could be modified to make it suitable for different manufacturing production methods.

Below is an example of target user feedback:

*Here, I have asked my target user what she thinks of each of my designs and recorded her feedback:*

1. *My target user said the design was a bit too unusual for someone to be going to Ascot, and not very appropriate for someone going to a very formal event, as it has many holes in it. However, it does reflect Moschino's styles with the colours and styles, especially the flowers around the collar and around the cuffs of the sleeve.*
2. *My target user said the style of the outfit is very suitable for Ascot as it is an appropriate length skirt, which is suitable for formal events; the textured fabric reflects Moschino's style as his work is quite random, and this aspect of the design stands out more because of the change in texture. My target user did not think the colours were suitable for spring/summer, and that she thought they would be more associated with winter.*
3. *My target user loved the leather jacket. However, she said people do not tend to wear leather jackets to Ascot. They tend to wear more formal jackets such as a blazer. She did not love the playsuit as much for this occasion, as she said it is not really formal enough; it is something she would rather wear to a party.*

Below is a good statement evaluating how well a jacket functioned when trialled:

*PERFORMANCE*

*The overall aesthetics of the jacket are emphasised through considered and appropriate use of functional fastenings.*

*The zip is the main fastening of the jacket. It works well as it is discreet so does not impact the appearance too much, but it also reflects the modern influence of utilitarian uniform and modern fastenings. It is much more practical and easy to use compared to a more traditional fastening such as buttons or frogging.*

*The false buttons on the panels and belt with poppers behind work well as the jacket gains the aesthetics of the traditional gold style feature, while not gaining the impracticality that comes with them. As the panels on the front are not the main fastenings, the poppers are sufficient enough to secure the decorative feature while not adding much inconvenience when putting on and taking off the jacket. The fact that the belt is also entirely decorative means that the poppers are sufficient enough to hold it tightly in place.*

*The jacket does not hinder movement and it is comfortable to wear. The satin lining means it is soft next to the skin, and is easy to slip on and off over other clothing. The pleat in the back of the lining allows more movement and allowance as the lining tends to have a smaller fit than the main jacket.*

*The fabrics used require careful aftercare, however this is not a problem as the jacket will not require much washing. The aesthetics of the fabrics were much more important than their care, although I only used high-quality materials so they should wear well and the dense, felted finish of the wool will not show dirt easily.*

Below is a useful summary of performance testing during user trials.

*PERFORMANCE TESTING*

1 **Is the jacket comfortable to wear? Is it restrictive?**

*I think the jacket fits nicely and is comfortable, especially with the soft satin against the skin. It was not restrictive when wearing or moving around in, although I am not sure I would be able to lift my arms up entirely due to the tight fit and padded shoulder. One thing that I noticed was that it was very warm to wear!*

2 **What do you think about the aesthetics of the jacket? What is your favourite feature?**

*I like the modern style and structured fit – I think it is very flattering, especially with the emphasised waist and belt. Black is always a good colour as it goes with everything and never goes out of style! My favourite features would be the belt and panels across the front, and also the embroidery across the back. The gold works really well against the black, and shows off the military style well. I like how the embroidery design takes a modern approach to a traditional technique. Although you cannot see the red lining, it is a nice touch, and adds to the overall quality and aesthetics.*

3 **What aspects would you change and would you add anything to the design?**

*I definitely would not add anything. There is the perfect balance of detail, so adding anything else would overcrowd the design. As for changing things, I think I would possibly reduce the height of the collar slightly, or make it come in closer to the neck, as I think my neck disappears slightly behind it. I have never been a fan of broad, padded shoulders and although I would not wear this style day to day, it works well for its intended purpose as it adds structure to the silhouette.*

4 **Are the functional aspects, including the zip and the poppers, a good addition or do you think it impacts the aesthetics?**

*Uniforms are supposed to be practical so I think they work well with the theme. The poppers are great because they are so much easier than buttons, and you cannot see them. The zip is very subtle and adds to the more modern concept, although I think an invisible zip would be even better. I always like my jackets to have pockets so I think if they could be discreetly added into the jacket then it would be ideal. Obviously function is not the main purpose of the jacket, however I think it would add to overall aesthetics and quality, which you said were such important factors.*

5 **Do you think it would work well with a hat? And would it appeal to you if you saw it in a magazine in the photoshoot?**

*It is definitely eye catching, and I think it would appeal in a wide market because of the modern, structured style and timeless features. I think it would work well with a hat but it would have to be a carefully selected one that complemented the fit and aesthetics. It would be cool if the hat mimicked or highlighted the gold of the jacket as this would also link them together nicely in a complementary way.*

Another student also analysed and evaluated their jacket through a comparison with an existing one. Wider issues have been considered before going on to assess its viability for industrial manufacture. The student evaluates the design and makes a concluding comment:

*'I think that my garment should be sold at a higher price than the existing coat because my raincoat has pockets and a hood. Also, my garment uses more colour. Since my garment requires more material, I believe it should be worth more. However, I must consider that my target market might not be able to afford this. As a result, the price that I have chosen is the most suitable for my garment.'*

Another student evaluated their bag design and manufacture in depth. The evaluation not only considers if the techniques used would be suitable for mass production, but there is also a focus on the needs of the consumer.

*'The main technique I used was decorative stitching, as it adds lots of intricate detailing to the bag, without being messy or overpowering. I also found it relatively quick and simple to do, so it was a useful technique for me. I also added a pompom trim to the main flap of the bag – this was a cost-effective way of including a 3D decorative element to the overall product, while fitting well with my chosen theme (Bohemian). In spite of this, based on the feedback from consumer trials, I would possibly reconsider the use of the pompoms if the item was to be mass produced, as although they add a good decorative aspect, they are quite fragile. If I decided to use them, I would have to look for a higher quality product, but consequently this would increase the costs. One technique I found to be effective – which could be replicated easily in mass production – was the quilting of the back panel. By adding wadding in between the outer fabric and the lining, I could provide additional comfort to the end user. Small details like this allow me to demonstrate how I have considered both the practical and aesthetic elements equally.'*

Modifications are made to product designs for several reasons:

- to improve the design so it is perfect for the intended user
- to make the design feasible for mass production
- to design more products based on the original design, which would create a full, marketable range.

When you have completed your project, it is an excellent idea to get someone else to read through it, looking for areas where you have not communicated your thinking clearly.

Check the following:

- The purpose of every activity on every design sheet is clear.
- Every piece of work is evaluated and a conclusion is specified.
- Through checking the above two points, your work should flow and your thinking be clear. Some students choose to have a short paragraph on every page which gives the reason for the work, an evaluation and a conclusion.
- Is your work presented well and is all written work accessible to the reader? If you are using plastic flip files, it is unwise to include folded pieces of work that cannot be seen unless the work is removed from the folder.
- Have you made effective use of space? Are there any areas of white space that need filling?
- Check your spelling, punctuation and grammar.
- Complete a bibliography so that the reader can see a full reference list of all the sources you have consulted when completing this work.

# Section 4

In this section you will learn about the following:

# 4.1 General exam advice

## General advice on answering exam questions

When the exam starts, do not be tempted to start writing immediately. Take a few minutes to read through the whole paper and get a feel for it. You can answer the questions in any order you want, and you may wish to start with a question that you feel you can answer well, in order to develop your confidence for the remaining questions. You should plan your time carefully so that you leave enough time to complete the paper.

Read the question carefully and think about what it is asking. Some of the longer answer questions may be based on a theme, but the different parts of the question will be about different things. Therefore do not fall into the trap of putting the same points in your answers to each section.

Answer the question that has been set, not the one that you would like or the one you answered for homework or in a mock exam. Repeating an answer to a question on last year's paper will not be right for the question you are attempting.

Plan your answers carefully – this can save time in the long run as you will be less likely to repeat things or give irrelevant information. It will also help you to write in a logical and coherent way.

You are encouraged to use diagrams where appropriate in your answers. This can be an efficient way to get your knowledge across, but you need to make sure that your diagrams are well labelled and clearly presented. Many students use a mixture of written description supported by a diagram.

Make sure your writing is legible. Use a black pen that gives a strong line so that your writing can be clearly seen.

Try to see the exam as an opportunity to show off your knowledge and understanding of the subject you have chosen to study at an advanced level.

## Command words

You are likely to encounter the following command words in exam questions.

**Table 4.1.1** Command words.

| Command word | Meaning | Example question |
|---|---|---|
| Analyse | Separate information into different components and identify their characteristics. | Analyse the ways in which the fashions from the early twentieth century showed a person's status in society. |
| Argue | Present a reasoned case. | Argue the case for using disposable fabrics for surgeon's gowns rather than ones that can be washed and used again. |
| Assess | Make an informed judgement. | Assess the importance of thermoplastic fibres in the finishing of fabrics. |
| Comment | Present an informed opinion. | Comment on the wearing of a uniform to show corporate identity. |
| Compare | Identify similarities and/or differences. | Compare the style of an outfit from 1900 with one from today's fashions in terms of their suitability for career wear. |
| Consider | Review and respond to given information. | Consider the way in which the designer has used different fabrics to provide interest in the fashion collection shown. |
| Contrast | Identify differences. | Contrast the use of a lining with that of an underlining when making fashion products |
| Criticise | Assess worth against explicit expectations. ('Criticise' is often used alongside terms 'analyse' or 'evaluate'.) | Criticise the use of a weft knitted wool fabric for a winter sweater. |
| Define | Specify meaning. | Define the term smart textile. |
| Describe | Set out characteristics. | Describe denim fabric. |
| Discuss | Present salient points. | Discuss the issues facing major retailers of textile products in relation to consumer demand for ethical trading. |
| Evaluate | Judge from available evidence.<br>You should consider the pros and cons of the situation you have been presented with, especially if the question asks you to critically evaluate. | Evaluate the use of a polyester/cotton blend fabric for a fashion jacket. |
| Examine | Investigate closely. | Examine the reasons why manufacturers are increasingly using regenerated fibres to replace cotton in fashion products. |
| Explain | Set out purposes or reasons. | Explain the difference between the selvedge and the raw edge of a woven fabric. |
| Identify | Name or otherwise characterise. | Identify two different features of Pierre Cardin's designs which made them inspirational in the 1960s. |
| Illustrate | Present clarifying examples. | Illustrate the ways in which designers present their ideas to different client groups. |
| Interpret | Translate information into recognisable form. | Interpret the meaning of the symbols on the care label shown. |
| Justify | Present a reasoned case/support a case with evidence. | Justify the use of prototypes in the development of a new fashion product. |
| Outline | Set out main characteristics. | Outline some of the possible problems a manufacturer may experience when working with knitted fabrics. |
| Relate | Demonstrate interconnections. | Relate the importance of customer identification to the use of product branding. |
| State | Express in unequivocal terms. | State the meaning of the term colourfastness. |
| Summarise | Present principal points without detail. | Summarise the main reasons for using automated manufacturing systems for fashion products. |

# 4.2 The AS written exam

## Introduction to the paper

There is one written paper for the AS Level award. It will assess your knowledge of the subject content.

### When will the written paper be taken?

The written paper will be taken in May or June at the end of your AS Level course.

### How long will I have?

The exam will last 1 hour and 30 minutes.

### What format will the written paper take?

The paper will have a mixture of multiple choice, short answer and longer answer questions in a combined question and answer booklet. There are no optional questions so you will be expected to attempt all the questions on the paper.

## How will I be assessed?

The paper will test your knowledge and understanding of technical principles, and designing and making principles relating to fashion and textiles. It will have 80 marks and contribute 50 per cent of your AS Level marks.

There are four assessment objectives (AOs) that are examined across the Fashion and Textiles award. Only two of these are tested in in the written exam: AO3 and AO4.

AO1: Identify, investigate and outline design possibilities to address needs and wants.

AO2: Design and make prototypes that are fit for purpose.

AO3: Analyse and evaluate:

- design decisions and outcomes, including for prototypes made by themselves and others
- wider issues in design and technology.

AO4: Demonstrate and apply knowledge and understanding of:

- technical principles
- designing and making principles.

The following table shows you the weighting that each assessment objective carries for the written paper.

**Table 4.2.1** The weighting that each AO carries.

| AO weightings for written paper | |
|---|---|
| AOs | % weighting in the written exam |
| AO1 | 0 |
| AO2 | 0 |
| AO3 | 15 |
| AO4 | 35 |
| Total weightings for the exam | 50% |

The written exam will allow you to demonstrate your ability to:

- recall information
- analyse and evaluate
- bring together knowledge and understanding from different areas of the specification.

You will need to demonstrate knowledge and understanding of the subject content relating to technical principles and designing and making principles. You may need to combine your knowledge of different areas of textiles and fashion in one answer to show your understanding of the subject as a whole.

The various activities you have completed for your NEA will have helped develop your knowledge and understanding of the subject. Where possible, you should use the knowledge you have gained from these activities when answering the questions on the exam paper.

## Types of questions

The written paper will have a mixture of different types. Some questions will be multiple choice style questions, where you will need to choose the correct answer from a number of options. Other questions will be short answer questions, where you may need to complete a table or write a short account. There will also be extended response questions, which require longer written answers. There may be images or illustrations on the paper that you need to refer to in your answer.

You will learn more about each of these question types and have a chance to practise them below.

## Multiple choice questions

- Each question carries one mark.
- For each question, you will be given **four possible answers** to choose from. Only one of the answers is the correct response.
- You will need to shade the box next to your answer.

### Question

Which one of the following is a mechanical fabric finish?

**A** Brushing ◯

**B** Gore-Tex ◯

**C** Proban ◯

**D** Teflon ◯

### Answer

The correct answer is brushing, which is the name of a raised finish. Gore-Tex is a laminated finishing process, and Proban and Teflon are chemical finishes.

Which one of the following is a mechanical fabric finish?

**A** Brushing ⬬

**B** Gore-Tex ◯

**C** Proban ◯

**D** Teflon ◯

Notice that in the example answer, only one box has been shaded in. This is the correct way to answer a multiple-choice question. If you shade in more than one box, your answer will be marked as incorrect, even if one of the answers you shade in is the correct answer. If you make a mistake, you should put a cross through the incorrectly shaded box and shade in the correct box.

Multiple choice questions look straightforward, but you will need to think carefully about the answer. Some of the possible answers may look very similar with only slight changes to the wording, and you may need to work out what each of the other possible answers mean before you can be sure which one is the correct answer to the question.





## Short answer questions

These questions will typically ask you to:

- label and complete drawings
- use notes and sketches to answer questions
- recall knowledge
- justify your answers further.

The number of marks allowed and amount of space provided in the exam paper are good indicators of the amount of detail that is required in your answer. Aim to fill the space that has been provided. Remember to read each question carefully, and underline the command word that has been used.

## Question

Place each of the fibres listed below in the correct box of the table.

You should use each fibre once only.

Acetate Acrylic Polyamide Polyester

Ramie Silk Modal Wool

| Natural cellulose | Natural protein | Regenerated | Synthetic |
|---|---|---|---|
| | | | |
| | | | |
| | | | |

## Answer

| Natural cellulose | Natural protein | Regenerated | Synthetic |
|---|---|---|---|
| Ramie | Silk | Acetate | Acrylic |
| | Wool | Modal | Polyamide |
| | | | Polyester |

This question is about recalling knowledge of fibre classification. As with multiple-choice questions, you need to think about the answers and be sure to use each fibre once only. It is a good idea to cross the fibres off the list as you place them.

## Extended response questions

Extended response questions require longer and more detailed answers. It is likely that these questions will ask you to:

- analyse and evaluate information
- draw comparisons and discuss
- describe a process or technique
- show your knowledge and understanding of a specific area of expertise from within the course.

The mark allowed for the question is written at the side of the question, and this should give you an indication of how much detail and what level of depth you need to go into in your written answer. For example, if there are six marks, writing two simple points will not be enough.

You will need to plan what you are going to write so that you do not repeat points, and to ensure you include all the points you believe are relevant. Think about the key terms, phrases or stages that you will need to explain or evaluate. Your plan does not need to be lengthy – it should act as a focus and give you time to stop and structure your thoughts. Planning can help you to construct a better answer, but try not to waste too much time as your plans will not gain you any marks in the exams.

## Question

The lady's suit shown in Figure 4.2.1 was worn by career women at the beginning of the twentieth century.

**Figure 4.2.1** A lady's suit from the 1900s.

The lady's suit shown in Figure 4.2.2 was a fashionable outfit for career women in the 1980s.

**Figure 4.2.2** A woman's career outfit from the 1980s.

Analyse how the different outfits were influenced by attitudes to women's position in society at the times when they were fashionable. **[9 marks]**

What is the question asking you to do?

You are being asked to:

- compare women's career outfits from the 1900s and 1980s
- explain how women's roles in society affected what they wore.

# 4.3 A-level Paper 1: Technical principles

## Introduction to the paper

There are two written examinations for A-level and between them, they assess your knowledge of the subject content. Paper 1 is based on technical principles which are covered in Chapters 1–14 of this book.

### When will the written paper be taken?

Paper 1 will be taken in May or June at the end of your A-level course. This is likely to be in the second year of your studies.

### How long will I have?

The exam will last 2 hours and 30 minutes.

### What format will the written paper take?

The paper will have a mixture of short answer and longer answer questions in a combined question and answer booklet. There are no optional questions so you will be expected to attempt all of the questions on the paper.

## How will I be assessed?

The paper will test your knowledge and understanding of technical principles relating to fashion and textiles. It will have 120 marks and contribute 30 per cent of your A-level marks.

There are four AOs that are examined across the fashion and Textiles award. Only two of these are tested in Paper 1: AO3 and AO4.

AO1: Identify, investigate and outline design possibilities to address needs and wants.

AO2: Design and make prototypes that are fit for purpose.

AO3: Analyse and evaluate:

- design decisions and outcomes, including for prototypes made by themselves and others
- wider issues in design and technology.

AO4: Demonstrate and apply knowledge and understanding of:

- technical principles
- designing and making principles.

The following table shows you the weighting that each AO carries for Paper 1.

**Table 4.3.1** The weighting that each AO carries.

| **AO weightings for Paper 1** | |
|---|---|
| AOs | % weighting in the written exam |
| AO1 | 0 |
| AO2 | 0 |
| AO3 | 7.5 |
| AO4 | 22.5 |
| Total weightings for the exam | 30% |

Paper 1 will allow you to demonstrate your ability to:

- recall information
- analyse and evaluate
- bring together knowledge and understanding from different areas of the specification.

You will need to demonstrate that you know and understand the subject content relating to technical principles. You may need to combine your knowledge of different areas of textiles and fashion in one answer, to show your understanding of the subject as a whole.

The various activities you have completed for your NEA will have helped to develop your knowledge and understanding of the subject. Where possible, you should use the knowledge you have gained from these activities when answering the questions on the exam paper.

## Types of questions

Paper 1 will have a mix of different types of questions; some may be multiple-choice-style questions where you will need to choose the correct answer from a number of options. Others will be short answer questions where you may need to label a diagram, complete a table or write a short account. There will also be extended response questions which require longer written answers. There may be images or illustrations on the paper that you need to refer to in your answer. You will learn more about each of these question types and have a chance to practise them below.

### Multiple choice questions

- Each question carries one mark.
- For each question, you will be given **four possible answers** to choose from. Only one of the answers is the correct response.
- You will need to shade the box next to your answer.

## Question

Which of the following is the name of a fabric colouring method?

**A** Batik ◯

**B** Bleaching ◯

**C** Calendaring ◯

**D** Photochromic ◯

## Answer

The correct answer is batik, which is the name of a resist dyeing method finish. Bleaching is a process that removes colour, calendaring is a fabric finish and photochromic is a light sensitive finish.

Which one of the following is the name of a fabric colouring method?

**A** Batik ⬬

**B** Bleaching ◯

**C** Calendaring ◯

**D** Photochromic ◯

Notice that in the example answer, only one box has been shaded in. This is the correct way to answer a multiple-choice question. If you shade in more than one box, your answer will be marked as incorrect, even if one of the answers you shade in is the correct answer. If you make a mistake, you should put a cross through the incorrectly shaded box and shade in the correct box.

Multiple choice questions look straightforward, but you will need to think carefully about the answer. Some of the possible answers may look very similar with only slight changes to the wording, and you may need to work out what each of the other possible answers mean before you can be sure which one is the correct answer to the question.

## Short answer questions

These questions will typically ask you to:

- label and complete drawings
- use notes and sketches to answer questions
- recall knowledge
- justify your answers further.

The number of marks allowed and amount of space provided in the exam paper are good indicators of the amount of detail that is required in your answer. Aim to fill the space that has been provided. Remember to read each question carefully, and underline the command word that has been used.

## Question

Explain what is meant by a fad design. Give an example. **[4 marks]**

## Extended response questions

Extended response questions require longer and more detailed answers. It is likely that these questions will ask you to:

- analyse and evaluate information
- draw comparisons and discuss
- describe a process or technique
- show your knowledge and understanding of a specific area of expertise from within the course.

The mark allowed for the question is written at the side of the question, and this should give you an indication of how much detail and what level of depth you need to go into in your written answer. For example, if there are six marks, writing two simple points will not be enough.

You will need to plan what you are going to write so that you do not repeat points, and to ensure you include all the points you believe are relevant. Think about the key terms, phrases or stages that you will need to explain or evaluate. Your plan does not need to be lengthy – it should act as a focus and give you time to stop and structure your thoughts. Planning can help you to construct a better answer, but try not to waste too much time as your plans will not gain you any marks in the exams.

### Question

Fabric finishes are important to make sure that fabrics are fit for their intended purpose.

Analyse the need for a wide range of fabric finishes used on a variety of textile products.

Include relevant examples of fabrics and typical finishes to illustrate the points you make. **[12 marks]**

What is the question asking you to do?

You are being asked to:

- identify the reasons why fabric finishes are needed and used
- give examples of products and finishes that show your knowledge of a range of different fabric finishes and understanding of why they are needed.

# 4.4 A-level paper 2: Design and making principles

## Introduction to the paper

Paper 2 is based on designing and making principles which are covered in Chapters 2.1- 2.10 of this book.

### When will the written paper be taken?

Paper 2 will be taken in May or June at the end of your A-level course. This is likely to be in the second year of your studies.

### How long will I have?

The exam will last 1 hour and 30 minutes.

### What format will the written paper take?

Paper 2 will have two sections in a combined question and answer booklet:

- Section A will be based on product analysis, and will have up to six short answer questions based on visual images of one or more products. This section will carry 30 marks.
- Section B will be based on commercial manufacture and will carry 50 marks. This section will have a mixture of short answer and longer answer questions.

## How will I be assessed?

This paper will test your knowledge and understanding of designing and making principles relating to fashion and textiles. It will have 80 marks and contribute 20 per cent of your A-level marks.

There are four AOs that are examined across the Fashion and Textiles award. Only two of these are tested in Paper 2: AO3 and AO4.

AO1: Identify, investigate and outline design possibilities to address needs and wants.

AO2: Design and make prototypes that are fit for purpose.

AO3: Analyse and evaluate:

- design decisions and outcomes, including for prototypes made by themselves and others
- wider issues in design and technology.

AO4: Demonstrate and apply knowledge and understanding of:

- technical principles
- designing and making principles.

The following table shows you the weighting that each AO carries for Paper 2.

**Table 4.4.1** The weighting that each AO carries.

| AO weightings for Paper 2 | |
|---|---|
| AOs | % weighting in the written exam |
| AO1 | 0 |
| AO2 | 0 |
| AO3 | 7.5 |
| AO4 | 12.5 |
| Total weightings for the exam | 20% |

Paper 2 will allow you to demonstrate your ability to:

- recall information
- analyse and evaluate
- bring together knowledge and understanding from different areas of the specification.

You will need to demonstrate that you know and understand the subject content relating to technical principles. You may need to combine your knowledge of different areas of textiles and fashion in one answer, to show your understanding of the subject as a whole.

The various activities you have completed for your NEA will have helped to develop your knowledge and understanding of the subject. Where possible, you should use the knowledge you have gained from these activities when answering the questions on the exam paper.

## Types of questions

Paper 2 will have a mix of different types of questions as described in Chapter 4.3. Examples of multiple-choice questions are provided in Chapter 4.2 and 4.3.

## Short answer question

Identify three different environmental issues related to the growing of cotton. **[3 marks]**

## Answer

The issues include:

- the use of pesticides
- the use of fertilisers
- the use of large quantities of water
- deforestation of land.

One mark for each correctly identified issue.

## Extended response question

Explain the safety standards that are used to protect the consumer of textile products.

Include relevant examples of products to illustrate the points you make. **[12 marks]**

What is the question asking you to do?

You are being asked to:

- identify safety standards related to the manufacture and testing of textile products
- give examples of products where specific safety standards are used.

# 4.5 Mathematical skills for the written exams

The written papers are required to test your mathematical skills. The questions will be included within a design and technology context, and will count for 15 per cent of the overall marks for the written papers.

The mathematical skills required will be equivalent to those for the higher level of the GCSE Mathematics course applied to Fashion and Textiles.

## Number and percentages

You will use number and percentages when calculating quantities of materials, costs and sizes.

## Ratios

In Fashion and Textiles, you will use ratios when scaling drawings and pattern grading.

## Calculating surface area and volume

When determining quantities for materials you are likely to need to be able to calculate surface area and volume.

## Trigonometry

When calculating sides and angles as part of fashion and textiles product design, you will be using your trigonometry skills.

## Construction, use and analysis of charts and graphs

Being able to construct, use and analyse graphs and charts is an important skill in fashion and textiles. You will need to represent the data you use to inform design decisions and evaluate outcomes. You will also need to use charts and graphs to present market data, user preferences or outcomes of market research data.

## Co-ordinates and geometry

Setting out patterns requires you to use datum points and geometry.

## Statistics and probability

Statistical analyses are important when determining user needs and preferences.

You will also use data related to human scale and proportion to determine required sizes and dimensions for fashion products.

**The application of these skills can be seen in the 'Maths link' boxes throughout this book.**

# Index

Definitions appear in **bold**

# Photo credits

All photos that have not been listed below have been kindly supplied by the author team.

**p.11** *cl* © Zero Creatives/Cultura/Getty Images, *bl* © missisya/Adobe.stock.com; **p.12** © SATRA Technology Centre; **p.22** © Charles Stirling/Alamy Stock Photo; **p.24** © Jessica Lynn Culver/Getty Images; **p.25** *tl* © Li Ding/Alamy Stock Photo, *cl* © Hendrik Schmidt/DPA/PA Images; **p.36** *tl* © ACORN 1/Alamy Stock Photo, *cl* © uanateutzi/Shutterstock.com, *bl* ©35mmf2/Shutterstock.com; **p.37** © Dontree/Shutterstock.com; **p.39** *tl* © Mike Flippo/Shutterstock.com, *cl* © Hemis/Alamy Stock Photo; **p.47** © INVISTA; **p.53** © Sunshine Pics/Alamy Stock Photo; **p.56** © Amorphis/123 RF; **p.58** *tl* © Mihai Daniel/Shutterstock.com, *bl* © callmerobin/Adobe.stock.com; **p.60** © Krzyzak/Alamy Stock Photo; **p.61** *cl* © Dragan Nikolic / Alamy Stock Photo, *bl* © haris M /Shutterstock.com, *br* © Wingedbull/Shutterstock.com; **p.62** © Dorling Kindersley/GettyImages; **p.63** *tl* © Paul Fearn / Alamy Stock Photo, *bl* © Dorling Kindersley: Lynda Kelly/GettyImages, *bc* © imageBROKER / Alamy Stock Photo, *br* © Darkkong/Adobe.stock.com; **p.64** © Yinkor/Adobe.stock.com; **p.65** *cl* © dpa picture alliance/Alamy Stock Photo, *c* © Mahmut Akkaya/Shutterstock.com, *r* © nara Prusakova/Adobe.stock.com, *bl* © Diana Archive/Getty Image; **p.66** © alekleks/Adobe.stock.com; **p.71** *cl* © Andreas Berheide/123RF, *bl* © heart design/Shutterstock.com; **p.72** © Angel_fff /Adobe.stock.com; **p.73** © 3M.co.uk; **p.75** © sanitized.com; **p.79** *tl* © fresh & green / Alamy Stock Photo, *clt* © Keith Webber Jr./Alamy Stock Photo, *clb* © Nhorizon/Shutterstock.com, *bl* © macbrianmun/Adobe.stock.com; **p.80** *tl* © H. Mark Weidman Photography/Alamy Stock Photo, *cl* © imageBROKER/Alamy Stock Photo, *bl* © Clynt Garnham Products/Alamy Stock Photo; **p.82** © Roger Grayson/Alamy Stock Photo; **p.85** *tl* © Monty Rakusen/Cultura Creative/Alamy Stock Photo, *cl* © Sirikorn Techatraibhop/Alamy Stock Photo, *bl* © imageBROKER / Alamy Stock Photo; **p.86** *tl* © Suriya Desatit/Alamy Stock Photo, *tc* © R_Boe /Shutterstock.com, *tr* © Ari N/Adobe.stock.com, *cl* © malven57 /Shutterstock.com, *bl* © Dmitry Melnikov / Alamy Stock Photo; **p.87** *c* © Elizabeth Whiting & Associates / Alamy Stock Photo, *cr* © Pieter Estersohn/Alamy Stock Photo; **p.89** *tl* © Kadmy/Adobe.stock.com, *bl* © Sean Gallup/Getty Images; **p.93** © Illustration by Meni Tzima www.yupyland.com; **p.96** *tc* © NearTheCoast.com / Alamy Stock Photo, *tr* © Sergio Azenha / Alamy Stock Photo, *cl* © Iain Masterton/Alamy Stock Photo; **p.102** *tl* & *tr* © Assyst Bullmer, *bl* © Sergey Ryzhov/Shutterstock.com; **p.103** *cl* © Emre Yen/Shutterstock.com, *bl* © dpa/Alamy Stock Photo; **p.105** *tl* © warloka79/Adobe.stock.com, *cl* © PETER MORRIS/Fairfax Media/Getty Images, *bl* © AMF Reece; **p.106** *tl* © Agencja Fotograficzna Caro/Alamy Stock Photo, *cl* © FUN FUN PHOTO/Shutterstock.com, *bl* © Pascal Le Segretain/Getty Images; **p.108** © Bacho Foto/Adobe.stock.com; **p.113** © Christopher Peterson/Splash News/Alamy Stock Photo; **p.114** © Jeff Gilbert/Alamy Stock Photo; **p.115** © CandyBox Images/Adobe.stock.com; **p.117** © tiero/123RF; **p.118** © dpa picture alliance/Alamy Stock Photo; **p.122** © Andrii Malysh/123Rf; **p.129** © Carolyn Jenkins/Alamy Stock Photo; **p.131** *tl* © fishvector/Shutterstock.com, *cl* © Clynt Garnham Products/Alamy Stock Photo, *bl* © Carolyn Jenkins/Alamy Stock Photo, *c* © Andrew Paterson/Alamy Stock Photo, *bc* © By Ian Miles-Flashpoint Pictures/Alamy Stock Photo, *br* © Anatoly Vartanov/123RF; **p.132** © Anatoly Vartanov/Alamy Stock Photo; **p.135** *cl* © Radim Beznoska/Alamy Stock Photo, *bl* © JABPromotions/WWD/Shutterstock/Rex Features; **p.136** *tl* © Malcolm Fairman/Alamy Stock Photo, *cl* © Tom Hanley/Alamy Stock Photo; **p.139** *tl* © Jim Parkin/Alamy Stock Photo, *cl* © Dinodia Photos/Alamy Stock Photo, *bl* © Joerg Boethling/Alamy Stock Photo; **p.140** *tl* © Innocenti/Cultura Creative/Alamy Stock Photo, *bl* © tatiana1987/Adobe.stock.com; **p.141** *tl* © doethion/Adobe.stock.com, *cl* © Graham Corney/Alamy Stock Photo; **p.142** *tl* © Sippakorn/Shutterstock.com, *cl* © TA images / Alamy Stock Photo, *bl* © dpa picture alliance/Alamy Stock Photo; **p.143** © imageBROKER/Alamy Stock Photo; **p.144** *tl* © Cseh Ioan/123 RF, *c* © moodboard / Alamy Stock Photo, *cr* © GzP_Design/Shutterstock.com, *bl* © valeriyakozoriz/Adobe.stock.com; **p.146** © javiindy/Adobe.stock.com; **p.147** © RichardBakerWork/Alamy Stock Photo; **p.152** *tl* © dpa picture alliance/Alamy Stock Photo, *bl* © David Grossman/Alamy Stock Photo; **p.153** © RichardBaker/Alamy Stock Photo; **p.154** *tl* © SuperGroup plc/Alamy Stock Photo, *cl* © Images of Birmingham Premium/Alamy Stock Photo; **p.155** *tl* © pmgimaging/Alamy Stock Photo, *cl* © Joerg Boethling/Alamy Stock Photo; **p.156** © dpa picture alliance/Alamy Stock Photo; **p.157** © See Li/Alamy Stock Photo; **p.160** *tc* © Everett Collection Inc/Alamy Stock Photo, *tr* © Asia Images Group Pte Ltd/Alamy Stock Photo, *cl* © Everett Collection Historical/Alamy Stock Photo, *bl* © Robin Skjoldborg/Cultura/Alamy Stock Photo; **p.161** *tl* © Oscar Elias/Alamy Stock Photo, *cl* © CatwalkFashion/Alamy Stock Photo, *bl* © Trinity Mirror/Mirrorpix/Alamy Stock Photo; **p.162** © Cultura Creative/Alamy Stock Photo; **p.163** *tl* © Alberto Pezzali/Alamy Stock Photo, *cl* © Stock Rocket/Adobe.

stock.com, *bl* © Armen Gharibyan/Alamy Stock Photo; **p.172** *tl* © oliver leedham/Alamy Stock Photo, *cl* © ton koene/Alamy Stock Photo; **p.188** © Archivart/Alamy Stock Photo; **p.189** *tl* © Pictorial Press Ltd/Alamy Stock Photo, *cl* © Heritage Image Partnership Ltd / Alamy Stock Photo; **p.190** © dpa picture alliance archive/Alamy Stock Photo; **p.191** *tl* © Virginia Turbett/Redferns/Getty Images, *cl* © Richard Young Photographi/REX/Shutterstock, *br* © Anton Oparin/Alamy Stock Photo; **p.192** *tl* © Reflex Picture Library/Alamy Stock Photo, *bl* © Pictorial Press Ltd/ Alamy Stock Photo; **p.193** *tl* © Peter Horree/Alamy Stock Photo, *cl* © Granger, NYC/Alamy Stock Photo, *bl* © Pictorial Press Ltd/Alamy Stock Photo; **p.194** *tl* © Pictorial Press Ltd/Alamy Stock Photo, *cl* © Rob Rich/Everett Collection/Alamy stock photo, *tc* © INTERFOTO/Alamy Stock Photo, *tr* © Elaine Lesser/Alamy Stock Photo; **p.195** *tl* © Mirrorpix/Alamy Stock Photo, *bl* © TASS/Alamy Stock Photo; **p.196** *tl* © Mirrorpix/Alamy Stock Photo, *tr* © Image Scotland/Alamy Stock Photo, *bl* © Nick Savage/Alamy Stock Photo; **p.200** *tl* © Hi-Story/Alamy Stock Photo, *tc* © Trinity Mirror/Mirrorpix/Alamy Stock Photo, *bl* © The National Trust Photolibrary / Alamy Stock Photo; **p.201** © Vintage Images/Alamy Stock Photo; **p.202** *tl* © Chronicle/Alamy Stock Photo, *cl* © Everett Collection Historical/Alamy Stock Photo, *bl* © W. and D. Downey/GettyImages; **p.203** *tl* © Popperfoto/GettyImages, *cl* © Vintage Images / Alamy Stock Photo; **p.204** Easier fitting children's clothes in 1910; **p.205** © Roger-Viollet / Topfoto; **p.206** *tl* © Pictorial Press Ltd/Alamy Stock Photo, *bl* © Christopher Stewart/Alamy Stock Photo; **p.207** *tl* © Horst P. Horst/Conde Nast Collection/Getty Images, *cl* © ClassicStock/Alamy Stock Photo, *bl* © Chronicle/Alamy Stock Photo; **p.208** *tl* © H. Armstrong Roberts/Retrofile/Getty Images, *clt* © H. Armstrong Roberts/Retrofile/Getty Images, *clb* © War Archive/Alamy Stock Photo, *bl* © Hulton Archive/Getty Images; **p.209** *tl* © War Archive/Alamy Stock Photo, *cl* © Everett Collection Historical/Alamy Stock Photo, *cr* © FPG/Hulton Archive/Getty Images; **p.210** *cl* © H. ARMSTRONG ROBERTS/ClassicStock/Alamy Stock Photo, *bl* © Granger Historical Picture Archive / Alamy Stock Photo; **p.211** *tl* © Granger Historical Picture Archive / Alamy Stock Photo, *clt* © Interfoto/History/Alamy Stock Photo, *clb* © Bettmann/Getty Images, *bl* © Joseph McKeown/Picture Post/Getty Images; **p.213** © Granger Historical Picture Archive/Alamy Stock Photo; **p.214** *tl* © Everett Collection Historical/Alamy Stock Photo, *clt* © Keystone-France/Gamma-Keystone/Getty Images, *clb* © Trinity Mirror/Mirrorpix/Alamy Stock Photo, *bl* © Interfoto/Alamy Stock Photo; **p.215** *cl* © Harry Hammond/V&A Images/Hulton Archive/Getty Images, *bl* © Neil Baylis/Alamy Stock Photo; **p.216** © Harvey Lloyd/Photolibrary/Getty Images; **p.217** *tl* © McKeown/Daily Express/ Hulton Archive/Getty Images, *cl* © H. ARMSTRONG ROBERTS/ClassicStock/Alamy Stock Photo, *bl* © Wesley/ Keystone/Hulton Archive/Getty Images; **p.218** *tl* © Popperfoto/Getty Images, *bl* © Chris Barham/Associated Newspapers/Shutterstock/REX; **p.219** *tl* © Ken Towner/Associated Newspapers/Shutterstock/REX, *cl* © Trinity Mirror/Mirrorpix/Alamy Stock Photo, *bl* © PYMCA/Universal Images Group/Getty Images; **p.220** © Erin Combs/ Toronto Star/Getty Images; **p.221** *tl* © AF archive/Alamy Stock Photo, *cl* © Roger-Viollet/TopFoto, *bl* © Pierre Vauthey/Sygma/Getty Images; **p.222** *tl* © KATHY WILLENS/AP/Shutterstock/REX, *bl* © PYMCA/Universal Images Group/Getty Images; **p.223** *tl* © Daniel SIMON/Gamma-Rapho/Getty Images, *clt* © Sarah Edwards/WENN Ltd/ Alamy Stock Photo, *clb* © Gareth Cattermole/Getty Images Entertainment/Getty Images, *bl* © Andrew Gombert/ EPA/Shutterstock/Rex Features; **p.224** *tl* © Tim P. Whitby/Getty Images, *cl* © PIERRE VERDY/AFP/Getty Images, *bl* © Giovanni Giannoni/Penske Media/Shutterstock/Rex Features; **p.226** © Martin Brayley/Alamy Stock Photo; **p.227** © Ruslan Kudrin/Alamy Stock Photo; **p.228** © PJF Military Collection/Alamy Stock Photo; **p.229** © Yodchai Prominn/Shutterstock.com; **p.230** © Hulton Archive/Getty Images; **p.231** © Iamnee/Adobe.stock.com; **p.233** *tl* © Angela Hampton Picture Library/Alamy Stock Photo, *bl* © Valentin Sama-Rojo/Alamy Stock Photo; **p.234** *tl* © NASA Photo/Alamy Stock Photo, *cl* © Jessica Richmond/Shutterstock/Rex Features; **p.247** © moodboard/Alamy Stock Photo; **p.254** © Hero Images Inc./Alamy Stock Photo; **p.258** © xPACIFICA/Alamy Stock Photo; **p.259** © marco matteucci/Alamy Stock Photo; **p.260** © Stocksnapper/Adobe.stock.com; **p.266** *tl* © Kzenon/Alamy Stock Photo, *cl* © Maria Kraynova/123RF, *bl* © Miyuki Satake/Alamy Stock Photo; **p.267** *tl* © Johner Images/Alamy Stock Photo, *cl* © Keerati Thanitthitianant/Alamy Stock Photo, *bl* © Valery Voennyy/Alamy Stock Photo; **p.268** *tc* © Eastman Machine Company, Buffalo, New York USA, *tr* © Eastman Machine Company, Buffalo, New York USA; **p.269** *cl* © Mila Gligoric/123 RF, *bl* © Duane Howell/Denver Post/Getty Images; **p.272** *tr* © Angela Hampton Picture Library/Alamy Stock Photo, *crt* © Ashley Cooper/Alamy Stock Photo, *crb* © Realimage/Alamy Stock Photo, *br* © Pulsar Imagens/Alamy Stock Photo; **p.273** *tr* © Janet Hostetter/AP/Shutterstock/Rex Features, *cr* © ZUMA Press, Inc./Alamy Stock Photo, *br* © Fotohunter/Shutterstock.com; **p.274** © Donna Sgro 'Morphotex dress with tucks' A/W 2009/10; **p.275** © Scott Houston/Alamy Stock Photo; **p.278** © Joerg Boethling/Alamy Stock Photo; **p.279** © age fotostock/Alamy Stock Photo; **p.280** *cl* © Joerg Boethling/Alamy Stock Photo, *bl* © Natalie Behring/ Aurora Photos/Alamy stock photo; **p.284** *c* © Hugh Threlfall/Alamy Stock Photo, *cr* © Hugh Threlfall/Alamy Stock Photo, *bl* © Elenovsky/Shutterstock.com; **p.287** *tl* © Agencja Fotograficzna Caro/Alamy Stock Photo, *cl* © Kzenon/

Alamy Stock Photo, *bl* © Carolyn Jenkins/Alamy Stock Photo; **p.288** *tl* © imageBROKER / Alamy Stock Photo, *b* © OEKO-TEX; **p.291** © Anatoly Vartanov/Alamy Stock Photo; **p.292** *tl* © Adrian davies/Alamy Stock Photo, *bl* © 67photo/Alamy Stock Photo; **p.327** © Classic Image / Alamy Stock Photo; **p.328** © ClassicStock / Alamy Stock Photo.